Routledge
Taylor & Francis Group

www.routledgesw.com

Alice A. Lieberman, The University of Kansas, Series Editor

An authentic breakthrough in social work education . . .

New Directions in Social Work is an innovative, integrated series of texts, website, and interactive cases for generalist courses in the social work curriculum at both undergraduate and graduate levels. Instructors will find everything they need to build a comprehensive course that allows students to meet course outcomes, with these unique features:

- All texts, interactive cases, and test materials are **linked to the 2008 CSWE Policy and Accreditation Standards (EPAS)**.

- **One web portal with easy access** for instructors and students from any computer—no codes, no CDs, no restrictions. Go to www.routledgesw.com and discover.

- **The series is flexible and can be easily adapted for use in online distance-learning courses as well as hybrid and bricks-and-mortar courses.**

- Each text and the website can be used **individually** or as an **entire series** to meet the needs of any social work program.

TITLES IN THE SERIES

Social Work and Social Welfare: An Invitation, Second Edition by Marla Berg-Weger
Human Behavior in the Social Environment, Second Edition by Anissa Taun Rogers
Research for Effective Social Work Practice, Second Edition by Judy L. Krysik and Jerry Finn
Social Policy for Effective Practice: A Strengths Approach, Second Edition by Rosemary K. Chapin
Contemporary Social Work Practice, Second Edition by Martha P. Dewees

Social Work and Social Welfare

An Invitation

Second Edition
by Marla Berg-Weger, Saint Louis University

In this book and companion custom website you will find:

- An emphasis on a **strengths-based perspective** and attention to diversity, social environment, theory and theoretical frameworks, levels of social work practice, and an array of fields of practice.

- The histories of social welfare and the social work profession presented as the **intertwined phenomena that they are.**

- A profile of the **contemporary landscape of the society in which social workers practice.**

- Social work practice within the framework of **planned change, encompassing: engagement, assessment, intervention, and evaluation and termination.**

- The opportunity to **hear from social work practitioners working in eight diverse and challenging practice settings.**

- Three unique, in-depth, interactive, easy-to-access cases, which students can easily reach from *any* computer, provide a **"learning by doing" format unavailable with any other text(s).** Your students will have an advantage unlike any other they will experience in their social work training.

- A wealth of **instructor-only resources** also available at www.routledgesw.com/intro provide: **full-text readings** that link to the concepts presented in each of the chapters; a complete bank of objective and essay-type **test items, all linked to current CSWE EPAS standards; PowerPoint presentations** to help students master key concepts; annotated **links to a treasure trove of social work assets on the Internet**; and a forum inviting all instructors using texts in the series to communicate with each other, and share ideas to improve teaching and learning.

Social Work and Social Welfare

An Invitation

Second Edition

Marla Berg-Weger
Saint Louis University

Routledge
Taylor & Francis Group

NEW YORK AND LONDON

First published 2010
by Routledge
270 Madison Avenue, New York, NY 10016

Simultaneously published in the UK
by Routledge
2 Park Square, Milton Park, Abingdon, Oxon OX14 4RN

Routledge is an imprint of the Taylor & Francis Group, an informa business

Typeset in Stone Serif by RefineCatch Limited, Bungay, Suffolk
Printed and bound in the United States of America on acid-free paper by
Edwards Brothers, Inc.

Library of Congress Cataloging-in-Publication Data
Berg-Weger, Marla, 1956–
    Social work and social welfare : an invitation / Marla Berg-Weger.—2nd ed.
       p. cm.—(New directions in social work)
    Includes bibliographical references and index.
    1. Social service—United States.   2. Poor—Services for—United States.   I. Title.
    HV91.B384 2010
    361.30973—dc22   2009023085

ISBN10: 0–415–80503–1 (hbk)
ISBN10: 0–415–80504–X (pbk)
ISBN10: 0–203–86412–3 (ebk)

ISBN13: 978–0–415–80503–2 (hbk)
ISBN13: 978–0–415–80504–9 (pbk)
ISBN13: 978–0–203–86412–8 (ebk)

BRIEF CONTENTS

DETAILED CONTENTS

PREFACE

MAJOR CHANGES TO THE SECOND EDITION

Like the first edition of *Social Work and Social Welfare: An Invitation*, this edition introduces students to the knowledge, skills, and values that are essential for working with individuals, families, groups, organizations, and communities in a variety of practice settings. With updated demographic, statistical, legislative, policy, and research information; sensitive discussions of contemporary ethical issues; and new first-person narratives from social workers in a variety of fields, the second edition provides an up-to-date profile of the world in which today's social workers practice.

For the new editions of all five books in the New Directions in Social Work series, each addressing a foundational course in the social work curriculum, the publisher has created a brand-new, uniquely distinctive teaching strategy that revolves around the print book but offers much more than the traditional text experience. The series website www.routledgesw.com leads to custom websites coordinated with each text and offering a variety of features to support instructors as you integrate the many facets of an education in social work.

At www.routledgesw.com/intro, you will find a wealth of resources to help you create a dynamic, experiential introduction to social work for your students. The website houses companion readings linked to key concepts in each chapter, along with questions to encourage further thought and discussion; three interactive fictional cases with accompanying exercises that bring to life the concepts covered in the book, readings, and classroom discussions; a bank of exam questions (both objective and open-ended) and PowerPoint presentations; sample syllabi demonstrating how the text and website used together through the course satisfy the 2008 Council on Social Work Educational Policy and Accreditation Standards (EPAS); annotated links to a treasure trove of articles, videos, and Internet sites; and an online forum inviting all instructors using texts in the series to share ideas to improve teaching and learning.

ORGANIZATION OF THE BOOK

Social Work and Social Welfare: An Invitation introduces students to the profession they are considering for their life's work. From a strengths-based perspective, students will be provided with a comprehensive overview of the major areas relevant for social work practice, including diversity, social environment, theory and theoretical frameworks, levels of social work practice, and an array of fields of practice. Presented as the intertwined phenomena that they are, the histories of social welfare and the social work profession are presented to help the student gain insight into the context of the social work profession. *Social Work and Social Welfare* offers a profile of the contemporary landscape of the world and the society in which social workers practice within the concept of planned change, encompassing engagement, assessment, intervention, and evaluation and termination. Students have the opportunity to read first-hand accounts of social work practice in an array of diverse and challenging practice settings and gain insights in to the future of the social work profession.

The following paragraphs serve to briefly introduce each of the chapters included in this book, with emphasis on the updated content.

Chapter 1

A Glimpse into the World of Social Work begins by grounding the students in a definition of social work, the ways that social workers help people, the people with whom social workers work, and the places where social workers practice. Current demographic and employment data for the social work profession is presented. In this first chapter, students are introduced to Emily. Throughout each chapter of the book, Emily's experiences as a social work student and later a practitioner, provide insights into the rewards and challenges of a career in social work that are addressed in that chapter.

Chapter 2

History of Social Work and Social Welfare enables student readers to understand and appreciate the historical backdrop of the social welfare system and the profession of social work that has produced the systems and profession that exist today. The dynamics of history as it impacts social work and social welfare is emphasized in this chapter.

Chapter 3

U.S. Poverty and the Implications for Social Work provides students with both an historical and contemporary look at poverty and the programs aimed at alleviating poverty within our society. As economic philosophy and status is everchanging, this chapter provides an up-to-date exploration of the current status of those persons living in poverty and the effectiveness of the legislation and programs that are intended to improve the quality of their lives.

Chapter 4

The Social Work Environment is, in fact, the global environment in which modern-day social workers live and practice. This chapter focuses on helping students understand the social forces and changes that influence our society. Within the context of the political, economic, and social environments that impact life for the clients systems served by social workers, current information is provided on such issues as race, ethnicity, age, gender, income (social class), sexual orientation, and religion.

Chapter 5

Diversity in Social Work Practice introduces the students to key areas of social work practice that will impact virtually every dimension of their lives as social workers. With an emphasis on self-awareness, students are challenged to consider the evolution of their own views on persons who may be different from themselves whether it be in the area of race, ethnicity, culture, religion, sexual orientation, age, or lifestyle. Framed within theoretical perspectives for understanding diversity, students are offered an overview of the skills required to be a culturally competent social work practitioner.

Chapter 6

While challenging for the beginning social work student to grasp, **Values and Ethics in Social Work Practice** are introduced in this chapter as the foundation that guides social work practice. Utilizing value and ethical dilemmas that challenge social workers, students have multiple opportunities throughout the chapter to consider the origins of their own value and ethical beliefs and to apply them to situations in which they will likely find themselves as they develop as practitioners.

Chapter 7

Social Work Perspectives and Methods conceptualizes generalist social work practice within the levels of practice with individuals and families, groups, and organizations and communities. Students are introduced to a range of theoretical frameworks that guide social workers as they practice, including strengths-based perspective, systems theory, and a model for solution-focused interventions.

Chapter 8

Fields of Social Work Practice provides students with up-to-date perspectives on social work practice in the first decade of the 21st century. Eight social workers share their experiences in eight different practice settings, ranging from health and mental health, and criminal justice settings, practice with persons with addictions, practice with immigrants and refugees, children and youth, and older adults, and rural practice.

Chapter 9

Social Work Practice with Individuals and Families is the first of the levels of practice to be presented. Students are exposed to the concepts of planned change. They will learn about the phases of the social work intervention, including engagement, assessment, intervention, and evaluation and termination. Linked to the EPAS, these areas of practice help students gain insights into the knowledge and skills required for competency-based social work practice. Students will become familiar with effective social work practice behaviors they will need as they practice at all levels.

Chapter 10

Social Work Practice with Groups continues the students' exposure to the facets of generalist social work practice. Students are presented with three models of group-level practice. Engagement, assessment, intervention, and evaluation concepts are applied at the group level of social work practice.

Chapter 11

Social Work Practice with Organizations and Communities and Policy Practice utilizes the insights gained about practice at the individual, family, and group levels to expand the students' awareness of social work practice areas to include organizations, communities, and policy. Added to the second edition, policy practice is presented to students as a career opportunity as well as a critical part of any area of practice.

Chapter 12

The Social Work Profession brings to a close this introduction to the social work profession. Trends in social work employment opportunities are included along with up-to-date information on salaries.

INTERACTIVE CASES

The website www.routledgesw.com/cases presents three unique, in-depth, interactive, fictional cases with dynamic characters and real-life situations that students can easily access from any computer and that provide a "learning by doing" format unavailable with any other text. Your students will have an advantage unlike any other they will experience in their social work training. Each of the interactive cases uses text, graphics, and video to help students learn about engagement, assessment, intervention, and evaluation and termination at multiple levels of social work practice. The "My Notebook" feature allows students to take and save notes, type in written responses to tasks, and share their work with classmates and instructors by email. Through the interactive cases, you can integrate the readings and classroom discussions by acquainting the students with:

The Sanchez Family: Systems, Strengths, and Stressors. The 10 individuals in this extended Latino family have numerous strengths but are faced with a variety of challenges. Students will have the opportunity to experience the phases of the social work intervention, grapple with ethical dilemmas, and identify strategies for addressing issues of diversity.

Riverton: A Community Conundrum. Riverton is a small midwest city in which the social worker lives and works. The social worker identifies an issue that presents her community with a challenge. Students and instructors can work together to develop strategies for engaging, assessing, and intervening with the citizens of the social worker's neighborhood.

Carla Washburn: Loss, Aging, and Social Support. Students will get to know Carla Washburn, an older African American woman who finds herself living alone after the loss of her grandson and in considerable pain from a recent accident. In this case, less complex than the Sanchez family, students will apply their growing knowledge of gerontology and exercise the skills of culturally competent practice.

IN SUM

I have written this book with the hope that it will provide you and your students not only with an introduction to our profession but also with deep insight into the knowledge, skills, and values that are required for a competent and effective social work practitioner. The multiple options for supporting your teaching of this content are intended to help you address the diverse range of student learning styles and needs. The design of this text and the instructor support materials optimize the experiential focus of facilitating students' introduction to the social work profession. I hope this book and the support materials will be of help to you and your students as they embark on their social journey.

ACKNOWLEDGMENTS

I would like to extend my appreciation to the many social workers who helped this book to become a reality. To Alice Lieberman and the other authors of this book series, Rosemary Chapin, Anissa Rogers, Judy Krysik, and Jerry Finn. I thank you for your vision, support, and feedback through this enriching and invigorating process. To my colleagues at Saint Louis University, Julie Birkenmaier, Jane Sprankel, Pam Huggins, Ellen Burkemper, Sue Tebb, and Sabrina Tyuse, I appreciate your willingness to provide resources, review chapters, and serve as a sounding board for my ideas. To the practitioners who contributed their "voices from the field," I am grateful for your willingness to share the stories of your professional lives. Thanks to Michael Cronin for his contributions to the test bank and website and sharing his experiences. To the staff of Routledge, Taylor & Francis, thank you for believing in the potential of this book series.

ABOUT THE AUTHOR

Marla Berg-Weger is a professor in the School of Social Work at Saint Louis University, Missouri, and serves as the Senior Associate Provost for Academic Affairs and Dean of the School for Professional Studies. Dr. Berg-Weger holds social work degrees at the bachelor's, master's, and doctoral levels. Her social work practice experience includes public social welfare services, domestic violence services, mental health, and medical social work. Her research and writing focuses on gerontological social work and social work practice. With Julie Birkenmaier, she co-authored the textbook, *The Practicum Companion for Social Work: Integrating Class and Field Work.* She is the past president of the Association of Gerontology in Social Work and currently serves as the Chair, of the *Journal of Gerontological Social Work* Editorial Board Executive Committee.

CHAPTER 1

A Glimpse into the World of Social Work

ASK SOCIAL WORKERS WHAT DREW THEM TO THE PROFESSION, and you will hear one common message: They liked the idea that they would be helping to better people's lives. In fact, the primary reasons that people become social workers are to: (1) help others; (2) advocate for those who are disadvantaged; and (3) provide mental health services (Whitaker, 2008, p. 4). Although many might have considered one of the other helping professions, such as psychology, sociology, teaching, or medicine, they chose social work. As you will learn throughout this book, social work is unique among other helping professions because of its broad scope of concern, its strong core values, and its commitment to social and economic justice.

Social work has goals and methods in common with other helping professions, and social workers have adopted useful knowledge from many of these professions. From psychology, social workers learn to understand the impact of emotional and psychological factors on the individual. From sociology, they gain insight into populations of people. From the medical professions, they learn of the relationships between biological functioning and health/illness and the impact of these factors on psychosocial well-being. The health professions also emphasize the value of the interdisciplinary team approach. Social work and other helping professions certainly overlap; however, social work is also distinctive in a number of ways (see Table 1.1).

The social work profession emphasizes a holistic, or interpersonal, perspective as opposed to the individual (intrapersonal) perspective of other helping professions. The National Association of Social Workers (NASW), the professional organization for the social work profession, issued a policy statement supporting "the promotion of social work as a distinctly different profession from other human service disciplines (such as counseling, clinical psychology, nursing, marriage and family therapy, and so forth) as it focuses on the intra- and inter-personal aspects of clients' lives" (National Association of Social Workers [NASW], 2009–2012b, p. 80).

A hallmark of providing social work services to people is to consider their social environment: their family, home, work, state of health, community, and the interactions that they have with all those areas of their life. Perhaps the most important

	DISCIPLINE	SIMILARITIES	DIFFERENCES
TABLE 1.1 *What Makes Social Work Unique*	**Psychology**	(1) Both are practice professions (2) At the graduate level, both are trained to provide psychotherapy (3) Both may work in the same settings with the same clients	(1) Psychology focuses on internal issues as the source of the problem/social work focuses on the person within the environment (PIE) (2) Psychology focuses on the individual as the target of the intervention/social work interventions encompass the individual and those in his/her environment (3) Psychologists administer and interpret psychological tests/social workers are typically not trained in this area of practice (4) In some states, psychologists can prescribe medications/social workers cannot (5) Clinical practice often requires a Ph.D. for psychologists and an MSW for social workers (social workers are licensed to practice as BSWs in many states)
	Sociology	(1) Both are interested in the patterns of behaviors of people	(1) Sociology is not a practice profession, but a social science that considers the population, often in the context of communities
	Health Professions (nursing and medicine, in particular)	(1) Both are practice professions (2) Both recognize the influence of health on well-being (3) Both work in community/hospital settings with the same patients (4) Both have generalist and specialist expertise	(1) Health professions often focus primarily on physical health issues, while social work assessments routinely include biological, psychological and social perspectives/factors (2) Social workers are expert about community resources (3) Physicians and some nurses can prescribe medications/social workers cannot

DISCIPLINE	SIMILARITIES	DIFFERENCES	TABLE 1.1 *continued*
Marriage and Family Counseling	(1) Both are practice professions (2) At the graduate level, both are trained to provide psychotherapy (3) Both have licensing and certification requirements (4) Both can conduct clinical practice with a master's degree (5) Neither discipline can prescribe medications	(1) Like psychologists, counselors focus primarily on the individual as the source of the problem for assessment and intervention (2) Counselors are not typically trained in community practice (e.g., advocacy, organizing, etc.)/social work training emphasizes competence at the individual/family/community levels	

Note: Additional sources used here include: Ginsberg, 2001; Peck, 1999.

distinction between social work and other helping professions is the emphasis on social action through advocacy for those oppressed or discriminated against by society. Although social workers often help people by providing services in an agency setting, the profession also advocates addressing social conditions such as homelessness, hunger, teen pregnancy, poverty, and discrimination.

This chapter will illustrate the meaning of social work. In the remaining chapters, a more detailed picture will emerge of what social work is and what you need to learn to be an effective social worker.

A DEFINITION OF SOCIAL WORK

Developing an accurate and comprehensive definition of social work requires an expansive view of the profession and the positions that social workers hold. As you might already know, social workers are employed in such helping institutions as schools, hospitals, mental health facilities, older adult service programs, and children's residential settings. You might not know, however, that social workers also work in banks, large corporations, theater groups, community gardens, military installations, police stations, and internationally. Social work professionals work with people in all segments of society, from those who are disenfranchised or devalued by society and living in poverty to those in the middle and upper socio-economic segments of society. They work with the young and the old, with people in good health and poor health, with people from diverse cultures and backgrounds, including those who may be immigrants or refugees or who have survived a disaster or traumatic experience.

Let us see how the profession itself defines social work. The profession's definition of social work has evolved over time. A 1973 definition developed by the National Association of Social Workers described social work as the "professional activity of helping individuals, groups, or communities to restore their capacity for social functioning and creating societal conditions favorable to that goal" (p. 4). This definition includes four basic goals for the profession: (1) linking people to resources; (2) providing direct services to individuals, families, and groups; (3) helping communities or groups provide or improve social and health services; and (4) participating in relevant legislative processes (pp. 4–5).

As the profession has continued to grow and change, so has the self-definition. Developed in 1996 as part of the profession's *Code of Ethics*, the current definition remains relevant today:

> The primary mission of the social work profession is to enhance human well-being and help meet the basic human needs of all people, with particular attention to the needs and empowerment of people who are vulnerable, oppressed, and living in poverty. A historical and defining feature of social work is the profession's focus on individual well-being in a social context and the well-being of society. Fundamental to social work is attention to the environmental forces that create, contribute to, and address problems in living.
>
> (NASW, 2009–2012b, p.1)

Common to both definitions, the goal of social work is to empower people to optimize their abilities and quality of life, whether through working directly with people or through taking action to change society. The openness and flexibility of these definitions enable social workers to respond to those needs that exist within their communities. The populations, health crises, social conditions, and ethical dilemmas with which social workers are engaged may vary, but the work transcends time and individual circumstance because of its all-encompassing nature. This diversity and the activist bias attract many people to the social work profession.

THE WORK OF SOCIAL WORK

Consider the experiences of a midcareer social worker named Emily. Like many of her professional counterparts, Emily has worked in a number of different social work positions and settings. Early in her career, she worked in the public welfare system in several different areas ranging from child protective services, to services for older adults and persons with visual impairments, to outreach work in a domestic violence program. Later, Emily obtained a graduate degree and, over the years, held social work positions in a mental health center, home health agency, hospital, and medical outpatient clinic.

One of the things that Emily has found especially rewarding about her profession is the variety of experiences she has had because she has degrees in social work. When she worked in the program that serves persons who have experienced domestic violence, for instance, she responded to calls from emergency rooms where women had gone after being battered by their partners. Emily met the woman at the hospital and assessed her current situation, abuse history, safety needs, and resources. She then arranged housing either at the shelter or at a safe house for the woman and her children. Emily worked with the woman during her stay to explore options and make long-term plans. Sometimes, this effort involved helping the woman leave her partner for a new life, but other times it meant watching her return to the relationship. In these cases, Emily always worked out a safety plan with the woman in the event the violence occurred again. Emily used a number of social work skills in this position: crisis intervention, interviewing, assessment, providing information and referral, brokering, intervention planning, evaluation, and documentation.

At the mental health center, Emily conducted intakes for persons requesting therapy services. She met with those persons for an hour-long assessment of their presenting concern, social situation, and mental health status. After completing this assessment, she compiled a report and recommended a treatment plan. In this job, Emily used such skills as assessment, diagnosis, preparation of documentation, and crisis intervention.

As a medical social worker in an acute care hospital setting, Emily provided services to patients and their families upon the request of the medical staff. She often assisted the patient and her or his family in making discharge plans. This process could include arranging for financial assistance, home health or hospice services, residential care, medications, medical equipment, and possible relocation. Emily was also there to support families when a patient died. When she was on call for the social work department, she covered the emergency room, which could involve just about any situation. Her crisis intervention skills clearly were a major asset here.

Because social work training provides a core set of knowledge and skills that can be applied in a variety of settings with a diverse population, Emily has been able to work in a number of challenging but rewarding positions: investigating adult and child abuse and neglect, working with women who have experienced domestic violence and their children, conducting assessments for therapy in a mental health center, arranging discharge plans for hospitalized patients, and providing therapy for persons experiencing such conditions as depression, a new medical diagnosis, or family and marital problems. You can see that Emily has enjoyed a broad and diverse career that was made possible by her social work degrees. She thrives on the opportunity to work with different types of people who are experiencing different life situations. In addition, she welcomes the opportunity to move into a new position if she chooses. Most of all, Emily enjoys being able to help people through difficult life experiences.

What Social Workers Do

While over 800,000 self-identify as social workers, approximately 595,000 of those employed as social workers in 2006 were professionally educated as social workers (Hopps et al., 2008; U.S. Department of Labor, 2008). Nearly half (42%) are engaged in practice in agencies in the private, not-for-profit sector, while thirty percent work in public or governmental organizations (28% government and 2% military); and one quarter (28%) work in the private, for-profit sector (Whitaker & Arrington, 2008).

The majority of social workers work with individuals, couples, families, and small groups (Whitaker & Arrington, 2008). In fact, most social workers who responded to a 2007 NASW Workforce survey reported that they provide services in the areas of mental health (35 percent), physical health (14 percent), family/children's services (11 percent), schools (6 percent), adolescent programs (5 percent), or addiction treatment (4 percent)—all of which are types of direct practice. Social workers in the United States provide more mental health and therapy services than any other discipline does, including psychology or counseling (NASW, 2005). In fact, social workers provide more than 60 percent of mental health services. In this field of practice, social workers provide crisis intervention and counseling services to individuals, families, and groups experiencing difficulty in coping with a life crisis or transition, such as a relationship problem, death or injury, divorce, or illness.

While the majority of social workers spend much of their time providing direct services to individuals and families, a significant number of social work professionals are engaged, in whole or in part, in policy development and analysis, advocacy, and in supervisory, administrative, and fund-raising activities. A survey of licensed social workers reports that most social workers spend at least a portion of their time in one or more of these activities (Center for Health Workforce Studies (CHWS) & Center for Workforce Studies (CWS), 2006). Almost one-third of the social workers surveyed in an earlier study did not have just one primary function; rather, they were engaged in multiple areas and levels of social work activities (Gibelman & Schervish, 1997).

Supervision and teaching are the most frequently mentioned secondary areas of work. In the areas of administration and policy, social workers are often the initiators of new social programs because they have been in the field and are able to see where the needs exist. This experience also helps social workers to understand and influence social policies because they have observed the impact of those policies on the client systems with whom they work. Social workers can share real-life stories with legislators to help them understand the effects of their votes on constituents. Not only do social workers inform legislators of needs, but they become those policy makers. Hundreds of social workers serve their communities and states as elected officials, including two in the U.S. Senate and seven in the House of Representatives (NASW, 2009b).

Social workers' skills enable them to work in a broad range of areas and specializations (Barker, 2003; NASW, 2009b):

- Conducting needs assessments, providing information and referrals, and accessing resources in social casework/**case management**.

- Serving as a case manager and counseling around specific health-related issues in medical social work.

- Working with students and their families on emotional, social, and economic concerns to enable them to focus on the student's education in school social work.

- Counseling individuals, families, and groups in such settings as hospitals, schools, mental health facilities, and private practices in **clinical social work.**

- Supervising programs and people in **administration and management**.

- Working to influence the development, implementation, and evaluation of policies aimed at creating social justice for those impacted by the policies in policy practice.

- Working with groups and communities to identify conditions and develop strategies to address them in **community organization**.

- Analyzing conditions, programs, and policies and conducting and studying research in an effort to improve the social service system in **social policy research**.

On a daily basis, social workers may find themselves engaged in these common work activities:

- Determining the social, emotional, and economic concerns and needs of persons for whom they provide services.

- Providing services to address the needs of people, or referring clients for appropriate professional or community services.

- Developing resources, programs, and social policies to address unmet community needs.

- Assessing, diagnosing, and/or treating mental health and emotional conditions.

- Working to improve social programs and health services by conducting research and encouraging communities and organizations to be responsive to identified needs.

- Helping people improve personal and/or social functioning by providing or referring for education, training, employment, and personal growth services.

BOX 1.1

Who Needs a Social Worker?

YOU'LL NEED A SOCIAL WORKER . . .

When you come into the world too soon

When you can't find anyone to play with

When you are left home alone

When you hate the new baby

When you don't think your teacher likes you

When you are bullied

When you don't want your mommy and daddy to divorce

When you miss your big brother

When you don't like how the neighbor touches you

When you get into fights at school

When you don't make the team

When your best friend moves away

When you get poor grades

When you always fight with your siblings

When your friends pressure you to get high

When you can't adjust to the move

When you can't talk to your parents

When you want to quit school

When your friends don't like you anymore

When you didn't want this baby

When you feel like running away

When your friend swallows an overdose

When you are the only one that thinks you're fat

When you can't find someone who speaks your language

When you can't forget the assault

When you can't decide on a career

When your family pressures you to marry

When your boss is hitting on you

When you can't stick to a budget

When you want to adopt

When you wonder if you are drinking too much

When you can't find good day care

When you think you are neglecting your kids

When you are hated because of who you are

When you lose your baby

When your community has gang problems

When your kids want to live with your ex

When your partner is unfaithful

When you want to meet your birthparent

When your disabled child needs friends

When your step-kids hate you

When your mother won't speak to you

When you can't face moving again

When your spouse wants a divorce

When you want to be a foster parent

When your city officials don't respond

When your best friend has panic attacks

When you find drugs in your son's room

When your job is eliminated

When your mother-in-law wants to move in

When your neighborhood needs a community center

When you find there is no joy in your life

When your car accident destroys your career

When you sponsor a refugee family

When your legislature passes a bad law

When your brother won't help care for dad

When your partner has a mid life crisis

When you are stressed by menopause

When your mom gets Alzheimer's

When you are caring for parents and children

When you want to change careers

When you lose your home in a fire

When you are angry all the time

When your nest really empties

When your partner insists you retire

When you can't afford respite care

When you can't find a job and you're sixty

When your kids demand that you move in with them

When your daughter suddenly dies

When you are scared about living alone

When you can't drive any more

When your children ignore your medical decisions

When your retirement check won't pay the bills

When you learn you have a terminal illness

When you need a nursing home

LIFE'S CHALLENGES – SOCIAL WORKERS ARE THERE FOR YOU!

BOX 1.1

continued

Source: © 2001, Darlene Lynch and Robert Vernon. For free distribution information visit: http:// hsmedia.biz

- Coordinating and working with governmental, private, civic, religious, business, and/or trade organizations to combat social problems through community awareness and response programs.
- Researching, planning, and developing social and health policies and programs.

Social workers' skills afford them the opportunity to work with any population in any situation or setting.

Who Is Served by Social Workers

If you are interested in being a social worker, it is important to understand that many of the people with whom you will work are struggling to function within their setting. Fortunately, most people have strengths on which to draw, and activating those strengths is the social worker's specialty. From the beginnings of the profession, social workers have worked one-on-one primarily with persons facing discrimination because of ethnic background, race, gender, ability, or age, or with those experiencing life crises, or physical or mental health issues. When asked to identify where they focus their professional resources, many social workers indicate a desire to work with family issues and with persons who have limited incomes (Gibelman & Schervish, 1997). However, the scope of practice and service boundaries for social workers has expanded throughout history to keep up with societal needs. Today, for example, social workers assist teens with pregnancy and HIV/AIDS prevention and sex education. Box 1.1 provides some insight into the range of people who might find themselves in need of a social worker's services.

As an adult service worker in the public welfare agency, Emily started off one typical day by visiting Mrs. H., a woman who was 70 years old and widowed with no family. Mrs. H. lived alone in a small house that Emily could see was not well maintained or clean. Mrs. H. was referred to Emily's agency by her minister because he was concerned about her. Mrs. H. was visually impaired due to glaucoma, had severe arthritis, and diabetes. She had been trying to cover up for her increasing debilitation by isolating herself and not participating in her usual social activities. These may seem like insurmountable problems, and the only reasonable response might seem to be, at first contact, to put Mrs. H. in a nursing home. However, Mrs. H. desperately wanted to continue living independently. Moreover, she was financially independent, and she had a small circle of caring people, such as her minister and neighbors, who provided social support. Through Emily's social assessment, which included family, financial, and health information, she concluded that Mrs. H. was a candidate for a number of social services: homemaker/chore (help with housekeeping tasks), home health services (nursing assistance to monitor her diabetes), services for persons with visual impairments (a rehabilitation teacher to help her adjust to her visual impairment), and telephone reassurance services (a daily telephone check-in service). With the help of these services, Emily's ongoing case management, and a willingness to build on her strengths, Mrs. H. remained independent and functional until her death 10 years later.

Where Social Workers Work

Emily's social work degrees and experience have enabled her to change positions within the social work field. Her social work training prepared her to work with varied groups of people in direct practice—children, families, older adults, and persons with disabilities or persistent illness. Her knowledge and skills have also enabled her to facilitate groups and to work at the administrative and educational levels. Emily values the learning she has gained in each of these settings.

Nevertheless, she has developed her preferences. Emily's social work experience began with a community service assignment in her introductory social work course. She found an opportunity at a nursing home, helping older adults. With her under-graduate degree in social work, Emily found a job in the public social service sector. However, Emily developed an extensive knowledge of the public welfare system that was an asset in being accepted into graduate school and in being hired to work in a shelter program for women who have been abused and their children. Her experiences in public welfare and domestic violence were viewed favorably when she applied for a position at the mental health center.

Although each setting offered a different experience and enabled her to develop her knowledge and skill as a social worker, Emily also found that her personality was better suited for some settings than others. For example, she learned that she enjoys working in an agency in which she has a large group of co-workers with whom she can interact on a daily basis.

Like Emily, most social workers gain experience in a variety of settings. Such settings include (1) organizations that primarily provide social services; (2) host settings, or secondary organizations such as schools, correctional facilities, or health care facilities; (3) voluntary nonprofit agencies; and (4) governmental or public agencies. Although some social workers are in private practice, most work in an organization. As for specialty, Exhibit 1.1 describes the settings in which most practicing social workers were employed in the year 2006 (U.S. Department of Labor, 2008). Social workers most frequently work in such settings as mental health agencies, child welfare programs, and elementary and secondary schools (Doelling, Matz, & Kuehne, 1999). Between one-half and two-thirds of all social workers are employed

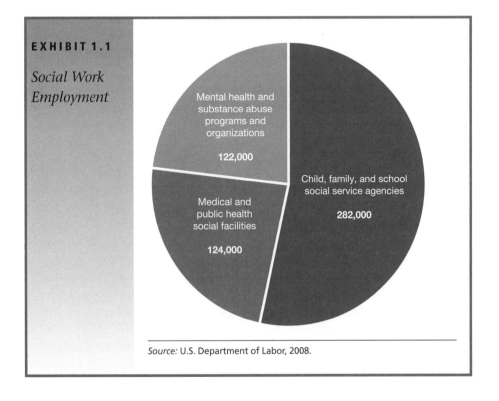

EXHIBIT 1.1

Social Work Employment

Mental health and substance abuse programs and organizations

122,000

Child, family, and school social service agencies

282,000

Medical and public health social facilities

124,000

Source: U.S. Department of Labor, 2008.

in the private social service sector (U.S. Department of Labor, 2008; Whitaker & Arrington, 2008). A majority work in nonprofit settings such as social service agencies, hospitals, residential care facilities, home health agencies, health centers, and criminal justice programs. These privately funded agencies are administered by boards of directors, and their profits are retained or reinvested in the programs to enhance service delivery. These agencies raise funds through individual and corporate donations, grants, fundraisers, and public sector contracts. In addition, an increasing number of social workers (over one-quarter) are working in for-profit settings such as corporations (for example, in employee assistance programs) and private schools (Whitaker & Arrington, 2008). The private social service delivery system in the United States consists of approximately 77,000 organizations—59,000 (two-thirds) serve individuals and families; 9,000 provide food, housing and other relief services, and 9,000 focus on vocational rehabilitation (U.S. Department of Labor, 2008).

Although a majority of social workers are employed in the private sector, public or governmental settings remain an important source of jobs for social workers. Reports suggest that an estimated one-third of social workers are employed in publicly funded settings that provide services in the areas of mental health, social services, child welfare, housing, education, and corrections (U.S. Department of Labor, 2008). The overwhelming majority of social workers in the public sector are employed at the state and local levels, with a smaller number working in programs at the federal level. These local, state, and federal settings include state-funded public welfare/human service departments; mental health agencies; child welfare agencies; housing programs; veterans' administration organizations; military installations; local, state, and federal court/justice systems; public schools; hospitals; and policy-making organizations.

The number of social workers in the public sector has continued to decrease due, in large part, to cutbacks in local, state, and federal budgets (Gibelman, 2004). However, the public setting remains an important arena for social workers to assist with enhancement of welfare programs.

PATHS TO BECOMING A SOCIAL WORKER

Emily's path to becoming a social worker is her own, but it is typical for many social workers. It began with a significant personal experience. Emily married shortly after graduating from high school, and she clearly did not expect that domestic violence would occur in her marriage. But when it did, Emily ended the marriage in a relatively short time. With her family's support, Emily headed off to college. She had no idea what she wanted to major in, but she was influenced by her past life experiences.

Emily was intrigued by a psychology course she took to fulfill her university's general education requirement. She liked the idea of trying to understand the ways that people think and behave. She had often been the person among her friends in whom others confided—maybe because she was a good listener. Next, Emily took sociology and anthropology courses. She was drawn to the idea of thinking about people within their societies, but she also liked the possibility of being able to help people.

One of Emily's instructors commented that she seemed to enjoy these classes, and she asked if Emily had considered social work. Emily had never met a social worker, but she began to investigate the social work program. The rest, as they say, is history. Emily went on to get her bachelor's and master's degrees in social work, and she has worked in a variety of settings. And yes, she has worked in many situations that involved domestic violence. Because of her training as a professional social worker, Emily recognized the importance of exploring her own life experience in relation to her professional work, and she has continued to do just that throughout her career.

Emily's story is not an uncommon example of a social worker's journey into the profession. Many social workers come to the profession through interest in helping people, a psychology or sociology course, or past personal experiences. Emily happened to have all three. The psychology course helped her to find a connection with one of her strengths—an interest in helping people. Her personal experience as a survivor of domestic violence helped her tap into a reservoir of empathy to help others. Knowing your strengths and developing skills for working with people are essential for considering a career in social work.

You might wonder, though, why Emily decided to major in social work instead of psychology or sociology. Had it not been for that insightful faculty member, Emily would likely have graduated with a psychology degree. Having a degree in psychology could have taken Emily down a different career path. She might have gone on to complete a graduate degree in psychology, which would have led her to focus primarily on psychological testing. A doctorate in psychology could have taken her into private practice, research, or academic life. You can see how psychology can overlap with social work, but there are differences, too. Emily can become a therapist with a master's degree in social work and a clinical credential (license). In psychology, she would require a doctorate.

SOCIAL WORK EDUCATION

To practice social work, social workers need the proper credentials. Professional social work can be performed only by a person who has been awarded a bachelor's or master's degree from a college or university social work program that is accredited by the Council on Social Work Education (CSWE). NASW has issued a policy statement that conveys the importance of the title of social worker being used only for persons who hold social work degrees (NASW, 2009–2012b). In fact, many states have passed title protection legislation stipulating that only persons with social work degrees from CSWE-accredited programs may refer to themselves as social workers. In addition, all states have enacted social work credentialing legislation that enables degreed social work practitioners to obtain a license or certification to practice social work. These laws vary from state to state and by area of practice expertise. Further, NASW actively advocates against laws and rules that do not stipulate that social work positions must be filled by degreed social workers.

Perhaps the social workers of your state have lobbied for legislation to protect the title of social worker or require social work positions to be filled by degreed social workers. You can check with your state's NASW chapter. U.S. social work programs grant three types of degrees:

- Bachelor of Social Work (BSW) prepares the graduate for generalist social work professional practice.

- Master of Social Work (MSW) prepares the graduate for advanced professional practice in an area of concentration.

- Doctorate of Philosophy in Social Work (PhD or DSW) is typically considered a research-oriented degree with a focus on preparing the graduate for a teaching and/or research career. However, several programs offer a doctorate degree in social work that emphasizes clinical practice.

Social work education is multifaceted, interdisciplinary, and diverse. The BSW exposes students to a wide range of content areas. A liberal arts background provides students with basic knowledge and skills that are an asset in social work practice, including an appreciation for scientific methods and historical development; skills for effective communication and critical thinking; awareness of the human condition and the contribution of the arts to society; openness to diversity, difference, and improvability; and knowledge of human biological function. For their elective coursework, many undergraduate social work students gravitate to courses that will strengthen their knowledge of human behavior or social policy development. An area of growing interest is fluency in a second language, such as Spanish or American Sign Language (ASL). As our society becomes increasingly ethnically diverse, bilingual skills and knowledge of global issues will become more important within the social work profession.

Within the BSW program, an array of courses covers the areas that have been identified as essential competencies for the professional social worker (Council on Social Work Education [CSWE], 2008):

- Identify as a professional social worker and conduct oneself accordingly.

- Apply social work ethical principles to guide professional practice.

- Apply critical thinking to informal and communicate professional judgments.

- Engage diversity and difference in practice.

- Advance human rights and social and economic justice.

- Engage in research-informed practice and practice-informed research.

- Apply knowledge of human behavior and the social environment.

- Engage in policy practice to advance social and economic well-being and to deliver effective social work services.

- Respond to contexts that shape practice.

- Engage, assess, intervene, and evaluate with individuals, families, groups, organizations, and communities.

Among the helping professions, social work is the leader in preparing graduates with a bachelor's degree to work effectively in social services. The BSW permits such quick entry into professional practice for three reasons:

(1) students in the BSW program are required to participate in two or three service-learning experiences in a social service agency; (2) the BSW program is accredited by a professional body; and (3) the BSW enables graduates to obtain a state license or certification (no other discipline credentials baccalaureate level professionals) (Boyd, 1996). Licensure signifies to society that the social worker has completed the required level and type of education and ensures that only those with those credentials can obtain the license (Hopps et al., 2008).

The distinction between the BSW and the MSW is primarily in the areas of content, program objectives, and depth, breadth, and specificity of knowledge and skills (CSWE, 2008). According to one NASW survey, nearly 80 percent of practicing social workers that responded possess an MSW degree, while 12 percent of respondents had the BSW as their highest degree (NASW Center for Workforce Studies, 2005). Social workers with BSWs and MSWs often work in the same settings and with the same client systems, but each functions at different levels and performs different tasks.

For example, at the BSW level, Emily worked directly with women and children in the domestic violence program. She helped them gain admittance to a safe-house program and to obtain legal, financial, health, and mental health services. In contrast, at the MSW level, Emily actually provided mental health treatment for the women and children in the shelter.

FIELD EXPERIENCES

Whichever level of social work education you might pursue, you can expect the theory learned in the classroom to be integrated with actual practice. The field education experience promotes the application of knowledge, skills, and values through at least 400 hours of supervised practice in a social work setting. This training enables social workers to work effectively and ethically with people facing real challenges. Members of the profession feel strongly that social workers should be mentored and supervised by other social workers.

Actual experience is invaluable. In fact, one strategy for determining whether social work might be the profession for you is to gain exposure to social work practice through a volunteer or service-learning experience. Whether or not you have engaged in community service in the past, now is an excellent time to seek a learning experience through volunteer service with the aim of working with and observing social workers as they perform their activities. Take full advantage of this opportunity to challenge yourself. Seek out a population with whom you are familiar, or even not familiar, and imagine yourself as a social work professional in that setting. If you are not required to engage in a community or service-learning project as part of your introductory coursework, do it anyway. In addition to providing an opportunity for you to gain experience, your community service can be an asset in other ways (Dale, 2001):

- Helping you to identify interests (or areas in which you are not interested) and goals.

- Enhancing your résumé, future marketability, and social work network.

- Building self-confidence and guiding your career directions.

Most social service agencies welcome—and actually rely on—the contributions of volunteers. Here are some suggestions for learning about service opportunities in your community:

- Consult with faculty members, your academic advisor, and/or the field education department.

- Contact your state's NASW chapter office.

- Contact your local United Way.

- Check your university's community service or volunteer clearinghouse office.

Like Emily, you may find yourself unexpectedly drawn to the profession of social work. And, like Emily, you will find that every little bit of experience helps. In each of the jobs in which Emily has worked, she has used the skills that she learned during her training and in previous jobs. Each job led to the next, and each job built on the last.

CONCLUSION

We have arrived at the end of the first chapter of this book. In this chapter, you have been introduced to the definition of social work, areas in which social workers practice, and the education required for becoming a social worker. I hope your perception of the social work profession is beginning to encompass the diversity and breadth that the profession itself encompasses. After reading this chapter, you may have developed more questions about the social work profession than you had when you began.

In this chapter, you have gained more insight into this career you are exploring, but we have a long way to go. We will continue our journey through the social work profession by exploring the history of social work, current challenges that influence social work, areas of practice, cultural competence, values and ethics, theoretical frameworks for guiding practice, fields of practice, and the possibilities for the future of the social work profession.

As you proceed, keep in mind the following, written by an MSW student (Walton, 1996, p. 63). Her words not only capture her enthusiasm for her new profession, but they also provide a sense of the work that social workers do.

> Social work is a career you can't leave at the office. You are committed to facilitating change in people's lives and the environment in which they live. You often work with, or on behalf of, individuals who have difficult problems and lack the resources with which to cope. It can be inspiring to see your client help themselves out of a crisis using skills you helped them find within themselves.

I hope that you, too, can be inspired and that you are now beginning to consider whether you want to be a social worker. Check out the top 10 reasons for being a social worker in Box 1.2 for some insight into a profession whose mission is to help others, make the world a better place, and perform meaningful work.

BOX 1.2

Top Ten Reasons for Being a Social Worker

10. Help People
9. Do what Counts
8. Practice Your Principles
7. Foster Success Stories
6. Match Skills with Life's Challenges
5. Change the Future
4. Make the World a Better Place
3. Satisfaction Guaranteed
2. World-Class Peers
1. Career of Champions

Source: National Association of Social Workers

MAIN POINTS

- Social work is a professional activity that provides the opportunity to work with individuals, families, groups, organizations, and communities. Over a half-million people in the United States are practicing social workers.

- Other professions, such as psychology and sociology, have contributed to the development of social work, but the profession of social work also has unique values, knowledge, and practice skills.

- Social workers provide an ever-changing array of services such as counseling, advocacy, case management, education, prevention, support, and crisis intervention.

- Social workers work with persons throughout all areas of our society, including children, adolescents, and adults experiencing life changes or crises; persons who are struggling with an illness, disability, addiction, or homelessness; persons who are the victims of oppression, discrimination, or social injustice, and persons who have survived a disaster who have emigrated from their home country.

- Social workers work in a variety of settings, including schools, hospitals, mental health facilities, addiction treatment programs, advocacy programs, and residential facilities for children, youth, persons who are homeless, and older adults.

- Social workers can obtain degrees at the bachelor's, master's, and doctoral levels. The National Association of Social Workers (NASW) and the Council on Social Work Education (CSWE) have defined the criteria for competence in a degreed social worker.

EXERCISES

1. In this exercise, you will meet the Sanchez family. Go to: www.routledgesw.com/cases and click on the Sanchez Family case. Read the introduction to the case and explore how the interactive program can be used. Activate each button to familiarize yourself with the presentation of information, the questions and tasks, and the Case Study Tools.

   Go to the Engage tab and complete Tasks 1 and 2 to better understand the needs of the Sanchez family. Use My Notebook to reflect on the roles that a social worker can play; describe the types of things a social work professional might be able to do to help the Sanchez family.

2. Visit one of the following websites to obtain information about the social work profession:

   a. National Association of Social Workers, www.naswdc.org or http://www.help startshere.org/. Click on "State Chapters" to get information about NASW programs in your state, including community service opportunities. You may also want to check out the NASW Twitter at www.twitter.com/nasw to learn more about NASW.

   b. Council on Social Work Education, www.cswe.org.

3. Describe yourself (character, traits, and values) in terms of how you perceive the world and human nature. Discuss how these qualities may impact your professional work.

CHAPTER 2

History of Social Work and Social Welfare

The exact beginnings and origins of the profession of social work are difficult to determine, but ample evidence throughout history suggests that what has come to be recognized as social work has been performed for thousands of years. This work, often performed by persons affiliated with religious institutions, usually took the form of providing tangible goods and services to impoverished people confronted with health problems. As you will learn in this chapter, this "charity" work evolved over the centuries to include the provision of mental health services, community organization and development work, and advocacy for groups of people experiencing oppression whose voices are not heard by decision makers.

Imagine what it was like, though, to be one of the pioneers who began to practice social work before it had a name. What would it have been like to pursue social work before much of society acknowledged the idea that we should care for all our citizens? Try to grasp the struggles that these heroes and heroines faced. Imagine that you are in 17th-century England trying to help poor families obtain enough food to eat; in 18th-century America trying to gain support to open that first orphanage; in 19th-century America working in one of the new settlement houses helping immigrants adjust to their new home; in 20th-century America working for school desegregation, elimination of domestic violence, or one of the other new areas for social work. In the 21st century we are still working in the same areas— new challenges, but the same areas—along with new areas of social problems and needs.

As we begin this discussion of the history of social work and social welfare, clarifying the difference between the two is important. Although the terms are often used synonymously, they are not the same. As you learned in Chapter 1, social work is the practice of a professional activity of helping individuals, groups, and communities. In contrast, **social welfare** is a system aimed at creating social and economic justice. Social welfare services and programs have been part of society for centuries, and they provided the cornerstone for the emergence and development of the social work profession. Our discussion here will include a chronicle of the history of social welfare programs and services in which many social workers are active as well as the history of the social work profession. It will end with an overview of the development of social work education. Two informative references are used here as the primary sources for compiling the following historical perspective (NASW's *Milestones in the Development of Social Work and Social Welfare* (1998) and the 20th edition of Mizrahi & Davis's *Encyclopedia of Social Work* (2008)).

DEVELOPMENT OF SOCIAL SERVICES

The roots of the social work profession lie within the religious community and the religious teachings of a range of different religious groups. For many centuries, the provision of charity (or alms) was entirely within the purview of churches. As early as 1200 BC, religious leaders urged Jews to help the poor of their communities. Reflecting those tenets, historical Jewish documents describe charitable services that actually resemble modern-day mediation and casework (Senkowsky, 1996b). A man named Stephen, working as a representative of his religion, has been called the "first" social worker. Seven Jewish deacons were selected by Christian leaders to see to the needs of Jews who had been enslaved. One of these seven men, Stephen, was particularly effective in this mission. Along with his six peers, his efforts have been described as the first social work because he collected food and money for distribution to the "needy." These activities themselves were not innovative; however, designating specific persons to do the work was innovative. Stephen was commended by many for his work, but the leaders of Jerusalem were not in support of his work. He was tried by the High Court of the Great Temple and executed for his values and beliefs by the religious leadership (Marson & MacLeod, 1996). For examples of the influence of the largely religious doctrine on modern-day social services, see Exhibit 2.1.

Beginning in the 14th century, social changes in Europe began to transform attitudes toward the poor and the provision of charity. The feudal system of payment for services in land was beginning to shift to a more wage-based economic and social system, which led to increased trade within the towns and cities, thus creating a new "middle class" (Reid, 1995). In 1349, the Statute of Labourers was established in England to create a distinction between the "worthy" and the "unworthy" poor. Under this law, only the elderly and people with disabilities were deemed worthy to receive charity.

Two centuries later, this concept was expanded into the Henrician Poor Law of 1536. Through this law, Henry VIII created even more restrictive categories of persons eligible to receive aid. He also developed governmental regulations for the collection and disbursement of mandatory donations (taxes) from the general citizenry. One effect of this law was to transfer the responsibility of charity from the church to the state. Together, the Statute of Labourers and the Henrician Poor Law established the precedent for public social services and provided the framework for the enactment of the Poor Laws of 1601.

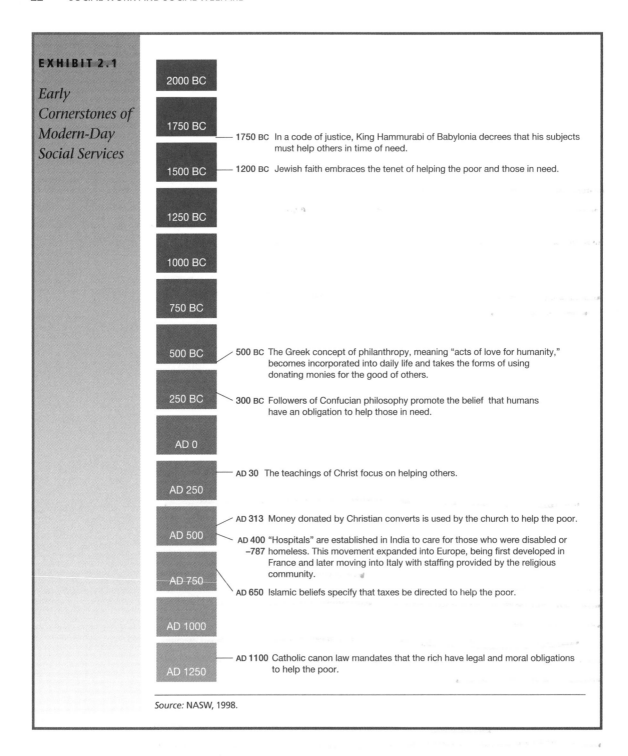

EXHIBIT 2.1

Early Cornerstones of Modern-Day Social Services

2000 BC

1750 BC
— **1750 BC** In a code of justice, King Hammurabi of Babylonia decrees that his subjects must help others in time of need.

1500 BC
— **1200 BC** Jewish faith embraces the tenet of helping the poor and those in need.

1250 BC

1000 BC

750 BC

500 BC
— **500 BC** The Greek concept of philanthropy, meaning "acts of love for humanity," becomes incorporated into daily life and takes the forms of using donating monies for the good of others.

250 BC
— **300 BC** Followers of Confucian philosophy promote the belief that humans have an obligation to help those in need.

AD 0

AD 250
— **AD 30** The teachings of Christ focus on helping others.

AD 500
— **AD 313** Money donated by Christian converts is used by the church to help the poor.
— **AD 400 –787** "Hospitals" are established in India to care for those who were disabled or homeless. This movement expanded into Europe, being first developed in France and later moving into Italy with staffing provided by the religious community.

AD 750
— **AD 650** Islamic beliefs specify that taxes be directed to help the poor.

AD 1000

AD 1250
— **AD 1100** Catholic canon law mandates that the rich have legal and moral obligations to help the poor.

Source: NASW, 1998.

Elizabethan Poor Laws of 1601

A defining point in the history of social services was the passage of the Elizabethan Poor Laws of 1601. These English laws are thought to be the single most significant event that defined the social service and welfare delivery system for the next 300 years. Many historical accounts of the development of the social work profession actually begin with the institution of these history-making laws. Advancing the philosophy of Henry VIII toward caring for those persons in need, the Poor Laws of 1601 were established in England during the reign of Queen Elizabeth I. Building on the efforts of the previous century, specifically the Henrician Poor Law and the Parish Poor Rate, that were aimed at placing responsibility for charity with the government and categorizing levels of charity based on worthiness, the Poor Laws employed the concept of mandatory local taxation to fund social and financial assistance (Corbett, 2008). Public assistance was provided to persons deemed eligible in three distinct categories: (1) monetary help for poor people who were deemed unemployable (older persons and persons with disabilities); (2) work for persons of limited income who were not elderly or disabled; and (3) apprenticeships for orphaned and dependent children. In order to receive assistance, recipients were often required to live in residential institutions known as workhouses, poorhouses or almshouses for adults and orphanages for children. Known as "indoor relief," this practice continued well into the 19th century, and in some areas of Europe and the United States could be found into the mid-20th century.

The European social and political climate was changing due to an increasing number of persons being displaced from rural areas as a result of restrictions on their rights to farming land. Known as the Enclosure Laws, these restrictions resulted in increased unemployment and homelessness. Such changes served as the impetus for the creation of the Poor Laws. These laws were an attempt to (1) extricate the church from the delivery of social services, (2) eliminate begging and criminal behavior, (3) centralize assistance within the government, and (4) standardize the types and amounts of assistance provided for the growing class of workers. The Poor Laws made a significant, long-term impact on the development of policies for providing aid to those persons in need by creating a clear-cut distinction between persons deemed worthy of receiving assistance and those deemed unworthy of receiving help. Persons deemed unworthy of aid were considered to be responsible for their situations. This belief continues to be at the core of the debate regarding funding for social programs. The Poor Laws represent a clear shift away from the private sector involvement in social service (that is, by the church) to governmental responsibility for the poor. This controversy over private versus public responsibility also continues to the present day. A form of the Poor Laws was eventually adopted in the North American colonies, as you will see in the next section.

Social Services in the 17th and 18th Centuries

Despite the overarching pervasiveness of the English Poor Laws, other events and advances that occurred during the next two centuries also had a profound effect on the future of social services in Europe and, later, in North America. For example, in the early 1600s, Father Vincent de Paul founded charity and religious organizations in France that established formalized structures for providing food, clothing, and financial support for those persons in need. The St. Vincent de Paul Society operated solely on voluntary contributions from parishioners, a model that prevails in the social service delivery system today. You might recognize the name, as the Society itself is still active in many communities.

Also during the 1600s, the Protestant ethic was gaining popularity in England and other parts of Europe. The **Protestant work ethic**, a belief system and way of life that emphasizes self-discipline and frugality, has had a significant influence on societal attitudes toward the poor. The Protestant work ethic perspective has taken on a negative connotation, as many people believe that all persons, through hard work and discipline, should be able to care for themselves at all times without help from others. Such thinking often translates into opposition to funding for social service and domestic programs.

Further efforts in 17th-century England to restrict access to aid by the poor took the form of the 1662 Law of Settlement, which stipulated that aid was based on one's place of residence. This law discouraged aid recipients from moving to other areas where they might find work (Reid, 1995).

Meanwhile, in England's North American colonies, the colonists began formulating social welfare policy in the form of poor laws fashioned after those in England. By 1657, Boston was home to the first private social welfare agency, the Scots' Charitable Society. In the same year, New York was the site for the first almshouse with others following soon thereafter in Plymouth (1658) and Boston (1660). In 1729, the first residential facility for orphans was opened in the French colony of New Orleans by the Ursuline Sisters, and the first psychiatric institution was established in 1773 in Williamsburg, Virginia. As you can see, even while the colonists were focused on expanding into new territory, establishing themselves in a new world, and grappling with the issue of colonization versus independence, they also devised plans to care for poor, sick, and disadvantaged persons. Most of these newly created organizations were private and often religiously affiliated.

Soon after independence, the government of the United States made its first major efforts to create public social and health services. A governmentally funded orphanage opened in Charleston, South Carolina, in 1790, and the U.S. Public Health Service was established in 1798 by a legislative act aimed at creating a health care system for merchant seamen. The Public Health Service still exists today to provide health care and mental health care to underserved populations around the world, to prevent and control disease, and to conduct research.

In sum, the 17th and 18th centuries were a time of expansion for social services.

Although the primary focus of most charitable programs was the alleviation of poverty by providing financial aid, they helped to educate future generations regarding the importance of addressing other aspects of the individual's life in order to facilitate a move out of poverty. The seeds for modern-day social casework and clinical treatment were being planted even at this point in our history in an effort to help those living in poverty to gain economic stability. A social system was literally built from scratch in the American colonies, becoming institutionalized as the country gained independence from England. However, as you will see, the belief in public responsibility for social and health services among American citizens would wax and wane from this point on—and it continues to be a source of controversy in the 21st century.

The 19th Century—a Defining Era in the United States

The 1800s were a boom time for the development of social welfare programs and the social work profession, particularly in the United States. This century witnessed progress in such areas as the creation of public and private agencies and organizations to address the country's growing social problems. During this century, the United States grew substantially in both size and population. In addition, the population became more diverse due to the increasing rates of immigration. Following the Civil War, the U.S. experienced a fluctuating economy that produced many periods of depression. Thus, the time was ripe for the formation of a more organized system of social service delivery. With the growth of the social service system came a dawning awareness that qualified and trained persons were needed to provide these services and to work with the increasingly diverse populations.

Exhibit 2.2 highlights some of the advancements that were made in our country's burgeoning system for taking care of all our citizens. Most important was the fact that a belief was developing during this time that certain groups within our population needed help in having their voices heard. The new United States was becoming humane with respect to the needs of those citizens living in poverty. Still, children, African Americans, widows and children of war veterans, persons with mental illnesses, and people devastated by disasters were just a few of the groups whose voices were then—and are now—often not heard by the majority of society. Advocates faced considerable adversity as they defended the rights of these marginalized groups. They often risked their reputations, safety, and personal funds to start programs to enhance the quality of life for these groups.

Although still considered by many authorities to be the preferred method for providing aid, indoor relief eventually gave way to "outdoor relief," the provision of services outside the institutional setting. From this paradigm shift came the founding of two movements that are of particular importance in the 19th-century history of social work and social welfare. The settlement house and Charity Organization Society movements, similar in intent but different in function, changed the nature of social service delivery and are proclaimed as being responsible

EXHIBIT 2.2

19th-Century Advances in Social Services

1810

1812 Societies for the Prevention of Pauperism were founded in New York, Baltimore, and Philadelphia aimed at providing aid to those who were suffering as a result of the War of 1812.

1820

1824 The Bureau of Indian Affairs was created as well as the House of Refuge—the first program for juvenile delinquents that was state-funded.

1830

1835 Boston followed other cities by establishing the Society for the Prevention of Pauperism, which became the forerunner of the Charity Organization Society movement that we will discuss in greater detail.

1836 Passage of child labor laws in Boston.

1840

1841 The first investigations of services provided to "insane people" were conducted by Dorothea Dix, who went on to help create 41 state and federal hospitals for persons with mental illness.

1845 The first public mental health facility (or "asylum") was opened in Trenton, New Jersey.

1850

1853 Children's Aid Society (still in existence in many states today) was organized in New York.

1863 First oversight organization for social services programs was founded in Massachusetts.

1860

1865 As a partnership between the federal government and private philanthropies, the Freedmen's Bureau was created as the first federal welfare entity to help freed slaves find new lives, gain education, and be protected from abuse and violence (ceased services in 1872).

1868 Public monies were used to pay "foster" families in Boston for housing children (New York followed in 1875).

1870

1870 A forerunner to the modern day long term care facility, the Home for Aged and Infirm Hebrew of New York City was established.

1877 Society for the Prevention of Cruelty to Children is organized in New York. The first Charity Organization Society (COS) began serving clients in Buffalo.

1880

1880 The Salvation Army was expanded to the U.S. (began in 1878 in England).

1886 First U.S. Settlement House opened in New York followed by the now famous Hull House in Chicago in 1889.

1890

1896 Public education became available to the "mentally deficient" in Providence, Rhode Island.

1900

Source: Corbett, 2008; NASW, 1998.

for the birth of the social work profession. Both movements share a philosophy that has become synonymous with American culture—individualism and personal freedom. However, efforts to integrate capitalistic individualism and charitable altruism have not always been successful, often resulting in a "patchwork of programs" (Reid, 1995, p. 2209). Nonetheless, settlement houses and charity organizations became the cornerstone of the American social service delivery system, despite the contradictions.

Settlement House Movement   Originating in England, the settlement house is a facility based in a geographically bound neighborhood whose purpose is to provide a center for the neighbors to come together for educational, social, and cultural activities. Settlement houses also provided social services and financial assistance. The first settlement house, Toynbee Hall, opened in London in 1884. It was not long before this model spread across England and the United States. In fact, just two years later, rooted in the Progressive Reform movement, the first American settlement house began operation in New York under the leadership of a former resident of Toynbee Hall, Stanley Coit. By the early 20th century, the number of settlement houses in the U.S. had grown to over 400 (Hopps et al., 2008). The best-known U.S. settlement house is Hull House, opened in Chicago in 1889 by Jane Addams and colleagues. (See Exhibit 2.3 to learn more about Jane Addams.)

The settlement house idea is based on three concepts: (1) social change can occur, (2) social class distinctions can be narrowed through information and education, and (3) change can come only when the settlement house workers immerse themselves in their clients' community (Blank, 1998). Simply stated, settlement houses were created as an attempt by socially minded persons to engage in "friendship with the poor through sharing their lives" (Kendall, 2000, p. 16). A key belief of this movement is that the social structure and society overall are responsible for individual problems. Originally aimed at serving the growing immigrant population, the early settlement houses focused on education and socialization into the American culture of the time (Blank, 1998). Jane Addams described her approach to the settlement house movement this way:

> Teaching in a Settlement requires distinct methods, for it is true of people who have been allowed to remain undeveloped and whose facilities are inert and sterile, that they cannot take their learning heavily. It has to be diffused in a social atmosphere, information must be held in solution, in a medium of fellowship and good will . . . . It is needed to say that a Settlement is a protest against a restricted view of education. (Urban Experience in Chicago)

Settlement house workers were typically young, well-educated adults (mostly women) interested in social issues and the arts. Because settlement house workers lived in the same neighborhoods as those with whom they worked, they could not ignore the mounting social concerns. These workers found the living and sanitary conditions, housing, child care, education, and worker exploitation in these neighborhoods to be unacceptable. The settlement house workers soon were in the forefront of controversial and much-needed social change and advocacy for marginalized groups. Thought by many to be the beginning of the social work profession's long history in social action and policy practice, workers in the early settlement houses played roles in the development of such social entities as juvenile courts, mothers' pensions, child labor laws, and workplace protections (McNutt & Floersch, 2008, p. 3). They also instituted training programs that would later become a component of the social work profession.

The settlement house concept is still in existence today, but it has undergone considerable reconstruction. The centers where idealistic, youthful volunteers lived and made efforts at teaching the arts and literature have been replaced by neighborhood-based community centers that provide a wide array of goods and services, including food and clothing, health care, after-school and summer recreation, crisis intervention, and counseling. The basic ideal on which the settlement houses were founded still exists today—change is most effective if it comes from within the community itself. One example, Grace Hill Settlement House, is profiled in Box 2.1.

Charity Organization Society   During the same period that the settlement houses were improving life for immigrants and influencing the formation of social welfare services in the United States, another movement that would impact the future of social work was under way. Like those of the settlement houses, the roots of charity organizations can also be found in 19th-century England. The London-based Society for Organising Charitable Relief and Repressing Mendicity provided the framework for the first North American **Charity Organization Society (COS)** in Buffalo, New York, in 1877. The concept of a charitable service that did not involve living with the persons being served quickly spread throughout the country; by 1892 there were 92 such societies in operation (Brieland, 1995).

The philosophical underpinning of the charity society movement was a morally based belief that the person was responsible for his or her own difficulties but could be rehabilitated through individual sessions with a "friendly visitor" as opposed to a financial handout (Brieland, 1995). "Not alms but a friend" was the motto of the early COS workers, who believed that extending friendship and sympathy would enable persons living in poverty to feel better about themselves and rise out of poverty (Kendall, 2000). The principles on which the COS was founded include: (1) detailed investigation of applicants; (2) central system of registration to avoid duplication; (3) cooperation between the various relief agencies; and (4) extensive use of volunteers in the roles of "friendly visitors" (Corbett, 2008, p. 7).

The first workers in the movement, the "friendly visitors" that would eventually become modern-day social workers, were primarily middle-class women who voluntarily ventured into neighborhoods in which persons of low income lived in

Jane Addams holding the peace flag standing with Mary McDowell.

Photo provided by University of Illinois at Chicago, The University Library, Department of Special Collections, Jane Addams Memorial Collection, JAMC neg 64.

EXHIBIT 2.3

Profile in Innovation: Jane Addams (1860–1935)

Synonymous with the origins of social work in the United States, Jane Addams opened Chicago's Hull House in 1889. Partnering with Ellen Gates, Addams established Hull House after visiting the original settlement house, Toynbee Hall, in London. Ever the activist, Addams fought for improved sanitary conditions in Chicago and, as a result, was appointed neighborhood sanitation inspector. Many organizations had their roots among the activism of Hull House. One example is the organization that later became the Children's Bureau. Quaker and staunch pacifist, her contributions go far beyond the work of Hull House. She was a community organizer, peace advocate, 1931 co-winner of the Nobel Peace Prize, and one of only two social workers inducted into the Hall of Fame of Great Americans. In 1909, Addams was elected president of the National Conference of Charities and Correction (later to be called National Council on Social Welfare), the first woman to hold this post. As pictured here, her dedication to the issue of world peace resulted in her active involvement in a number of peace organizations, including the Women's Peace Party, the National Progressive Party, and the Women's International League for Peace and Freedom. A prolific writer, Addams' works include six books on her life and her views. She accomplished all of this despite the fact that as a woman she did not acquire the right to vote until 1920.

Source: Barker, 2003; Corbett, 2008; Hopps et al., 2008; NASW, 1998; Quam, 2008.

order to share their wisdom and advice on good living. Organizers of this movement believed that visiting people in their homes and encouraging them to live a moral life was a more effective method of intervention than giving them financial aid. As a result, the COS entities engaged in such activities as individual assessments and registration of those "worthy" of receiving charity and, ultimately, employment and

BOX 2.1

*Grace Hill
Settlement
House*

Grace Hill Settlement House

Grace Hill Settlement House, located in St. Louis, Missouri, can trace its origins to a decision in 1844 by leaders of the town of North St. Louis to donate land for a church. Grace Episcopal Church was built in a neighborhood in which most residents were Episcopalians. As wealthier residents moved out of this neighborhood, it became home to a middle-class and then a low-income population, including many recent immigrants. In response, Grace Episcopal Church founded the Holy Cross Mission in 1903 to meet the changing needs of the neighborhood.

To expand their mission into the delivery of health care services, the Episcopal Diocese began the Holy Cross Dispensary in a nearby location in 1906. In 1914, Holy Cross Mission was incorporated. In 1923, the organization joined with the Community Fund (now United Way) to provide kindergarten, health clinics, recreation, and classes in crafts, dance, athletics, and music. From 1938 to 1944, Grace Hill gained recognition as a settlement house and instituted such changes as accepting African Americans and replacing religious staff with social workers. By 1965, Grace Hill had established its first Head Start program for preschool education. Shortly thereafter, Grace Hill, using neighbors (residents of the neighborhood) as advisors to program operations, began a meal program for older adults and developed a 10-year neighborhood improvement plan that resulted in the construction of low-cost apartments and the rehabilitation of existing housing stock.

By the 1980s, the philosophy of the agency was that the neighbors should be involved in developing training programs, forums, a resource bank, self-help groups, and communication centers. Keeping the settlement house model alive, services are now provided in the areas of child and older adult care, housing for low-income persons and families, self-help, job skills training, and community and economic development.

legal services (Brieland, 1995). Although the value-laden component of these early social services continued and became a pervasive part of social work for many decades, the work of these well-intentioned volunteers laid the groundwork for such advancements as social casework and the formation of family and children's service agencies.

Contributions of the Settlement House and Charity Society Movements   To grasp the significance of the events of 19th-century social services, let us compare and contrast these two major movements. The settlement house movement taught the importance of assessing and understanding the conditions in which client systems live as well as their cultures, the impact of environmental conditions on the quality of people's lives, and the effectiveness of empowerment through education, information, and group work. The friendly visitors of the Charity Organization Society movement taught the value of assessing each individual situation and developing an intervention specific to the individual, coupled with the knowledge that money alone does not always facilitate change. The COS movement was focused on relief, while the Settlement House vision was that of reform (Hopps et al., 2008).

Although both movements—in particular, the COS movement—have been criticized for being shortsighted and judgmental, together they provided the first steps that enabled the social work profession and society to move forward in our treatment of poor, abused, and oppressed groups.

Social Services in the 20th Century

The dawning of the 20th century brought with it even more changes in our society, in general, and the social services community, in particular. Economically, the country was emerging from the depression of the late 1800s. The first two decades of the 1900s were a time of economic prosperity. Socially and politically, the 1890s and early 1900s, known as the Progressive Era, were a time of significant reform in such far-ranging areas of women's rights (specifically suffrage), health care and social service programs, education, political practices, occupational and consumer safety, child and social welfare laws, environmental preservation, and socialization for immigrants. The leaders of the progressive movement successfully advocated for changes in social insurance, government regulation, and the professionalization of helping professions (Reid, 1995, p. 2212).

By this time, social work was established as a profession that responds to current economic, political, and social events and trends. Therefore, in times of economic booms, leaders in the social service movement had the opportunity to focus on coordinating services and organizing coalitions to enhance service delivery. The Progressives, a group of social and political activists that included Jane Addams, founder of Hull House, encouraged a number of social changes during this time. The Progressives gained national recognition for the need to establish a federal infrastructure for financial assistance, public health interventions, and social work professionalization that would concretize the delivery of social services for many years to come (Reid, 1995).

During the early decades of the 1900s, social workers and government officials formed organizations and government agencies that solidified the place of social services in U.S. society. Three organizations that grew out of the progressive movement and had an impact on the work of social workers were the National Urban League, the Children's Bureau (first headed by Hull House alumnae, Julia Lathrop), and the Child Welfare League of America. Despite social workers having a role in the founding of these organizations, the influence of such organizations on social work may not be readily apparent, the endorsement of governmental agencies and the merging of smaller groups into larger groups strengthened the position and voice of those committed to serving the poor.

Of particular importance during this period was the implementation of social policy and programming aimed at workers, women, and children. Workers' compensation legislation was first passed in 1910, and within ten years most states had followed suit. The Mothers' Pensions program that provided assistance for women and children were launched. Recipients of the Mothers' Pensions were typically Caucasian widowed mothers. Modeled after traditional charity programs in which the financial benefits were minimal and the goal was moral reform, this program was the first nationwide public program that provided financial assistance to women who were rearing families on their own and attempted to destigmatize recipients (Seccombe, 1999).

Also of importance during the early part of the 20th century was the emerging presence of social service departments being housed within institutions. The Massachusetts General Hospital in Boston was the first to create a department to serve patients' social and psychiatric needs. Soon there would be over one hundred hospital social service units. "Psychiatric social worker" was, in fact, first used in Boston in 1914.

Developments During the Depression and the New Deal   The stock market crash of 1929 sent the country spiraling downward into an economic and social depression that would last through the next decade. The Great Depression of the 1930s was a time of suffering and unrest. Nevertheless, as had become the tradition for the profession, social workers once again rose to the occasion.

When Franklin D. Roosevelt, a Democrat, was elected to the presidency in 1932, nearly one-third of Americans were living in poverty, manufacturing and agriculture had been devastated, and the breadlines were long and getting longer. In response, the Roosevelt administration instituted a number of New Deal programs that would have a lasting effect on our society.

Probably the most important New Deal legislation was the Social Security Act of 1935. Originally championed by members of the progressive movement since the early years of the century, the Social Security Act was passed as a measure to alleviate the poverty of the elderly, widows and widowers, the unemployed, persons with disabilities, and dependent children. The legislation became the foundation of our public welfare and retirement systems. Social worker Jane M. Hoey was appointed by the president to direct the Federal Bureau of Public Assistance, the entity that over-saw distribution of aid through this legislation. In addition to providing a retirement income for older adults, the Social Security Act ultimately resulted in the develop-ment of public assistance programs that would include such services as health care, employment services, transportation, and child day care for persons living in poverty and with disabilities, as well as impoverished women and children (known as Aid to Dependent Children, then, **Aid to Families with Dependent Children—AFDC** and now, **Temporary Assistance to Need Families (TANF)**). The Social Security Act and other New Deal reforms affirmed the role of the federal government in the administration of social services. This development would later serve U.S. society well, because structures were in place during times of economic crisis.

Other social and economic programs implemented during the New Deal include:

- *Federal Emergency Relief Administration (FERA):* Headed by social worker, Harry Hopkins, FERA formed a system of state grants to provide financial assistance. FERA later became the *Works Progress Administration (WPA)*, an agency that created employment from 1935 to 1943 for over eight million people in such diverse areas as construction of roads and bridges to development of cultural programs.

- *Civilian Conservation Corps (CCC):* In existence from 1933 to 1942, the CCC was designed to conserve and develop the nation's natural resources, while creating employment opportunities for unemployed men.

- *National Youth Administration (NYA):* Out of concern for ensuring that the country's high school and college students be able to complete their education, the NYA provided funding for part-time employment.

Developments During World War II and the 1950s   As often occurs during war-time, the United States experienced an economic recovery during the 1940s. World War II had a significant impact on the social work profession as well. For example, social workers developed and administered mental health programs for military personnel. This activity ultimately led to the creation of the nationwide, community-based mental health system that remains the basis for the provision of mental health services (Reid, 1995).

Nevertheless, there was little expansion of the social welfare system during the latter half of the 1940s. The focus during these years was on the returning veterans, one million of whom used the 1944 GI Bill of Rights to acquire a college education and purchase homes. In 1946, the group now known as the Baby Boomer generation was being born. This period provided a segue into the 1950s, which was clearly a strong economic period as well as a relatively conservative era in politics.

One of the most important 1950s events for social welfare and social work was the creation of the cabinet-level Department of Health, Education, and Welfare (HEW) in 1953, during the administration of Republican president Dwight D. Eisenhower. This was the first acknowledgment by the federal government that the well-being of all people in the United States was a high priority. This department—which in 1979 was divided into the Department of Health and Human Services (HHS) and the Department of Education—has been instrumental in formulating and administering virtually every federally funded social welfare program in existence in this country.

Other than establishing HEW, the 1950s, like the 1940s, are not well known for advances in the social service arena. Historically, the combination of Republican presidential administrations with prosperous times often means little attention (and funding) is devoted to the social service community; the 1950s are a prime example of that historical pattern.

Developments During the 1960s and 1970s   The 1960s have become well known as a tumultuous time on many fronts. In 1960, the nation elected a Democratic president, John F. Kennedy. The civil rights movement was heating up. The war in Vietnam would soon take center stage, bringing with it civil unrest here at home. The youth were headed in a different direction from those of the previous decades. Many young people opposed the Vietnam War and military service in general, participated in the sexual revolution, and experimented with illicit drugs.

From the social work perspective, the 1960s were an interesting time, indeed. Many social workers feel that the 1960s were one of the most significant times for the profession due to the creation of a number of social programs, advances in civil rights, and the willingness of U.S. citizens to confront injustices in a public way. The Kennedy administration established the Peace Corps in 1961 and encouraged Congress to pass the 1963 Community Mental Health Center Act. Kennedy's successor, Lyndon B. Johnson, another Democrat, oversaw passage of the Civil Rights Act of 1964 as well as the Economic Opportunity Act of 1964—an array of social welfare legislation known collectively as the Great Society. Although some critics consider Johnson's War on Poverty and the Great Society to have been a failure, the 1964 legislation was responsible for the creation of numerous social programs, many of which still exist in some form today: Job Corps, Head Start, Volunteers in Service to America (VISTA—the domestic version of the Peace Corps), and the Neighborhood Youth Corps.

Five major social programs were enacted during the Great Society that enhanced—and perhaps saved—the lives of the people they serve:

- *Medicare:* Health insurance for those who receive Social Security passed in 1965.

- *Medicaid:* Health insurance for those who receive public welfare benefits also passed in 1965.

- *Older Americans Act:* A nationwide system of community-based services for older adults was created in 1965.

- *Food Stamp Act of 1964:* This Department of Agriculture program provides food assistance to people living on limited incomes.

- *Elementary and Secondary Education Act:* In 1965, federal funding was directed for the first time in history toward the goal of providing services in the public school system for an array of services and students.

Although not as glamorous and exciting as the 1960s, the 1970s was a decade of progress in social services. Despite the ultimate downfall of the Republican administration of Richard M. Nixon, a significant number of programs were created under his leadership. The focus of his administration was a traditional Republican one in that "charity" was not endorsed, but work incentives were supported (Reid, 1995). The laws passed during the administrations of Nixon and his successor, Gerald Ford, that had far-reaching effects on social service delivery include:

- Supplemental Security Income (SSI) was made available in 1972 for older persons and people with disabilities whose income was still well below poverty standards.

- The 1974 Comprehensive Employment and Training Act (CETA) program provided educational and job opportunities for persons of limited income.

- The Education for All Handicapped Children Act (1975) required all public schools to provide educational experiences for children with disabilities that are comparable to those available to children without such disabilities.

- The Title XX amendment to the Social Security Act (1975) provided funds for the purchase of social services, training, and housing for persons who qualified based on their income.

- The 1974 Child Abuse Prevention and Treatment Act created a comprehensive approach to the prevention, investigation, and treatment of child abuse that was expanded in 1978 to address inadequacies of the adoption system.

Developments during the 1980s and 1990s   Those in the social work community do not typically view the 1980s with favor. The Republican administrations of Ronald Reagan and George H. W. Bush followed the traditional pattern of decreased spending on domestic and social programs. Specifically, two legislative acts passed during Reagan's first term severely cut social service funding: the Omnibus Budget

Reconciliation Act (OBRA) of 1981 and the Tax Equity and Fiscal Responsibility Act of 1982. OBRA gave more authority and less funding to states for administration of public assistance programs and made it more difficult for those living in poverty to access services, as states could individually determine eligibility and access. The 1982 law resulted in decreased Medicare, Medicaid, AFDC, SSI, and unemployment funds. Continuing in his predecessor's footsteps, George H.W. Bush advocated for increased privatization of the social service system based on a belief that the public should not be responsible for the welfare of the general population. Enacted in 1988, the Family Support Act was an attempt to positively impact the welfare system by providing improved employment and training programs, child support enforcement, and child care services. Ironically, it may be argued that the attempts of Reagan and Bush (senior) to disempower the social welfare system resulted in a strengthening of sorts. Increased funding and management options at the state level and a renewed interest in the nonprofit sector helped bring the attention of the general public to the need for a centralized social service system (Reid, 1995).

President Bill Clinton's campaign platform in the early 1990s was designed to redirect the public's attention to domestic issues. Clinton's presidential years focused on reviewing and revamping a number of domestic programs. His administration took on such intractable social issues as health care, family health and well-being issues, abortion, discrimination against gays and lesbians in the military, welfare reform, and distressed communities (Green & Haines, 2002). Despite the failure of the effort to embrace universal health care and a Republican-controlled congress, the Clinton administration made significant strides in revitalizing the economy, increasing the minimum wage to $5.15/hour, creating new jobs, and eliminating the budget deficit (Hopps et al., 2008).

For social workers, the most significant issues addressed during the 1990s were welfare reform and community development. The 1996 Personal Responsibility and Work Opportunity Reconciliation Act (PRWORA) became law, replacing Aid to Families with Dependent Children with Temporary Assistance to Needy Families (TANF). TANF continues to provide cash assistance to women who are low-income and their children, but with greater restrictions, mandated work requirements, and a five-year lifetime cap on the receipt of benefits. Proponents believe that the welfare-to-work programs created by this welfare reform are responsible for positive changes, while others (mostly those on the front lines) believe they are a deterrent to getting out of poverty. Many former welfare recipients gained employment during the prosperous 1990s, but many critics question whether this trend can be maintained during weaker economic times (Green & Haines, 2002). Many persons working full time for minimum wage still live in poverty without health care and other resources.

The 1990s saw an array of new legislation aimed at protecting the rights of certain populations and ensuring access to services. Passed in 1990, the Americans with Disabilities Act (ADA) guarantees that persons with disabilities can have access to public facilities and live without fear of employment discrimination. The

Individuals with Disabilities Education Act (IDEA) addressed the gap of services to children with disabilities who attend public schools. The Mental Health Parity Act (1996) mandates that insurance companies must provide coverage for mental health services as well as physical health services.

In spite of changes pursued and achieved by the Clinton administration, critics question whether real change occurred and, if so, who benefited from that change. For example, homosexuality was publicly addressed for the first time by the military with the creation of the "don't ask, don't tell" policy. This policy, which meant that the military could not officially inquire about a service member's sexual orientation, and service members could not offer that information, was viewed as a setback by the gay and lesbian rights movement.

Social Services in the 21st Century and Beyond

The new millennium saw the inauguration of a Republican president whose campaign platform let us know that he is not a supporter of increased funding for social programs. In fact, one of George W. Bush's early efforts in this area was to make federal monies available to faith-based social services. In many ways, this is a continuation of the agenda promoted by his father, George H. W. Bush, who launched the 1,000 Points of Light project in which private-sector agencies were showcased for their efforts. Both efforts aim at increasing the private sector's responsibility for social programs. Through the two administrations of the 21st century Bush presidency, social services experienced continued and increasing privatization of services—an action that decreases the governmental responsibility for funding. Despite the fact that the budget was in surplus in 2000, the 2005 Deficit Reduction Act (DRA) was passed to offset deficits due to tax cuts, the Iraqi war, and natural disasters (Hopps et al., 2008).

The 2008 Presidential elections marked a dramatic shift on several levels. We have elected Barack Obama, the first African American president in our history, whose candidacy was focused on turning the economic, educational and social tide in our country. Within the first month in office, the new President's history-making economic stimulus package is an effort to stabilize the country's economy by creating new employment and opportunities. The President has also made a commitment to tackle other areas of crisis within our country, to include housing, educational and social services.

Although historical trends can be a guide, predicting what will happen in the coming years would still be speculation. However, we can predict which issues among the current social, economic, and political challenges that confront our social service system will affect social work practice. For example, welfare reforms, changing family demographics, restricted access to benefits, an aging society, and the need for greater understanding of global issues are all expected to provide opportunities for social workers to test their skills. Here are some observations from current research:

- Approximately two-thirds of our population will use public assistance benefits at some point in their adult life (Rank & Hirschl, 2002). In fact, over a three-year period, approximately one-third of Americans spent at least two or more months living in poverty (DeNavas-Wait et al., 2008). More funding will be needed to support welfare-to-work programs, particularly for single, female-headed households.

- Both domestically and internationally, the population will continue to become older, creating new challenges for the older adults, their families and their societies.

- Immigrants and refugees are at higher risk for living in poverty, particularly those who enter the U.S. as undocumented persons.

PROFESSIONAL EDUCATION IN SOCIAL WORK: AN HISTORICAL PERSPECTIVE

As you have seen, the social work profession has been evolving for centuries. However, the term "social work" was not commonly used and formalized social work education did not exist until the late 1800s and early 1900s. In a sense, social work education began in the early settlement houses, which served as "social laboratories" for university students. As Exhibit 2.4 shows, though, not all the training originated at the university.

Despite the fact that social work was not fully recognized as a profession until the 1930s, the term social work was first used in 1900 by an educator, Simon Patten, to refer to the work of friendly visitors and settlement house workers. This bit of social work trivia indicates that the emergence of the profession coincided with the growth of these two movements during the late 1800s. In fact, the volunteers that were prominent in the early movements were motivated to "address the 'social question,' the paradox of increasing poverty in an increasingly productive economy" and recognized the need to move their voluntary efforts to an occupation and then to a profession (Hopps et al., 2008, p. 1).

Educating Social Workers

As in England, U.S. social work training emerged from the COS and settlement house movements, taking the form of apprenticeships and in-house training. The leadership of the burgeoning profession quickly determined that more formal training was needed. By 1893, a call had been issued for "formal education in applied philanthropy" because the "on-the-job" training offered within the agency setting was deficient in the provision of principles and theory (Leighninger, 2000, pp. 1–2). In 1894, the first social welfare textbook, *American Charities*, was published.

Exhibit 2.5 discusses Mary Richmond and the seminal textbook that she developed two decades later.

Recognizing that, in order to be a profession, a shift was needed to move from volunteers to trained professionals, the idea of formalized social work training quickly gained appeal throughout the United States. These early educational ventures were agency-based, but within a brief period, the training programs were increasingly located in university settings, with input provided by agency personnel (Frumkin & Lloyd, 1995). Many people believed that the early British social work educational approach was more advanced than U.S. methods because the training was entirely university-based. Many English social workers, however, considered the slower-developing American system—with its independent schools of social work heavily influenced by community agencies—to be superior to their university-based system (Kendall, 2000).

The founding of the program considered to be the first social work training program in the United States occurred in 1895 at the Chicago School of Social Economics at Chicago Commons. By 1903, the program was known as the Chicago School of Civics and Philanthropy (which later became the University of Chicago School of Social Service Administration) and was offering a year-long training program. By 1918, seventeen social work training programs had been established (Frumkin & Lloyd, 1995)—an average of one new program per year. Most programs emphasized a casework curriculum, thus carving out a niche for clinical social work.

A little-known charity organization worker from an upper-middle-class English family, Octavia Hill entered the "charity" world by working with young girls in a toy-making project under the guidance of her mentor, social reformer John Ruskin. Hill soon became aware of the appalling conditions in which the girls lived. By 1869, she had moved from the toy project into recruiting and training other volunteers to help improve housing for low-income persons. These female volunteers, known as Housing Estate Managers, collected rents and engaged in individual work that would later be known as social casework.

Hill's contribution to the development of the social work profession around the world is that she trained the volunteers to work with tenants on an individual basis in a caring, respectful manner, affirming their dignity and autonomy—the cornerstone of what we now know as social work. In fact, Hill's group discussions about cases, facilitated by a mentor, were the origins of organized social work training. Hill is also credited with establishing an organization that became the model for the Charity Organization Society movement.

EXHIBIT 2.4

Profile in Innovation: Octavia Hill (1838–1912)

Source: Barker, 2003; Kendall, 2000.

EXHIBIT 2.5

Profile in Innovation: Mary Richmond (1861–1928)

The "foremother" of American professional social work, Mary Richmond was a social activist and prolific writer on social issues (Kendall, 2000). Starting out as a treasurer for a Maryland COS, Richmond also served as a friendly visitor (Longres, 2008). In 1897, Richmond, then secretary of the Charity Organization Society of Baltimore, delivered a speech at the National Conference of Charities and Corrections in which she said "we owe it to those who shall come after us that they shall be spared the groping and blundering by which we have acquired our own stock of experience" (Richmond, 1897, p. 181). Richmond argued that workers needed training as "relief and child-saving agents" with "shoulder-to-shoulder contact which makes cooperation natural and inevitable" (p. 181). She went on to state that theory and practice should be concurrent, with students beginning in a

Mary Richmond

general area of study and moving into a specialization—the model still used as the basis of social work education today. Richmond's definition of social casework set the stage for the future of social work practice.

Richmond's call for the formalized training of "charity" workers had previously been made by a Massachusetts community activist, Anna Dawes, but it was not acted on until 1898 when the New York School of Philanthropy (now the Columbia University School of Social Work) offered a six-week summer school session that was extended in 1910 to two years. Richmond went on to become a faculty member in this program. She is best known for her 1917 book, *Social Diagnosis*, which was a compilation of her own lectures and interdisciplinary reading. This book became the primary text used by early social work educators. Interestingly, Richmond debated with Simon Patten (who coined the use of the title "social worker") on the issue of the focus of social work, whether it should be working with individuals or serving as advocates.

Source: Barker, 2003; Brieland, 1995; Longres, 2008.

Despite the rapid growth of educational endeavors, however, the profession was still in its infancy, and it was generally unorganized and fragmented.

Abraham Flexner (1866–1959), an educator and not a social worker, made a major contribution to the growth of the social work profession, although his efforts initially were viewed as devastatingly negative. His 1915 critique on the profession resulted in some of the most important advancements in the profession's history. At the time of his analysis, Flexner was the assistant secretary of the General Education Board for New York City. Speculation has been offered that the profession's leadership asked Flexner, an educational reformer, to offer his thoughts on the social work profession because they had already begun to realize that the profession needed to change (Leighninger, 2000). Although the enhancements that Flexner recommended took many years to achieve, and, in fact, are ongoing, his report did serve to solidify social work as a profession. Flexner recommended that social work become better organized, and he identified a set of criteria that he viewed as minimal for any discipline to be considered a profession. Flexner's report states that a profession must

- Involve intellectual operations with large responsibility.
- Derive raw material from science and learning and apply it to a practical and definite end.
- Possess educationally communicable techniques.
- Have self-organization.
- Be altruistic in motivation.

Recognizing that social work possessed character, practicality, a tendency toward self-organization, and altruism, Flexner stated that it was not yet a profession due to deficits in individual responsibility and educationally communicable techniques (Syers, 2008).

Social work professionals of the time rallied in an effort to strengthen the profession. As a result of Flexner's critique, social work training programs became more formalized. In addition, social workers began to conduct their own research, thus generating their own theories. Finally, the profession began to articulate its own methods of practice and focused on organizing social workers into a professional group. One response to Flexner's concerns was Mary Richmond's 1917 book, *Social Diagnosis*, which outlined assessment techniques for use with clients.

By 1917, seventeen of the social work education programs that were in operation in the United States and Canada came together to establish the Association of Training Schools for Professional Social Work. Reorganizing later, the group became known as the American Association of Schools of Social Work (AASSW). By 1952, the AASSW joined forces with the National Association of Schools of Social Administration to become the Council on Social Work Education (CSWE)—the organization that now accredits bachelor and master of social work programs. In addition, the National Association of Social Workers was established in 1955 when seven previously separate professional social work organizations joined to form one national organization that could represent the interests of the profession.

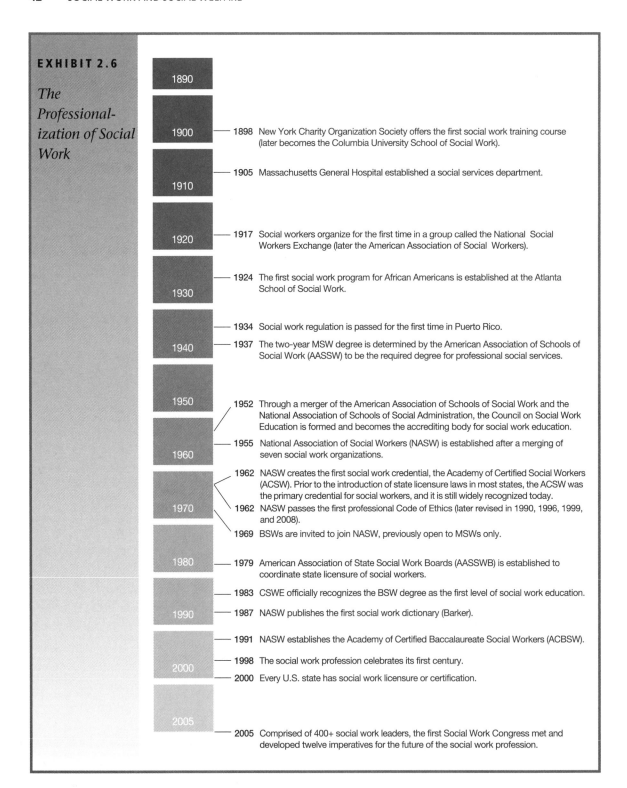

EXHIBIT 2.6

The Professionalization of Social Work

1890

1900

1898 New York Charity Organization Society offers the first social work training course (later becomes the Columbia University School of Social Work).

1905 Massachusetts General Hospital established a social services department.

1910

1920

1917 Social workers organize for the first time in a group called the National Social Workers Exchange (later the American Association of Social Workers).

1924 The first social work program for African Americans is established at the Atlanta School of Social Work.

1930

1934 Social work regulation is passed for the first time in Puerto Rico.

1937 The two-year MSW degree is determined by the American Association of Schools of Social Work (AASSW) to be the required degree for professional social services.

1940

1950

1952 Through a merger of the American Association of Schools of Social Work and the National Association of Schools of Social Administration, the Council on Social Work Education is formed and becomes the accrediting body for social work education.

1955 National Association of Social Workers (NASW) is established after a merging of seven social work organizations.

1960

1962 NASW creates the first social work credential, the Academy of Certified Social Workers (ACSW). Prior to the introduction of state licensure laws in most states, the ACSW was the primary credential for social workers, and it is still widely recognized today.

1962 NASW passes the first professional Code of Ethics (later revised in 1990, 1996, 1999, and 2008).

1970

1969 BSWs are invited to join NASW, previously open to MSWs only.

1980

1979 American Association of State Social Work Boards (AASSWB) is established to coordinate state licensure of social workers.

1983 CSWE officially recognizes the BSW degree as the first level of social work education.

1987 NASW publishes the first social work dictionary (Barker).

1990

1991 NASW establishes the Academy of Certified Baccalaureate Social Workers (ACBSW).

1998 The social work profession celebrates its first century.

2000

2000 Every U.S. state has social work licensure or certification.

2005

2005 Comprised of 400+ social work leaders, the first Social Work Congress met and developed twelve imperatives for the future of the social work profession.

Expanding Professional Boundaries

Establishing social work education was not the only activity of the social work profession that was occurring during the late 19th and early 20th centuries. Professional social work was gaining recognition in three fields of practice: medical social work, psychiatric social work, and child welfare. In 1905, the first hospital social work department was organized at Massachusetts General Hospital, and just two years later, the same institution offered psychiatric social work services. Interestingly, the title "psychiatric social worker" was not used until 1914.

In the realm of child welfare services, a variety of practice activities were emerging. Social workers were being trained in the area of mental health diagnosis at the same time that juvenile court systems were being established to address the issue of juvenile crime and delinquency (Brieland, 1995). Social workers were also making their presence felt in the public school systems, where they worked with children whose home lives were dysfunctional. These areas remain a central part of social work today.

While much of the early period of the profession's formation focused on developing knowledge and skills for working with individuals and families, other concepts and areas of practice have emerged. By the 1930s, group work and community organizing were gaining recognition as areas of practice (Hopps et al., 2008). Since the 1960s, we have seen an expansion of these areas as well as the introduction of generalist practice, ecological and systems theory and, most recently, evidence-based practice (McNutt & Floersch, 2008). As you will learn throughout this book, each of these areas has found its place in contemporary social work practice.

An additional area of activity for the social work profession was the creation of professional associations. See Exhibit 2.6 for some of the highlights of the profession's organizational efforts.

In 1977, a special issue of the journal *Social Work* was devoted to defining, describing, and discussing conceptual frameworks that were pertinent to social work practice at that time. This effort to further refine the definition of the profession of social work addressed such issues as the mission, objectives, professional oversight, knowledge and skills, and educational implications associated with the profession (Minahan, 1981).

This special issue generated such attention that a second special issue appeared in 1981. This second effort to frame social work as a strong profession included a working statement on the purpose of social work. I want to share the complete statement with you so that we can use this as a point from which to build our collective understanding of the social work profession (Minahan, 1981, p. 6):

> The purpose of social work is to promote or restore a mutually beneficial interaction between individuals and society in order to improve the quality of life for everyone. Social workers hold the following beliefs:

- The environment (social, physical and organizational) should provide the opportunity and resources for the maximum realization of the potential and aspirations of all individuals, and should provide for their common human needs and for the alleviation of distress and suffering.
- Individuals should contribute as effectively as they can to their own well-being and to the social welfare of others in their immediate environment as well as to the collective society.
- Transactions between individuals and others in their environment should enhance the dignity, individuality and self-determination of everyone. People should be treated humanely and with justice.
- Clients of social workers may be an individual, a family, a group, a community or an organization.

The social workers who developed this working statement also conceptualized a list of objectives that were (and still are) essential for the practice of social work (Minahan, 1981, p. 6). These objectives include

Social workers focus on person-and-environment *in interaction*. To carry out their purpose, they work with people to achieve the following objectives:

- Help people enlarge their competence and increase their problem-solving and coping abilities.
- Help people obtain resources.
- Make organizations responsive to people.
- Facilitate interaction between individuals and others in their environment.
- Influence interactions between organizations and institutions.
- Influence social and environmental policy.

WHERE WE HAVE COME FROM AND WHERE WE ARE GOING

We began this odyssey into the history of social work and social welfare more than 3,000 years ago with the concept that we, as citizens, have a moral obligation to help others. You have seen, throughout the centuries, the ways in which an entire profession has been molded from those early hints of altruism. Our profession came into existence out of a need to respond to the "social question" of the 19th century, specifically, how could poverty and social need exist in a country of prosperity (Hopps et al., 2008). In just over 100 years, the term social work came into use, and the definition of a social worker has evolved from an occupation for "anyone involved in activities with a social purpose" (Kendall, 2000, p. 93) to a professional who completes a degree from an accredited social work program and who is engaged in a theory-based practice of helping others to optimize their potential in life. As a profession, social work has moved from a belief system that blamed the individual for creating her or his pauperism to an understanding that environmental conditions are the precursors for poverty. In addition, both social action and individual casework are now recognized parts of the profession (Kendall, 2000).

Social work education has also evolved from a model of informal apprenticeships to one of a three-level, accredited professional education built on a framework of knowledge, skills, and values. While Flexner's 1915 report may have spurred the profession into a critical review of our educational and practice models, it is through the work of the many and visionary educators and practitioners that our educational system has continued to be on the forefront of meeting the needs of our society. As leaders in our field note in a 2008 overview of social work education, our current and future focus is on strengthening our accountability to those we serve, specifically in terms of developing key competencies for students and practitioners (particularly in the area of multiculturalism—the ability to work with diverse populations), determining appropriate outcomes for education and interventions and evaluating our practice (Hoffman et al., 2008; Hopps et al., 2008). Developing educational delivery systems that are responsive to the needs of social work students is critical for our profession to continue to reach all segments of our population. To remain on the cutting edge of human service education and delivery, we continuously review our educational programs and explore ways to make social work education available and effective. Providing distance education programs in alternative formats and venues is just one example. Having made the journey from the origins of the profession to the present day, you can see that a long and rich history will guide social workers into the future.

CONCLUSION

This chapter has described the history of social welfare and the social work profession. Many innovative and courageous women and men helped shape the profession that is so integral to our modern-day society. I hope that this gives a meaningful context to learning about the values and ethics embraced by the profession, the fields of practice in which social workers engage, and some of the skills needed to be a professional social worker.

The history of social work and social welfare has been and continues to be linked to the events of the time. As social workers respond to the changing needs of the client systems that they serve, new knowledge and skills are developed. One thing that we now know about social work is that our history still serves as a guide to our future. To be effective practitioners, we must be acutely aware of the dynamic and constant changes that occur in economic, political, social policies while, at the same time, being mindful to adhere to our professional values and ethics—more about which will be discussed in Chapter 6.

As this chapter has highlighted, our profession was founded on a need to help people who are impacted by a changing environment and, as McNutt and Floersch (2008) point out, we are still engaged in that quest today. While the definitions of the social work profession have evolved over the history of the profession, a common theme and commitment has been woven throughout. That is, social workers have long been committed to perceiving client systems within the context of the environment in which they live and interventions have been targeted at individuals, families, groups, communities, and societies (Gibelman, 2004).

MAIN POINTS

- Social welfare is the system of programs and services that respond to social and economic needs and injustices. The first organized attempt at mandating the provision of social services was the 1349 Statute of Labourers that designated categories of need in England.

- The Elizabethan Poor Laws of 1601 established an approach to the delivery of financial and social aid that continues today. Intended to transfer the authority for charity from the church to the government, standardize aid programs, and decrease criminal activity, these laws dictated that public aid could be given to the unemployable, but that the employable must work and children that were orphaned or dependent would serve as apprentices.

- The roots of the U.S. social service system can be found in the British system's settlement houses and charity organizations. In the settlement house movement, young people lived and worked in poor neighborhoods to help improve living conditions; in the charity organization movement, caseworkers focused on helping individuals overcome their problems.

- The 20th century saw the formalization of the social work profession and growth in the social service delivery system. The Depression of the 1930s prompted a shift of services from the private to the public sector. The civil unrest of the 1960s and 1970s prompted new social initiatives created to address issues of poverty and the needs of women, children, and older adults.

- Demographic changes in the 21st century are creating a society with widening economic gaps and an older, more diverse population with greater social, economic, and physical needs.

- In existence for a century, social work education has continued to change in response to societal needs. Flexner's 1915 report on the profession had the effect of solidifying social work as a profession.

EXERCISES

1. Go to the Sanchez Family interactive case (go to www.routledgesw.com/cases). You will note from Celia Sanchez's history that Celia uses the food bank at her church as a resource for her family. The Catholic Church has a long and venerable history of caring for the poor in its communities. Describe a faith-based organization in your community that offers services to persons with limited incomes. How does it differ from sectarian institutions that offer the same or similar services?

2. Select one of the concerns or needs identified in the Sanchez Family case. Citing examples from this chapter, speculate on the ways that the concern or need would have been addressed in different eras.

3. Review the case file for Hector Sanchez. You will note that Hector was given amnesty under a 1986 federal amnesty program. Using the Internet, conduct a search to learn about federal amnesty programs.

4. Go to the Carla Washburn interactive case at www.routledgesw.com/cases and familiarize yourself with the case. You will note that the social worker is employed by the Area Agency on Aging (AAA). The AAA was established through the Older Americans Act. Develop a brief report on the history and current focus of the Older Americans Act, specifically as it relates to the Area Agency on Aging. Identify those services provided by the AAA that Mrs. Washburn could receive.

CHAPTER 3

U.S. Poverty and the Implications for Social Work

How did I get to be eighty
  And
    Never
      Get over
        Being
          Poor?
When I was little
  I was poor.
    But playing
      And
        Dreaming
        Kept some of the pain
          Of
            Being poor
              Away
    And my folks
      Kept
        Lots of the worries from me.
When I was a teenager
  I just knew I'd marry a good man
    With work
      And
        Things would be all right.
And I did.
But he was poor, too.

Work was steady for a while,
  But so were the children.

There were good days
  And warm times
But there were lots of times
  When his work died off

And
  His worrying
    Brought pain.
He worked any kind of job
  In
    Any kind of weather
      Till
    The fever got him
      And
    The Lord took him
      And I had to go to welfare.
Then
    They cut that—some.

Reverend,
  Do people born poor?
    Have
    To stay that way—always?
  Ain't there any other way—
                Even when we get to be eighty?
  Does "poor" always have to be
      A
        Life sentence?

From *If . . . A Big Word With the Poor* by Don Bakely, Faith & Life Press,
Newton, Kansas. Used by permission.

This 1976 poem, composed by a social activist, focuses on the plight of an impoverished 80-year-old woman. At the same time, the poem raises a number of issues that continue to plague our society more than 30 years after its publication. The woman in this poem contacted Don Bakely for help one Thanksgiving Day because she was out of food and fuel. His powerful words move us as we read this poem because they address the issues of lifelong poverty, being an older adult and poor, and the inadequacy of the public welfare system. His words, however, also capture the hope that this woman continued to have throughout her life—a phenomenon we do not usually associate with chronic poverty and advanced age.

The social issues raised in this poem provide us with a beginning point for a discussion of the needs of many persons in our society and the approaches that have been devised to address those needs. Specifically, we will continue our journey through the social work profession by discussing the issues of poverty and society's historical response to eliminating poverty. Understanding poverty, welfare programs, and social services are critical for all social workers. As noted in Chapter 1, the mission of social workers is to enhance the capacity of their clients. To be an effective social worker, you need to understand your clients' concerns, challenges, and needs—whether they are related to poverty, health, employment, or safety. This chapter covers the origins of poverty, the ways in which the public and private sectors have attempted to minimize poverty and its effects, and the role of a social worker in optimizing clients' capacities.

DIMENSIONS OF POVERTY

Emily did not have much experience with or knowledge of poverty before deciding to be a social worker. Actually, Emily had no personal experience with poverty. She certainly knew there were people in the world and in her community who lived in poverty, but she did not think about their situations, so they were not real for her. She had no insight into the realities of living in poverty. She had heard people say that poor people could escape poverty simply by "pulling themselves up by their bootstraps." Not being sure about the truth of that adage, Emily found herself wondering about the reasons for so many people to become impoverished.

Emily's first experience with persons living in poverty came during her community service for her introductory social work course. While Emily had no life experience with poverty, she believed that, as a social worker, she needed to gain insight into the lives of persons living in poverty. Therefore, she opted to complete her service learning experience at Oasis House, a shelter for families who are homeless. There, she began to gain insight into poverty and the ways in which living in poverty affected people. As she worked with children on their homework, they shared with her stories about having utilities cut off, being hungry, getting evicted, and living in the car—all because a parent was laid off from her or his job. Emily learned that poverty is not simple or just, and it is not caused by a lack of motivation. Rather, poverty is a complicated phenomenon that has many faces, some that are 9 years old.

If asked such questions as what does being poor mean, who are the poor, how do people get to be poor, what keeps people in poverty, many people in our society would have opinions, but those opinions are often not fact based. The definition of poverty, profiles of those who live in poverty, and the causes of poverty have been and continue to be emotional and value-laden issues with which our society struggles in the political, social, religious, and public and private social service arenas.

Defining Poverty

A simple definition of **poverty** would be having inadequate financial resources. Stated more poignantly:

Poverty is hunger. Poverty is lack of shelter. Poverty is being sick and not being able to see a doctor. Poverty is not being able to go to school and not knowing how to read. Poverty is not having a job, is fear for the future, living one day at a time. Poverty is losing a child to illness brought about by unclean water. Poverty is powerlessness, lack of representation and freedom. (Worldbank Group, 2003)

The concept of quantifying poverty was first documented in 1795 in England when the government subsidized wages that fell below a designated level. Known as the Speenhamland system, the amount of the subsidy was determined by the current price of bread and the number of members in the family (Barker, 1999). It was not until 1964 that the U.S. federal government devised the poverty line as an official measure of poverty. The **poverty line** is the amount defined by the federal government as the minimal income level at which a family or individual can meet their basic needs. The measure was originally based on research from 1955 that suggested that people spend one-third of their post-tax income on food (Sherraden, 1990). Known as the Thrifty Food Plan, the government thus calculated the poverty line by identifying the amount needed for the minimum subsistence diet and then multiplying that number by three. Based on this formula, in 2009, a family of four living in the contiguous U.S. with a total household income of $22,050/year ($1,467/month) meets the poverty guidelines (Center on Budget and Policy Priorities [CBPP], 2009; U.S. Department of Health and Human Services [DHHS], 2009).

Current spending patterns differ dramatically from what they were in 1964. Today families spend a smaller percentage of their income on food and a much larger percentage on transportation, housing, and medical care. Moreover, poverty is measured on income before taxes are deducted, and some nonmonetary items (such as food stamps) can be considered a part of income. These strictly economic measures of poverty (though still used) are considered outdated by welfare rights advocates, and many social workers think that poverty can best be understood in social, political, economic, and emotional terms. Economically, "absolute" poverty occurs when an individual's income is less than the amount needed to obtain the minimal necessities for living. On an emotional level, "relative deprivation" is the perception that an individual does not possess as many assets as others (Hopps & Collins, 1995). Both types of poverty are real and interrelated, and both can be devastating for the individual and the family.

Who Are the Poor?

Many people believe the stereotype that people who are poor are nonwhite unemployed single mothers with lots of children, who subsist on welfare and are homeless or live in dilapidated housing in "bad" areas. Most unfortunate is the widespread myth that people who live in poverty are lazy and unmotivated to change their situations. Many people living in poverty are employed, have two or fewer children, and are very motivated to move out of poverty. In spite of this, the percentage of Americans living in poverty in 2007 was 12.5 percent, an increase from 36.5 million in 2006 to 37.3 million in 2007 (U.S. Census, 2008c). While this number has ranged between 11 and 15 percent throughout the past thirty years, the number of Americans living in poverty has steadily increased since 2001 when it was 11.7 percent of the population, with the greatest increases occurring in the Midwest and southern states and among immigrants (Rank & Hirschl, 2001a; Sherman et al., 2008). Did you know that nearly three-quarters of persons receiving public cash assistance (welfare) are working (Nagle & Johnson, 2006)?

By age 65, some 64 percent of Americans will require assistance from at least one form of a social welfare or "social safety net" program such as Medicaid, food stamps, and cash assistance (Rank & Hirschl, 2002). In fact, over half of persons 20–65 years will receive food stamps, with a startling 42 percent of those suffering from "food insecurity" (i.e., lack of adequate nutrition) (Rank & Hirschl, 2001a). The fact is that a large percentage of U.S. citizens will live in poverty at some point during their lives (see Exhibit 3.1).

Although many of the stereotypes of poverty are unfounded, the reality is that certain groups are vulnerable for living in poverty. For example, women are more likely to experience poverty than men. Over one-fourth of female headed households in which there is no husband/father present have incomes that fall below the poverty line (DeNavas-Wait et al., 2008). Women at each end of the age continuum are particularly at risk for living in poverty, with 15 percent of women aged 18 to 44 and 11.5 percent of women aged 75 and over living in poverty. Nonwhite women are at the greatest risk for poverty among all groups, with rates ranging from 20.2 percent (Hispanic women) to 23.4 percent (African American women) to 27.6 percent (Alaska Native/American Indian women) (U.S. DHHS, 2008).

In addition to gender, another significant factor in being poor is race and ethnicity. While over one-third of Americans will live in poverty at some point between 20 and 40, being African American and having limited education places one at higher risk for poverty (Rank & Hirschl, 2001a). In 2007, 24.5 percent of African Americans and 21.5 percent of Hispanics/Latinos were reported to have incomes below the poverty line as compared to 8.2 percent of non-Hispanic whites. For families, African American and American Indians are the most likely to live in poverty (nearly 22 percent each) followed closely by Hispanic families (20 percent), while the national average for all racial groups is less than 10 percent (U.S. Census, 2008b).

Nearly one-third of African American female-headed households in which no husband is present have incomes that are less than the poverty line. By age 75, ninety-eight percent of African American women and 96 percent of African American men with less than a high school education will have spent at least one year of their lives living in poverty, compared to 65 percent of white women and 74 percent of white men (Rank & Hirschl, 2001b). These statistics provide justification for the power of education.

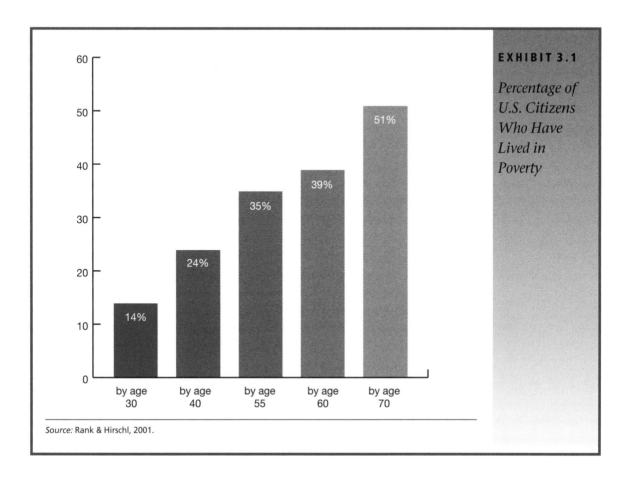

EXHIBIT 3.1

*Percentage of
U.S. Citizens
Who Have
Lived in
Poverty*

Source: Rank & Hirschl, 2001.

Age is also a factor. Approximately 18 percent of all children in the United States (up from 17.5 percent in 2006) live in poverty (U.S. Census, 2008b), many of whom have at least one working parent (Johnson, 2001). While children make up one-quarter of the population, they are over one-third of those living in poverty (DeNavas-Wait et al., 2008). Within the older adult population, approximately 10 percent have incomes below the poverty line (DeNavas-Wait et al., 2008).

Employment is no guarantee that a person will escape poverty. In fact, approximately two-thirds of poor families had at least one adult employed full time, but over half of those families still fall under the poverty line (Nagle & Johnson, 2006). The total income for a family of four in which one member is earning minimum wage still falls $1,550 under the poverty line (Furman & Parrott, 2007). Clearly, working full time in a minimum-wage position does not raise an individual above the poverty line.

In fact, consider the situation for a family of four represented in Table 3.1. As you can see, based on $22,050 being the poverty line for a family of four, this four-person family is able to have a total income that is slightly above the poverty line,

TABLE 3.1

Profile of the "Working Poor"

Annual net income from full time employment at $7.25/hour	$13,391
Plus tax credit	$5,260
Food Stamps	$4,464
Total Annual Income	$23,115

Source: Furman & Parrott, 2007.

but would fall short of the poverty line each year with the aid of earned income, child tax credits (to be discussed later in this chapter) and food stamps despite the fact that the "breadwinner" is working full time. Even with these benefits, the family may struggle to make ends meet, but without those additional benefits, the family's income would fall $7,400 under the poverty line (Furman & Parrott, 2007). By the way, the wage earner is making $7.25 per hour, the federal minimum wage (effective July, 2009). A minimum wage of $8.28/hour would enable a small family to live above the poverty line (Rank, 2006). It is important to note that six states do not have a minimum wage. However, 27 states and the District of Columbia have enacted laws that require higher minimum wages with the highest being $8.55 in Washington (U.S. Department of Labor, 2009b). Finally, did you know that the current federal minimum wage has the same purchasing power as it did in the 1970s?

Causes of Poverty

One of the most controversial issues in U.S. society today concerns the causes of poverty. Most opinions will be in one of two directions: (1) the individual is responsible, or (2) societal structure is responsible. We will examine both arguments.

Pre-dating even the Charity Organization Society movement, individuals have long been viewed as being responsible for their inability to earn an adequate income. This philosophy, which is sometimes referred to as "blaming the victim," is rooted in the belief that all individuals can and should be self-sufficient and should not require any outside assistance for themselves or their families. A related belief is that persons living in poverty are "different from mainstream Americans" and this difference explains their poverty, lack of motivation, and poor life choices (Rank, 2006, p. 22). In fact, half of the persons surveyed believed that those living in poverty are not working hard enough to bring themselves above the poverty line (NPR, 2001). This belief system presents an ongoing challenge for those who advocate for the poor, particularly when funding decisions are at stake. Voters and policy makers who adhere to the "pull yourself up by your bootstraps" philosophy are typically less supportive of spending tax dollars on programs to combat poverty. Interestingly, these views fall neatly along political lines. Examining beliefs by political affiliation has historically suggested that Republicans typically believe that lack of hard work and an unwillingness to be employed are the major causes of poverty, whereas Democrats more often cite external circumstances as the cause of poverty (National Public Radio et al., 2001). Research, however, consistently confirms that the attitudes and values of those living in poverty mirror those of mainstream society, but "human capital" plays a significant role in determining one's earning potential (Rank, 2008). Influenced largely by the parental human capital, one's ability to earn is related to such factors as parental income, education, health, and wealth.

The alternative view places the blame for poverty on societal structures. Much like the founders of the settlement house movement, proponents of this approach believe that a number of external factors over which the individual has no control make certain individuals vulnerable to a life of poverty. Simply stated, structural vulnerability occurs when the number of employment (those that will pay a living wage), child care, and housing opportunities are not adequate (Rank, 2008). The prevalence of low-paying employment opportunities that do not offer adequate benefits and the possibility for advancement creates situations in which low-income persons cannot gain economic stability. As one example, even in economic boom times, there is no guarantee that jobs will be accessible to those who lack training and technical sophistication. In addition, as you have seen, when jobs become available to such groups, the salaries are frequently insufficient for these workers to climb out of poverty. Other causal factors related to human capital that cause poverty include being female, nonwhite, too old, or too young; being a victim of domestic violence as a child, an adult, or both; being a victim of institutional oppression or discrimination based on disability or social class.

Rank (2006) offers a new paradigm for understanding poverty that encompasses five components that build on the structural perspective: (1) poverty occurs when the structure, not the individual, fails; (2) over a life time, people move in and out of poverty; (3) poverty creates deprivation that goes beyond income and includes quality of life, health, and opportunities; (4) poverty is an injustice because it can be prevented; and (5) poverty affects everyone through creating problems in the areas of health, education, and crime. Viewing poverty as a societal issue moves us away from holding the individual responsible for both the cause and solution and makes us all responsible.

You will be interested to learn that a fourteen year study of social work students found that their perceptions of the causes of poverty are structural and that poverty can only be eliminated through societal change. Further, social work students also believe that those living in poverty are the best determiners of their own lives (Clark, 2007).

Poverty has many different faces; therefore, understanding the longevity of poverty adds a useful dimension to our definition. Living in poverty is typically short-term (fewer than two years), but can be chronic, lasting for years. Even those living in poverty for briefer periods of time can move in and out of poverty depending on their life circumstance. For example, a person is laid off from her or his job or has a short-term disability. Individuals in this situation may receive public assistance until able to rejoin the labor force. Thus, they live in poverty only for a short period of time. Recent immigrants who receive public assistance until they find work also fall into this category.

Another group, known as the **working poor**, are those who are typically employed, but poverty occurs when the job is only part-time or does not compensate the employee enough to move above the poverty line, resulting in the individual being marginally poor.

Those persons who live in poverty for longer periods of time have often been at higher risk due to: physical or mental health disabilities; being female or a member of a female-headed household; being a member of a racial or ethnic minority; or living in an economically disadvantaged area (Rank, 2008). Poverty of this type may continue through multiple generations. Being reared in a family that receives public assistance places individuals at risk for this type of poverty cycle (Rank, 1994).

CHALLENGES AND BARRIERS TO MOVING OUT OF POVERTY

Living in poverty can become chronic and cyclical for those individuals who begin their lives in poverty and may later move in and out of poverty, particularly with changes in employment, health, and child care status. To understand this concept, recall the older woman in the poem at the beginning of the chapter. She was born into poverty, a life that may not provide adequate opportunities for health care, education, or career choices. She probably did not complete high school. She and her husband worked in a series of low-paying jobs that did not offer opportunities for upward mobility or even stability and certainly not for saving for old age or their children's education. Her children grew up in an environment of deprivation and lack of choices, thereby creating another generation of a family who will rear their children in poverty. Thus, the cycle continues.

Consider the teenaged girl who experiences an unplanned pregnancy and applies for public assistance (welfare) as a single parent. As a result of her pregnancy, she may not be able to complete high school or pursue any post–high school education. If she obtains full-time employment, she will lose the financial assistance that she currently receives for child care. Moreover, if her car breaks down, she may not be able to afford the repairs. In such a case, she could lose her job due to absenteeism and may consequently be forced to reapply for public assistance. Thus, the cycle continues.

Another scenario to consider is the woman who married at a young age and had several children. Her husband insisted that her job was to take care of the children, so she did not work outside the home. Over the years, the husband's occasional outbursts of violence became more frequent until he was physically abusing her on a regular basis, mostly when he was intoxicated. When he turned his violence toward the children, the woman decided she and the children had to leave. She sought safety for herself and the children in a shelter for survivors of domestic violence. The shelter staff helped her to apply for public assistance, food stamps, and housing and to file for divorce. The court ordered her husband to pay child support, but payments were erratic at best. Because the woman had never held a full-time job, she had no work history or discernible skills to market to potential employers. She found a few minimum-wage jobs, but she was always the first worker to be laid off. Between her frequent layoffs and unreliable child support, she moved in and out of the welfare system. Even when she was able to survive without public assistance, she could never move herself out of poverty. Thus, the cycle continues.

These are just three examples of the challenges of moving out of the cycle of poverty. To gain insight into the role of the social work profession in helping poor people receive services to meet basic needs and in working toward change in society to alleviate poverty, let us now turn to a review of the approaches that have been adopted in the United States to address the issue of poverty.

APPROACHES TO POVERTY IN THE UNITED STATES

Defining the best strategy for eliminating poverty has long been a hotly debated issue in the United States. Strategies for raising people's incomes above the poverty line are controversial because public tax dollars are the primary funding source for welfare programs. As you know, the issue of helping the poor is a value-laden one. This already emotional issue is further complicated by the fact that all U.S. taxpayers have a vested interest in the way their money is spent. For this reason, funding for social programs is a consistently volatile issue for politicians, special interest groups, and those agencies responsible for implementing the programs.

Let us not forget, though, the group that has the most vested interest in the ways in which public funds are spent—the persons themselves who are living in poverty. Unfortunately, this group often has the least influence over the decisions that affect their well-being.

Another group that has a keen interest in social welfare programs is social workers. It is much easier for social workers to fulfill their mission of empowerment if they have adequate funding and support to do so.

Before reviewing the strategies that have been employed here in the United States, it is important to understand the philosophy that underpins the strategies. Let us start by reviewing definitions that are relevant for our discussion of social welfare. As you review the following pages, keep in mind the words offered by Rank

(2006) "how we view poverty is critical to guiding how we will address it. Part of America's ineffectiveness in reducing poverty during the past three decades stems from a skewed and incorrect perception of impoverishment."

Terminology of the Social Welfare System

In its literal interpretation, the word *welfare* means "good health, prosperity and social respect" (Albelda et al., 1996). However, in the context of our discussion, the modern-day intent of **welfare** is a societal effort to help people achieve and maintain physical, emotional, and financial well-being. Since the early 1900s, when social services were being formalized in the United States, the term welfare has come to have a negative connotation and has become synonymous with poverty and the public assistance programs that provide cash assistance to single mothers and their children (AFDC, now known as TANF). Although typically associated with programs for persons who are low-income, welfare, if taken in its literal sense, also comes in the form of corporate and realty investor tax benefits, corporate bailouts, home mortgage deductions, tax abatements for home ownership in economically depressed areas, and farm and low-income housing development subsidies.

The term social welfare has also taken on a dual meaning. Following the literal definition for *welfare*, social welfare describes a group's level of stability. However, it also refers to our country's system of programs, benefits, and services that supports those in need of financial, social, and health care support. The term **public welfare**, often used synonymously with *public assistance*, also refers to the policies that a country develops to provide for the well-being of its citizens.

Social welfare programs are guided by **social policy**, defined as governmental rules and regulations that are used to develop and guide the practices and procedures related to social issues. These policies guide social workers' practice. Social policies address programs in such areas as education, health, corrections, and social welfare, but are aimed at creating resources needed to meet the basic needs of society. Social policies can be of two types: residual and institutional. **Residual social policies** address a social need that is specific to a population and will continue to exist regardless of the policies' effectiveness or ineffectiveness. Services for pregnant women and disabled persons are examples of programs that result from residual social policies. In contrast, **institutional social policies** address a social need that is universal to a population. Social Security is an example of an institutional social policy that provides retirement insurance for all older adults who have invested in that system. The work of the social work profession is inextricably linked to the social policies (perhaps even dependent on the policies) that underlie the laws, funding, insurance reimbursements, and authority to enact, implement, and oversee the programs.

A subset of social policies, **social welfare policies** allocate financial, social, and health resources. Social workers' activities are impacted by social policies, in general, and social welfare policies, in particular.

Now that you have acquired a basic understanding of the terms that are so integral to any discussion of social welfare issues, let us examine the historical underpinnings of our modern-day social welfare system. As you know from Chapter 2, the social welfare system in the United States is based on the English model but adapted by the United States. As the country was founded on the principle of independence and autonomy, it is not surprising that the basis of the welfare system is "competitive individualism and the validity of market-based economics" (Hopps & Collins, 1995, p. 2268). The historical review of the social work profession in Chapter 2 focused on the development of the social service structure. For our review of the evolution of the public welfare system, we will again take a tour through history, but this time we will target the important events that led to the creation of our contemporary programmatic approaches to social needs.

Social Welfare in the 17th–19th Centuries

Although considerable progress was made in social service–related areas in the first two centuries of our country's history, much of the accomplishment was in the private sector. Before 1862, all welfare benefits provided by the government were administered at the local, rather than the federal, level. However, the widespread disability and death rates caused by the Civil War created the need for a comprehensive national response. Therefore, in 1862, the federal government enacted legislation to provide pensions for Union soldiers and their dependents or survivors in the event of a soldier's death (Albelda et al., 1996). Other public assistance programs triggered by the Civil War included the Freedmen's Bureau, which provided help for freed slaves from 1865 to 1872, and an 1890 law that awarded pensions to all veterans who served in the Union army.

Social Welfare in the 20th Century

During the late 19th and early 20th centuries, in addition to the emergence of the settlement house and Charity Organization Society movements, public programs were being created to combat the results of the economic depression that had beset the country in the 1890s. Many of these programs were initiated at the state level, but they spread from state to state. Groups such as orphaned or fatherless children and older adults were being marginalized by the lack of a comprehensive approach.

In addition, a new paradigm for assisting the increasing populations of children, single mothers, and older adults was introduced during these years. In 1909, a White House Conference on Children recommended that children should remain with their parents whenever possible (Albelda et al., 1996). As a result, public funds were shifted toward providing services in homes versus automatic institutionalization. One law that reflected this new approach was the 1921 Sheppard-Towner Act, the first federal program to fund maternal and child health care for low-income

BOX 3.1

New Deal Programs

1933—The Federal Emergency Relief Act (FERA) provided temporary financial support to unemployed persons. The Civilian Conservation Corps (CCC) was an early federally funded employment program that became the forerunner to the Job Corps program of the 1960s.

1935—The Social Security Act provided assistance to fatherless families through the Aid to Families with Dependent Children (AFDC) program. AFDC became the cornerstone of the public response to poor families and remained essentially unchanged until the 1990s.

1935—Aimed at creating employment opportunities, the Works Progress Administration (WPA), employed 8 million workers in the building of parks, bridges, and roads.

women and children, thought by many to be the forerunner to modern-day public assistance for single women and their children.

New Deal Welfare Reforms   The drastic times of the Great Depression of the 1930s called for drastic measures. To alleviate the suffering of millions of Americans, the administration of Franklin Roosevelt created a number of public welfare programs. With nearly one-third of the workforce unemployed at the height of the Depression, a stronger, more comprehensive federal response was necessary. Perhaps the most famous federal initiative from this period is the Social Security Act of 1935. However, under the umbrella of Roosevelt's New Deal, a number of welfare programs were established (see Box 3.1).

With the exception of the Social Security legislation, most of these interventions were repealed or discontinued following the Depression. Programs developed to address crisis situations are typically intended to exist only for the duration of the crisis. Social Security is the exception, and it created a comprehensive system for providing an income for older adults and later for the children of deceased workers and workers that suffered disabilities.

Social Welfare from World War II through the 1970s   Welfare programs established during the economically prosperous late 1940s were primarily aimed at war veterans and their dependents and survivors (although it is doubtful whether many people considered these programs to be welfare).

The 1950s continued to be a prosperous decade for the United States, with moderate growth in the development of social welfare programs. The Social Security Act was expanded in 1950 to include benefits for low-income children and the disabled. The U.S. Housing Act of 1954 prompted urban renewal projects across the country. In 1953, the Department of Health, Education, and Welfare (HEW) was created as a cabinet-level department to oversee funding and programs in these three areas.

From a public welfare standpoint, the 1960s were a boom time. As part of Lyndon Johnson's War on Poverty, new programs were established through the Economic Opportunity Act of 1964. The Economic Opportunity Act funded training and community action programs such as the Job Corps, which provided employment training for youth; Volunteers in Service to America (VISTA), which sent volunteers into poor neighborhoods; Community Action Programs (CAPs), community-based antipoverty programs; and **Head Start**, the program that provides early childhood development services to low income children. Additional efforts included the food stamps program, which helped low-income people to purchase food, and the Older Americans Act of 1965, which dispersed funds to communities to develop programs for older adults.

Despite the fact that new programs were being created to decrease the numbers of persons receiving public assistance, the welfare rolls increased in both size and composition. AFDC recipients were increasingly families headed by single mothers and families of color. Opponents of welfare programs called for making the benefits more restrictive and requiring welfare recipients to work.

In an effort to respond to the criticisms of public assistance programs, the Work Incentive Program (WIN) was established to provide training, job placement, child care, and transportation. But the program failed due to lack of adequate funding to provide the comprehensive services that were intended.

In contrast to the 1960s, during the 1970s few new programs were introduced. Rather, adjustments were made to existing programs. For example, the 1975 Title XX amendment to the Social Security Act provided additional funding for personal social services for low-income persons, including services to promote economic independence (for example, employment training and placement), child and elder abuse and neglect prevention, and community-based services to prevent institutionalization of older adults and persons with disabilities. The exception is the **Supplemental Security Income (SSI)** program, established in 1972. This program provides public financial assistance for low-income persons who are elderly, visually impaired, or have disabilities. Unlike Social Security, assistance is not based on previous employment, but on current income.

Following the demise of the Nixon administration, Presidents Ford and Carter endeavored to continue the "welfare revolution" begun in the 1960s but had only moderate success. The number of recipients of welfare programs was reduced, but at a high financial cost to taxpayers because social welfare program funding was increased using tax dollars. Proponents of the work-ethic school of thought perceived that these programs were only increasing the dependence of the poor on public assistance and were not reforming them (Reid, 1995). The "revolution" as such ended with the election of Ronald Reagan in 1980.

Turnabout: Social Welfare in the 1980s and 1990s   Reminiscent of the Nixon era, the Reagan and G.W.B. Bush administrations of the 1980s and early 1990s focused on a supply-side economics approach that decreased resources for public welfare programs resulting in anti-welfare sentiments and increased tensions between the social service and political communities (Hopps et al., 2008). Known as "Reaganomics," both administrations subscribed to the philosophy that welfare should be a private business, not a public responsibility. To implement this philosophy, Reagan proposed, and Congress passed, the 1981 Omnibus Budget Reconciliation Act (OBRA), which eliminated public-service jobs, decreased benefits for low-income workers and AFDC recipients, and granted authority for resource distribution to the states (Albelda et al., 1996). The Family Support Act of 1988 emphasized work requirements and brought support for the perceived need to make welfare benefits more punitive and restrictive by making eligibility more limited. Issues such as AFDC, homelessness, and AIDS took a backseat to supporting corporate America and military spending (Segal, 2007). Many critics contend that the policies adopted by the Reagan and Bush administrations constituted a significant setback for the gains that had been made in social welfare policy throughout the 20th century.

The 1990s brought a renewed focus on public responsibility for social needs. Clinton's election strategies focused on returning the nation's attention to domestic issues, specifically, health and education. During the 1990s Congress passed several laws that had economic implications for impoverished families, people with disabilities, and minority populations. For example, the 1990 Americans with Disabilities Act, the Civil Rights Restoration Act, the 1993 Family and Medical Leave Act, the Brady (gun control) Bill, and the Anti-Crime Bill were all aimed at enhancing the quality of life for large groups of Americans and, in many cases, the quality of their economic well-being (Segal, 2007).

The tides soon shifted again, however. Promoted by Newt Gingrich, a member of the House of Representatives, the Republican-based Contract with America was introduced in the mid-1990s. The Contract was an effort by political conservatives to reverse the more liberal social welfare policies of earlier decades (for example, the Great Society). Responding to the economic recession and the increased number of people living in poverty, the political community shifted their focus to welfare reform legislation aimed at reconceptualized welfare as temporary and strengthened states' control over allocations (Gibelman, 2004). After numerous revisions, the Clinton administration agreed to support the Personal Responsibility and Work Opportunity Reconciliation Act (PRWORA) in 1996, which replaced AFDC with Temporary Assistance to Needy Families (TANF). The PRWORA was intended to decrease dependence on welfare. Moreover, because the federal government would fund TANF through block grants to the states and would not provide a uniform set of guidelines, the PRWORA authorized each state to determine (1) the ways that funds would be allocated and the amounts that would be awarded, (2) time limits for cash assistance, and (3) eligibility requirements for Medicaid health coverage. States that did not comply with general federal regulations regarding the restrictions for receiving TANF benefits jeopardized continued funding. One condition of the PRWORA was a five-year lifetime cap on public assistance benefits. In addition,

TANF recipients are required to be engaged in a work-related activity for at least 30 hours per week. The first five year period ended on September 30, 2002. Welfare reform required the social work profession to reconceptualize the way in which programs were delivered. Despite the lack of any major positive strides being made in social welfare policies and programs, the Clinton administration was generally viewed as more supportive of the social work profession and those served by social workers (Gibelman, 2004).

Social Welfare in the 21st Century   The 2000 election of George W. Bush returned the country to an earlier era of decreased public funding for social welfare programs and pressure being placed on the non-profit and faith organization sectors to carry the burden for meeting societal needs. In fact, the first executive act of the new president was to create the White House Office of Faith-Based and Community Initiatives that continued the shift from public to private responsibility. A commitment to "compassionate conservatism" and a supply-side economic philosophy (i.e., tax benefits benefit higher socioeconomic level citizens and corporations, but exclude the middle and lower economic levels) resulted in a continued shift toward political and social conservatism and decreased governmental support—a move that historically means fewer resources for social welfare programs (Gibelman, 2004; Hopps et al., 2008).

The 2006 elections brought a change of legislative leadership as the Democrats gained control of Congress. This shift resulted in enactment of several more progressive moves: a voluntary prescription drug plan through Medicare (2006) and legislation to raise the minimum wage from $5.15 to $7.25 by 2009.

Concern for the well-being of TANF recipients who would have difficulty gaining and maintaining employment motivated welfare rights advocates to lobby state legislatures to reauthorize TANF benefits. While the Deficit Reduction Act of 2005 served to re-authorize TANF, more stringent requirements were placed on states and, ultimately, the recipients themselves that determine the level of federal funding that states will receive (Hagen & Lawrence, 2008). Effective October 1, 2008, the Final Rules of TANF went into effect with a loosening of the activities that "count" as work. Critics, however, remain unconvinced that the TANF requirements are sensitive to employment barriers for all TANF recipients, particularly those with disabilities (Schott, 2008).

A fierce debate continues between those who emphasize decreasing welfare rolls and increasing employment, and those who stress alleviating poverty through the provision of funding for training and employment (Coven, 2005; Peterson, 2002). There has been and continues to be considerable concern and controversy over the impact of TANF legislation. Despite the fact that the number of families receiving TANF has decreased, advocates for children and welfare recipients have long feared that the lives of these individuals will get worse instead of better because states that have not budgeted well for a particular year can refuse or decrease the amount of aid granted for each applicant (Segal, 2007).

Although many people agreed that the welfare system was in need of reform, opponents of TANF view it as coercive regarding work requirements, inflexible regarding time limits, and shortsighted as the approach is one focused on the labor force as opposed to investing in human capital (Hagen & Lawrence, 2008). Critics view welfare reform as based on what they consider to be an incorrect assumption that poverty is a temporary situation that can be rectified by a stable national and global economy (NASW, 2006–2009a).

Other criticisms leveled against the reforms suggest that little change has occurred since the passage of the PRWORA. Requiring TANF recipients to work has only minimally decreased national poverty rates, primarily because TANF recipients have been unable to obtain employment with wages high enough to lift them out of poverty. In most US states, families receiving TANF are under 75 percent of the poverty line which is further below than it was in 1996 (Schott & Levinson, 2008). Therefore, the next steps to supporting TANF recipients in their struggle for self-sufficiency are to focus on the factors that would help them find employment that pays a living wage (for example, education, training, social and health-related services, and transportation) and to advocate for higher overall wages (NASW, 2009–2012n).

The momentum of the 2006 elections and an increasing dissatisfaction with governmental spending priorities created an environment that enabled the 2008 election year to be monumental in a variety of areas. The election of Barack Obama, who campaigned on a platform of social and economic reform, along with a Democratically-controlled Senate and House of Representatives bodes well for social welfare initiatives.

Entering office in the throes of a major economic crisis, President Obama's first focus was to stabilize the economy. With the U.S. Department of Labor (2009a) reporting over 12 million people (9.5%) unemployed and that rate expected to rise to 10 percent before the recession ends, those hardest hit are those on the lowest end of the socioeconomic spectrum. To revitalize the economy, Obama introduced the American Recovery and Reinvestment Act within his first month in office. Aimed at re-stabilizing the nation's economy, the Economic Stimulus Bill infused $789.5 billion into the economy to strengthen the infrastructure, support state and local governments, provide tax assistance, and invest in health care, energy, the environment, and education (CSWE, 2009). Social workers and those we serve will be positively impacted by a number of the areas of designated spending. The projected breakdown of spending includes: (1) tax relief ($288 billion); (2) state and local relief ($144 billion); (3) infrastructure and science ($111 billion); (4) protecting the vulnerable ($81 billion); (5) health care ($59 billion); (6) education and training ($53 billion); (7) energy ($43 billion); and (8) other ($8 billion). Not only will social workers be interested in the outcomes produced by the stimulus initiative, we will be on the forefront of the implementation. Specific social service-related expenditures are planned in the areas of: food stamps (SNAP) ($20 billion); unemployment benefits ($40 billion); low income tax credits

($34 billion); TANF ($5 billion); and over $1 billion for veterans' benefits (Pace, 2009).

While the nation is optimistic that the economic stimulus initiative will enable our country to return to a stable economic status, we must continue to strive for a just solution to the issue of poverty. Rank (2006) offers a new paradigm for allowing people to live a life without poverty: (1) ensure a minimum wage that will enable individuals and families to work full-time and expect to live above the poverty line; (2) better utilize the taxation system to better support low-income persons through Earned Income Tax Credit and other tax credits; (3) ensure that basic goods and services are available to all—education, health care, affordable housing and child care; and (4) create a culture and structure for developing individual assets through Individual Development Accounts (IDAs).

IMPACT OF THE CHANGING APPROACHES TO POVERTY ON SOCIAL WORK

This brings our discussion to the present day. As you have learned, sentiments regarding public welfare resources and programs are complex and closely linked to the political, economic, religious, and social spheres of U.S. society. Our discussion raises the question, what are the implications of this changing tide for the social work profession? Social and economic needs inevitably prompt a societal and political response. This response, in turn, determines the amount of money that politicians, bureaucrats, private foundations, and individual donors will spend. This availability of funding determines the extent to which social workers will be engaged (funded) to provide social work services. The public child welfare system provides an example of this model. When the political climate is unfavorable for public social services, funding is decreased, and the number of social work positions is lowered. Although the demand for social work services in this case may remain high, the funding is not adequate to support all the positions required to meet this demand. Such situations result in fewer workers with larger caseloads. During these times, politicians often suggest that the private sector should fill the gap created by decreased public funding. Yet another example is the treatment of persons with mental illness. Research conducted by Vaughn and colleagues (2009) indicates that persons experiencing mental illness, specifically personality disorders, utilize social welfare programs and services at levels higher than others in the population; suggesting that funding of prevention and treatment programs could reduce the burden on the public welfare system.

There will always be a role for social workers regardless of the political and economic climate. However, social workers' jobs may become more or less challenging depending on the political affiliation of the people or group in the political majority, the state of the economy, and the prevailing sentiments regarding social welfare programs. In the most recent policy statement, the National

Association of Social Workers (2009–2012n) calls for social workers to advocate for policies and plans that will:

- create a safety net for persons that are experiencing poverty;

- help persons living in poverty to build personal and financial assets through such programs as individual development accounts;

- enable those persons living in poverty to integrate work, education, and family life; and

- promote services to focus on the underlying economic causes of poverty, including the impact that such factors as substance abuse, domestic violence, health problems, and illiteracy play in preventing an escape from poverty. (pp. 357–358)

One of the roles of an effective social worker is to facilitate the client system's access to services. When functioning in this role, the social worker assists client systems of all sizes in identifying and connecting to all the resources for which the client is eligible. For example, helping a family locate in-home services to avoid placing their elderly mother suffering from dementia in a long-term care facility is an example of linking a client to needed resources. To fulfill that objective, social workers must possess a working knowledge of existing social welfare programs and keep themselves updated on the ever-changing policies, eligibility requirements, application protocols, and benefits associated with these programs.

Although programs come and go with political and funding changes, a core group of programs have seemingly weathered the political and economic storms. These programs fall into one of two general categories: universal or selective. Let us look at a sampling of both types of programs with which social workers need to be familiar.

Current Social Programs

Social programs currently available are typically eligibility-based and include:

- Authorized by the Social Security Act of 1935, **Social Security** provides a retirement income for all workers who have paid into the system during their years of employment. The benefit that a person receives is based on the amount that she or he "invested." The act also provides income to survivors (spouses and children) of deceased workers and to workers who become disabled, if they have worked long enough to qualify. While Social Security benefits are adjusted based on the rate of inflation, they are not increased until after the cost of living has risen; therefore, the benefits are often not consistent with the current cost of living (Hoefer, 2008).

- Part of the Great Society movement of the 1960s, **Medicare** is health care coverage for persons who receive Social Security benefits. Any person who receives any type of Social Security payments is automatically eligible for Medicare.

- Temporary Assistance to Needy Families (TANF) provides monthly cash assistance to eligible low-income families with children under age 18. Within the first two years of benefits, TANF recipients who are able bodied must be engaged in work or work-related activities (for example, job training or seeking) or lose benefits. Over a lifetime, an individual can receive benefits for a total of five years only. Because each state determines the eligibility criteria and amount of assistance received, TANF benefits vary from state to state. However, the average monthly cash benefit is $354 overall, ranging from $296 for a single parent with one child to $521 for a single parent with four or more children (U.S. Department of Health and Human Services (U.S. DHHS), 2006). Each state determines its own amount with the lowest being $170 per month in Arkansas and the highest being $923 per month in Alaska (Schott & Levinson, 2008). Ironically, only 40 percent of eligible low income families actually receive cash assistance through TANF (Parrott, 2008).

- Funded through the Social Security program, **Social Security Disability (SSD)** provides cash assistance for persons deemed to be unable to work for a period of at least one year for reasons of physical or mental disability. Restrictions enacted as part of the Contract with America deemed workers who become disabled due to drug or alcohol addiction to be ineligible for SSD (Dickinson, 1997).

- Begun in 1972 as a merging of several different federal and state programs, **Supplemental Security Income (SSI)** provides cash assistance to low-income adults, older adults, and persons with disabilities or visual challenges who meet income and health standards. SSI funds are administered by the Social Security Administration, but the funding is separate from the funds allocated for other Social Security programs. SSI recipients can receive other benefits (such as Medicaid and food stamps) while receiving SSI. The federal government bears the cost of this program, but a number of states add to that amount.

- Introduced in 1965 along with Medicare as an amendment to the Social Security Act, **Medicaid** is the health coverage that is available to some recipients of the eligibility-based programs (TANF, SSI, and SSD). Social Security recipients may also receive Medicaid, but eligibility is based on need; that is, recipients must qualify based on their income. Each state sets the criteria for Medicaid.

- Instituted in 1964, the **Food Stamps** program administered by the Department of Agriculture provides an electronic card that can be used to purchase food items. This program is intended to supplement a family's income and is based on the assumption that families spend 30 percent of their total income on food. Renamed the **Supplemental Nutrition Assistance Program (SNAP)** in 2008, the program serves over 28 million persons each month. As part of President Obama's American Recovery and Reinvestment Act of 2009, beginning April, 2009, the maximum allotments will be raised 13.6 percent—from $200 for a one-person household to $1,202 for an eight-person household (U.S. Department of Agriculture, 2009). Approximately 80 percent of TANF recipients receive food stamps (DHHS, 2006).

• Aimed at enhancing the physical health of poor women, infants, and children, **Women, Infants, and Children (WIC)** has been in operation since 1974. Primarily a federally funded program, it provides vouchers to poor women who are eligible based on their income and current health status. They can purchase certain foods for themselves and their children. Mothers and their children can receive WIC benefits along with other assistance programs such as TANF and Medicaid.

• For those low-income adults who do not qualify for any other cash assistance programs, states have historically made small, short-term cash benefits available through **General Assistance (GA)**, sometimes called general relief. As welfare cuts and reforms have proliferated, most states have opted to eliminate this program.

• In effect since 1975 and expanded in 1986, 1990, 1993, and 2001, low income working persons are eligible to receive the **Earned Income Tax Credit (EITC)**, a refundable tax credit based on the number of children and the total household income. The federal EITC program, which is administered through the Internal Revenue Service, is designed to help the working poor retain a larger percentage of their income. Because applicants simply request these funds when they submit their federal tax returns, this program involves less paperwork than many others. As of 2009, twenty-four states have also enacted EITC legislation that can be received in addition to the federal credit (Levitis & Koulish, 2008). One in every seven individuals and families that submit federal income tax returns applies for federal EITC, making this program the most successful government effort for alleviating poverty for children as over 4 million were saved from living in poverty (Nagle & Johnson, 2006). The maximum federal EITC benefit for a family with two or more children is $4,824 (Levitis & Koulish, 2008). An effort is currently underway at the federal level to expand the EITC program, including the Child Tax Credit. If approved, this legislation would enable more than 2.5 million persons to escape poverty—800,000–1 million of whom are children (Sherman, 2009).

- Begun as part of the 1960s War on Poverty, **Head Start** is a child development program for low-income children. Head Start services include preschool, health, and nutrition programs.

- An emerging response to eliminating poverty is the **Individual Development Account (IDA)**. One in five Americans have no financial assets with that number being higher among persons of color (Sherraden, 2008). Initially funded by non-profit organizations, as persons with low incomes save, those savings are matched 1:1, 2:1, or even 3:1. These funds can then be used for purchasing a home or business, education or other investments to achieve financial well-being. IDAs have been so successful that over 30 states and the federal government have passed legislation supporting this program.

Like many social work students, Emily questioned the value of studying social welfare history and the myriad government programs. After all, she just wanted to help people, and spending time reading about policies had nothing to do with helping people, or did it? One day at Oasis House, Emily and her social work supervisor, John, met with one of the shelter's residents, Tonya. Tonya's TANF and Medicaid benefits were about to be terminated because she was not employed full time. Instead, she was enrolled in a licensed practical nurse program and working part-time at a skilled nursing facility. She had only three months until graduation, and her only income was the public assistance she received. Since she and her two children fled from her violent husband, Tonya had tried to comply with the TANF work requirements. However, she had difficulty keeping a job because the LPN program is full time. In addition, she had to make frequent medical visits related to her older child's cerebral palsy. She had held several part-time jobs while she was in the LPN program, but she either had to quit each one or she was fired due to absenteeism because her child was hospitalized or had medical appointments.

In his role as an advocate, John telephoned Tonya's income-maintenance caseworker to request that Tonya be scheduled for a hearing at which she could request a work waiver to complete training. He also requested that the agency allow him to accompany Tonya to the hearing and present photographs verifying that she was a victim of domestic violence. As a result of John's knowledge of governmental benefits and Tonya's rights, Tonya obtained a waiver to allow her to finish training. John also helped Tonya apply for SSI for her child who had a disability. Through her experience with Tonya and John, Emily learned the importance of being knowledge-able about policies and programs if she intends to become an advocate for people in need.

This chapter has described key governmental programs that are available to the people with whom you will be working as a social worker. Remember that regardless of the area of social work in which you specialize, you are responsible for staying current with the myriad changes made to these programs every year.

CONCLUSION

The arrival of a new millennium provides us with an opportunity to look both to the past and to the future. While our social services continue to be delivered by both public and private entities, governmental sources provide the majority of the funding. We continue to be predisposed to explaining poverty and need as being individually-based—a situation that can result in decreased funding from public sources (Hoefer, 2008). As we all know, the U.S. is rooted in a capitalist economic philosophy, but how do our views on individualism versus community responsibility change during economic crisis? When a wage earner of a family living at a middle-class socioeconomic level is laid off and the family's home is lost to a foreclosure and they have no health insurance coverage, suddenly they are now living below the poverty line. Can our society shift from an individualistic perspective to one focused on the community coming together to help those in need during times of crisis?

The causes of poverty are multifaceted and complex, as are the solutions. The dynamics of political, social, and economic factors interact to create an economy and a culture in which poverty exists. Social welfare policy and, subsequently, programs change frequently related to the prevailing economy and society's views on the level of funding and how much of a safety net to provide.

Understanding the historical roots of contemporary social welfare philosophy and programs is essential for a practicing social worker. Social workers' knowledge, skills, and values give them valuable insights into the systemic impact of poverty on those with whom they work.

More policy changes are needed to address a growing number of people, especially children, living in poverty. To help people achieve economic stability, social workers can advocate for policy changes in such areas as TANF, health care and insurance, the minimum wage, tax structures, and educational benefits. But you cannot advocate for your position unless you know the varied positions of others involved. Social workers have long been on the forefront of advocacy efforts, and they will continue to use their knowledge of systems, organizations, and communities to advocate for and with others at the local, state, national, and international levels to alleviate poverty.

Even in this era of uncertainty, another of Don Bakely's poems captures a sense of optimism and hope.

When I was a kid,
  I looked to the day when
    I would stop dreaming those wild hopes
  and
    I'd be old enough
      to make real life
        out of
          unreal dreams.
But I still catch myself
    hanging onto dreams—
  and I'm forty.
Sometimes I catch myself thinking
  maybe today
    a big, beautiful car is going to pull up out front
      and
        the rich man is going to get out
          and say,
  "I heard about you,
    that
      you are a good man
        and work hard
          and love your kids
            and are down on your luck.
  Here's a check.
  Come by the office. I've got a good job for a man like you.
  By the way, keep the car.
        I see you need one.
        I'll catch a cab back."
  Of course,
    he never comes.
  I really know
        he
          never
            will.
  But, see,
    with poor folks
      even wild hopes
        are
          hopes worth thinking.
            kind of fun, in fact.
Then, too.
    if we can't have some glimmer
                in
                  tomorrow.
    even a
      long-shot,

> *never-happen*
> *glimmer.*
> *Then each today*
> *is always*
> *only*
> *darkness.*

Excerpt from "The family of poor: Part three)," From *If . . . A Big Word With the Poor* by Don Bakely, Faith & Life Press, Newton, Kansas. Used by permission.

MAIN POINTS

- Poverty is a complex political, economic, and social issue, but essentially is not having enough money to live adequately.

- The poor are not just the stereotype of the homeless man or woman sleeping in a doorway or pushing a shopping cart on the downtown streets of a city; those groups at highest risk for living in poverty are women, persons of color, older adults, and children (who cannot work).

- The causes of poverty continue to be hotly debated. Some people believe that the individual is responsible for her or his economic plight, while others believe that external factors (such as employment and economic conditions) place people at risk for living in poverty.

- Poverty can be short-term or episodic in which the individual is working but cannot earn enough money to move out of poverty; or chronic in which the individual's poverty is long term.

- Understanding both the literal meanings and societal connotations of terms such as welfare, public assistance, and social policy helps in understanding society's perception of poverty.

- A variety of federal, state, and local government agencies are involved in the administration of social welfare programs. Societal responses to poverty tend to reflect the current political climate, with conservative political administrations restricting social programs and more liberal administrations expanding social programs.

- Social welfare programs fall into two categories: universal (Social Security and Medicare) and selective (for example, TANF, SSI, and SNAP). Social workers are responsible for being familiar with these programs and staying current with the myriad changes made every year.

EXERCISES

1. As you have learned from the Sanchez Family interactive case (go to www.routledgesw.com/cases), the family has struggled financially throughout the years. Hector has prevented the family from taking advantage of many of the resources available to them. Complete the following two exercises:
   a. Using the information and the websites provided in this chapter along with those from your state government, identify benefits that may be appropriate for various members of the Sanchez family.
   b. Reflect on the reasons that Hector may feel resistance to utilizing social services. Additionally, reflect on how you think Hector and the members of his family may feel in the client role.
2. Review the case file for Junior Sanchez. Answer Junior's Critical Thinking Questions.
3. As you learned from this chapter, Tonya is a single mother with two children. Her son, William, is 3 years old and her daughter, Erica, is 6 years old. For the purpose of creating a budget, Tonya's current employment or welfare benefits are not to be considered. Develop a budget that would be required for Tonya and her two children to live for one month. You may want to have a calculator available to help you in this exercise.

   This budget should not reflect a luxurious lifestyle or a life at bare minimum, but rather should show what you believe are essentials for living and their costs for one month. For each basic human need, enter an amount that you think is a true monthly cost regardless of who would pay for it. For example, the cost of food will be the same if the family receives food stamps or not. In actuality, the family may not have the resources to purchase that amount of food, but it is still a cost. As you are creating this budget, identify your reasons for deriving that particular amount.

   Once you have developed a picture of Tonya's needs for one month, you can compare your amounts with the actual amounts required if this family lived in your state by calculating a family budget at the Economic Policy Institute Basic Family Budget Calculator located at www.epi.org/content/budget_calculator. As you progress with this exploration, consider Tonya's situation from two different perspectives. First, assume that Tonya and her children receive TANF benefits and compare your budget with the amounts of benefits that they will receive. Second, consider the scenario in which Tonya is employed full-time in a minimum wage job. Decide if she receives health/dental benefits for herself and/or her children. In order to make these comparisons, you will need information on living costs in your community.

   Questions to consider as you complete this exercise:
   a. What information do you need to know to be able to develop a monthly budget?

    b. What categories of expenses would a single mother with two children have during the month?

    c. What is the amount of TANF provided by your state for a mother and two children?

4. Interview friends, family members, co-workers, and/or others about their definitions of and attitudes about "welfare." Reflect on the similarities and differences in their responses and the way in which their definitions and attitudes compare to the definitions described in this chapter.

CHAPTER 4

The Social Work Environment

THE SOCIAL WORK PROFESSION HELPS INDIVIDUALS, FAMILIES, groups, organizations, and communities. The profession's helping mission places it in the center of people's lives and the societal issues that influence their lives. Social work "is created within a political, social, cultural, and economic matrix that shapes the assumptions of practice, the problems that practice must deal with and the preferred outcomes of practice" (McNutt & Floersch, 2008). Therefore, social workers must be knowledgeable about the makeup of society in general and the populations who use social workers' services in particular.

In this chapter, you gain an understanding of the diversity of the U.S. population and then examine the challenges that confront social workers in contemporary society. The social work profession exists within an environment that encompasses the economic, social, cultural, political, and religious issues (Gibelman, 2004). It is often those same political, economic, and social issues that present obstacles for those persons served by social workers that also provide opportunities for growth and social change. We will explore these issues from the perspectives of both challenges and opportunities for social work practice.

Recognizing that demographics are constantly undergoing shifts, let us first turn our attention to an overview of the current demographic profile. Within each category that creates the portrait of U.S. society are the links to the knowledge and skills that social workers will need to practice with that particular segment of the population.

AMERICA'S CHANGING PROFILE

As of March 1, 2009, the world is comprised of over 6.7 billion people, 305+ million of whom live in the United States. A new American is born every eight seconds, one dies every twelve seconds, and one immigrates every 36 seconds which results in an overall population increase of one person every fourteen seconds (U.S. Census Bureau, 2009). The U.S. is made up of diverse people, but government policies are not always supportive of all segments of the population. Recent demographic shifts

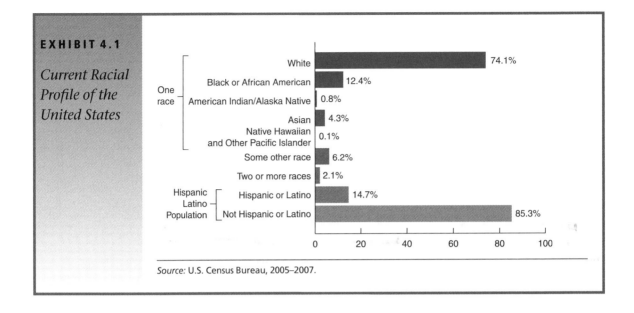

EXHIBIT 4.1

Current Racial Profile of the United States

Source: U.S. Census Bureau, 2005–2007.

have made the population more diverse than at any previous time in history. Using data from five primary sources—the U.S. Census Bureau (2009b), the Current Population Reports Projections (Day, 1996), *Women's Health USA 2008* (U.S. DHHS), *Income, Poverty, and Health Insurance Coverage in the United States: 2007*, and the *2009–2012 Statistical Abstract of the United States*—this chapter presents highlights of the diversity of the present population with projections for the future. The discussion focuses on five demographic characteristics: race and ethnicity, age, gender, income, and religion.

Changes in Race and Ethnicity

A racial and ethnic profile of the United States is shown in Exhibit 4.1. The United States experienced greater population growth between 1990 and 2000 (32.7 million people) than during any other 10-year period in history, with the largest growth occurring in the western states and metropolitan areas. Going further, from 1995 to 2050 the U.S. population is expected to increase by 50 percent, with the largest growth occurring within the Hispanic/Latino and Asian populations, primarily due to immigration. Thus, racial and ethnic diversity clearly is increasing, particularly among older adults, in general, and older adults of color, in particular. One reason for this trend is that persons of color are gaining better access to health care and are therefore living longer. In addition, fertility is expected to remain constant while mortality declines.

One consequence of this increased diversity is that the U.S. population will include greater numbers of people whose first language is not English and who identify with more than one racial or ethnic group. Over 6,000 languages exist across the globe, with nearly 400 different languages represented within the U.S. population alone. Nearly one in five residents of the U.S. speak a language other than English when they are in their homes. Over 1.3 million persons will immigrate to the U.S. in 2010—a number that will rise to an annual rate of over two million by 2050. Of those, nearly 50,000 are **refugees** (persons who seek refuge from danger or persecution in their home country) who were resettled in the U.S. in 2008 alone (U.S. Committee for Refugees and Immigrants, 2008). These numbers do not include those persons who are in the U.S. in an undocumented status. For social workers, increased diversity requires that they have culturally competent skills to meet the needs of clients whose experiences, cultural heritage, language, values, and traditions are different from their own.

The Aging Population

Not only is the U.S. population becoming more diverse racially and ethnically, but it is also aging. Since 1990, the median age has increased from 32.9 to 36.6 years, and it is expected to increase to 38.1 years by 2050. Significantly, a greater percentage of the population of persons of color falls within the under-18 category, whereas whites make up the largest percentage of older adults. Based on current demographic projections, by 2030 more than 40 percent of the total U.S. population will be either under age 17 (21 percent) or over age 65 (22 percent). As children and older adults tend to be the most vulnerable segments of the population, such increases will result in a greater need for social work competence in working with these groups.

Life expectancy is currently at 77.8 years for all groups. Men and persons of color have lower life expectancy. However, longevity is on the increase for all groups; by 2050 life expectancy is projected to be as high as 83.9 years overall, although still lower for persons of color and men. The fastest growing segment of the population will be those over 85—this group will double by 2025 and increase five times by 2050. As the population gets older, social workers need skills to work with the entire continuum of ages, particularly in multigenerational family situations.

More older adults are rearing grandchildren as a result of the children's parents being unavailable for a variety of reasons, including substance abuse, incarceration, and divorce. Current trends suggest that multigenerational families will reside together more often, and more older adults will live in congregate living situations such as retirement communities, assisted living facilities, and long-term care facilities. These arrangements will require social workers to be as skillful in working with older adults as with children and younger adults.

Gender Makeup of the Population

Today, women make up nearly 51 percent of the U.S. population, although the male population experienced more growth between the 1990 and 2000 censuses. Men outnumber women until age 24, but for the 65-and-older segment, women make up 58 percent of the population. By age 85, women outnumber men by two to one. Male mortality begins to increase initially due to professional and recreational activities and later due to chronic fatal illnesses such as heart disease and cancer. These patterns are expected to continue, as the older adult proportion of the female population increases. As the number of older women increases, social workers need to be aware of the issues that confront this population. Compared to older men, older women are more likely to live alone, to have lower incomes, to experience more chronic health problems, and to assume more caregiving responsibilities (for example, for spouses or grandchildren). With the changes that have occurred in recent decades regarding women's roles in society, women's aging will be changing as well due to increased participation in the workforce, and social workers need to be preparing proactively for the new generations of older women.

For social workers, links to gender are significant in the areas of employment, public assistance programs, education, health and mental health, and global women's issues. For this reason, NASW, in the 2009–2012 policy statement, calls for equity and social and economic justice in these areas (NASW, 2009–2012h).

Income Levels and Poverty

In 2009, the median household income for all Americans was $48,201/year with a range of $37,781/year for Hispanic Americans to $64,238/year for Asian Americans and a state-based range from a high of $68,080/year in Maryland to $36,338/year in Mississippi. From 2000 to 2006, overall median household incomes fell 2 percent, while median household incomes for African Americans, Asians, and Pacific Islanders fell 3.4 percent to 6.4 percent. The number of people living in poverty rose by 1.2 percent. In a review of the past 30 years, the number of persons living in poverty has climbed steadily, although the percentage of the population living in poverty fluctuates. Thirteen percent of women and 11 percent of men currently live in poverty.

High divorce rates and more single women heading households also contribute to a concept known as the "feminization" of poverty, as more women, making less money, will be heading households by themselves. Interestingly, overall incomes for women rose (5 percent), bringing the female-to-male earnings ratio to an all-time high of .78 (women earn 78 cents per every dollar earned by men). Despite the Equal Pay Act being passed in 1963, women's incomes still lag behind their male counterparts in all 50 states (U.S. Census Bureau, 2008d). Addressing the structural causes of poverty by increasing opportunities for education, health coverage, child care, and employment that provide a living wage may serve to close that gap (NASW, 2009–2012h).

A startling fact is that the richest 20 percent of the population receive almost 50 percent of household incomes, while the poorest 20 percent receive 3.5 percent of overall household incomes. Poverty rates rose from 11.3 percent of the population to 12.5 percent, with non-Hispanic whites, Hispanics, urbanites, Southerners, and children being most affected. The poverty rate for the white population is approximately 8 percent, while the rates for African Americans and persons of Hispanic/Latino origin are over 24 percent and 21 percent, respectively (U.S. Census Bureau, 2008b; 2009a). For those U.S. residents who immigrated to this country, 16 percent live below the poverty line, ranging from a high of 51 percent for Somali immigrants to a low of 5 percent for European-born residents.

These demographic shifts have implications for social work practice. As poverty rates increase, more people will need assistance with finances, health, employment, food, housing, utilities, and child care. In addition, family crises and violence often increase when families are experiencing stress. Therefore, social workers increasingly will need the necessary skills to work with diverse families in crisis.

Religious Affiliations

At the beginning of the 21st century, approximately 1,600 different religions and denominations were being practiced in the United States, almost half of which have been established in the past 40 years (Mindell, 2007). Exhibit 4.2 shows two ways of looking at religion that have implications for social workers. Although people who self-identify as Muslim are a small percentage, their number, and the number of people who self-identify as members of other religions, are increasing. Increases reported include Islam—109 percent; Buddhism—170 percent; Hinduism—237 percent.

Despite the number of different religious affiliations, the United States is far from being free of religious segregation and discrimination. The events of September 11, 2001, for example, prompted a rash of discrimination directed toward Muslims. Muslims have been subjected to physical, verbal, and written assaults, threats against their lives, and damage to their businesses and homes.

For social workers, this means that they should be aware of their own religious and spiritual beliefs as well as those of others. They can then work to promote religious acceptance and understanding and to incorporate spirituality into their practice. Because the population is aging and religious affiliation increases with age, social workers will benefit from knowledge of religion and sensitivity to the role of religion and spirituality in the lives of older adults. Integrating religious and spiritual information into the information gathering process can expand your perspective of the client's situation. For example, being aware of a client's religious involvement can be a resource in the social work intervention whether the client is an older adult, an immigrant or a refugee (Sheridan, 2002).

EXHIBIT 4.2

Self-Reported Religious Affiliation in the United States

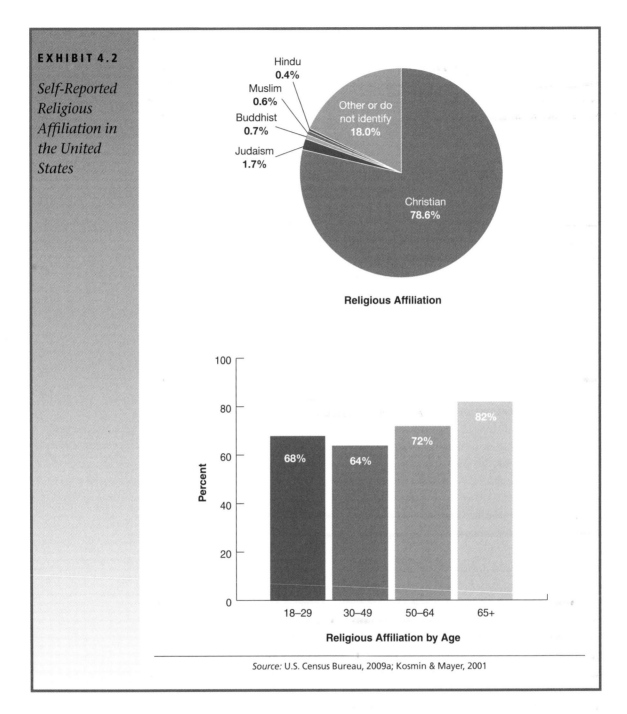

Hindu **0.4%**
Muslim **0.6%**
Buddhist **0.7%**
Judaism **1.7%**
Other or do not identify **18.0%**
Christian **78.6%**

Religious Affiliation

68% 64% 72% 82%

Percent

18–29   30–49   50–64   65+

Religious Affiliation by Age

Source: U.S. Census Bureau, 2009a; Kosmin & Mayer, 2001

CHALLENGES AND OPPORTUNITIES FACING SOCIAL WORKERS

Emily began to notice that the domestic violence shelter program where she worked was serving an increasing number of women whose first language was not English and who frequently had limited English-speaking skills. The women were being identified primarily as victims of domestic violence through hospital emergency rooms where they were seeking emergency medical treatment. The community in which Emily worked was experiencing an overall increase in the number of refugees and immigrants from Eastern Europe, Russia, African countries, and several Spanish-speaking countries; therefore, multiple languages were involved. The domestic violence program staff and volunteers spoke only English and therefore had to rely on the women's family members (often their children who were more proficient in English) or the on-call interpreters engaged by the hospitals. Emily and her co-workers also realized that their understanding of domestic violence within other cultures was limited. Providing services to non-English-speaking women in crisis without regular interpreters hampered Emily's ability to establish rapport, gather information, and develop supportive and helpful interventions with this client group. Consequently, Emily and her co-workers were growing increasingly concerned that their non-English-speaking clients were not being effectively served by their agency or other agencies that provided services to victims of domestic violence and their children.

As you have learned, social work practice is often shaped by current political, economic, and social philosophies and events. Although the political, social, and economic issues of today and tomorrow may be different from those that affected past generations, the social work profession must be prepared to influence and respond to the effects of such changes on the individuals, families, organizations, and communities that it serves. Changes will bring new and controversial issues for social workers, but it will be the profession's "values and mission that will anchor the profession in the sea of change" (Allen-Meares, 2000, p. 179).

A major issue that has long confronted social workers is the political, economic, and social oppression and discrimination faced by those groups with whom practitioners work. Although oppression and discrimination are closely related, they are distinct concepts. **Oppression** occurs when the actions or beliefs of individuals, groups, or institutions are controlled or repressed by other persons or groups within a society. Oppression can be formalized and overt, as in the case of the historical treatment of gay, lesbian, bisexual, and transgendered persons in society. However, it can also be informal and covert, such as the continued mistreatment of these groups following passage of hate crimes legislation.

In contrast, **discrimination,** in a social context, is the behavior that results from possessing a bias toward an individual or group based on such characteristics as race, ethnicity, gender, religion, age, sexual orientation, mental and physical conditions, class, and lifestyle (Barker, 2003). Both concepts involve actions whereby an individual or group exerts power over a less-powerful group, often through force, violence, or restriction of resources (Van Soest, 2008).

In spite of the fact that many people come to the U.S. to escape oppression and discrimination in their homelands, the history of both the country and the social work profession has been fraught with devastating and long-standing examples of both oppression and discrimination. We can see this in the ways in which persons of color, women, homosexual, transsexual, or transgendered persons, persons living with a disability, and many immigrant, refugee, and religious groups historically have been mistreated. If such treatment goes unchallenged, both the oppressed and the oppressors can rationalize oppression and discrimination, which in turn perpetuates these behaviors. For example, such rationalizations often include beliefs by both the oppressed and the oppressors that those in power are superior to or protective of those being oppressed or have control of needed resources (Van Soest, 2008).

Regardless of the form that oppression takes, four commonalities can be found: (1) those perceived to be "normal" are perceived to have power and those who are different are viewed as being lesser; (2) violence or the threat of violence is at the root of oppressive acts; (3) to persist, oppression must be institutionalized; and (4) because oppression becomes a part of the fabric of the oppressing group, those being oppressed become devalued or invisible (Van Soest, 2008, p. 323).

Exhibit 4.3 can help you understand how oppression is perpetuated. This framework illustrates how oppression is perpetuated because we are exposed and socialized to misinformation in our youth, which is reinforced by the people and entities within our individual environments. Continued socialization then becomes internalized as the person being oppressed begins to believe the stereotypes that the dominant culture has about the group, resulting in the inability to distinguish truth from misinformation. Feelings generated by this socialization process can include anger, guilt, confusion, and alienation. Each phase of the cycle of oppression can elicit a variety of reactions from the individual or group. Four responses are depicted in Exhibit 4.3:

- *Emotions:* Emotional reactions can range from anger to sadness.

- *Internalization:* Attitudes and behaviors can manifest at either the conscious or the unconscious levels.

- *Dissonance:* As a result of the emotions, attitudes, and behaviors that occur through socialization, individuals often respond by examining and exploring their feelings about the oppression they have observed.

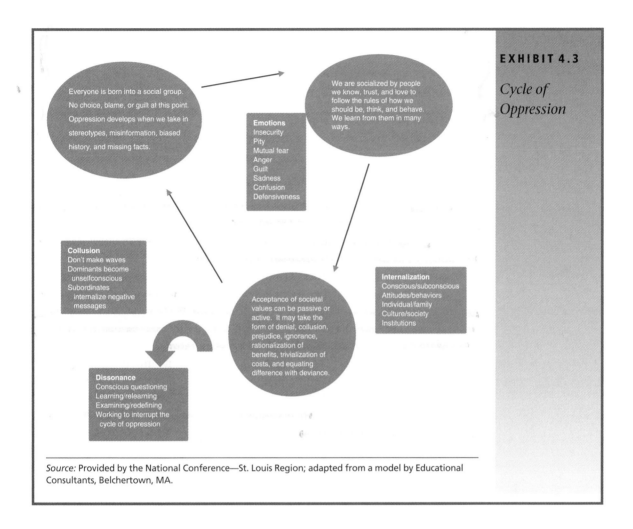

Source: Provided by the National Conference—St. Louis Region; adapted from a model by Educational Consultants, Belchertown, MA.

- *Collusion:* Through nonaction, individuals may participate in the perpetuation of the cycle of oppression.

We all possess assumptions about others. These assumptions can lead to prejudicial or discriminatory attitudes and behaviors, but can also provide a basis for cultural insight. A sampling of such assumptions includes

- People are not born with prejudice.

- Prejudice and bias are learned.

- Devaluation and disempowerment are the preconditions for prejudice and oppression.

- Prejudice is learned and can be unlearned.

- Privilege, recognized or not, is a social and economic (or political) benefit.

- All people have prejudices, but not all people can enforce their attitudes through institutions and systems of power.

- Discrimination is a real problem.

- Guilt immobilizes. Our work here is about issues, not blaming.

- People need a safe place to work.

There will always be diversity and difference; unity is possible only through understanding, accepting, and valuing diversity. Throughout the history of the profession, social workers have played an active role in working to eliminate social injustices that lead to oppression and discrimination. For example, they have helped vulnerable groups band together, as in the case of welfare rights organizations, and they have advocated for change at the legislative level. Social workers have lobbied and, in some cases, sought elected office to work for justice for victims of domestic violence and hate crimes and have campaigned for access to housing and public facilities for older adults and persons with disabilities. Current changes in the demography of our country challenge social workers to maintain an awareness of the social forces that face society so that the profession can respond to the needs of diverse and changing client groups.

Now that you understand the role of social workers in combating oppression and advocating for social justice, let us consider some of the political, economic, and social challenges and opportunities that will confront society and, in particular, the social work profession in the coming years. We will also explore the knowledge and skills that social workers will need to acquire in order to competently practice in an ever-changing society.

Political Environment

Because funding for social services is often a volatile and controversial political issue, the political climate in the United States has always had a significant impact on the social work profession. As you saw in Chapters 2 and 3, the political climate of the early part of this century shifted to a more conservative direction, resulting in decreased political and financial support for many social service programs and resources. Some observers speculated that the beginning of the 21st century, much like the beginning of the 20th century, will be known as a "period of increasing political tension" with issues of race, culture, diversity, civil rights, immigration, religion, abortion, gun control, and nontraditional families on the forefront of the political scene (Austin, 1997, p. 398). Because the issues with which practitioners work have long been "politicized," social workers cannot view their work as apolitical. Therefore, they assume responsibility for understanding and participating in the political process (Haynes, 1996). The 2008 elections provided considerable hope for those working in the social service arena. President Obama's campaign agenda and his economic stimulus package and health care reform are evidence of his administration's strong commitment to strengthening not only the economy but the social infrastructure of our society. Hundreds of millions of dollars are designated for services for health, children and families, older adults, Native Americans, education, persons with disabilities, employment, and housing. Elements of the American Recovery and Reinvestment Act of 2009 that are specifically focused on those with low and moderate incomes will infuse funds into TANF, employment and educational programs, unemployment insurance, child care, and support, SNAP, emergency shelter, and tax credit programs—Child Tax (up to $1,000/child) and Making Work Pay ($400/worker) (Center on Budget and Policy Priorities (CBPP), 2009).

Challenges in the Political Environment   Although social workers historically have maintained a "love/hate" relationship with the political system and the politicians who spearhead political change (or lack thereof), social workers can initiate change by working inside the political system as opposed to attempting to change the system from the outside (Reisch, 2000). A comment by Reisch (1997) is an apt descriptor of this relationship:

> We have long operated under the illusion that compassion alone will produce change. Although compassion motivates some people to act and think differently, it is insufficient to transform the deep-rooted institutional indifference of our society. (p. 90)

The continuation of many social service programs, however, will likely require social workers to integrate "political action into a broader pro-social welfare strategy" (Reisch, 1997, p. 81). In other words, in order to continue to work with individuals, families, groups, organizations, and communities, social workers are active at the political level to ensure that adequate funding and resources continue to be available for those services.

The National Association of Social Workers has long been committed to helping social workers be involved in political activity. Through PACE (Political Action for Candidate Election), national, state, and local candidates from any party whose political platforms are consistent with the NASW agenda are endorsed and financially supported.

The conservative political times of the first years of this decade have created a transfer of policy making from the national to state level, thus creating widespread inequities in the way that individual states administer social policies and programs (Schneider, 2002). Moreover, in an effort to cut costs and transfer power to the states, the role of the federal government shifted from one of a service provider to that of a monitor of services (Reisch & Jarman-Rohde, 2000). Given the increasing diversity of our population, such a shift meant that social workers had to become the advocates for social service programs that are socially just and equitably delivered.

The American voting public called for a change. With the election of Barack Obama came a shift in the political climate and, hopefully, a commitment to bipartisan collaboration aimed at enhancing the quality of life for Americans, particularly those in need. The American Recovery and Reinvestment Act is a result of a cooperative effort on the part of politicians in the House of Representatives, the Senate, the Obama transition team and the newly appointed Administration (CSWE, 2009). History will be the test to determine if these efforts will be effective.

Opportunities in the Political Environment   Strategies that social workers employ to affect political change include both an educational and participant focus. From an educational perspective, social workers raise the awareness of client systems, community residents, organizational staff, and policy makers regarding the inadequacies of the political and social service systems (Reisch, 1997). From a participant perspective, social workers can engage in the electoral advocacy and lobbying process by (1) becoming candidates for political office, (2) encouraging candidates to support issues that are important to the client systems served by social workers, (3) supporting candidates who may be excluded from political office due to the exorbitant costs of contemporary political campaigns, and (4) working to promote governmental monitoring of the social service delivery system (Reisch, 2000).

With much of the decision making for social services now occurring at the state level, the closer proximity to legislators allows social workers and client systems to provide input regarding contradictory policies and inefficiencies in service delivery (Jacobson, 2001). Social workers can embrace opportunities to influence political decision making through a variety of strategies. Strengthening the role of social work in the public sector can help social workers better understand the needs of client systems. Such understanding can contribute to the ability of social workers to advocate for policy changes that address the inequities of the service delivery system.

The ever-changing relationship between the social work profession and the sociopolitical environment of that period are both frustrating and exhilarating, but provide our profession with the opportunity to develop new knowledge and skills to better serve our client systems (Gibelman, 2004). Gaining a better understanding of the impact of global influences on social work practice can enable social workers to better serve the increasingly diverse client systems.

Economic Environment

Inextricably linked to the political climate, the economy has a powerful influence on the social work profession. Social workers need to understand the U.S. and global economies as they relate to daily work with client systems. For example, assisting persons with securing a job depends on overall employment opportunities in a community.

As with the political roller coaster of modern times, the economic status of life in the United States has its ups and downs. The effect of increased social and economic inequities (the rich becoming richer and the poor becoming poorer) creates increasing poverty rates for persons of color, children, women, immigrants, and older adults. Due to economic downturns, many employers lay off workers, consolidate jobs, use temporary workers who do not receive costly employee benefits, and move companies out of the country to less-expensive work environments. Such employment instability has historically resulted in increased unemployment and underemployment (Reisch & Jarman-Rohde, 2000). For social workers, these trends mean more persons with greater economic needs. The U.S. economy at the end of the first decade of the 21st century is an unfortunate, but accurate, depiction of this historical trend.

Challenges in the Economic Environment The implications of economic turbulence for social work practice can be pervasive and challenging because they seriously affect both the lives of client systems and the social worker's ability to provide services. For example, the economic impact of the billions spent on the second war in Iraq and the rebuilding effort can affect areas ranging from social service funding to the availability of employment for returning service personnel. An unstable economy can generate greater financial, social, and emotional needs for client systems. Women and persons of color may present with greater needs, as these two groups often have the least stable employment histories and are the first to be laid off in times of economic hardship.

Social service workers whose agencies are experiencing downsizing as a result of decreased funding and private contributions can be faced with increased workloads. Larger caseloads can mean that the social worker has less time to devote to client systems. An increased emphasis on cost-effectiveness in social service delivery can result in fewer resources being allocated to client systems. Governmental downsizing often triggers decreased funding for social programs, a particularly devastating outcome for children, who are often pitted against older adults in terms of resource allocation (Reisch & Jarman-Rohde, 2000).

A nation's economic philosophy and policy is key in determining the availability and type of employment, the amount of salaries paid, and the role of the government in employment areas (NASW, 2006–2009a). In the years immediately prior to 2008, there were signs that the economic policy of the previous administration was not working. Increases were seen in the unemployment rates for those with limited income and education levels, food stamp applications, and those living in "deep poverty" (income is less than half of the poverty line). The recession of the latter years of this century is doubly challenging due to weakened safety nets in unemployment insurance and cash assistance for families who are poor (Parrott, 2008). As a result, increases are expected over the next several years in the number of people, including children, living in poverty, particularly "deep poverty."

Opportunities in the Economic Environment   A first step in understanding and participating in the economic process is to develop a working knowledge of economics. Understanding economic trends and implications can improve the social worker's ability to serve and advocate for social service resources. Armed with knowledge of social work and economics, social workers can influence the economic system by advocating for **economic justice**—"an ideal condition in which all members of society have the same opportunities to obtain material resources necessary to survive and fulfill their human potentials" (Barker, 2003, p. 137). For example, we can call for increasing the number of jobs and for employers to pay a living wage to promote self-sufficiency that can, in turn, decrease the need for a number of social services (such as financial assistance, housing, and health care). **Living wage** is defined as the amount needed to ensure that the standard of living for a person/ family does not fall below the poverty line. Community-based advocates across the country have equated that amount to be an hourly wage ranging from $6.25 to $12.00 an hour, with many advocating for $8.20 an hour. On an optimistic note, the first legislation enacted by the Obama administration in 2009 was the passage of the Lilly Ledbetter Fair Pay Act. This new law holds employers responsible when they have discriminated against employees in the area of wages.

Public welfare policies that embrace a true multicultural vision as opposed to those that work to separate and isolate ethnic groups, and the development of more equitable family and labor policies and job opportunities, will begin to address the underlying economic injustices (Reisch & Gorin, 2001). Educating others regarding the relationships among economic instability, decreased resources, and social stressors (such as chemical dependency and addiction, domestic violence, child/ older adult abuse and neglect, and mental illness) is another strategy for positively impacting the lives of the client systems served by social workers. During challenging economic times, social workers have the opportunity and an obligation to develop and learn new practice methods to meet the needs (McNutt & Floersch, 2008). We can advocate with policy makers to increase opportunities for employment, education, and tax credits and allocations for food, housing, and cash assistance—all areas that will serve to buffer the impact of the current recession (Parrott, 2008).

Social Environment

Although deeply embedded within the political and economic controversies that exist, several social issues emerge in their own right as themes for the future of social work practice. We look at some of them in this section, including inequities in health care access, the aging of the U.S. population, and the need for increased knowledge of multicultural issues.

Challenges in the Social Environment   As previously highlighted, the U.S. population is expected to experience considerable growth within the populations of persons of color and older adults over the next several decades. This has significance for the future of social work practice in the area of health care. Projections suggest that health care needs, particularly for persons of color and older adults, will increase, but the available resources will decrease. The number of older adults living in long-term residential care facilities will increase, requiring considerable increases in both financial support and staff trained in gerontological care areas.

In the workplace, downsizing and increasing use of temporary workers can lead to decreased social relationships, which in turn can result in increased isolation, morale problems, and reduced productivity. Increases in single-parent (mostly female and many persons of color) households will result in greater financial and social service needs. Related to increases in single-parent households, decreases in average household incomes will lead to more households, particularly those with children, being considered "poor." As the number of families living in poverty increases, so will the need for social services (Reisch & Jarman-Rohde, 2000).

Opportunities in the Social Environment   Social workers have the knowledge, skills, values, and the vantage point for creating changes that occur as a result of social influences. Opportunities for change within both the profession itself and the social service system include:

- Diversifying the makeup of the profession to include more persons of color and males (Gibelman & Schervish, 1997). The profession is largely white and female and does not and will not accurately reflect the overall populations served.

- Working toward expanded socioeconomic opportunities, particularly for children who grow up in poverty, persons of color, and immigrants, all of whom utilize social services more than other groups (Murdock & Michael, 1996).

- Becoming more globally sophisticated in order to intervene successfully with the increasing numbers of client systems who live in or have emigrated from other countries. Changes may include self-assessment and expansion of global awareness as well as developing knowledge and skills related to cultural norms, beliefs, behaviors, language, values, culture, and policy (Hoffman, et al., 2008; Ramanathan & Link, 1999).

- Creating more ethnically sensitive social and health care programs that focus on localized community building. Such efforts can help to develop services for the diverse and changing client populations. Such enhancements can help reduce the lack of coordination and communication that currently exists among agencies in the social service delivery system. Client systems must often travel to multiple agencies in varying locations to complete applications for services.

- Developing programs and services that emphasize a multicultural perspective by ensuring that a consistent program ideology, culture, and practice are embraced by the agency (Gutiérrez & Nagda, 1996).

Although the future of the social service delivery system seems fraught with challenges, and social workers might have diminished resources with which to respond to these challenges, the profession can look to its strengths and to the practice of seeking change from an individual level to the larger society. Many aspects of the social service system may not work as efficiently or effectively as they could or should; however, the social work profession will work to build and strengthen the system for those who count—their clients and their communities. Social workers will be participants in shaping the future, but first, they must recognize that change is needed within both society and the social work profession (Raffoul, 1996). From that perspective, the profession can assess, intervene, and evaluate the change efforts—just as you will learn in generalist social work practice.

Emily's and her co-workers' concern about communicating effectively with the increasing number of women appearing in emergency rooms who did not speak English led them to face one of the challenges of the changing profile of U.S. society. They saw this situation as an opportunity to assess the need for interpreters, determine the availability of interpreting resources, and develop a network of interpreters who could supportively and accurately translate for this client population during times of crisis.

The staff conducted interviews with agencies that typically provided services to victims of domestic violence—public welfare, health care organizations, schools, mental health agencies, and housing programs—to determine their needs and resources for translation services. Following this assessment, Emily's agency contacted other agencies and organizations that had access to the ethnic communities that spoke the languages of the women who were being abused. As a result, the staff were able to create a database of volunteer interpreters who spoke a variety of languages, and they sent the list to all the organizations that provided services to victims of domestic violence.

CONCLUSION

Social work is a profession that functions within the context of the larger society; therefore, social work practitioners must have a comprehensive set of knowledge and skills that enables them to understand the social environment in which the client systems live. Not only do social workers need to maintain current knowledge of the shifts in the global and domestic population and, in particular, the population being served by their agency, but it is critical that social work professionals utilize our skills to raise awareness of the perspective that our profession has about society within the larger context. Specifically, social workers are on the frontlines of social issues; therefore, we have insights about the political, economic, and social environments that we are obligated to share with decision and policy makers.

The projections related to shifts in the U.S. demographic profile included in this chapter give you insights into the knowledge and skills that you will need in order to practice social work in the coming decades. To provide an additional perspective, consider these projected population trends (U.S. Census Bureau, 2009). By 2050:

- The U.S. population will be 439 million.

- 54 percent of the population will be persons of color.

  ○ Hispanics will triple to one-third of the population.

  ○ African Americans will increase from 14 percent (2008) to 15 percent.

  ○ Asian Americans will increase from 5 percent to 9 percent.

- 62 percent of the child population will be children of color.

- 88.5 million Americans will be 65 years or older.

- 19 million Americans will be 85 years or older.

You have seen how understanding diverse racial and ethnic groups and their languages and cultures, the needs of older adults and their families and caregivers, and the impact of religious and spiritual beliefs on behavior will be critical in the coming years. These are just a sampling of those competencies needed for effective social work practice.

Social workers must also be vigilant in their efforts to maintain up-to-date knowledge of the political, economic, and social issues that impact their work and their clients' lives. Social work is built on the premise that we can respond to societal needs; therefore, it is our "capacity to change that gives hope for the profession's future" (Kindle, 2006, p. 17). It is for this reason that social work students must take coursework in such areas as economics, political science, and philosophy along with sociology and psychology. Regardless of the path that you pursue in your social work career, responding to contemporary societal issues and advocating for social and economic justice is going to be a part of virtually every social worker's professional life.

MAIN POINTS

- The demographic profile of the United States is becoming more diverse. This country is now a multicultural, multiethnic, aging, and socially diverse society whose members have differing beliefs and value systems.

- The largest growth in U.S. history occurred between 1990 and 2000, with the largest increases being among the Hispanic/Latino and Asian populations.

- By 2030, nearly one-fourth of the U.S. population will be 65 years or older, with the fastest growing segment of the older-adult population being in the 85 and older group. Women make up the majority in this age group, and social workers will need to be aware of gender-related issues.

- Religious diversity is increasing and in some cases means increased religious discrimination.

- Demographic shifts require social workers to be aware of the trends and the needs of the changing society. To be effective social workers, professionals need knowledge and skills to work with diverse client systems.

- Both challenges and opportunities exist for the social work profession, specifically within the context of the political, economic, and social changes.

- Social workers remain advocates of social and economic justice while working with individuals and groups that continue to experience discrimination and oppression.

EXERCISES

1. Using the Sanchez Family interactive case (go to www.routledgesw.com/cases), respond to the following:
   a. What are the political, economic, and social issues that are present in this case?
   b. Identify the information from the case that helped you to determine the political, economic, and social issues.
2. Select one of the policy areas identified and examine the evolution of that issue through the case. Identify the relevant societal, economic, political, or religious implications of the policy.
3. In reviewing the information regarding Hector Sanchez, you learned that Hector may be laid off from his job at the construction company. Reflect on the implications for Hector and his family if he were to be laid off. What benefits will he/they be eligible to receive? What strengths does Hector possess that will enable him to obtain employment? What barriers exist that may present challenges for Hector in obtaining employment?

4. Understanding the environment in which social workers practice can be complex and span the spectrum from micro to mezzo to macro-level interventions. Go to the Riverton interactive case at www.routledgesw.com/cases. Upon familiarizing yourself with the community, particularly the Alvadora neighborhood, choose either a social, political, or economic perspective and respond to the following:
   a. Describe the community from the perspective that you have chosen.
   b. What are the issues and challenges that exist within the Alvadora neighborhood?
   c. Describe your perspective on the reasons for the presence of the issues and challenges you identified.
   d. Within the perspective that you have selected, identify the opportunities for the Alvadora community.
5. In an effort to gain insight into the societal and legal protection for gay, lesbian, bisexual, and transgendered individuals, search the Internet to identify a city or municipality in your state that includes sexual orientation in their city or municipal codes. Write a reflection paper on the number of communities that have included protection for sexual orientation. Are you surprised by your findings?
6. From a recent issue of your local newspaper, identify the key political, economic, and social issues. Reflect on your thoughts regarding whether these issues are consistent with social work concerns.
7. Describe the social class with which you identify and respond to the following:
   a. Do you believe your class influences your attitudes toward others in society?
   b. Do you believe your class influences your behaviors and life choices?
   c. If so, how? If not, explain.

CHAPTER 5

Diversity in Social Work Practice

As a result of increased globalization, enhanced communication, and greater access to transportation, the world in which social workers function has expanded. The population of the United States has become more diverse in the areas of race, ethnicity, culture, age, and sexual orientation. Diversity is a concept that is woven throughout every facet of social work practice. Since practitioners work with the entire spectrum of society, they must be keenly aware of the social and cultural environments in which they work, and they must possess knowledge and skills to be effective in working with all people, whether they are similar to or different from themselves. Through the accreditation standards for social work education programs, the Council on Social Work Education (2008) requires that students learn about diversity and use knowledge and skills that demonstrate their understanding of and appreciation for the diversity of those persons and groups they serve. Working effectively with diverse populations is a lifelong learning and growing process, as social workers encounter diversity of all kinds throughout their careers. Competent practice requires social workers to continually learn about other cultures and aspects of a diverse society. The first step in becoming an effective social worker is to embrace **cultural competence** as a vital social work skill. Culturally competent social workers understand the need to address diversity and examine individual awareness and experiences. The social work profession defines cultural competence as:

> the process by which individuals and systems respond respectfully and effectively to people of all cultures, languages, classes, races, ethnic backgrounds, religions, and other diversity factors in a manner that recognizes, affirms, and values the worth of individuals, families, and communities, and protects and preserves the dignity of each. (NASW, 2007)

Achieving **linguistic competence** is also critical for a social worker to become culturally competent. Linguistic competency is commitment by individuals and organizations to communication that can be understood by all and encompasses such strategies as multicultural staff, language and sign interpreters, multilingual

94

written and electronic materials, and information that is sensitive to a diverse audience (Goode & Jones, 2006).

In two policy statements issued by the National Association of Social Workers (2006–2009c), the social work profession is called to view language as one expression of an individual's culture and to promote and support the "implementation of cultural and linguistic competence at three intersecting levels: the individual, institutional, and societal" (p. 81).

Such workers are equipped to explore the meaning of their own life experiences and the impact of their personal beliefs on their ability to be effective practitioners. Understanding your own identity and experiences helps to understand the identities and experiences of others.

In this chapter, we explore the reasons that diversity is a key facet of the profession of social work, the theoretical concepts of oppression, and the roles that language plays, both negative and positive. We also review the areas of diversity that have presented challenges for social workers and the practice skills necessary for working effectively with diverse client systems.

DIVERSITY AS A COMPONENT OF THE EDUCATIONAL PROCESS

One of Emily's child protective service cases provided her with a new perspective on the meaning of culture and family. Emily was assigned to investigate the alleged neglect of Shanté, a 6-year-old African American child who lived with her mother, Jerilyn. Shanté had missed a number of days of school and often came to school unkempt and hungry. During her investigation, Emily learned that Jerilyn had sustained a head injury during a car accident several years earlier and was now living with a physical disability. Until recently, the two had lived with Jerilyn's mother, who had been the primary caregiver for both Jerilyn and Shanté, but the mother had recently died following a stroke. Recognizing that she was unable to care for Shanté, Jerilyn agreed to award custody to her sister, Roberta. Roberta lives in the house next door to them.

The case went to court to finalize the custody arrangement, and during Roberta's testimony, the fact emerged that she was not Jerilyn's biological sister. The two women had been lifelong friends and belonged to the same church, one whose members referred to one another with the honorifics of "sister" and "brother." Emily had assumed that sister meant a familial connection because her cultural experiences had not included in-depth knowledge of the African American culture or the religion practiced by the two women. From this experience, Emily learned some valuable lessons related to making assumptions, particularly when working with persons whose cultures are different from her own. Ultimately Roberta was awarded custody of Shanté, who was well cared for and saw her mother on a daily basis.

The U.S. and global societies are multicultural, and all citizens need an understanding of the cultures of others. In considering cultures, social workers learn about the history, beliefs, family structure, religion, dress, food, and lifestyles of a group. Although the specific issues related to diversity may be different today than they were during earlier periods of social work, the profession continues to advocate vigilance in regard to such issues of social justice as discrimination, oppression, and inequalities. Emily's experience demonstrates that attention to diversity and culture is as important as ever.

The National Association of Social Workers and the Council on Social Work Education, through their publications, mandate that social workers acquire the knowledge and skills necessary for culturally competent practice. The NASW *Code of Ethics* (2008) calls for social workers to respect the inherent dignity and worth of a person, to be sensitive to cultural and ethnic diversity, and to work toward ending discrimination, oppression, poverty, and social injustice. The *Code* further charges social workers with the obligation to practice within and develop their areas of competence and directs social workers to understand human behavior within the context of culture and to use a strengths-based perspective when viewing all cultures. In 2008, language was added to the *Code* that calls on the profession to respect and protect gender identity and immigrant status. The *Code* thus binds all social workers to practice competently and without discrimination. Given that the majority of social workers surveyed report their practices to be comprised of a racially and ethnically diverse group of clients, it is critical for social workers to possess multiculturally competent knowledge, skills, and values. Groups represented in social work caseloads include clients who are: non-Hispanic white (99%); African American (85%); Hispanic (77%); Asian (49%); and Native American (39%). Over 40 percent of social workers work with a caseload that is largely non-Caucasian.

As an extension of the *Code of Ethics*, the NASW membership, in 2001, developed the Standards for Cultural Competence in Social Work Practice, a set of 10 standards for culturally competent practice. Culturally competent practice requires more than knowing about diversity; it requires the ability and skills to take action (Simmons et al., 2008). As an acknowledgement of this premise, the profession moved cultural competence to a higher level in 2007 by adding indicators for demonstrating the achievement of those standards. The standards and indicators are shown in Box 5.1.

As the information in Box 5.1 demonstrates, to practice social work with cultural competence, you need an extensive knowledge of persons different from yourself, an awareness and understanding of yourself, and skills that are appropriate for application with persons and groups different from yourself. In essence, cultural competence is the ability to examine your own attitudes, beliefs, and values and to gain knowledge and skills that will enable you to adapt your practice to the unique needs of all client systems. It is important to note that culturally competent knowledge, skills, and values extend beyond racial and ethnic differences. Being culturally competent "can mean the difference between a person making it or falling through the cracks" (NASW, n.d.a).

STANDARD	INTERPRETATION	INDICATORS	
Ethics and values	Within the context of the client system's culture, the profession's values mandate that social workers respect the individual and her or his right to self-determination, and confront any ethical dilemmas that result from conflicts.	Knowledge of the NASW *Code of Ethics* and social justice and human rights principles. Ability to recognize and describe areas of conflict and accommodation in values. Awareness of differences and strengths.	**BOX 5.1** *Standards and Indicators of Culturally Competent Social Work Practice*
Self-awareness	Culturally competent social workers are responsible for being aware of their own cultural identities as well as "knowing and acknowledging how fears, ignorance, and the 'isms' have influenced their attitudes, beliefs, and feelings."	Examine and describe cultural and social heritage and identities, beliefs, and impacts. Ability to change attitudes and beliefs and increase comfort. Demonstrate understanding of limitations. Work with others to enhance self-awareness.	
Cross-cultural knowledge	Baseline and ongoing knowledge of cultures other than one's own is an expected component of culturally competent practice.	Gain knowledge of: client groups, dominant and non-dominant groups, privilege, and interactions of cultural systems.	
Cross-cultural skills	Because culturally effective social workers intervene with a wide range of people who are different from them, they must remain open to learning new knowledge and skills.	Gain skills to communicate, interact, assess, intervene, and advocate with diverse groups. Effectively use clients' natural supports.	
Service delivery	Interacting with co-workers, agencies, and the community to maintain awareness of cultural diversity and to ensure the provision of culturally competent services is critical to effective practice.	Utilize formal and informal community resources. Advocate for and help to build culturally competent services.	

BOX 5.1
continued

STANDARD	INTERPRETATION	INDICATORS
Empowerment and advocacy	Within the context of the client system's culture, social workers advocate for and with client systems toward consciousness raising, development of personal power, and social change.	Advocate for culturally respectful policies. Utilize appropriate methods and interventions. Be aware of own values and their impact on client systems.
Diverse workforce	Social workers advocate for maintaining the diversity of the social service delivery system.	Advocate for and support a diverse workforce that reflects the needs of the client systems being served.
Professional education	Social workers advocate for cultural-focused education and training for the social work profession.	Advocate for and participate in education to ensure culturally competent knowledge, skills, and values.
Language diversity	Social workers are obligated to ensure that services are provided in a linguistically competent manner.	Advocate for and implement use of culturally competent written, electronic, and verbal communications.
Cross-cultural leadership	The profession is committed to sharing the profession's values and ethics training knowledge with others.	Social work leaders model culturally competence through interactions, communications, policies, and hiring.

Source: Adapted from NASW, 2007.

SELF-AWARENESS: AN EXPLORATION

For those who are members of a majority group in the U.S., there is not a "lived experience" of being in a minority group. Think of a time when you felt you stood out or were a minority in a group. What emotions does that memory evoke? Why did you feel different—was it race, gender, age, economic level, religion, sexual orientation, or maybe your dress or speech? What was the outcome of that situation? Getting in touch with the experience and feelings of being different can help you develop empathy for others and their experiences of difference.

While raising your self-awareness about issues of diversity, oppression, discrimination, and social justice is critical for effective social work practice, it can be exhilarating and liberating as you learn more about your own culture and heritage. At the same time, however, delving into your own culture, your place in society, and the impact of your behavior on others can be a painful process, as you may discover biases about which you were unaware.

To understand the meaning of social justice, it is important to identify the ways in which you knowingly or unknowingly speak or act in ways that can result in the discrimination of other persons. You may come to terms with the fact that you have biases (we all do) or that you or others have engaged in or supported behaviors that have been disrespectful or hurtful to others. Recognizing these facts will likely be painful and difficult, but it is an important step toward achieving cultural awareness and sensitivity and, ultimately, cultural competence.

Another useful strategy to heighten your self-awareness is to examine your own diversity and its impact on your life. To identify issues related to your own culture and experiences, consider the questions posed in Exhibit 5.1. Compare your culture and experiences to other cultures by considering the similarities and differences in the ways in which you celebrate special occasions, interact with others, and use language to describe your group and other groups, for example.

Having strategies for broadening your awareness of other cultures is also useful in achieving cultural competence. You can use these strategies to acquire knowledge about the practices of other cultures, compare and contrast these practices with those of your own culture(s), and develop an understanding of the culturally competent skills that are needed to be an effective social worker with specific groups. Some suggestions for exposing yourself to new experiences are listed here. Each of these experiences will be most educational and meaningful if you are with other people with whom you can compare observations and feelings.

- Seek out interactions with persons or groups who are different from you. For instance, engage someone you see on a regular basis but have never talked with.

- Attend international festivals, museums, or arts events, and ask questions about the culture. It is ideal to attend an event with someone familiar with that culture or heritage.

- Read a magazine or newspaper targeted to a specific group with whom you are not familiar.

- Attend a service in a religious institution that is new to you. This experience will be even more meaningful if you attend the service with a member of that religious group.

- Read a book that portrays a culture with which you are not familiar.

- Watch a television show or movie in a language other than your first language or one that portrays a culture with which you are not familiar.

- Visit a restaurant or eat food that is new to you (or better yet, organize a potluck gathering in which people bring food of their culture).

EXHIBIT 5.1

Self-Awareness: Cultural Identity

Who are you?

⬇

With which racial, ethnic, religious, gender, age, social class, and sexual orientation groups do you identify?

⬇

Into which of these groups were you born, and which have you joined since birth?

⬇

What unique characteristics do your affiliations have that other groups do not?

⬇

What do you like about your culture(s)? What do you not like about your culture(s)?

⬇

Have you ever experienced discrimination as a result of your affiliation with one or more of the cultures to which you belong?

⬇

What was the nature of that discrimination?

⬇

Consider the language that you use. What terms do you use to refer to other groups? How do others refer to you?

- Identify a controversial issue that is currently plaguing society or your community and identify your thoughts and feelings about the issues. Talk with others, seek out information from credible sources on the issues, and reflect on strategies for resolving the dilemma on the individual, community, or societal level.

- Observe the conversations of others: Do they use discriminatory language, make inappropriate jokes, or engage in offensive behaviors? If so, what is your response (or lack of response)? Are you silent and, if so, why?

- Volunteer with an age or a cultural group with whom you have little experience. Senior centers, skilled nursing facilities/adult day care, child day care centers, and programs for persons who are developmentally disabled, new to this country, or experiencing poverty or homelessness are all good choices.

Moving out of your "comfort zone" and having new experiences is a positive step toward understanding more about yourself and your cultural origins. It also serves to expand your comfort zone so that you can be effective with others who are different from you. Gaining cultural competence will be a lifelong endeavor, but one that we are all obligated to.

THEORY THAT HELPS US UNDERSTAND DIVERSITY

In order to practice competently with diverse populations, social workers understand issues related to diversity from multiple perspectives. Having explored these issues from the historical and demographic perspectives in earlier chapters, we will now consider working with diverse populations from a theoretical perspective. We will focus on two theoretical frameworks that can help social workers understand, engage, assess, and intervene with clients from different cultures: the ecological perspective and the strengths perspective. By using an appropriate theoretical approach, social workers are already sensitized to the need to include cultural information in the assessment and intervention process. Culturally competent knowledge and skills are essential for the application of theoretical frameworks to social work practice.

The ecological and strengths perspectives are strategies that can guide social workers in conducting an engagement, assessment, intervention, and evaluation with all client systems, but they are particularly helpful in working with client systems whose cultural experiences are different from their own. When working with persons with diverse backgrounds, social workers should note differing home environments and family cultures so that identifying culturally related strengths becomes key to the assessment process. As you come to appreciate how theory can help in understanding diversity, you can focus on the language and challenges of multicultural social work practice.

Ecological Perspective

A theoretical approach to social work practice that views the client system within the context of the environment in which the client lives is known as the **ecological perspective** (Germain & Gitterman, 1980). The concept of "environment" includes family, work, religion, culture, and life events (for example, developmental issues and life milestones and transitions). This perspective directs the social worker to consider each aspect of the client system's life when establishing rapport, conducting an assessment, and developing an intervention plan with the client system. Known as the **person-in-environment** perspective, it emphasizes the fact that clients' beliefs, emotions, behaviors, and interactions are influenced by their past and present life experiences as well as the larger society in which they live. Within each client system encounter, the social worker must be aware of the influence of such cultural factors as race, ethnicity, place of origin, age, gender, social class, religion, and sexual orientation. Culturally competent practitioners incorporate those societal, cultural, and personal influences that impact the client system's experience with the world in which they live.

Another fundamental component of the ecological perspective is recognition of the impact of oppression on the client system's life experiences. As an example, consider a scenario in which you are a social worker working with a client who is Native American and you are not Native American yourself. Native Americans have long been oppressed by society in such areas as resource allocation, education, and employment. They have been victims of exploitation, abuse, segregation, open hostilities, and violence. In working with the client, you would be remiss if you did not consider the historical, political, and societal issues related to Native Americans, in general, and to individual tribes, in particular. Client systems that have experienced institutionalized oppression are likely to feel powerlessness and a lack of trust, particularly regarding members of the oppressing group. As social workers, we are bound by our *Code of Ethics* to not only oppose such oppression, but to understand its origins and impact, to actively advocate against it and develop interventions that will combat it (Van Soest, 2008).

In building rapport, the effective social worker will gain knowledge of the client system's history of oppression and experiences of discrimination, while not promoting either. At the same time, the social worker is responsible for striving to understand the client system's values, beliefs, and cultural practices and the ways each impacts the perspective and interaction the client has with her or his environment. Such sensitivity to issues of diversity takes into consideration multiple aspects of the client system's environment and conveys to the client the worker's respect for the client's cultural heritage and experience. For example, the social worker assigned to work with a Native American family can be more effective if armed with knowledge about that client system's tribal affiliation, history, traditions, and current issues.

Strengths-Based Perspective

A concept embedded within the ecological perspective is the **strengths-based perspective**. Viewing the client's cultural experiences and beliefs as strengths on which to build an assessment and intervention is an extension of the ecological model of social work practice. Too often in the past, practitioners have seen culture, ethnicity, religion, and sexual orientation as irrelevant, different (a deficit), or an area for change, rather than as an asset or resource in problem solving. Incorporating the client's cultural characteristics and experiences into the social work strategy as a strength is consistent with the social work value of respecting each individual's uniqueness and worth. Applying the knowledge and skills of the strengths-based perspective along with those of culturally competent practice, social workers can promote a multicultural environment.

The strengths-based perspective is particularly important for practicing social work with cultural competence at all levels (Saleebey, 2006). Using a strengths perspective, the social work relationship is built around the experience and life of the client system, thus demonstrating respect for culture, lifestyle, and client right to self-determination. Framing cultural diversity issues as part of the client system environment provides the social worker with additional resources for understanding the stressors being experienced by the client system, aids in building rapport and trust, and contributes to culturally appropriate intervention plans.

Consider a scenario in which you are a social worker working with an older Jewish woman who immigrated to this country from Europe following World War II. She is a widow and a retired teacher who lives alone and has no immediate family nearby. Since the death of her husband, she has become more withdrawn, and you are concerned that she is depressed. While conducting an assessment, you learn that she is a survivor of the Holocaust and the concentration camps. You help her to see her life experiences as a resource for educating others about the atrocities committed during the Holocaust, and you arrange for her to join a speaker's bureau for the local Jewish Community Center. She travels to schools to share her story with children, most of whom have never met a Holocaust survivor. Her depression dissipates; she is now feeling useful because she is using her skills as a teacher and her life experiences as a survivor.

THE LANGUAGE OF DIVERSITY

Social workers must not only become familiar with the language of diversity if they wish to be effective practitioners and advocates for marginalized and oppressed populations, but also understand, use, and advocate for language that is respectful and nondiscriminatory. Language is a powerful tool and can be used to encourage as well as demean individuals or groups. Social workers are mindful not to use negative language that can perpetuate stereotypes. Currently in use is **person first language.**

Person first language refers first to the person and then to the situation (for example, "person with a disability" instead of "disabled person"). As evidence that our attitudes and language continues to evolve, Mackelprang and colleagues (2008) note that disability advocates are challenging the use of person first language, citing that disabilities are a form of diversity, not a pathology.

Throughout history, society has developed, used, and misused a variety of terms to describe groups that are different from one another. Because of differences of opinion, changing perceptions, and the dynamics of language, the meanings of terms—particularly terms related to race and ethnicity—have become inconsistent. Box 5.2 presents many of the terms and their meanings, which are necessary to understand in order to practice social work ethically and responsibly. These are not the only terms you may find in the social work literature, but are an inclusive and appropriate sampling.

THE "ISMS"

The following statement by Martin Luther King Jr. speaks to pervasiveness of discrimination: "Injustice anywhere is a threat to justice everywhere" (King, 1963).

Throughout history, social workers have been on the forefront of challenging the ever-present **isms**—doctrines, causes, or theories, which within the social work profession, typically imply negative attitudes or beliefs regarding a specific population of people, although they can connote positive belief systems as well.

Once a person has been identified as a member of a group that is targeted as a vulnerable group, society tends to view that person only by her or his membership in that group. For example, a person with a physical disability is often viewed only as a person with a disability and not in light of father, mother, teacher, or other possible roles and memberships. As you read the following sections, keep in mind that each group comprises individuals who are also members of other groups. We are more than our race, gender, sexual orientation, age, abilities, or religious affiliations.

The following discussion is not intended to be an all-inclusive list but rather a sampling of those areas that social workers encounter on a routine basis. Awareness and knowledge of these isms are part of becoming a culturally competent social worker. Because the demographic characteristics of the United States are changing, social workers are also responsible for acquiring and maintaining cutting-edge skills in order to serve the changing population and also to advocate for oppressed and marginalized groups.

Racism

Probably the most common "ism" challenging modern-day society, **racism results from the categorization and stereotyping of groups by racial characteristics or ethnic origins**. Whether on a personal or societal level, racism is defined as the belief that

Accommodation/acculturation/assimilation: Used interchangeably, these terms are, in fact, distinct concepts regarding a majority group's treatment toward a minority group within a society. **Accommodation** refers to the efforts of one group to make changes to enable another group to live within society. For example, offering printed materials in multiple languages to enable persons whose first language is not English is a form of accommodation. **Acculturation** is the socialization of one culture into the ways (that is, values, beliefs, and behaviors) of another culture. In contrast, **assimilation** is adoption of one group's cultural practices (for example, values, norms, and behaviors) by another group. For example, refugees become "Westernized" when they immigrate to the United States. Assimilation can be viewed as a form of oppression when the traditions of the assimilated group are ignored or its members are forced to give up those traditions and values.

Despite the fact that the United States has always been a diverse society, considerable inconsistency exists in the ways in which the majority culture has interacted with persons of color. At various points in history, the majority group has attempted to achieve acculturation, assimilation, and accommodation, while only recently recognizing that each racial, ethnic, and religious group can retain its own culture without being "changed."

Although members of the majority culture often recognize that minority groups could retain their cultures, some question whether such ties to their origins would hamper their ability to become truly American.

Bias/prejudice: Positive or negative prejudgments or attitudes toward a person, group, or idea. Not typically based on fact or evidence, **bias**, or **prejudice**, grows out of misperceptions.

Color: Despite the political, social, and emotional connotations that this word conveys, remember that *color* literally refers only to the pigmentation of a person's skin.

Culture: One of the terms that has been defined differently at different times and in different sources, **culture** can be considered as the way a group of people perceive the world around them and structure their interactions within and outside their unique group (Schlesinger & Devore, 1995). Specifically, a culture is defined by the many characteristics and components possessed by a group, such as values, beliefs, religious and political tenets, and behaviors. Culture is an *overall* social construct encompassing such issues as race, ethnicity, and group membership that individuals and groups use in interacting, communicating, and interpreting information (Okun et al., 1999).

Ethnicity: Determined by the cultural group with which an individual identifies, **ethnicity** can be characterized by national origin, race, language, and/or religious beliefs and practices. Depending on the culture, country, region, and religion into which a person is born, she or he can self-identify with multiple ethnicities.

Ethnocentrism: Group members who practice **ethnocentrism** believe that their culture is the norm and that other cultures with different practices or beliefs are therefore outside the norm (Okun et al., 1999). Ethnocentric attitudes and behaviors generally result when members of a group perceive themselves as superior to other groups.

Integration: Just as segregation has been institutionalized (formalized) within our society, so too has **integration**, in which diverse groups such as those in public schools, the military, and the workplace have been brought together as equals.

Marginalization: The subordination of individuals or groups who possess less power, **marginalization** occurs as a result of the perpetuation of stereotypes and oppression.

BOX 5.2

Terminology for Culturally Competent Social Work Practice

BOX 5.2
continued

Multicultural competence: The practice of multicultural competence, or **multiculturalism**, is the practice of understanding, recognizing, and respecting the cultural values, beliefs, and behaviors of others.

Pluralism: Aimed at increasing inclusiveness, **pluralism** values all groups and provides a basis for understanding the way members of a society interact with one another and the environments in which they live (Logan, 2003).

Race: The term **race** refers to human characteristics that can be determined by physical traits (such as skin color or hair texture); geography (for example, place of origin); or culture. The U.S. Census Bureau (2009) separates race from Hispanic/Latino origin and uses five categories:

● White—origins in Europe, the Middle East, or North Africa.

● Black or African American—origins in any of the black racial groups of Africa.

● American Indian or Alaska Native—origins in any of the original peoples of North, Central, or South America.

● Asian—origins in any of the original peoples of the Far East, Southeast Asia, or the Indian subcontinent.

● Native Hawaiian or Other Pacific Islander—origins in any of the original peoples of Hawaii, Guam, Samoa, or other Pacific Islands.

Besides having a physical meaning, race has assumed a meaning that carries intensely emotional and personal implications.

Segregation: Racial and religious **segregation**—the separation of one group from other groups—are two forms of institutionalized segregation that our society has deemed unlawful. In contrast, informal segregation, which can be just as devastating, cannot be legislated.

Social class: An individual or group may be categorized in a **social class** depending on characteristics such as income, social status, education, and religious affiliation.

Stereotyping: Similar to bias and prejudice, **stereotyping** occurs when someone assumes a person possesses the same characteristics as all other individuals within his or her group.

one group is superior to another group(s) based solely on race. Racism in its most extreme form is typically perpetrated by a majority or dominant culture and serves to segregate, isolate, and disempower a minority or less powerful group of people. In the United States, the Caucasian population has historically held the majority position due to population composition, but as you read in earlier chapters, demographic trends indicate, the population ratios are changing, but that has not resulted in the end of racism (NASW, 2009–2012j). Despite a shifting of the population, anti-immigrant sentiment continues to exist in such areas as access to social services, education, and housing.

Racism has permeated essentially every aspect of U.S. society. Racism exists on two levels: institutional racism and individual racism. Institutional racism refers to discrimination against persons of color in accessing such resources as employment, education, financial assistance and credit, organizational membership, and home ownership. In contrast, individual racism is abuse or mistreatment propagated by a person or group. For example, the uttering of a racial slur by one person to another is individual racism.

Over the past 50 years, U.S. society has dramatically modified its definitions of and approaches to race-related issues. During the mid-20th century, a "melting pot" approach in which sameness among the races was emphasized aimed at creating a society in which all cultures become blended into a single culture without the distinctions of diversity. Not all segments of society embraced such an approach; for example, a forced segregation approach was the dominant philosophy in most southern U.S. states. Then, during the late 1950s and 1960s, support grew for an approach that embraced a "world of difference" philosophy that focused on racial uniqueness. However, others within the civil rights movement advocated for total racial integration.

The decades of the 1970s and 1980s began to emphasize a multiculturalist perspective that valued individual ethnicities. This perspective met with intense intellectual and political opposition from persons and groups that wanted to maintain racial separateness. For some, this view again shifted during the 1990s to a pluralistic conceptualization in which people exist within a society of groups that are distinctive in ethnic origin, cultural patterns, and relationships. As evidenced by the 2009–2012 policy statement, the social work profession embraces an "inclusive, multicultural society in which racial, ethnic, class, sexual orientation, age, physical and mental ability, religion and spirituality, gender and other cultural and social identifies are values and respected" (NASW, 2009–2012j, p. 286).

For most people, racial issues can evoke intense emotional reactions. Most people have been either a victim or perpetrator of racist thoughts or behaviors, and many people have been both at one time or another. As students and instructors, we must all bring our life experiences to the social work classroom. As long as we remain open to expanding our cultural awareness and sensitivity, the social work classroom can be an excellent environment in which to learn and grow. Some students, both white students and students of color, report being uncomfortable in a classroom in which racism is discussed because of feelings of discomfort regarding the behaviors of their racial group, anger regarding the treatment of persons of color, or resentment toward students who have not experienced discrimination. However, when students agree to create a safe environment in which issues, and not people, are confronted, they can initiate stimulating and meaningful discussions. Known as critical multiculturalism, this paradigm goes beyond race to include education on culture, oppression, multiple identities, power, whiteness and privilege, historical context, and social change (Daniel, 2008).

Social workers can confront racism in many ways. The most obvious strategies include advocacy, education, and, sometimes, mediation (for example, serving as an agent to promote effective communication). To be effective in any of these areas, social workers engage in self-awareness, particularly the willingness to recognize areas in which their own knowledge and skills are lacking. Social workers confront racial injustices at any and all levels and areas of practice. We must ask ourselves if we are implementing approaches that take into consideration the culture of the client system (Golden, 2008).

The status of racial justice at the beginning of the 21st century remains controversial and is, as yet, undetermined. While considerable strides have been made by society and the social work profession in recent years to eradicate racism, we are reminded to continue our efforts (Blank, 2006). Think about your own knowledge and skills and, more importantly, what your role is in promoting justice.

Ageism

When most people hear the term *ageism*, they immediately think of the mistreatment of older adults. In fact, ageism refers to discrimination based on *any* age. The two groups most at risk for age bias and discrimination are children and older adults. Being on the two ends of the age spectrum places these groups in vulnerable positions regarding access to resources. Moreover—and perhaps even worse—the two groups are sometimes pitted against each other when resources are allocated.

While we all have experienced being on the youthful end of the age spectrum, most of us have yet to experience life as an older adult. Therefore, we rely on our perceptions of older adults, which may be biased and stereotypical. In one study of social work students' perceptions of themselves at age 75, most students expected to have health and memory problems, but would still be attractive, valued and active (Kane, 2008). A useful exercise in understanding the needs of older adults that you will encounter in your social work practice, consider how you see yourself as an older adult and how you would like to be perceived.

As the sheer number of older persons has risen and will continue to rise dramatically, their collective "voices" are increasingly being heard, in part because they have become highly organized and are diligent advocates for their own rights and benefits. Even so, older adults continue to need support from social workers and others who will advocate on their behalf. Children have a difficult time being heard by policy makers and funders and must depend on adults to champion their causes.

Dealing effectively with ageism begins on a personal level. Conduct an inventory of your ageist experiences. Have you ever purchased a greeting card that lamented the fact the person was over the hill? Have you ever been dismissed by someone because you were too young (or too old) to understand something? Have you heard or made stereotypical remarks about the driving abilities of either young or old people? Have you ever referred to a person's age in a derogatory manner—

"geezer" or "baby," for instance? As a part of any diversity self-awareness campaign, checking ourselves and our society on ageism issues is our obligation as social workers. In social work specifically, all practitioners are ethically bound to acquire knowledge and skills that will enable them to be effective in working with persons of any age.

Sexism

A part of U.S. history and still pervasive today, sexism has been defined as the belief that men are superior to women as a result of gender. Sexism occurs when women are discriminated against because they are women. Consider just a few of the institutionally enforced examples of sexism that were in place for most of the history of this country: Women could not own property, vote, run for public office, or divorce their husbands, and they were prevented from being trained in many professions. Although our nation has made considerable strides toward improving the status of women, significant gender-based inequities remain. As you read earlier in this book, women's earnings continue to be lower than men's for the same positions. Women are still in the minority in most traditionally male-dominated professions (such as medicine, engineering, and politics), and when women achieve a major presence within a professional discipline, the salaries of both men and women tend to decrease. The majority of persons who are victims of violence or living in poverty (particularly for female-headed households) continue to be women.

Although equal employment and sexual harassment policies have eradicated institutional sexism, other forms of sexism continue to exist but appear to have gone "underground." For example, both genders continue to make sexist remarks, particularly in the areas of domestic and sexual violence, clothing, and behaviors. When women engage in traditionally male activities, they may be criticized, particularly when the women excel in the activity. Women continue to function as the primary caregivers for the family, even when they work full time outside the home.

Social workers have an ethical responsibility to address issues of gender equality for all women. We can begin by taking into account the interplay of characteristics that make her vulnerable to discrimination and oppression (Worden, 2007). Consider the female client who is also a woman of color, a religious minority or economically disadvantaged and the way in which those factors impact her life experience and self-perception. Social workers can work at the prevention level by dispelling stereotypes and myths about women's rights and abilities. Social workers can also empower women by informing them that they do not have to let a sexual assault go unreported or remain in a violent relationship. Social workers can work at the policy level to ensure that policies are crafted to guarantee gender equity. Every social worker can write letters to the media when women are portrayed unfairly, stereotypically, or as inferior to men. You might take a minute to consider other types of activities that you can do to combat sexism.

Classism

Based on social class (for example, economic and social status), classism can occur as a result of occupational status (for example, blue collar or white collar) or income (for example, lower socioeconomic class, lower-middle class, owning/ ruling classes). Although some philosophers have claimed that the United States can and should be a classless society, the reality is that our society has distinct classes that have evolved over time to include categorized values, expectations, beliefs, and lifestyles (Okun et al., 1999). In fact, the distinctions between the richest and the poorest in our society reached an all-time high in the last century (Yeskel & Leondar-Wright, 1997). Moreover, based on the last official census, the economic gap between the richest and the poorest is widening (U.S. Census Bureau, 2004).

Most often defined as socioeconomic status, social class is used prejudicially as a mechanism for labeling people in formal and informal ways. Classism, thus, is the discrimination that occurs as a result of this compartmentalization by income and wealth. Some people believe that membership in a particular social/economic class is based on the person's willingness to work hard—the philosophy of pulling yourself up by your bootstraps, discussed in earlier chapters. Because of this, people on the low end of the economic continuum are characterized as simply lacking ambition, without consideration for such factors as race, ethnicity, gender, disability, and access to resources and opportunities.

Your experiences with and views on socioeconomic class are yet another issue to consider as you conduct your diversity self-assessment. Consider the following messages that you have received throughout your life regarding social class and income:

- Have you ever thought about the socioeconomic class into which you were born? If not, in which class does your family of origin belong?

- Do you continue to be a member of that class? If you have changed socioeconomic class, how did that occur?

- What does membership in your socioeconomic class, or any other socioeconomic class, mean in terms of your education, resources, opportunities, place of residence, and employment?

- Have you been a victim of classist remarks, or (be honest here) have you made classist remarks?

- Do you perceive a difference between those students whose parents pay for college and those students who must take out loans?

As with all the isms, the social worker's role in combating classism is often one of advocacy and education. Countering the "bootstrap" myth, empowering people to reach their optimal functioning and quality of life, and confronting classist language are just three anticlassism activities in which social workers can engage proactively.

Ableism

A recent addition to the language of diversity, *ableism* is defined as "discrimination and exclusion that oppresses people who have mental, emotional, and physical disabilities" (Rauscher & McClintock, 1997, p. 198). Disabilities can be perceptual, illness related, physical, developmental, psychiatric, psychological, mobility related, or environmental (for example, allergies). Unfortunately, U.S. society again has a long and shameful history of discrimination against persons with disabilities. From the language used to refer to a person with a disability, to the restriction of access to schools and buildings, and to the penchant for "warehousing" people with disabilities in institutions and separate schools, the United States has oppressed this population for centuries.

Despite the fact that one-third of us will experience a disability within our lifetime, it has only been in recent years that ableism has been considered in such areas as policy making, funding, and public sensitivity with over a dozen major legislative acts passed (NASW, 2009–2012g). In particular, two legislative mandates, the Rehabilitation Act of 1973 and the Americans with Disabilities Act of 1990, established institutional support for assuring the civil rights of, and providing supportive accommodations and services for, persons with a wide range of disabilities. Think for a moment of all the disability-related terms you have heard or used throughout your lifetime. Box 5.3 lists some common terms and provides alternative language, known as "words with dignity," that is more likely to preserve the dignity of people with different abilities.

In striving to eradicate ableism, the social work profession has long championed equity, respect, and physical accommodation. Although our society has made strides in many areas—particularly education, accessibility, employment, and benefits—the professional challenge is to continue to draw attention to the abilities and strengths of persons with different abilities. As with other isms, social workers are ethically obligated to be on the cutting edge of services and resources for persons with disabilities. They must also combat both the use of inappropriate language and discrimination in the provision of services. Finally, they should fight to ensure the rights of any person with a disability. The following are principles of practice to keep in mind when working with persons with disabilities:

- All people are capable or potentially capable.

- Persons with disabilities do not need to be "fixed" in order to function in society.

- Disabilities are a social construct, and interventions therefore must target the political realm.

BOX 5.3	WORDS WITH DIGNITY	AVOID THESE WORDS
Substitutes for Ableist Terms	Person with a disability, disabled	Cripple, handicapped, handicap, invalid (literally invalid means "not valid")
	Person who has, person with (e.g. person who has cerebral palsy)	Victim, afflicted with (e.g. victim of cerebral palsy)
	Uses a wheelchair	Restricted, confined to a wheelchair, wheelchair bound (the chair enables mobility, without the chair, the person is confined to bed)
	Non-disabled	Normal (referring to non-disabled persons as "normal" insinuates that people with disabilities are abnormal)
	Deaf, does not voice for themselves, nonvocal	Deaf mute, deaf and dumb
	Disabled since birth, born with	Birth defect
	Psychiatric history, psychiatric disability, emotional disorder, mental illness	Crazy, insane, lunatic, mental patient, wacko
	Epilepsy, seizures	Fits
	Learning disability, mental retardation, developmental delay, ADD/ADHD	Slow, retarded, lazy, stupid, underachiever

Other terms which should be avoided because they have negative connotations and tend to evoke pity and fear include: abnormal, burden, condition, deformed, differently abled, disfigured, handi-capable, incapacitated, imbecile, manic, maimed, madman, moron, palsied, pathetic, physically challenged, pitiful, poor, spastic, stricken with, suffer, tragedy, unfortunate, and victim.

   Preferred terminology: blind (no visual capability), legally blind, low vision (some visual capability), hearing loss, hard of hearing (some hearing capability), hemiplegia (paralysis of one side of the body), paraplegia (loss of function in the lower body only), quadriplegia (paralysis of both arms and legs), residual limb (post-amputation of a limb)

Source: Paraquad (n. d.).

- Persons with disabilities have more common characteristics than differences.

- Disability does not imply dysfunction.

- Persons with disabilities have a right to self-determination. (Mackelprang & Salsgiver, 1999, pp. 241–243)

Heterosexism

Heterosexism, the belief that heterosexuality is the only acceptable form of sexual orientation, exists at all levels of our society and is perpetuated formally and informally. Linked to religion, morality, and deviance, a nonheterosexual orientation has been and continues to be considered by many people to be a choice, a defect, or a perversion and therefore "curable." As a result of such homophobia, lesbians, gay, bisexuals, and transgendered persons (persons whose gender identity is counter to traditional definitions of heterosexual or homosexual) have been prohibited from employment in many areas, from legally marrying, adopting children as a couple, receiving partner benefits, serving in the military if they disclose their sexual orientation, and making legal and medical decisions for their partners. The LGBT community has often been the victim of hate crimes that range from verbal harassment, to physical assaults, or "gay bashing," to murder. As a result of the overwhelming biases that have prevailed in our society, these groups have historically been highly reluctant to disclose their sexual orientation in any but the safest places, often not even "coming out" to their families, co-workers, or some friends.

Recent years have seen significant progress in the area of gay rights as a result of the mobilization of the gay community and their supporters. The recognition of same-sex partners and marriages by some states and employers is one example of the progress made.

More than with most of the other isms, talking about homosexuality makes some people uncomfortable. Talking about sexuality, in general, is awkward for many of us, but a lack of knowledge, fear of offending the person, deep-rooted religious beliefs, or even fears about our own sexuality make talking about homosexuality particularly difficult for some of us. In fact, for some students, their first social work course might also be the first time that they engage in a discussion in which homosexuality is not framed as deviant. Social work classrooms can be a safe place to share thoughts and feelings about working with sexual orientation issues.

As it has for other social work practice issues, NASW formally took, in two separate policy statements, a stand against LGBT discrimination and prejudice in such areas as inheritance, insurance, marriage, child custody, employment, credit, immigration, health and mental health services, and education (2009–2012f, m). To become culturally competent to intervene successfully with LGBT clients, social workers must be mindful of the historical issues that surround the oppression of this population. Adhering to the values of the social work profession, social workers' work should be a "celebration of the strengths of this largely invisible minority," not just an acceptance or tolerance (Boes & van Wormer, 2009, p. 938). Social workers must also learn and use appropriate language, be open to understanding differences, and see beyond the person's sexual orientation. Confronting organizations' heterosexist policies and eligibility criteria and ensuring LGBT inclusive language and materials are additional strategies we can employ (Gates, 2006). Finally, as with all the other areas, social workers can advocate for equality and respect in legislation, policies, service delivery, and practices for these groups.

Religious Discrimination

Religious oppression and discrimination have existed for thousands of years. People have been persecuted for practicing a variety of religions by being physically separated, denied employment, and even tortured and killed. Even in recent times in the history of this country, religious discrimination has taken the form of formally and informally restricted educational and employment, political, and social opportunities.

Although religion has always been a part of the lives of the people served by social workers, religion has not always been included in social work education and practice in the mainstream of the profession. In recent years social workers have recognized the important role that religion and spirituality play in their clients' lives. Consequently, they have begun to incorporate these issues into their assessments and intervention plans. Along with knowledge of biological, sociological, cultural, and psychological development across the life span, spirituality is now required content in human behavior and the social environment courses for CSWE-accredited programs.

The profession recognizes that incorporating the "faith life" of a client system can be an important component of the social worker–client relationship and exploring, supporting, and connecting a client system with strategies for supporting spiritual beliefs and the person's faith life can be incorporated into the intervention strategy. In exploring a client system's spirituality, questions on satisfaction and meaning in life can arise. For example, when working with persons around death and dying issues, it can be important for the social worker to view the client's faith beliefs as a source of coping. As the profession continues to integrate faith beliefs into social work practice, social workers are exploring issues of religion and spirituality on both personal and professional levels. Although social workers cannot possibly be knowledgeable about all of the world's religions, they are professionally bound to consider each client's faith life as part of the client's environment and to learn the influence of faith, religion, and spirituality on the client system's life.

THE CULTURALLY COMPETENT SOCIAL WORKER

During the time Emily worked in the domestic violence program, she encountered a particularly challenging cultural dilemma that involved ethnicity, religion, and gender issues. Through the intervention of a neighbor, a woman who was a recent immigrant from South Asia and had limited English-speaking skills sought protection from the shelter. When the option was presented to her that she could pursue an Order of Protection through the court system, she stated that a legal order would have little to no influence with her husband. She told Emily and the staff that the only person who could help influence her husband would be the local religious leader for her faith community. She believed that her husband would be more responsive to the faith leader's rule than a court judge.

Emily's responsibilities in this situation were to conduct an assessment, offer the services of the domestic violence program, explore options for safety, and develop an intervention plan if the woman would agree to it. Being unfamiliar with the client's religion and customs, Emily was uncertain how to proceed. She consulted with her supervisor and together they contacted the religious leader who then intervened on behalf of Emily's client.

Consider for a moment the cultural competency skills that Emily was required to demonstrate in this situation:

- Knowledge of the client's faith beliefs, traditions, and values, particularly as they relate to women, marriage, and domestic violence.

- Ability to communicate with a reluctant person in crisis through an interpreter.

- Ability to relate to a woman whose values and religious beliefs differed dramatically from Emily's views on women, marriage, and violence.

- Willingness to affirm the woman's right to self-determination when she opted not to pursue legal intervention and to return to the violent situation.

As Emily's experience depicts, culturally competent practice comprises skills at multiple levels: cognitive (knowledge of diversity history and issues), affective (emotional), and behavioral (language and communication skills) (Schlesinger & Devore, 1995). An effective practitioner possesses a high level of awareness in each area as well as a commitment to the idea that cultural competence is a lifelong learning process that can be both challenging and rewarding.

The following discussion is intended to heighten your sensitivity regarding the basic practice skills in awareness, language, and communication that are critical for a multiculturist approach to cultural competence. Compiled from several sources, the skills offered here are not specific to any particular group, because it is important to recognize the diversity within client populations and refrain from practicing social work with a "cookbook" approach (Congress, 2009; Colon et al., 2007; Dunn, 2002).

Cultural Awareness

Increased self-awareness and knowledge of your own identity are the first steps in cultural awareness. Key skill areas include

- Every social worker–client system relationship is a cross-cultural experience in that everyone has distinct cultures and backgrounds.

- Do not assume anything based on the client's membership in a diverse group. You can assume there is as much diversity within a culture as there can be between cultures.

- If you share membership in a cultural group with the client system, do not assume that you have more in common than membership. Likewise, do not assume that you have nothing in common with a client who is in a different group than you are.

- Stay in touch with your own beliefs at all times—your biases and lack of knowledge as well as feelings of comfort.

- Before you encounter a client system or situation, identify the knowledge and skills that you may need. For instance, do you need to arrange for an interpreter, do you need information on religious practices, or do you need to ensure that the meeting location is accessible for the client(s)?

- If interpretation is needed, it is best not to use a family member, particularly a child, to provide interpretation unless it is appropriate or necessary.

- Know that you will make mistakes, and be open to the possibility that the client system can teach you about diversity and help you learn from your mistakes. When you make a mistake, do not attempt to cover it up. Rather, acknowledge the mistake, and take the opportunity to learn a better way to interact.

- Recognize that characteristics and differences can be a resource in the helping process.

- Recognize that the client system with whom you work may be uncomfortable with your cultural differences.

- Approach your assessment from a cultural diversity perspective and include such areas as home of origin, reason for relocation, language(s) spoken, beliefs about health, illness, family, holidays, religion, education and work. The "culturagram" (Congress, 2009) is one tool that can be used to conduct a culturally focused assessment.

- Monitor your communication style and the ways in which your verbal and nonverbal behaviors could be interpreted. For example, do you speak too quickly to be clearly understood by a person who is just learning English? Are you uncomfortable when people you do not know well get too physically close to you?

Your level of awareness may be different in different areas, such as sexual orientation, age, or class. Use the Action Continuum, shown in Exhibit 5.2, as a tool for determining your level of awareness. As you review the continuum, ask yourself these questions: (1) Where are you on the continuum? (2) Where would you like to be? (3) What will help you move to the next place on your journey?

Language and Communication Skills for Cultural Competence

As you have observed throughout this chapter, language and communication are particularly challenging areas of culturally competent practice. Language is intricately tied to the culture of any group. It is a powerful mechanism for imparting positive and negative messages, and for this reason it can serve both to perpetuate oppression and discrimination and to demonstrate respect and sensitivity. Therefore, social workers are responsible for using appropriate and culturally sensitive language and communication whenever they refer or speak to any group. Although slang may be acceptable in certain settings, social workers are always mindful of using language that is the most respectful and empowering and that is preferred by the group being addressed. Using culturally appropriate language and communication skills helps to create a safe environment for the client system that will foster trust and build rapport. Society and, in particular, social workers often struggle with being appropriate in the language of diversity. Terms change, they have regional connotations, and they are heard differently depending on the speaker.

Although learning, understanding, and using language correctly are essential components of culturally competent social work practice, effective multicultural practitioners also possess practice skills that enable them to communicate sensitively with diverse groups. When in doubt regarding the most appropriate language, you have several options for obtaining more information.

You can ask other professionals who work with the population or persons who are members of the cultural group with whom you are working to serve as your cultural guide. In cases in which you have established a rapport with the client system, you may ask the client system for help in understanding appropriate language. In addition, pay particular attention to the opening of any encounter with a client system by introducing yourself by name and title, referring to an adult client using an honorific that is respectful and culturally appropriate (for example, Mr., Mrs., or Ms.), and clarifying the pronunciation of the person's name and desired address. Then inquire about the person's culture, specifically the preferred name of the group in which the person is a member (for example, Cherokee versus Native American).

EXHIBIT 5.2

Self-Awareness:
Action
Continuum

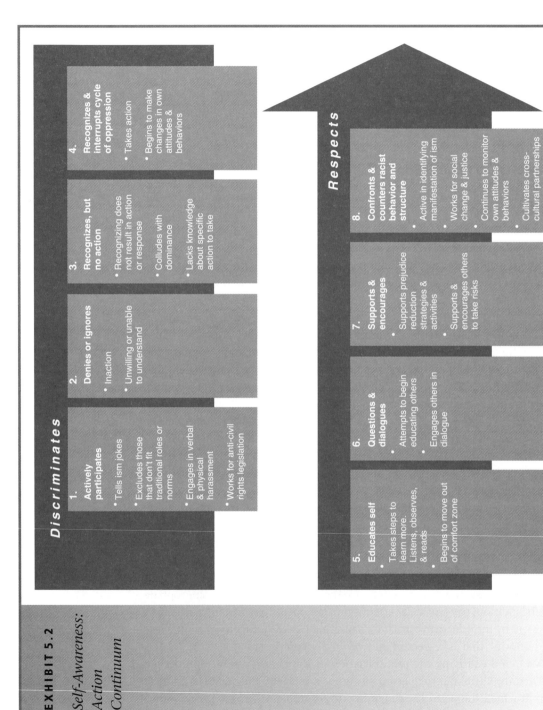

Discriminates

1.
Actively
participates
- Tells ism jokes
- Excludes those that don't fit traditional roles or norms
- Engages in verbal & physical harassment
- Works for anti-civil rights legislation

2.
Denies or ignores
- Inaction
- Unwilling or unable to understand

3.
Recognizes, but no action
- Recognizing does not result in action or response
- Colludes with dominance
- Lacks knowledge about specific action to take

4.
Recognizes & interrupts cycle of oppression
- Takes action
- Begins to make changes in own attitudes & behaviors

Respects

5.
Educates self
- Takes steps to learn more. Listens, observes, & reads
- Begins to move out of comfort zone

6.
Questions & dialogues
- Attempts to begin educating others
- Engages others in dialogue

7.
Supports & encourages
- Supports prejudice reduction strategies & activities
- Supports & encourages others to take risks

8.
Confronts & counters racist behavior and structure
- Active in identifying manifestation of ism
- Works for social change & justice
- Continues to monitor own attitudes & behaviors
- Cultivates cross-cultural partnerships

Source: Adapted from the National Conference for Community and Justice-St. Louis Region. Developed by Roni Branding AU:2002.

Here are further suggestions for communicating sensitively:

- Balance the use of professional language and language that is familiar to the client system. Client systems may misunderstand or be offended by professional jargon (particularly medical or legal terminology or acronyms), slang, or colloquialisms.

- Be genuine in your use of language and style of communication, particularly avoiding words or behaviors with which you are not familiar.

- Be aware of the meanings that different cultures attach to certain nonverbal behaviors. These meanings may be assigned or interpreted based on traditions, thus resulting in a misunderstanding (Okun et al., 1999). For example, eye contact is interpreted many different ways: as an invitation to continue speaking, as a sign of sexual interest, aggression, respect, or disrespect. Similarly, silence and facial and physical expressions convey different messages depending on the individual's culture, ranging from discomfort to anger to respect. Finally, space and physical touch can be interpreted as intimacy, aggression, or dominance based on cultural definitions.

- Be sensitive and aware of a person's culture, but do not discuss it unless it is relevant to the situation. For example, a disability or sexual orientation may not be pertinent to the reason for your encounter. Therefore, there is no need to focus the professional relationship on that aspect of the person's life. To avoid labeling, use person first language (e.g., person with a disability). Referring accurately to the client system's cultural background may include, for example, Asian American (citizen or born in the United States) or Asian (international person or non-U.S. citizen).

- Check regularly with a person whose culture is different from your own to ensure that she or he has understood what you have said or meant. Ask the person to repeat her or his understanding of the content of the conversation. This strategy will prevent you from assuming that you are being understood simply because the person nods in assent.

- If you are unsure of the meaning of a word, phrase, or behavior used by the client, ask the client in a nonjudgmental, nonpatronizing way to explain the meaning.

CONCLUSION

We have explored a range of issues related to diversity and culturally competent social work practice. Like other aspects of social work practice, striving to be a culturally competent practitioner requires that you continually seek out knowledge, skills, and self-insights. Being an expert in all areas of diversity is impossible, but social workers are obligated to acquire as much information as possible about the populations that are living in their communities and to whom they are providing services. Culturally competent practice means being proactive and assertive in your efforts to understand other cultures. Clients bring a rich and inspirational history of diversity and can serve as teachers for the social worker who views that diversity as a strength. To practice cultural competence in contemporary society, social workers must have knowledge, principles, and practices to embrace a more inclusive and just society (Daniel, 2008, p. 35).

Let us end this chapter with William M. Chace's 1989 perspective on diversity:

Diversity,
Generally understood and embraced, is not casual liberal tolerance of anything and everything not yourself. It is not polite accommodation. Instead, diversity is, in action, the sometimes painful awareness that other people, other races, other voices, other habits of mind, have as much integrity of being, as much claim upon the world, as you do. No one has an obligation greater than your own to change, or yield, or to assimilate into the mass. The irreconcilable is as much a part of social life as the congenial. Being strong in life is being strong amid differences while accepting the fact that your own self can be a considerable imposition upon everyone you meet. I urge you to consider your own oddity before you are troubled or offended by that of others. And I urge you, amid all the differences present to the eye and mind to reach out and create the bonds that will sustain the commonwealth that will protect us all. We are meant to be together.

MAIN POINTS

- Culturally competent social work practice is the ability to work respectfully and effectively with all persons. A key element is developing insights into your own beliefs and values regarding culture—your own and that of others—and continually learning about others.

- Social workers must routinely conduct a "reality check" regarding their beliefs and actions related to working with persons different from themselves as well as persons from similar backgrounds as themselves.

- Two theoretical frameworks, the ecological and strengths perspectives, help social workers understand and work with client systems that are different from themselves.

- Language and communications in all forms play a major role in both oppression and building respect for diverse groups. Social workers should understand the various ways certain terminology, such as race, ethnicity, and assimilation, have been used throughout history.

- Understanding the isms faced by many cultures in our society helps social workers to be more sensitive to people of different races, ages, and abilities.

EXERCISES

1. Using the Sanchez Family interactive case (go to www.routledgesw.com/cases), review the case file for Vicki Sanchez. Answer Vicki's Critical Thinking Questions. Next, review the case file for Hector Sanchez and answer Hector's Critical Thinking Questions.
2. Using the Sanchez Family case, imagine that you are a social worker newly assigned to work with Hector and Celia on the adoption of their grandson, Joey. Based on your own cultural heritage, select a description from the general list below:

- You are not of Hispanic or Latino origin and have had little experience with this population.

- You are not of Hispanic or Latino origin, but have had some experience with the Hispanic population and have limited Spanish-speaking skills.

- Your ethnic background is of Latino origin, but you have not lived in or near a Latino community.

- Your ethnic and cultural background is Latino. You speak fluent Spanish and your upbringing is similar to that of the Sanchez children.

  Having identified your personal characteristics as they relate to the Sanchez family, consider the following social work skill issues:

- What are the differences that you may encounter?

- What are the similarities that you may encounter?

- What are your feelings about working with the Sanchez family, including stereotypes, biases, feelings of familiarity, or anxiety?

- Given your knowledge of the Latino culture (or lack of), what information, knowledge, or skills do you need to acquire before meeting with the Sanchez family?

- How might you respond if you make a cultural mistake (speak or behave in such a way that you offend the person(s))?

- What might you ask the Sanchez family to help you in establishing a rapport?

- Who or what resource can be helpful to you in preparing for your meeting with the Sanchez family?

- If you do not speak Spanish, how will you communicate with Celia? If you are bilingual, will you speak in Spanish or English? How will you determine which is appropriate?

Although your responses to the above questions are speculative at this point, you have engaged in an exercise that is critical to becoming an effective and culturally competent social worker.

3. Using the Carla Washburn case (go to www.routledgesw.com/cases), write a narrative description of Mrs. Washburn and her current situation. Review your narrative for any evidence of ageist terms or attitudes. If evidence of ageism is noted, re-write your description of Mrs. Washburn from an ageist-free perspective. Lastly, write a brief reflection on this experience (i.e., how were you ageist, what are the origins of your ageist attitudes, etc.).

4. In order to better understand the origins of your thoughts, feelings, and stereotypes about the diverse range of persons in our society, consider each of the following social groups and the sources of your information about each group. List the specific information you gained from each of the sources in the two categories on the right of the table, below.

5. Consider an experience that you have had with diversity at any point in your life. This experience may be one in which you were the recipient or perpetrator of discrimination or oppression, or an experience in which you felt uncomfortable due to your lack of familiarity with the situation or person(s). After you have identified the experience, write a narrative that includes the following:

- A description of the experience.

- What was uncomfortable, awkward, or painful about this situation?

- Which of the "isms" is relevant to this situation? Why?

- How did you respond to the experience?

- If you were to encounter this situation again, would you respond differently? Why? How?

- How might this experience influence your future professional life?

Now that you have completed this portion of the exercise, stop and read the narrative that you have written and answer these questions:

- Did you learn anything new about yourself?

- Have you changed since this experience? How?

THINGS I LEARNED GROWING UP

SOCIAL GROUPS	FROM FAMILY, TEACHERS, AND FRIENDS	FROM MEDIA* or INTERNET
Persons with disabilities		
African Americans		
Asian Americans		
Latino Americans		
American Indians		
Americans of European descent		
Persons of dual racial heritage		
Women		
Men		
Persons who are gay, lesbian, bisexual or transgender		
Persons who are economically disadvantaged		
Persons who are financially affluent		
Older adults		
Persons who practice religions different from my own		
Other+		

* Media can include television, radio, Internet, magazines, and advertisements
+ Fill in other groups by whom you have been influenced.

Source: Adapted from the National Conference for Community and Justice–St. Louis Region.

- What would you say to someone else who has had this experience?
- What culturally competent skills did you use? If you were to encounter this situation again, which culturally competent skills would you use?

You have begun a lifelong journey of self-reflection that is essential for culturally competent social work practice. You can continue to use this exercise as you encounter future issues of diversity.

6. In an effort to gain further insight into yourself, respond to the following:

   - When you see an older adult in a wheelchair, what are your thoughts?

   - When you see someone who is cognitively impaired, what is your reaction?

   - When you are on public transportation and you are sitting next to a person with a developmental disability or a possible mental illness, how do you react? What are your feelings in this situation?

   - When you see a person with Down Syndrome, what is your reaction?

   - When you see two persons of the same gender walking down the street holding hands, what is your reaction?

   - Can you think of other situations in which you have had a reaction?

   Once you have considered your responses to the above questions, identify the culturally competent skills that you feel you possess. How did you gain these skills? What skills do you lack?

7. Identify an area, event, or situation related to diversity (racial, ethnic, religious, economic, gender, age, sexual orientation, etc.) that has challenged you. Describe your response, how you might respond differently in the future, and how this experience may impact your professional work.

CHAPTER 6

Values and Ethics in Social Work Practice

Emily faced a difficult situation while completing the community service require-ment for her introductory social work course at Oasis House, a shelter for persons who are homeless. She was in the recreation room of the shelter talking with one of the residents, Lorinda, a single mother with two young children. Emily had talked with Lorinda on several previous occasions and felt a special bond with her. Lorinda and Emily were the same age and had many similar interests. They had both been on their high school track teams and had competed in the same events. During one conversation, Lorinda asked Emily for money. Lorinda told Emily that she needed the money to help her boyfriend get bus money to get back home. He had gone to another city to look for work so he could earn money and send for Lorinda and the children. He had not found a job and had no money for the trip back. Lorinda assured Emily that she would repay the money as soon as she and her boyfriend had jobs.

Emily did not know what to do. She liked Lorinda and wanted to help her, but was not sure that she should give Lorinda her own money. What would you do in this situation?

The situation that Emily encountered is considered an **ethical dilemma**, a commonplace occurrence in the social work profession. An ethical dilemma exists when the social worker "must choose between two or more relevant, but contra-dictory, ethical directives, or when every alternative results in an undesirable out-come for one or more persons" (Dolgoff et al., 2009, p. 9). A dilemma can occur when a social worker's ethical principles and standards conflict with those of the client, agency, or society. Areas of challenge can include the birth of a child, loss of a loved one, natural disasters, child or older adult abuse, neglect, or exploitation; mental or physical illness; financial or housing needs; discrimination; and domestic violence. Such value-laden issues create the potential for an ethical dilemma to occur because the social worker may have to involve authorities, challenge the client system's choices, or confront an injustice.

When a social worker intervenes in a situation, several value systems and ethical practices are already in place. Specifically, the values and ethics of the social worker, client system, agency, and society are all present, and they impact the social work intervention and outcome. In this chapter, we focus on values and ethics and the ways in which they relate to social work practice. We will begin our exploration of this topic by defining the terms and highlighting the reasons that values and ethics are central to competent social work practice. As part of this process we will consider the NASW *Code of Ethics* (2008). You will have an opportunity to examine your own values and to apply social work values and ethics to challenging social work practice.

SOCIAL WORK'S COMMITMENT TO VALUES AND ETHICS

National events determine our ideals, as much as
our ideals determine national events.
—JANE ADDAMS

Values can be defined as a society's system of beliefs, principles, and traditions that guide behaviors and practices. You might also think of values as the ideals by which we live. To rephrase the quotation from Jane Addams, our values are shaped by society and society is shaped by our values—a statement that is certainly still relevant in the U.S. today. For example, the social work profession believes that all people have a right to access the resources needed to optimize their quality of life.

The definition of **ethics** is somewhat different: "a system of moral principles and perceptions about right versus wrong and the resulting philosophy of conduct that is practiced by an individual, group, profession, or culture" (Barker, 2003, p. 147). You can see that values and ethics are closely related. As one example, the social work profession has turned the value regarding access to resources into a professional ethic by advocating with policy makers for groups marginalized by society (e.g., advocating for low-income families to gain better access to resources).

With this understanding of the interconnections between values and ethics, let us examine some issues that students in the introductory social work course frequently ask about. You will see that value conflicts and ethical dilemmas can be an everyday occurrence in the life of a social worker, but they take place on several different levels. An ethical code, such as NASW's *Code of Ethics*, provides guidelines for professional conduct in six key areas: clients, colleagues, practice setting, professionalism, the profession, and the broader society.

Why Values and Ethics Are Important in Social Work

Value and ethical issues are present in every encounter that a social worker has with a client system, but because the client systems with which practitioners often work are persons or groups who have experienced some form of discrimination or oppression, and may not have adequate resources, their "voices" are often not heard by society. The role of the social worker may be to advocate for a client system's rights, to help the client system access information and resources, or to assist the client in enhancing her or his quality of life. Therefore, at this level, a competent social work practitioner is aware of value and ethical issues and the implications of those values and ethics on the social work intervention.

Having an awareness and understanding of their own value system as well as the value systems of their clients, the agency of employment, and the larger society can help to ensure that social workers do not unknowingly discriminate against a client system through inappropriate language or behavior. Although social workers are not expected to *share* these value systems, they are ethically bound to *respect* the value systems of others. Moreover, having insight into the client's value system can help the social worker to understand the client's decision-making processes, choices and behaviors, and patterns of functioning and dysfunction.

In order to approach an ethical dilemma, the social worker needs to understand the value systems of all involved. This is the first step toward a resolution to the ethical challenge. The social worker does not attempt to change the client system by imposing her or his values on the client system, but instead strives to understand and respect the client's values.

Values and Ethics Issues in Social Work

Every client with whom a social worker interacts is different, and each conflicted situation is unique. Therefore, in order to maintain an individualistic perspective, a social worker cannot formulate blanket responses to ethical dilemmas. Instead, social workers are mindful of the client system's values as well as any ethical implications that may result from the social worker–client system relationship.

As the social work's professional knowledge and skills grew and evolved, so did the profession's values. In response to the political, economic, and social environment changes, the profession's values moved through four phases: (1) the *morality period* of the late 19th century in which the client's morals were of primary interest; (2) the *values period* of the 20th century focused on the profession's development of core values; (3) the *ethical theory and decision-making period* of the latter 20th century emphasized the development of guidelines and protocols for responding to ethical dilemmas; and (4) the current period of *ethical standards and risk management* in which conduct and malpractice are emphasized (Reamer, 2009b). This evolution has enabled the profession to establish a core set of values, processes for ethical practice and guidelines for protecting client systems.

More than a century of focus on values and ethics has also highlighted awareness of the complex nature of social work and the fact that the values of the social work profession operate at multiple levels. That is, social workers are knowledgeable about values at the personal, professional, and societal levels. One popular model delineates values by level of involvement (Dolgoff et al., 2009):

- *Individual or personal values:* the values of one person.

- *Group values:* the values of groups within society (for example, religious and ethnic groups).

- *Societal values:* the primary values of the larger social system.

- *Professional values:* the values of a specific discipline or professional group.

An alternative framework for exploring individual, group, and societal values categorizes these values by type and outcome (Reamer, 1995):

- Ultimate values are those broad-based, societal values that guide a group's long-term aims. Our society's rules against discrimination and oppression are examples of ultimate values. For social workers, ultimate values are often though not always a consistent extension of societal values, including respect for people, equality, and nondiscrimination.

- Proximate values are specific, short-term values that relate to policies and rights. In the social work profession, for example, proximate values include the right to have access to services.

- Instrumental values are directed toward the process of attaining a desirable end through desirable means. Within a social work context, instrumental values refer to the client's right to confidentiality, self determination, and informed consent.

Having a conceptual basis for understanding your own, your client's, and societal values can help you to interpret the inevitable value conflicts that you will encounter as a social worker. Let us continue this examination of values and ethics by considering another situation in which Emily finds herself.

After Emily graduated with her BSW degree, she secured her first social work position. Finally, she was going to be in a position to really help people. Her first social work job was in the adult social service unit of a multiservice public community agency. When she interviewed for this position, she was told she would be working as a case manager with older adults to help them maintain their independent living situations. Emily enjoyed this position for three years, at which time the agency overhauled the structure of its social services, and all workers became "generic" workers, handling both child and adult services. Emily found herself being assigned child protection cases, in which she investigated allegations of abuse and neglect, testified in court, and often recommended that the child be removed from the home and placed in foster care. For the first time in her career, Emily felt conflicted regarding her role as a social worker. She felt her lack of knowledge about and interest in working with children and their parents would hamper her ability to serve the best interests of the clients.

Emily experienced a **value conflict**—a situation in which a social worker's values (or "shoulds") clash with the value system of a client, agency, co-worker, or society in general. In this case, Emily's dilemma was the result of her adherence to the social work value of practicing only in her areas of competence. Value conflicts present themselves in many different forms. You cannot possibly anticipate all the potential conflicts that await you, but you can anticipate that such conflicts *will* arise, and you can prepare yourself by developing a set of skills to respond to them when they do. The following sections describe some value conflicts that you may encounter as a social work professional.

Job-Related Value Conflicts   Emily's conflict is one example of a situation in which the social worker's value system comes into conflict with the duties that she or he has been hired to perform. Because social workers intervene in settings in which they assume a position of authority over the client system, such conflicts are not uncommon. Possible settings for value conflicts include the public welfare system, the criminal justice system, for example, an incarceration facility, a residential care facility, or an agency to which client systems are mandated for social work services by the judicial or legal system. Social workers working in host settings (organizations whose primary service is not social work such as schools, hospitals, or the court system) can find that their values are in conflict with that of their employer. While all professionals who work in these settings are there to serve the client or patient population, the avenues for fulfilling that goal can come into conflict with those of their co-workers' disciplines.

Value conflicts can also arise when social workers find themselves in the role of an authority or "pseudo-cop" (Baldino, 2000, p. 25). Pseudo-cop social workers may be torn, for example, between their duty to comply with the court's directives and their obligation to support their client. For social workers that find themselves in such a dilemma, observing and seeking the wisdom of other experienced workers in similar settings can be an effective strategy for gaining perspective and competence in this role.

Unethical or impaired behavior on the part of a co-worker may also create value conflicts. Consider a scenario in which you learn that a co-worker's drug or alcohol use is beginning to impair his ability to perform his job duties. Consider also the co-worker who defames or discriminates against clients and co-workers. What is your personal and professional obligation in these situations? Is it acceptable for you to look the other way? Do you confront the co-worker or report your suspicions to a supervisor? As a social work professional, you consider the potential conflict between your personal loyalty to a co-worker and the profession in the area of unethical or dangerous behavior (Wilshere, 1997).

Value Conflicts Related to Religion and Belief   Many people are drawn to the social work profession out of a sense of religious calling or obligation or as a result of experiences related to their religious beliefs. A number of social work practitioners are employed by faith-based organizations that espouse a religious mission and philosophy. Ideally, social workers in these situations will work with client systems and colleagues who share their religious beliefs. Although many social workers find that practicing social work and their religion go hand-in-hand, others experience conflicts between the two. In reality, religious differences are common, even in situations in which the client or colleague is of the same faith as the social worker. A value conflict can occur when the religious beliefs of the client and the social worker impede their ability to work together effectively or when the religious beliefs of the social worker and the agency conflict. For example, consider a situation in which the worker's position on abortion is pro-life and the client is seeking an abortion.

Although social workers are trained to maintain emotional objectivity, issues related to religious beliefs and practices are areas in which the social worker's experiences may be an asset for effective practice. For example, consider a situation in which a client appears to be uncooperative with the physician's plan for a medical procedure. Because the social worker is familiar with the client's religious beliefs, she recognizes that the client's lack of compliance is not resistance at all, but rather an expression of the client's religious beliefs, which make it impossible for the client to consent to the medical procedure (Senkowsky, 1996a).

Value Conflicts over Limited Resources   The social work profession values each person's right to have access to resources to optimize her or his quality of life. Although society as a whole supports this value, heated debates occur at the personal and policy levels regarding the distribution of those resources, most of which are limited. One example is the value held by many people that persons living in poverty do not deserve a "handout" but instead should have to work "like the rest of us" for their living. This value can be translated into an anti-poor attitude and further into supporting political candidates who oppose welfare. Social work students may struggle with this particular issue, which actually may be a conflict between values to which they have been exposed and different value systems that they are encountering in social work classes.

The Social Worker's Values

Although social work training emphasizes being nonjudgmental, the reality is that you cannot "check your values at the door." Your value system reflects the influences of the family who reared you; your educational, religious, spiritual, social, and professional experiences; and your formal social work training. You bring your value system into each and every social work situation. Before you can begin to determine strategies for understanding and working with the value systems of clients, agencies, or society, you must consider your own value system, its origins, and the implications of your values for your life and your future practice.

Throughout the history of social work, some social workers have espoused the views that social work practice should be value free and that values do not affect social work practice (Dolgoff et al., 2009). Over time, however, most social workers have recognized that personal, group, and societal values do influence their work. The challenge for the profession then becomes to enable social work students and practitioners to clarify their values, understand the profession's values, and acquire skills for ethical social work practice.

An important step in understanding values and their impact on ethical behavior is to clarify your own values. **Values clarification** is the process of exploring your values and comparing them to others for the purpose of developing an appreciation and respect for your values and the values of others (Barker, 2003). Clarifying your values does not mean that you automatically change them. In fact, taking the risk to learn other perspectives may confirm your commitment to your values. Sometimes, however, values do change as a result of efforts to clarify them. As you are exposed to new and different ideas or provided with different information, your previous perspective can be altered. The key is your willingness to risk change by exposing yourself to other views and value systems that may differ from your own.

Some people might go so far as to argue that attaining a social work degree is, in fact, an ongoing exercise in values clarification. As a social work student, you will find that your value system will constantly be challenged through your discussions with faculty and fellow students, readings, assignments, and field experiences. You can begin the process of clarifying your values by starting with casual conversations or issues that arise in your classes. Part of the process of understanding your own values is taking the risk of hearing ideas that are different from your own. Although that may not be a comfortable situation, it is an important process to engage in during your training so that you will be more comfortable and aware once you become a practitioner. Although you will continually encounter new situations throughout your career, you will eventually develop a strategy and a comfort level for these situations.

When you are involved in a conversation regarding ethics, you can initiate the process of clarifying your values by asking yourself these questions:

- What do I think about this issue?

- What are the origins of my values on this issue?

- What are the other person's values on this issue? Are our values similar or different? If they are different, does this difference create a dilemma for me? For the two of us?

How the Social Work Profession Defines Ethics

Action indeed is the sole medium of expression for ethics.
—JANE ADDAMS

Many professions have developed a standardized approach to guide their members in establishing a competent and effective practice. As the quote from Jane Addams implies, ethics is defined by action. By definition, a **code of ethics** is a document, created by the members of the profession, that provides specific guidelines for appropriate and expected professional behaviors. These behavioral expectations are rooted in the values and ethical standards deemed acceptable by the profession.

The social work profession has several codes aimed at promoting ethical practice. The most widely known, the NASW *Code of Ethics*, referred to many times in this book, was developed to clearly specify expected professional conduct for the members of the association. Other social work organizations have developed codes of ethics that are similar in intent to the NASW's but are specific to their organizational mission and membership.

The NASW Delegate Assembly, a body of NASW members elected by their state chapters, meets once every three years to debate and vote on NASW policies, including the *Code of Ethics*. Recognizing that social work changes as society changes, NASW has revised the *Code* several times since its inception in 1960, most recently in 1996, 1999, and 2008.

Although the *Code of Ethics* is intended as a guide, it also serves as a mechanism for monitoring social workers' practice competency and ethics. Violations can be reported to a state chapter or the national office. A committee of NASW members then reviews the complaint and can recommend any number of actions if the complaint is substantiated. Such actions may include corrective action (such as suspension from the organization, mandated consultation, or censure), informing the regulatory board of the state in which the social worker practices, or public sanction. Social work licensure or certification, which exists in every state and requires ethical practice. Social workers can risk being sued for malpractice in civil court if ethical practice is violated.

The initial NASW *Code of Ethics*, accepted by the membership in 1960, emphasized the primacy of professional responsibility over personal interests, the client's right to privacy, obligations for service during public emergencies, and a duty to contribute to the knowledge of the profession (Reamer, 2008a). The current version mirrors the earlier documents, despite its increased length and proliferation of legal terms. It consists of four sections: preamble, purpose, values and ethical principles, and ethical standards.

The preamble outlines the mission and core values of the social work profession. As stated in the 2008 *Code of Ethics*, the mission of the social work profession is to enhance human well-being and help meet the basic human needs of all people, with particular attention to the needs and empowerment of people who are vulnerable, oppressed, and living in poverty. A historic and defining feature of social work is the profession's focus on individual well-being in a social context and the well-being of society. Fundamental to social work is attention to the environmental forces that create, contribute to, and address problems in living. Social workers promote social justice and social change with and on behalf of clients. "Clients" is used inclusively to refer to individuals, families, groups, organizations, and communities. Social workers are sensitive to cultural and ethnic diversity and strive to end discrimination, oppression, poverty, and other forms of social injustice. These activities may be in the form of direct practice, community organizing, supervision, consultation, administration, advocacy, **social and political action**, policy development and implementation, education, research, and evaluation. Social workers seek to enhance the capacity of people to address their own needs. Social workers also seek to promote the responsiveness of organizations, communities, and other social institutions to individuals' needs and social problems.

From the profession's mission, we can derive the **core values** of the social work profession: service, social justice, dignity and worth of the person, importance of human relationships, integrity, and competence.

Following the preamble, the second section outlines the six purposes of the *Code:*

- Identify core values on which social work's mission is based.

- Summarize broad ethical principles that reflect the profession's core values and serve as the basis for a set of specific ethical standards to guide social work practice.

- Help social workers identify relevant considerations when professional obligations conflict or ethical uncertainties arise.

- Provide ethical standards to which the general public can hold the social work profession accountable.

- Socialize practitioners new to the field to social work's mission, values, ethical principles, and ethical standards.

- Articulate standards that the social work profession itself can use to assess whether social workers have engaged in unethical conduct.

The statement of ethical principles—highlighted in Table 6.1—is based on the six core values identified in the preamble. These ethical principles are the "ideals to which all social workers should aspire" (NASW, 2008). These help provide a guide for social work practice in challenging ethically laden situations.

The final part of the *Code* includes six sections that list ethical standards or categories of ethical responsibilities: (1) clients, (2) colleagues, (3) practice settings, (4) professionalism, (5) the social work profession, and (6) the larger society. Considered to be the substance of the *Code*, these six standards include 155 specific items that stipulate social workers' ethical responsibilities within each standard. The standards are intended to guide the conduct of social work professionals and serve as the basis for evaluating violations of the *Code of Ethics*. Box 6.1 discusses these ethical standards in detail.

The NASW *Code of Ethics* addresses a range of broad but important—and sometimes controversial—behaviors and practices. A number of themes recur throughout the standards encompassed by the *Code*. Possibly the most important theme is respect for the client, as reflected in such standards as the social worker's commitment to clients and client self-determination. As part of demonstrating respect for the client is the commitment and ethical responsibility to practice culturally competent social work (NASW, 2007). Another underlying theme is responsibility for the profession, as evidenced by those standards that address colleagues with impairments and unethical colleague behaviors. The *Code* also articulates the responsibility of the social work profession for society, which is attained through such efforts as advocacy, education, and political action.

The application of social work ethics evolves over time as social problems and issues evolve. For example, mandated reporting of suspected child abuse, neglect, and exploitation is an ethical practice issue that emerged in response to the changing social climate. Until the 1970s, social workers were not legally required to report incidents of suspected abuse. However, as society focused attention on this issue, the social work profession followed suit by supporting mandated reporting.

TABLE 6.1 *Ethical Principles Based on Core Social Work Values*	CORE SOCIAL WORK VALUES	SOCIAL WORK ETHICAL PRINCIPLES
	Service	Help people in need and address social conditions and concerns.
	Social justice	Challenge social injustice.
	Dignity and worth of the person	Respect the inherent dignity and worth of the person.
	Importance of human relationships	Recognize the central importance of human relationships.
	Integrity	Behave in a trustworthy manner.
	Competence	Practice within areas of competence, and develop and enhance professional expertise.

BOX 6.1

Ethical Standards for Social Workers

1. *Clients:* This grouping of ethical standards addresses the responsibilities to clients, including the topics of:

commitment to clients	client's right to self-determination
informed consent	competence and diversity
conflicts of interest	privacy and confidentiality
access to records	sexual relationships and harassment
physical contact	derogatory language
payment for services	interruption/termination of services
clients who lack decision-making capacity	

2. *Colleagues:* Ethical responsibilities in this standard relate to collegial behaviors, including guidelines for:

respect	confidentiality
interdisciplinary collaboration	disputes involving colleagues
consultation	referral for services
sexual relationships	sexual harassment
impairment of colleagues	incompetence of colleagues
unethical conduct of colleagues	

3. *Practice settings:* This set of ethical standards encompasses the social worker's responsibilities to the setting in which she or he practices, including employers, co-workers, supervisors, and supervisees:

supervision and consultation	education and training
performance evaluation	client records
billing client	transfer
administration	continuing education
commitments to employers	labor-management disputes

4. *Professionalism:* The NASW defines professionalism as the "degree to which an individual possesses and uses the knowledge, skills, and qualifications of a profession and adheres to its values and ethics when serving the client" (Barker, 1999, p. 380). Professionalism requires the social worker to practice ethically, competently, fairly, and honestly, and prevent such unethical behaviors as:

interference of private conduct	dishonesty, fraud, and deception
impairment of ability	misrepresentation
solicitations	failure to acknowledge credit
discrimination	

BOX 6.1
continued

5. *The social work profession:* This section of the *Code* addresses social workers' commitments to the entirety of the social work community in the areas of maintaining:

    integrity of the profession   evaluation and research

6. *The broader society:* Social workers are responsible to society (for example, the community in which they live and the community at large) in the areas of:

    social welfare   public participation
    public emergencies   social and political action

Why Have a Code of Ethics?

As you read this book, I hope that you have questioned why the social work profession needs any codes to dictate appropriate professional behavior. After all, don't we all become social workers because we are altruistic and giving persons? If this is true, then why should we require a formal document to guide and monitor our practice? Critics of the *Code of Ethics* argue that to be ethical, social workers need only "practice wisdom" (the knowledge, skills, and values that a social worker collects over the course of a career), instincts, and virtuosity and that being governed by a code is time consuming, coercive, and a wasted effort (Dolgoff et al., 2009, pp. 34–35). Now that you have reviewed the *Code of Ethics*, what do you think?

The profession's current interest in codifying values and ethical practice has been formalized largely since the 1960s and 1970s. This emphasis on formalizing ethical practice may be due, in part, to societal changes that have affected the clients served by social workers. Advances in such areas as medicine (for example, treatments, technology, and disease awareness), electronic technology, global awareness, resource management, and the social work mission continues to prompt social workers to consider the impact of these developments on their clients (Reamer, 2008b).

As the complexity of the social worker's job has increased, so has the potential for ethical dilemmas. When faced with multiple alternatives, directions, or potential contradictions of ethical principles, social workers can use a set of guidelines in establishing an ethical intervention that serves the best interests of the client and the system in a manner that is consistent with present-day cultural demands (Dolgoff et al., 2009).

Another issue that may occur to you as you read this book is the way the social work profession uses the various ethical codes. Most social workers view the codes as guides for their professional behavior, but many practitioners also recognize that even a well-developed, professionally binding code has its limitations. As you reviewed the standards in Box 6.1, you undoubtedly noticed that the items are broad in nature and leave particular situations open to interpretation. Nevertheless, despite its general approach to ethics, the *Code* remains the best resource to consult when you are faced with an ethical dilemma.

APPLYING VALUES AND ETHICS AT WORK

The potential for a value conflict or an ethical dilemma is something that social work practitioners keep in mind at all times. No matter how clear, simplistic, or mundane a situation may seem on the surface, social workers do not trivialize the situation or routinize the interpretation or the response. Instead, social workers keep in mind the value base that has long guided social work practice. The knowledge and skills developed by social work professionals are deeply rooted in this set of values, which have changed little since they were first introduced.

Although the core social work values and ethical principles are widely accepted by the profession, their meanings and the implications of those meanings are routinely open to interpretation and often result in disagreements (Dunlap & Strom-Gottfried, 1998a). To help in the application of ethical principles, social work theorists have developed tools for making ethical decisions. One is known as the Enhanced Ethical Decision-Making Matrix (D'Aprix et al., 2001). The model is based on the premise that the social worker (1) explores all options before taking action, (2) recognizes her or his personal values and biases, and (3) evaluates the effectiveness of the action. The first step in applying this model is to identify the ethical issues using the *Code of Ethics*. Table 6.2 presents a set of questions and the basis for those questions that can aid in the identification process.

Using a decision-making framework does not ensure "easy answers to the tough questions," but it does provide an approach for analyzing the situation and devising an ethical and thoughtful response. The model prompts the social worker to ask the questions that are relevant to the ethical dilemma, to compartmentalize the information, to establish priorities, and to consider the impact of the outcome on all the parties involved.

Although social work training places the utmost importance on respecting the client system's values, determining the client's values or understanding the implications of those values may not always be easy. For example, could you be an effective social work practitioner when the person with whom you are working has a history of abusing children? Would you be able to see the client as someone other than an abuser? Could you acknowledge the client's strengths and potential for change given that she or he has abused another person? These and most value-laden questions can be answered only when social workers review their own value system and the values of the profession. Emily was confronted with just such a situation.

TABLE 6.2	QUESTIONS TO IDENTIFY ETHICAL ISSUES	BASIS FOR QUESTION
Ethical Decision Making: Identifying the Issues	1. What are the interventions and ethical issues that make it difficult to choose a course of action?	Worker is able to address all potential ethical issues to be addressed. Worker determines if any *Code of Ethics* standards or laws are involved.
	2. What are my viewpoints about these issues?	Worker is able to recognize her/his personal biases and determine any impact of the biases on client system outcomes.
	3. Which actions (interventions) might address the practice and ethical issues listed in number 1?	Worker is able to consider all potential alternatives for intervention.
	4. What are the potential consequences/ outcomes of these actions?	Worker can conduct a cost-benefit analysis of the potential intervention.
	5. How would I prioritize the intervention and ethical issues using the Ethical Principles Screen (EPS)?	Using the EPS, the worker can rank-order priorities.
	6. Based on this prioritization, which issues will I address first and which action will address this issue?	After prioritizing the ethical issues, the worker can prioritize the proposed interventions.
	7. Throughout this process, have I consulted with colleagues for their professional opinions?	Worker can benefit from the practice wisdom of other social work professionals.
	8. How will I monitor and evaluate the effectiveness of this plan of action?	Ongoing monitoring enables the worker to know when to proceed to the next priority and to assess the status of the dilemma.

Source: D'Aprix et al., 2001.

ETHICAL DILEMMAS: WHEN THE PERSONAL AND THE PROFESSIONAL CONFLICT

During one of her practicum experiences, Emily was invited by her field instructor at a mental health center to co-lead a male batterers' group with a male colleague. You will recall from Chapter 1 that Emily was a victim of domestic violence several years earlier. She did not share that reality with her field instructor or her co-workers at the practicum site because she was afraid they would view her as inept.

After all, if she were a competent individual, would she have allowed herself to become involved in a violent relationship? Nevertheless, Emily agreed to partici-pate in the group, feeling that she would disappoint her supervisor if she rejected the invitation. She also believed that she had put the experience behind her and that because of her personal experience and social work training, she would bring a valuable perspective.

Unfortunately, Emily's experience was less than successful, to say the least. She was extremely uncomfortable as she listened to the men rationalize their violence against their female partners. Based on her value system, Emily viewed violence as reprehensible, and she was now solidly entrenched in that belief because of her own experience. Emily's belief system had evolved to believing that batterers could not be rehabilitated. She soon realized that she probably had not "put the experience behind her," and she was faced with ethical dilemmas:

- *In her current state of discomfort, she was not fulfilling her commitment to be a co-facilitator.*

- *If she left the group, she would be leaving her colleague without a co-facilitator.*

The agency was strongly committed to having a male/female team for this group. Because she had not told her supervisor or her colleagues of her past experience, Emily was fearful they would think she was hiding this information. This belief might lead them to question her ethical behavior. She questioned whether her personal values were impeding her practice obligations. She was especially fearful of her reactions if she continued in the group: Would she "lose it" during a group session, or would she continue to be immobilized? What would you do in Emily's situation: leave, stay, or seek help?

An ethical dilemma is most challenging when personal values and professional ethical obligations conflict. Most practitioners agree that the "best interests" of the client system should take precedence, but your personal values may override your professional duty in some situations. Consider Emily's dilemma, for example. Her experience with domestic violence made it difficult for her to work with male batterers at this early point in her career. Nevertheless, when she was given the opportunity to co-lead a group of men who had battered a female partner, she felt she could maintain enough emotional objectivity to be an effective co-leader. Clearly, her personal experiences and values clouded her objectivity. It was important for her to learn that putting personal values aside is not always an easy task. The negative group experience enabled her to confront her fears during supervisory sessions. With her supervisor's support and challenges, Emily was able to come to terms with her feelings and shift her belief to consider that treatment of violent behavior could be successful. As a result, she ultimately was able to co-facilitate the group.

Although the ethical dilemmas that you are likely to encounter in your practice will all have unique characteristics, some common areas that challenge social workers can be identified. Based on suggestions by Reamer (2008b), the ethical challenges presented in the following sections, when linked to the social values and ethical principles discussed earlier, can provide a context in which to consider appropriate responses to the situation. As you review these challenges, consider your own value system, your potential responses, and the intersection of the two. You may find that these situations prompt more questions than answers, but keep asking the questions.

Confidentiality

The social worker–client relationship is based on trust. When that trust is threatened or violated, an ethical dilemma may occur. A key to establishing a trusting relationship is for the social worker to respect the client's confidentiality. Defined as the disclosure of client-related information only with the permission of the client, **confidentiality** can be categorized as either absolute or relative. Absolute confidentiality means that all information is to be held in confidence; relative confidentiality means that some information can be disclosed. In cases of relative confidentiality, social workers frequently share information with colleagues or law enforcement officials, but only with client consent (Barker, 2003).

Because the social work profession places such importance on the issues of privacy and confidentiality, these issues are addressed in two of the profession's documents, the NASW Policy Statements and the *Code of Ethics*. The 2009–2012 Policy Statement on confidentiality and information utilization provides clear guidelines for obtaining, sharing, and utilizing information related to client systems. Additionally, Standard 1.07(a–r) of the NASW *Code of Ethics* addresses privacy and confidentiality in great detail because social workers are privy to considerable and intimate client information. The standard, derived from the social work value of viewing each person with dignity and worth, provides guidelines for protecting information related to the client's reasons for receiving services, her or his legal and financial status, and other personal life details.

Legally, social workers must share information in two situations. In cases of suspected abuse of children, older adults, and persons with disabilities, social workers are mandated to report the suspected abuse to the state agency. Secondly, in cases in which a person threatens harm to self or others, the social worker must report to the designated authority in that state.

Social workers can also share information when the client has granted **informed consent** through a signed release of information. Such consent is needed for the practitioner to share information regarding the content of the professional relationship, client information/statements, professional assessments, and information from client records (Burkemper, 2004; Dunlap & Strom-Gottfried, 1998b). In order to grant a valid informed consent, the client or the client's guardian must give written permission as in a release of information and be told what information is to be shared and the reasons for sharing it, with whom the information will be shared, and the date of expiration for the information. Most agencies have a standardized informed consent form.

Additional protection of client information is included in the Health Insurance Portability and Accountability Act of 1996 (HIPAA) (U.S. Department of Health and Human Services, 2004). The HIPAA legislation is designed to protect and enhance the rights of consumers of health care services without compromising the access to or effectiveness of the provision of services. The law mandates that consumers of health care services have the following rights: to see and obtain copies of their health care records; to be informed in writing about the ways in which health information is used by the health care provider; and to have assurance that their identifiable health information is protected. Privacy and confidentiality do, however, have limits. When the limitations of the social worker's ability to maintain privacy or confidentiality are challenged, an ethical dilemma can arise. For example, the social worker strives to maintain the client's confidentiality (and trust) but may have a legal or societal duty to divulge the information, as in the case of suspected abuse or harm to self or others (Dolgoff et al., 2009). In such situations, the social worker may face a conflict between maintaining the client's trust and recognizing the mandate to violate confidentiality.

For beginning social workers, the responsibility to maintain a client's privacy and confidentiality can become overwhelming. When do you share or not share client information? What can you write or not write in a client record? What if you accidentally breach a confidence? These are all questions that you should be routinely asking yourself. Here are recommended practices to maintain your client's privacy and confidentiality (Dunlap & Strom-Gottfried, 1998b):

- Be vigilant, including taking note of your location as you communicate information to or about the client. Make confidentiality foremost in your mind as you practice.

- Protect records by keeping them in a locked receptacle, and safeguard computer files with a firewall, password, or short-delay screen saver.

- Monitor your ongoing client-related activities by gathering only the information that is relevant to the services being provided.

- Learn and understand laws and agency policies and practices regarding the protection of information.

- Monitor yourself. Use your supervisor and colleagues for consultation, not the clients or your friends or family.

- Picture yourself as a consumer of your services—how would you like to be treated?

Client Self-Determination

The right to **self-determination** is also derived from the social work value and ethical principle related to dignity and worth of the person. Standard 1.02 specifies that the social worker is obligated to respect the client system's right to make decisions and choices and to determine her or his own goals. As with confidentiality, situations can arise that limit the social worker's ability to fully comply with this obligation. As mentioned earlier, when a person has threatened physical harm to herself or himself or to others, the social worker is ethically and legally obligated to protect the person and override the right to self-determination (Reamer, 2006).

Ethical dilemmas can also occur in non-life-threatening situations in which the social worker feels the client is making a decision that may have a negative or harmful outcome. Consider, for example, the person who resumes drinking or using drugs, who returns to a violent relationship, or who is mandated for services but refuses to participate even though noncompliance will result in a return to prison. In these situations, the social worker must balance the issue of respecting the client's right to self-determination with the competing obligation to help the client achieve a positive outcome (Dolgoff et al., 2009).

A useful guideline to follow in these difficult situations is to remember that the person's right to self-determination takes precedence whenever possible. Even the client who has not voluntarily come to the social worker for services has the "right" to choose nonparticipation. The social worker's responsibility is to offer or provide the opportunity to identify and examine the consequences of that choice. If social workers are to truly respect and value their client systems, they must diligently respect the client's right to self-determination. The reality is that all people have the right to make decisions about their lives.

Boundaries

The parameters that define your relationship with the client system as professional rather than social are called **boundaries**. Boundaries can be difficult to delineate and maintain because clients often share intimate details of their lives with their social worker, making the relationship appear to be personal and intimate. The social worker–client relationship can involve sharing, cooperation, and even liking each other, but it is not a friendship, romance, or business partnership (Strom-Gottfried & Dunlap, 1998). Having a personal as well as a professional relationship with a client is considered to be a dual relationship. For example, dating is a dual relationship and is considered unethical. Similarly, conflicts of interest are addressed in Standard 1.06 of the *Code of Ethics*, which states that a social worker must maintain separateness in personal, religious, political, or business areas. An example of an ethical violation would be to enter into a business venture with a client.

Becoming familiar with the profession's ethical standards as well as agency policies and practices will help you to avoid committing ethical infractions related to client–worker boundaries. Conducting periodic reality checks with colleagues and supervisors in cases of ambiguity can also help social workers maintain appropriate boundaries. Despite the best precautions, it is not always possible to maintain boundaries. You could encounter a client somewhere outside the social work setting, for example. In those instances, allow the client to acknowledge you first, and if you engage with the client, ensure that you do not discuss the professional relationship during the encounter. Be prepared for the possibility that the client may not choose to acknowledge you at all, or that she or he may openly acknowledge you and discuss the reasons why you know each other. In either case, it is the social worker's responsibility to maintain professional boundaries.

Self-Disclosure

Related to boundaries is the issue of **self-disclosure**, the sharing of personal informa-tion with a client. The *Code of Ethics* states that social workers should not allow their personal issues to interfere with the best interests of the client. Although this does not specifically address the issue of self-disclosure, it implies that social workers should approach self-disclosure with caution. Sharing personal information with clients may be done with the best of intentions. For example, substance abuse treatment programs may hire workers who are recovering from chemical depend-ency or addiction and encourage them to disclose their history of abuse to their clients to establish a rapport. The social worker may believe that if the client knows that the worker has had similar experiences, the client will be better able to work through the challenge. In fact, the social worker's self-disclosure may achieve that goal. The client may see the social worker as more credible or trustworthy, feel that her or his experience was normal, or feel more confident and inspired to change (Reamer, 2001).

In other cases, however, self-disclosure can sabotage the social work inter-vention. The client may become confused by the worker's disclosure, may try to mirror the worker's recovery, or may shift attention to the worker's life (Strom-Gottfried & Dunlap, 1999; Reamer, 2001). For example, consider Emily's experiences related to self-disclosure. In the case of the client at Oasis House, her self-disclosure prompted the client to feel comfortable asking Emily for money. In the situation with the domestic violence group, would Emily have wanted to share with the batterers her history as a victim of domestic violence?

Social workers monitor themselves closely regarding the disclosure of personal information. Here are some strategies for self-monitoring:

- Learn the agency policy and practice regarding self-disclosure.

- Determine the appropriateness, benefits, and costs of sharing the information and the client's ability to use the information (Strom-Gottfried & Dunlap, 1999).

- Consult with colleagues and supervisors regarding their experiences with self-disclosure.

Allocation of Resources

Particularly during challenging economic times, social workers are often faced with the dilemma of too few resources for too many client systems. They may have to deny an application for assistance because the funding has been exhausted or there are no beds in a shelter or food in the pantry. As social workers are often the first contact for the clients, they typically must shoulder the burden of informing them that there are no resources to meet a request.

Resources are typically allocated on the basis of equal-sized proportions, a lottery system, or on a competitive basis using financial need or past oppression as the criteria (Reamer, 2001). Ethical dilemmas involving resource allocations can be particularly challenging because there may be little that the social worker can do to influence the outcome. Nevertheless, social workers have an ethical obligation to play a role in the allocation of resources. Social workers who work directly with client systems can be the voice for these clients. Similarly, social workers who occupy supervisory, administrative, and policy positions in both public and non-profit organizations can advocate for equitable allocation of resources.

CASE: CARLA'S RIGHT TO PRIVACY AND CONFIDENTIALITY

We have explored a number of issues related to social work values and ethics. It is now time to apply the concepts and framework to an ethical dilemma. The dilemma is followed by the questions that might arise from the situation, and the issues are applied to the decision-making matrix presented in Table 6.2. Built on the Ethical Principles Rules and Screen developed by Dolgoff and colleagues (2009), D'Aprix and colleagues (2001) developed earlier a matrix for applying the screen. When presented with an ethical dilemma, the social worker should first apply the Ethical Rules Screen (Dolgoff et al., 2009, pp. 65–68) which requires the following:

- Examination of the *Code of Ethics* (2008) to determine if any of the *Code* rules are applicable.

- If one or more of the *Code* rules apply, the social worker follows the *Code* rules

- If the *Code* does not apply, the social worker moves to the Ethical Principles Screen.

The Ethical Principles Screen provides guidance for rank-ordering the issues using the seven ethical principles: (1) protection of human life, (2) equality and inequality, (3) autonomy and freedom, (4) least harm, (5) quality of life, (6) privacy and confidentiality, and (7) truthfulness and full disclosure. Using these seven principles prioritizes the ethical questions and enables the social worker to determine the issues that are most important to address.

Here is the ethical dilemma: You are a social worker at Oasis House, where your supervisor asks you to talk with a new resident, Carla. Carla told shelter workers that she is 18 and homeless. During your talks with Carla, however, she admits that she is really 15 and has run away from home. She further divulges that she does not want to go home because her mother's live-in boyfriend sexually abused her. She begs you not to share the information about the sexual abuse with anyone or to contact her mother.

The questions that might arise include the following:

- Does the adolescent have a legal right to make decisions about her life without parental consent?

- Would it be appropriate for you to discuss Carla's situation with her mother without Carla's informed consent?

- If Carla is being sexually abused, does she have a right to privacy after she has shared her secret with you?

- What is your responsibility to Carla's parents?

- Was Carla informed that you might not be able to maintain complete confidentiality *before* she confided in you?

- What are the agency's policies and procedures related to sexual abuse and Carla's status as a minor and a runaway?

You can analyze this practice situation by using the decision-making matrix in Table 6.2 as a guide. Table 6.3 uses that table's general categories in presenting possible ways of breaking down the problem to reach a satisfactory solution. As you can see, this ethical dilemma poignantly addresses the client's right to protection, self-determination, privacy, and confidentiality. At the heart of the NASW *Code*'s first ethical standard, Social Workers' Ethical Responsibilities to Clients, is client self-determination. Having respect for the client is based on the core social work value of "dignity and worth of the person" and the ethical principle of "respect the inherent dignity and worth of the person." Respecting Carla's right to self-determination, privacy, and confidentiality is key to upholding her dignity and worth. You are ethically bound to respect her dignity and worth, behave in a trustworthy manner, and practice with competence. By asking you to keep the alleged abuse in confidence and help her with emancipation, Carla is attempting to exercise her right to self-determination, privacy, and confidentiality. However, although you want to maintain her trust, as a social worker you are ethically and legally bound to report the abuse because she is a minor. The ethical dilemma here clearly is between client

TABLE 6.3

Ethical Decision-Making in the Case Study: Carla's Right to Privacy and Confidentiality

PRACTICE/ ETHICAL ISSUES	ETHICAL PRINCIPLE(S)	PERSONAL BIASES	ACTION(S) OPTIONS	POTENTIAL CONSEQUENCES/ OUTCOMES	ACTION(S) TAKEN	MONITOR/ EVALUATE EFFECTIVENESS
Client's request to not report the sexual abuse.	1) Protection of human life. 6) Privacy and confidentiality.	I think the mother is at fault.	a) Report the abuse to the public agency despite her opposition. b) Work with client to make the report together.	a) Report is made, but client's trust is lost. b) Build trust with client so report can be made.	Jointly work with client to make report.	Check with client at each step to determine her sexual safety.
Client's request to not contact her mother.	6) Privacy and confidentiality. 3) Self-determination. 1) Commitment to client.	I think her mother must be contacted.	a) By reporting to the public agency, the mother is contacted despite her opposition. b) Trust is built and mother is contacted.	a) Mother is contacted, but client's trust is lost. b) Trust is built and mother is contacted.	Jointly work with client to contact her mother.	Check with client at each step to determine her trust comfort levels with contacting mother.

Ethical Principles Screen:

1) Protection of life
2) Equality and inequality
3) Autonomy and freedom
4) Least harm
5) Quality of life
6) Privacy and confidentiality
7) Truthfulness and full disclosure

Source: Adapted from D'Aprix et al., 2001; Dolgoff et al., 2009.

confidentiality and mandated reporting of suspected abuse. Even having determined that, to best serve Carla, you must report the suspected sexual abuse to the child welfare agency. Moreover, you continue to respect her right to self-determination and privacy.

The challenge is to help Carla without losing her trust. Exploring her options and the pros and cons associated with the various options could help her to feel positive about reporting the abuse. Helping Carla to understand that reporting the abuse is part of the helping process can serve to maintain her trust.

CONCLUSION

To maintain a professional perspective and avoid feelings of being overwhelmed, remember that clarifying your own values and practicing social work in an ethical manner is a lifelong endeavor for social workers. As social workers interact with people in a changing society, new ethical challenges will continue to emerge. The effective practice of social work means that social workers approach each situation with questions regarding the ethical implications of their actions. I hope this chapter encourages you to begin to explore and expose your own values and ethics and their origins, and that such an exploration will become an ingrained part of your social work practice. Reamer's 2009 statement sums it up:

> To practice competently, contemporary professionals must have a firm grasp of pertinent issues related to ethical dilemmas and ethical decision-making. This knowledge enhances social workers' ability to protect clients and fulfill social work's critically important, value-based mission. (p. 120)

MAIN POINTS

- Social work values are defined as the beliefs that we hold for ourselves and others in our communities. Ethics are the behavioral manifestations of the values that we hold about the way we and others should behave toward one another.

- Ethical dilemmas can occur in every aspect of social work practice. Social workers face ethical dilemmas in the areas of legal and health care issues, client rights and responsibilities, allocation of resources, and maintaining privacy and confidentiality.

- To practice social work in an ethical manner, awareness of your own values and of the profession's code is key.

- Understanding values and ethics is a personal thought process that is difficult to measure, seldom has obvious or concrete solutions, may evolve and change over time as a result of culture, contemporary norms, and events, and is applicable at all levels of social work practice.

- The NASW *Code of Ethics* serves as the guide for ethical practice. Taking advantage of the practice wisdom of your social work colleagues, consulting the *Code of Ethics*, and familiarizing yourself with the laws, policies, and practices related to your position are three "musts" for being an ethical practitioner.

EXERCISES

1. To prepare yourself for working through the exercises in this chapter, go to the Sanchez Family interactive case (at www.routledgesw.com/cases). In the Assess tab, complete Task 3, "A Values Inventory for Social Workers."
2. Using the Sanchez Family case, review the case file for Junior Sanchez. Then select Carmen Sanchez and answer her Critical Thinking Questions. Next, answer Joey Sanchez's Critical Thinking Questions.
3. The best method for clarifying your values and developing responses to the inevitable ethical dilemmas that will arise is to practice. In this exercise, you can explore the values, ask the questions, and apply the ethical principles highlighted in this chapter. When you have read the following scenario, use the modified version of the Enhanced Ethical Decision-Making Model (D'Aprix et al., 2001) to complete the matrix. When you have completed the matrix, you can compare your analysis with mine to see how we compare. There are seldom "absolute" right or wrong answers in an ethical dilemma, just lots of questions and possibilities. As an ethical practitioner, you are obligated to have a reasoned approach.

   Using the Sanchez family interactive case study, imagine that you are a social worker in a not-for-profit agency that provides crisis services over the telephone and to walk-in clients. Emilia Sanchez, a 24-year-old who is two months pregnant has telephoned several times. In her last telephone call, she confided to you that she uses crack cocaine and drinks alcohol several times a week. You have expressed your concern that her drug use may be dangerous for her unborn child, but she does not seem worried. She has also stated that she is unable or unwilling to give up the drugs. In this telephone conversation, she told you that she is unsure if she wants to keep "it." You suspect that she has traded sex for drugs and she is not working or attending school. Emilia tells you that her Catholic parents do not know about the pregnancy and she does not want them to know anything because they will insist she have the baby. Her mother already cares for Emilia's son, Joey, and has two younger children still living at home, and Emilia's father works long hours. They have little money and she does not want to burden them with another mouth to feed.

Your Analysis:

MODIFIED VERSION OF ENHANCED ETHICAL DECISION-MAKING MODEL						
PRACTICE/ ETHICAL ISSUE	ETHICAL PRINCIPLE(S)	PERSONAL BIASES	ACTION(S) OPTIONS	POTENTIAL CONSEQUENCES/ OUTCOMES	ACTION(S) TAKEN	MONITOR/EVALUATE EFFECTIVENESS
1.						
2.						
3.						

Consider this question: If your best friend was in Emilia's situation, would your analysis change? If so, in what way?

4. Go to the Riverton interactive case at www.routledgesw.com/cases. The social worker in this case is both a professional working in the community and a resident of the community. Utilizing the information included in this chapter, identify the potential ethical implications for the social worker and develop a response to each issue identified.

5. Go to the Carla Washburn interactive case at www.routledgesw.com/cases and consider Mrs. Washburn's right to self-determination. Utilizing the information from this chapter, describe the issue of her right to refuse services and health care from the dual perspective, specifically responding to the following:

   a. Does Mrs. Washburn have a right to refuse services and treatment?

   b. What is the social worker's role/option should the client refuse services or treatment?

   c. Discuss the ethical implications of the client's right to refuse services and treatment.

   d. Cite the section of the NASW *Code of Ethics* that addresses this issue.

6. To better understand where your values come from, complete the following:

   a. Identify five values that are important in your life and consider the origins of those values.

b. Compare those values to those of the social work profession. You can then think about the ways in which you act on each value. Do you engage in activities or behaviors that enable other people to discern your value on that particular issue, or would other people have no idea about your value? Finally, consider whether this value has ever created a dilemma for you. If so, what was the dilemma, and how did you resolve it?

To help you compare your values with those of the social work profession, the six social work values are listed below:

Service

Social justice

Dignity and worth of the person

Importance of human relationships

Integrity

Competence

PERSONAL VALUE	ORIGINS OF VALUE	BEHAVIOR	RELEVANT SOCIAL WORK VALUE	DILEMMA
1.				
2.				
3.				
4.				
5.				

After you have completed this exercise, reflect on your work and consider these questions:

• Did you learn anything new about yourself?

• Did you learn anything new about anyone else?

• Are you satisfied with the ways in which you act on your value system? If not, what changes can you make?

- If any of your values created an ethical dilemma for you, were you satisfied with the way in which you handled the dilemma? If not, what could you have done differently?

- Do you feel your value system is consistent with the values of the social work profession?

- Which of the social work values is the most important to you?

- How do you currently see that you may be exercising this value in your life?

7. Identify a value conflict or ethical question you have encountered in your life. Include your thoughts and feelings, response to the dilemma, and what you might do in the future with a similar situation. Discuss how your values related to this issue may impact your profession.

CHAPTER 7

Social Work Perspectives and Methods

Emily's BSW provided her with the knowledge and skills to work with individuals, families, groups, and communities. In her first job as an adult services worker in a small multiservice community service agency, she intervened on all these levels. On the individual level, she worked with the older adults through the homemaker/ chore program as well as with persons with visual impairments and female recipients of public assistance who were seeking employment. In each of these programs, she also worked with the clients' families. On the group level, Emily facilitated a support group for persons who had recently lost their vision. Finally, at the community level, Emily helped a community group develop a telephone reassurance program in which volunteers from the Senior Center telephoned homebound older adults each day to ensure their safety and well-being. Emily helped the Center committee oversee this program and set policy. As a result of her involvement with the Senior Center group, Emily became part of a community task force that included community agencies and older adults to create an annual community-wide resource and wellness fair. Emily performed all these levels of social work in just one job. Her varied activities are an example of generalist social work practice.

Both the 2008 NASW *Code of Ethics* and the Council on Social Work Education (CSWE) describe bachelor-level social work practice in terms of the framework known as **generalist social work practice**. At this level, social workers have a broad-based set of knowledge and skills that they can use for assessing and intervening with competence at multiple levels. One of the six values included in the *Code of Ethics*, Importance of Human Relationships, calls on social workers to "strengthen relationships among people in a purposeful effort to promote, restore, maintain, and enhance the well-being of individuals, families, social groups, organizations, and communities." In the 2008 CSWE *Educational Policy and Accreditation Standards*, CSWE-accredited BSW programs are required to include content on working with individuals, families, groups, organizations, and communities. In this chapter, we define and explore the generalist area of social work education and practice from both theoretical and practice perspectives.

HISTORY OF GENERALIST SOCIAL WORK PRACTICE

Although the idea of providing services to individuals, families, groups, and communities is rooted in the origins of the profession, the framing of generalist practice is a relatively recent development in the profession. Historically, two movements that shaped contemporary social work practice helped both to separate and to unite the profession around the concept of generalist practice. Despite an ongoing philosophical competition, the Charity Organization Society, which emphasized the individual, and the settlement house movement, with an emphasis on groups and communities, paved the way for three distinct theoretical and service paths: individual casework, group work, and community organization (Hernandez, 2008). However, the social turmoil of the 1960s prompted the profession to consider an approach to social work practice that would integrate these three modalities in an effort to provide more comprehensive services (Landon, 1995). This shift of philosophy led to the emergence of the generalist perspective.

Interest in a universal approach to social work practice resulted in the emergence of the baccalaureate in social work. Beginning in the 1960s and 1970s, BSW programs emerged as a strategy for promoting the generalist social work practice model. Before this period, the only social work degrees granted were at the master's level. Social work scholars and practitioners agreed that practitioners with BSWs, trained in the generalist perspective, could best fulfill the needs for professional services, particularly in inner-city and rural areas and the public sector. The generalist practice model provides a solid preparation for the graduate social work degree, which focuses on a specialty area of concentration. The BSW curriculum prepares generalist practitioners, and the MSW curriculum begins with a generalist perspective, but offers specialization through concentration in particular areas of study.

After decades of debate, a consensus has been reached regarding the definition of generalist social work. In 2006, the Association of Baccalaureate Social Work Program Directors approved the following definition:

> Generalist social work practitioners work with individuals, families, groups, communities and organizations in a variety of social work and host settings. Generalist practitioners view clients and client systems from a strengths perspective in order to recognize, support, and build upon the innate capabilities of all human beings. They use a professional problem solving process to engage, assess, broker services, advocate, counsel, educate, and organize with and on behalf of client and client systems. In addition, generalist practitioners engage in community and organizational development. Finally, generalist practitioners evaluate service outcomes in

order to continually improve the provision and quality of services most appropriate to client needs. Generalist social work practice is guided by the NASW *Code of Ethics* and is committed to improving the well being of individuals, families, groups, communities and organizations and furthering the goals of social justice.

LEVELS OF GENERALIST SOCIAL WORK PRACTICE

Perhaps the greatest strength of the generalist approach is that social work skills can be transferred to different types of situations that allow for influencing social change on a structural as well as personal level. As you know, social workers work with client systems at the individual, family, group, organizational, and community levels. Within generalist practice, the nature of the intervention is determined by the "size" of the client system. Generalist social work practice takes place at three levels: the individual and family level, the group level, and the organization and community level. These levels are described here.

- *Individual and family level:* The most basic level of generalist social work practice is intervention with individuals and families. Interventions on this level can include working one-on-one with an older adult and her or his family toward developing a post–hospital discharge plan or with a victim of sexual assault and her or his significant others. Consider the social worker who conducts the home study for a couple seeking to adopt a child. The worker interviews the couple to determine their motivation and qualifications for adoption, compiles a written assessment, and guides them through the legal adoption process. Working with individuals and families can sometimes provide insight into the gaps and concerns of the larger service delivery system.

- *Group level:* While engaged in the process of working with groups, the social worker may discover that social work practice on the group level demands many of the skills developed for working with individuals. Group level practice can include assisting a group of families seeking family therapy, instituting a support group for persons with eating disorders, and providing guidance to a group seeking to eradicate the drug problems of young people in their neighborhood. Returning to the example of the couple seeking to adopt a child, the social worker may work at the group level by participating with the couple in a support group for adoptive parents.

- *Organization and community level:* At this level social work practice involves interventions with large groups, organizations, and communities of all sizes. The practitioner can be engaged in such varied activities as **locality or community development** (intervention targeted at enhancing a specific geographic area or region); analysis and implementation of policy; advocacy activities (for example, lobbying, letter writing, and public speaking); and administration (for example, personnel, supervision, budgeting, and grant writing). At the organization and community level, the adoption social worker may promote legislation that will open adoption records for adult adoptees, or create a community task force to address a need for improved economic stability.

Training in generalist practice enables the social worker to practice ethically and competently at all three levels. Moreover, most social work positions require the social worker to function at all three levels at some point. Most generalist practitioners develop a focus on one or two of the areas, although these preferences frequently change over the years of practice. For example, you might begin your career working with individuals in direct service but find later that you have a desire to move into social work administration. This is a major benefit of being a social worker: Your knowledge, skills, and values provide you with mobility.

GENERALIST SOCIAL WORK SKILLS AND ROLES

Regardless of where or with whom a beginning social worker intervenes, she or he must acquire a basic set of skills. Recently, one NASW chapter compiled a list, "100 Skills of the Professional Social Worker." Reproduced in Box 7.1, the list is a testament to the wide variety of skills that are part of the social work repertoire. This array of skills enables generalist social workers to function in a number of different and varied roles and in a variety of situations. Roles of generalist social workers who perform at the individual, family, group, organization, and community levels can be categorized as (Hepworth et al., 2010):

- Direct provider of services—counseling and therapy, group work, and educator.
- System linkage—broker, case manager, **mediator**, advocate.
- System maintenance and enhancement—organizational analyst, facilitator, team member, consultant, and supervisor.
- Researcher/research consumer.
- System development—program developer, planner, policy and procedure developer, and advocate.

To highlight several of these skills further:

Working with client systems to facilitate a planned change, the **direct provider** intervenes with individuals, families, and groups in therapeutic situations and with organizations and communities to identify needs and strengths and facilitate social change.

BOX 7.1

100 Skills of the Professional Social Worker

Activism	Fundraising	Post-discharge follow-up
Administration	Financial counseling	Political action
Adoption	Gestalt therapy	Prevention
Advocacy	Goal setting	Problem evaluation
Applied research	Grant writing	Problem-focused therapy
Assessment	Grass-roots organizing	Problem resolution
Basic skills training	Group therapy	Program administration
Behavior therapy	Health education	Program planning
Brief therapy	Health planning	Psychosocial assessment
Career counseling	Home studies	Public relations
Case management	Intake	Qualitative research
Child advocacy	Independent practice	Quantitative research
Client and family conferences	Information and referral	Rational-emotive therapy
Client and family education	Interagency collaboration	Reality therapy
Client screening	Interdisciplinary collaboration	Recording
Coaching	Interviewing	Referring
Coalition building	Intervention	Residential treatment
Cognitive therapy	Legislative advocacy	Resource allocation
Community organization	Life skills education	Role playing
Conflict resolution	Lobbying	Service contracting
Conjoint therapy	Mandated reporting	Service coordination
Consultation	Marital therapy	Short-term therapy
Continuity of care	Mediation	Social action
Coping skills	Milieu therapy	Social work education
Counseling	Needs assessment	Staff development
Crisis intervention	Negotiation	Supervision
Data collection	Networking	Support group
Direct practice	Outcome evaluation	Task-centered casework
Discharge planning	Outreach	Teach coping skills
Divorce therapy	Parent training	Team player
Empowerment	Placement	Termination
Expert witness	Planning	Treatment planning
Family therapy	Policy analysis	Utilization review
	Policy development	

Source: Akin, 1998.

As a **case manager**, the social worker's role is to help the client system mobilize itself to meet an agreed-upon goal. A generalist social worker can work one-on-one with individuals and families, with small-scale therapeutic or self-help groups, as well as with larger groups seeking social and political change. A frequently sought-after job for social workers with BSWs, case managers are on the front lines of social service delivery, where they coordinate the services and resources needed by clients.

For example, a case manager for a person with severe and persistent mental illness may coordinate housing, mental health, financial, employment, and transportation services for the client. Social work practice at the group, organization, and community levels is built on a working knowledge of case management skills that enables the social worker to understand individual group members' needs.

In functioning as a **broker**, the social worker facilitates a client system's access to needed resources. Broker activities could include helping an older adult apply for assistance with his heating bill, assisting a group of parents of children with attention deficit disorder to arrange a meeting with the school board to improve school-based services, or working with another social service agency to streamline their application process for their clients.

In the role of **advocate**, the social worker can work with the individual, family, community, or organizational level to voice the needs of a client group to a larger group or the entire society for the purpose of achieving social justice. For example, the social worker can advocate on behalf of a client at the adoption hearing, or she or he can lobby the state legislature to enact laws to address the needs of foster children.

Generalist practitioners can also engage in **planning and program and policy development**. With experience practicing social work at multiple levels, generalists gain insights into the effectiveness with which policies and programs are not meeting client systems' needs so they may facilitate the development of new or enhanced services. Social workers can use that practice wisdom to analyze policies and evaluate programs to determine if they are, in fact, effectively fulfilling their intended purposes.

THEORY IN GENERALIST SOCIAL WORK PRACTICE

The knowledge and skills of the competent generalist are based on a framework that is known to be effective for the client system. Theoretical frameworks that are empirically tested through research can provide the practicing social worker with a foundation for determining the type and direction of the assessment, intervention, and evaluation of the client relationship.

Intended to guide assessments and interventions, **theory**, as it is applied in the social work profession, encompasses both the traditional scientific concept of empirical tests that are used to explain behaviors and processes and the more contemporary concept of pragmatism—explanations that emanate from practice (McNutt & Floersch, 2008). A sub-set of theory, referred to as **practice theory**, are the perspectives specifically targeted at work with individuals, families, and groups (Walsh, 2010). A theoretically and empirically based practice approach is one that has been tested in controlled situations so that social workers have evidence that a particular approach is appropriate for specific populations. The practice methods are not speculative or performed by trial and error. Such practice, known as

evidence-based practice, uses research to guide the social worker in developing knowledge and skills for client system interventions. The ability to link theory with practice and articulate the who, what, when, where, why, and how of all interactions and activities in which social workers engage to influence or facilitate change differentiates the professional from the nonprofessional or the paraprofessional worker. Theory allows the social worker to move from the philosophical assumptions to practice realities (McNutt & Floersch, 2008, p.143). In applying theory in a practice situation enables the social worker to (1) predict and explain client behavior; (2) generalize among clients and problem areas; (3) bring order to intervention activities; and (4) identify knowledge gaps about practice situations (Walsh, 2010, p. 4).

In the following sections, we explore several of the theoretical frameworks that have become hallmarks of the social work profession, particularly generalist social work practice. Theory provides the basis for a perspective or frameworks which then guides practitioners to the appropriate practice methods or approaches. Remember too that although the integration of theory with practice is critical to effective interventions, applying theory in practice situations can be challenging. Therefore, social workers must be well trained in a variety of perspectives so that the application of theory becomes a natural part of the delivery of services.

You have already been introduced to two of these theories in earlier chapters—the ecological and strengths perspectives, for example. We will look at these in more detail here, along with systems theory and the solution-focused brief therapy perspective. These frameworks can be helpful in practicing at all levels. A final note will point out the way that social work draws on theory from other disciplines.

Person-in-Environment and Ecological Perspectives

In Emily's work with the senior homemaker/chore program, she came to appreciate the importance of viewing clients within the context of their social and physical environment. The homemaker/chore service provides in-home services to older adults who are unable to perform those tasks needed to maintain independent living. The typical homemaker/chore service client is an older adult with physical health problems who lives alone. Without the support of this program, the individual would likely have to enter a residential long-term care facility.

Marietta, a 78-year-old, widowed, African American woman living alone in a rental house, taught Emily the importance of seeing the "big picture." Marietta was referred to Emily's agency by her family physician, Dr. Stephens, who was concerned about Marietta's ability to care for herself. In her initial assessment of Marietta's situation, Emily was ready to recommend that Marietta be placed in a skilled care facility due to her physical frailty, vision problems, lack of ability to cook or maintain her house, limited income, and apparent lack of social support.

Through her assessment, Emily learned that Marietta's only son had recently died and she was estranged from her daughter-in-law and adult grandchildren because she believed they had not provided her son with adequate care during his illness. Marietta's daughter lived nearby, but they were frequently in conflict because Marietta believed her daughter should leave her husband because he was abusive to her when he was drinking. Marietta's only living sister suffered from Alzheimer's disease and was no longer able to care for herself. Marietta told Emily that she did not believe her children or sister would help her, and she refused to consider moving in with any of them.

Upon conducting a more thorough assessment, Emily learned that Marietta had close ties with her neighbors, church, and several of her nieces and nephews. Although she did need in-home services to continue living independently, she was part of a large, close, and supportive network of caregivers.

We begin our journey through the theoretical frameworks used in generalist social work practice by first examining two key perspectives: the person-in-environment and ecological perspectives. The profession has a long history of emphasizing the **person-in-environment perspective**, which perceives each individual as an interactive participant in a larger physical, social, communal, historical, religious, physical, cultural, and familial environmental system (Kondrat, 2008, p. 348). Specifically mentioned in the NASW *Standards for Cultural Competence* (2007), social workers are obligated to incorporate cultural factors and meanings when they are utilizing the person-in-environment framework.

More recently referred to as **People:Environment (P:E)** to denote the transactional relationship of people to their environment, this perspective enables social workers to understand the complexities of clients' lives by emphasizing the impact of the physical and social environment on the person (Gitterman & Germain, 2008). Had Emily not used this approach with Marietta, she would not have recognized that Marietta was only one part of a larger, supportive system.

During the 1950s, social work scholars were urging practitioners to consider the interaction between the individual and the larger world. This transition began in the 1970s, when interest in the social environment was heightened (Kondrat, 2008). A landmark event in this movement occurred in 1973, when social work scholar Carel Germain introduced the ecological perspective for social work. This perspective is based on the premise that the relationship between the individual and her or his social environment determines the individual's life situation. Examining the interaction between the client system and the larger social and physical environment is the focus for understanding human behavior, rather than looking to the cause of the interaction. For example, understanding the impact of a child's relationships with her family on her ability to perform well academically is more important than explaining the cause of the parent–child interactions.

The original ecological model encompassed ten conceptual components, with eight concepts added at later points as the framework has evolved (Germain &

Gitterman, 1995; Gitterman & Germain, 2008). The 18 concepts are described in Table 7.1. Aimed at helping client systems improve the level of fit with their environments by eliminating life stressors, the model provides a strategy for identifying the client system; assessing the client's dilemma in terms of strengths,

TABLE 7.1 *Basic Concepts of the Ecological Perspective*	ECOLOGICAL CONCEPTS	DESCRIPTION
	ORIGINAL MODEL:	
	Person–environment fit	The ability of client system to positively engage with the environment—a positive fit suggests the client system has adapted successfully.
	Adaptations	To maintain a stable person–environment fit, systems constantly adapt to changing environment.
	Life stressors	The person–environment fit may be compromised if the client system is unable to adapt to life crises.
	Stress	The individual's response to a life stressor.
	Coping measures	To maintain a desired person–environment fit, systems develop methods for adapting to life stresses.
	Relatedness	Connections that people make with others in their environment; they serve as resources for adaptations.
	Competence	Systems must have the resources to function effectively.
	Self-esteem	The person's self-perception influences her/his ability to feel competence.
	Self-direction	The client system's ability to feel control over itself impacts self-esteem, competence, and ability to adapt to life stresses.
	Habitat and niche	Referring to clients' physical space and place within that space, habitat and niche can determine the client system's well-being.
	ADDED CONCEPTS:	
	Coercive power	Poverty, "isms," and homelessness are examples of "social pollutions" that inhibit the client system's ability to adapt and fit with the environment.
	Exploitative power	Another stressor, exploitative power is the oppression of one group over another.
	Life course	Ecologically, the path of a client's life is fluid, changing, and unique.
	Individual time	The meaning that the client system attaches to life experiences.
	Historical time	The impact of historical and social change on the client system.
	Social time	The client system's transitions and life events are a product of social, biological, economic, demographic, and culture factors.
	Resilience	Protective factors enable people to thrive in spite of life stressors.
	Flexibility	In order to adapt to environmental changes, the network must have the ability to be diverse and responsive.

Source: Germain & Gitterman, 1995; Gitterman & Germain, 2008.

supports, resources, and previous coping and adaptive skills; and intervening with the client with a number of possibilities. The generalist social worker can intervene with the person and use different facets of the person's system (for example, family, employer, or church) to address the client's needs. The practitioner can then use an ecological perspective at the individual, family, group, organization, and community levels. For example, Emily identified existing family and community resources and mobilized those resources to enable Marietta to continue living in her own home.

Systems and Ecosystems Theory

Rooted in theoretical biology, the concept of viewing clients within a systems framework first emerged in the late 1950s and early 1960s and became the major guiding theoretical framework for the social work profession for several decades (Kondrat, 2008). **Systems theory**, logically enough, evolved from the concept that a system is comprised of multiple components that interact with one another to create an entire entity. From a social work perspective, a **system** can be a physical and/or social entity that includes individuals, families, groups, organizations, communities—local and global, and even nations. You have no doubt noticed from your reading so far that the persons or groups served by social workers are considered **client systems**, but the term is used interchangeably with **clients.**

Every system is made up of elements, which can be any physical, social, or personal entity that is orderly, interactive, and functional. For example, a person may be part of a system that is composed of physical elements such as the individual's household, neighborhood, community, city, country, and world. Social elements can include the client system's relationships with persons that make up the environment in which the client lives. A system is composed of the various parts that interact with one another to contribute to the overall functioning of the system. A change in one element affects all of the other elements.

Systems Theory Concepts   The systems theory framework helps social workers view client systems within the context of their interactions within a larger environment and explains human behavior in terms of the reciprocal relationships among the elements in the system. Whereas the ecological model illuminates the relationship between a client system and the environment, systems theory provides a way of understanding the change process that the client system undergoes.

To understand change from a systemic perspective, consider that when one part of a system changes, the entire system must change. For example, when a family member is added or removed from a family system for any reason, the system must change because the addition or loss creates a different configuration of people, relationships, required tasks, and available resources. Just as natural change can modify a system, a social work intervention can prompt a system to change. In fact, the mere presence of a social worker as a "change agent" means that the worker becomes part of the system, thus producing a change. To function, a system must be dynamic and flexible.

Viewing the person, family, group, or community as a part of a larger system has numerous implications for generalist social work practice. For example, a systems approach enables the generalist practitioner to consider the client system within the larger context of the environment in which the client lives. Such a framing enables the social worker to understand relationships and factors that affect the client system as a result of interactions between the client and the environment. Defining the client within a larger context further provides the social worker an opportunity to target multiple components of the system for intervention. Lastly, viewing the client system from a systemic perspective incorporates the unique qualities of the client and emphasizes the dynamic nature of human interactions.

As you have learned, it is critical for social workers to grow and change as our society changes. In recent years, social work scholars have incorporated the concept of the **ecosystem** into the guiding principles for practice. Building on to the general systems theory with a focus on the individual's relationship to the external environment, the ecosystem perspective emphasizes the dynamic and inter-dependent relationships that the individuals, family, or community has with the surrounding environment (Kondrat, 2008). There is clearly no one theoretical approach that will explain all situations, but frameworks that view the client system in terms of the environment have prevailed within the social work profession as they are most consistent with social work values and mission.

Applying Theory in Generalist Practice Now that you are familiar with the person-in-environment, systems, and ecosystems frameworks, let us apply these concepts to generalist social work practice. Due to the universality of these systems-based theories, the concepts can be applied to virtually every level and type of social work relationship. In order to apply systems concepts, social workers use tools to systemically assess and intervene in client situations.

One such tool is the **ecomap**. Developed by Ann Hartman in 1975 as a strategy for systemically assessing individuals and families, the ecomap depicts the type and quality of relationships along with the dynamic nature of those relationships (Hartman, 1978). The ecomap can be used at all levels of social work practice.

Using Emily's experience with Marietta, described earlier in this chapter, an ecomap is presented in Exhibit 7.1. As you can see, each component of the client system is identified within a circle. The quality of the relationships can then be coded using the various types of lines. In addition to identifying the quality of the relationship by drawing lines, arrows indicate the flow of energy and resources that are invested in and derived from that relationship. After lines and arrows are drawn from the individual to each part of the sub- or suprasystems, the social worker and the client can review the ecomap together to identify strengths, stressors, and areas for change. An imbalance of energy either flowing into or out of a relationship may indicate an area for change.

By placing the client and her or his household members in the center circle and other persons and resources in the circles that surround the client, the ecomap heightens a client's awareness of the strengths and patterns of current relationships in her or his life. In addition, it serves as a strategy to identify changes the client would like to make in those relationships. Specifically, if the client would like to change a part of her or his life, the resources and specific areas that would have to be changed in order to achieve that goal are laid out on the ecomap. The ecomap is useful with larger systems (for example, neighborhoods) to identify links within and outside the system. This tool can be used to establish a social work relationship at multiple levels, monitor change, and evaluate progress at the termination of the professional relationship.

Looking at the ecomap to assess Marietta's social environment, you can see that the relationships in her life are sources of both support and stress, and several are in a state of change. The relationships that Marietta has with her nieces and nephews, her neighbors, the members of her church, and her physician serve as strengths for her. Marietta's relationship with her sister is changing, as her sister's memory is deteriorating due to Alzheimer's disease. Stressors in Marietta's life include the relationships with her estranged daughter-in-law and her daughter. The new relationships that Marietta is developing with Emily and, later, the homemaker/chore worker have the potential to be sources of social support, but they are still being stabilized. Having the ecomap as a tool for assessment in Marietta's situation enabled Emily to identify existing resources and strengths and target areas for intervention.

Strengths-Based and Empowerment Perspectives

While working at the public welfare agency, Emily was taking her turn at "intake"—seeing walk-in or call-in clients who were in crisis. Sarah, a 16-year-old, walked into the office and explained that she found the agency address in the telephone directory. She had her one-day-old daughter with her, and she told Emily that she delivered the baby at her girlfriend's house (in the bathroom with only her friend present). Neither Sarah's nor her friend's parents were aware of the birth. The friend's parents were out of town. By Sarah's calculations, the baby was near full-term. Neither Sarah nor the baby had seen a health care provider. Sarah was nursing the baby, and from Emily's quick assessment, the baby appeared to be healthy. Sarah refused to identify the father, but Emily suspected the father might be her 21-year-old stepbrother. Her verbal and nonverbal cues raised Emily's suspicions.

Sarah appeared extremely distraught, asserting that she "had to do something with this baby now." However, she was also adamant that she would not involve her parents, or anyone else, in her situation. She reported that she was an above average student, she was active in a service organization, and she worked part time at a fast-food restaurant. She claimed to have dated casually, but denied that she was currently

EXHIBIT 7.1

Ecomap

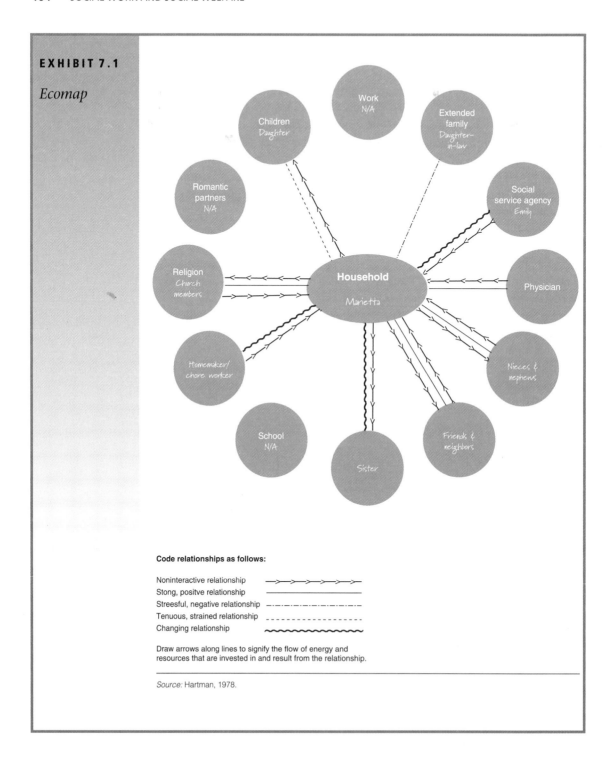

Code relationships as follows:

Noninteractive relationship

Stong, positve relationship

Streesful, negative relationship

Tenuous, strained relationship

Changing relationship

Draw arrows along lines to signify the flow of energy and
resources that are invested in and result from the relationship.

Source: Hartman, 1978.

involved in any serious relationship. She informed Emily that her family belonged to a conservative fundamentalist religion, and she feared severe consequences if they discovered that she had become pregnant.

Initially, this case may seem overwhelming, as Emily is faced with multiple challenges: Sarah, a minor who may have been sexually assaulted by a family member, delivers her own child without benefit of health care and is fearful of being discovered by her family. What strengths can there be in a situation such as this one? Let us look at this case more closely to determine the strengths that exist. First, Sarah was courageous and resourceful enough to deliver the baby safely (seemingly), nurse the baby, and come to Emily's agency for help. She has a supportive friend, attends school and performs well academically, has a job, and is involved in community service. Despite all the challenges Emily will face in working with Sarah's situation, there are strengths on which to build: Sarah has a history of being responsible, she is concerned for the child, and she is asking for help. Seeing Sarah through the eyes of her strengths as opposed to her deficits is the essence of strengths-based social work practice.

Focusing the client–worker relationship on client strengths has been a relatively recent revolution in the social work profession although it is a natural outgrowth of the concepts of a systems and ecological perspective. Historically, social workers were trained in the problem, or pathology, model of assessment and intervention. In this model, the social worker focuses first and foremost on the problems, deficits, and inadequacies of the client system. The shift to the strengths-based perspective occurred within the social work community during the late 1980s (Saleebey, 2006). Conceived originally as a strategy for working with persons with severe and persistent mental illness, the strengths approach is now used with an array of client populations, in large part because emphasizing client strengths is consistent with the values and ethical code of the social work profession. The social work value of recognizing client uniqueness and self-worth is inherently a strengths perspective.

Strengths-Based and Empowerment Concepts   "Problems versus possibilities" is the basis of the strengths-based perspective. Being a strengths-based social worker means that "*everything* you do as a social worker will be predicated, in some way, on helping to discover and embellish, explore, and exploit clients' strengths and resources in the service of assisting them to achieve their goals, realize their dreams, and shed the irons of their own inhibitions and misgivings, and society's domination" (Saleebey, 2006, p. 1).

Although the strengths approach is relatively simple to comprehend, it can be challenging to put into practice for both the client system and the social worker. Client systems in crisis, or who have multiple challenges, may have difficulty perceiving any strengths in either themselves or their situations. Social workers will work with clients who can be hostile, resistant, or who have a history of inappropriate or illegal behavior. Assessing strengths in these situations is just as important to building a collaborative working relationship. Change occurs best when working with clients' strengths and assets.

Considered the key to the implementation of the strengths-based perspective, **empowerment** is the process of the professional acting in a collaborative role with the client system to recognize the strengths possessed by the client in such areas as knowledge, resiliency, and goals (Blundo, 2008). Using a systems framework to understand the environment in which the client system functions and then building on the existing and available strengths, assets, and resources, empowerment becomes the process used by the social worker and the client system to facilitate the change process. Identifying and understanding the social environment and its strengths are the first steps in helping the client(s) feel empowered to make a change.

The strengths-based framework assumes that building on a client's strengths can serve to empower the client to change, a process that can be collaborative, dynamic, and evolving. This perspective is based on six principles, as follows (Saleebey, 2006, pp. 16–20):

- *Every individual, group, family, and community has strengths:* To discern client system strengths, the social worker must respect and value the client's "story" and knowledge of their situation. For example, the strength of a client suffering from severe clinical depression may be that she or he was able to get out of bed three days this week as opposed to only one day last week.

- *Trauma and abuse, illness, and struggle may be injurious, but they may also be sources of challenge and opportunity:* Without minimizing the emotional and physical scars that come from a painful or traumatic experience, the social worker helps the client to see that she or he can use the experience to learn and grow in order to move beyond the self-defeating perception of her- or himself as victim or failure. Think of the example of a neighborhood in which the older adult residents are afraid to leave their homes. Mobilized by the social worker, the residents are empowered to rally together and organize a community center where they can go and participate in safety.

- *Assume that you do not know the upper limits of the capacity to grow and change, and take individual, group, and community aspirations seriously:* The social worker can empower client systems to think beyond negative life experiences, disabilities, or challenges, with the aim of expanding the client's self-vision of capacities and possibilities. Consider, for example, a middle-aged mother who dropped out of high school and receives public assistance but who goes on to finish high school, community college, and college to become a social worker.

- *We best serve clients by collaborating with them:* Respecting clients' knowledge and expertise in their own lives or communities is the first step in developing a collaborative and empowering relationship. Collaborating with the client system creates the opportunity to use the worker's and client's strengths and resources—a strategy that diminishes the prospect for further victimization of the client. For example, consider a situation in which the social worker facilitates a meeting between police and a group of immigrants whose neighborhood is the target of hate crimes to discuss strategies for addressing the problem.

- *Every environment is full of resources:* Regardless of the level of chaos or the sparseness of obvious strengths, the strengths-based social worker can identify resources on which to build an intervention plan with the client system. For example, a person who is experiencing homelessness, has an addiction to drugs, and is estranged from his family comes to a program serving military veterans who are homeless. The very fact that the man has come for help constitutes a strength in this situation.

- *Caring, Caretaking, and Context:* The social work profession is deeply committed to the concept of caring for others, helping people care for themselves, and mobilizing communities and societies to care for their members. Based on the idea that the strengths perspective is about helping people to recognize their strengths and have hope, the concept of caring for others is a natural fit for strengths-based social work interventions.

Strengths-Based and Empowerment Perspectives in Generalist Practice

> *Do things with people, not for people.*
> —JANE ADDAMS

Working with people is to empower them. Approaching every social work situation with the six principles of the strengths-based perspective just described sets the stage for an empowering and liberating social work encounter. The concepts and skills promoted by the strengths-based perspective have relevance to every area in which social workers practice, including: working with diverse populations; advocating for social justice; respecting the client system's right to self-determination; and developing interventions for individuals, families, groups, organizations, and communities (Blundo, 2008). To further understand the strengths and empowerment perspectives, a social worker needs skills to act on the principles. A useful strategy is to compare the client–social worker relationship from both a strengths and a deficit perspective. Table 7.2 depicts a comparison of the two models (Saleebey, 1996, p. 298).

	THE ISSUE	FROM THE DEFICITS PERSPECTIVE	FROM THE STRENGTHS-BASED PERSPECTIVE
TABLE 7.2 *Comparison of Deficits and Strengths Model*	The person is . . .	the case, symptoms, and the diagnosis	unique and her/his traits are strengths
	The intervention is . . .	problem-focused	possibility-focused
	The client's "stories" are . . .	re-interpreted by the expert	a way to know and appreciate the client
	The social worker . . .	is skeptical of the client's "stories" and rationalizations	knows the person from the inside out
	Childhood trauma . . .	predicts adult pathology	can either weaken or strengthen the client in adulthood
	The expert on the client's life is . . .	the social worker	the client
	The intervention is determined by . . .	the social worker	the client's aspirations
	Possibilities and development are . . .	limited by the client's pathology	opened by the client's possibilities and development
	Resources and skills are possessed by . . .	the social worker	the client and the social worker
	The focus of the relationship is . . .	symptom reduction	moving, affirming, and strengthening

Source: Adapted from Saleebey, 1996.

A next step in becoming a strengths- and empowerment-based social worker is to develop the ability to identify strengths that will enable the client system to think and respond with a sense of empowerment. The following is a list of possibilities that a social worker might be able to identify in a given intervention (Saleebey, 2006, pp. 82–84). Can you think of other areas for developing questions to add to this list—from your own life experiences or those of others?

- Lessons learned about self, others, and the environment around the client system.

- Personal qualities, traits, and virtues.

- Knowledge of the world that surrounds the client system.

- Talents possessed by the client system.

- Cultural and personal stories.

- Resources found within the client system (e.g., the client's own pride).

- Resources found within the client system's community (e.g., people and organizations).

- Spirituality as a resource for finding meaning and hope in life.

Social workers who use strengths-based empowerment strategies should keep in mind that for many clients, this may be the first time a helping professional has prompted them to consider their life stories in terms of the successes instead of the challenges. In this sense, an empowerment-based approach can serve as a valuable learning experience for both the social worker and the client. As Saleebey (2006) states:

> The formula is simple: Mobilize clients' strengths (talents, knowledge, capacities, resources) in the service of achieving their goals and visions and the clients will have a better quality of life on their terms. (p. 1)

Particularly well-suited for social work practice, one approach that is grounded in the strengths-based perspective is motivational interviewing. First developed by Miller & Rollnick (2002) for clients struggling with change, motivational interviewing encompasses four principles: the expression of empathy, development of discrepancy; rolling with resistance; and supporting self-efficacy. Now in use with clients who confront addictions, high-risk behaviors and criminal charges, motivational interviewing places the client in charge of the change and employs the skills of reflective listening, empathy, and articulating the pros and cons of change (Corcoran, 2008).

Returning to Emily's experience in working with Sarah, consider the strategies she could use to empower Sarah to take action in her situation. Building on Sarah's strengths of being responsible, having concern for the well-being of the baby, and the fact that she sought help for herself and the infant, Emily may begin by commending Sarah for these actions. Acknowledging the client's strengths is a step toward establishing rapport and building trust so that the client views the social worker as a partner in resolving a crisis. Emily can then explore with Sarah the options that are desired, realistic, and necessary. From a legal and ethical perspective, it is unrealistic for Sarah's parents not to be informed about the birth and possible sexual assault by the stepbrother.

Working from an empowerment approach, Emily can help Sarah develop a strategy with which she can feel safe to talk with them. For instance, Emily can offer to be with Sarah when she talks to her parents. In addition, let us assume Sarah and Emily are in one of the 47 states that have "safe haven" laws that protect parents from prosecution if they take their newborn child to a designated site (for example, a hospital, police station, or child welfare agency) within a specified amount of time. If they are in one of these states, Emily can assure Sarah that she will have legal protection because she brought her child to a designated safe place. Can you think of additional strategies that Emily can use to help Sarah feel empowered?

Solution-Focused Model

While working as a social worker for a home health agency, Emily was assigned to work with Charlie, a 30-year-old man recently discharged from the hospital after experiencing a gunshot wound. The gunshot resulted in a spinal cord injury, leaving Charlie a paraplegic (paralyzed from the waist down). When Emily first visited Charlie, he was hostile and refused to discuss any further rehabilitation. Emily suspected that Charlie was frightened and depressed, so she began to talk with him about the aspirations he had as a child. Charlie wanted to be a minister in his church, but he strayed from that goal when he dropped out of college.

Through their conversations, Emily helped Charlie to realize that his disability need not prohibit him from returning to college and becoming a minister. Over time, Emily and Charlie reconstructed his misconceptions of his abilities, and they developed a plan for working with the occupational and physical therapists so that Charlie could reapply to college and achieve his goal of joining the ministry.

Solution-Focused Concepts The **solution-focused model** is a strengths-based approach in which the social worker helps the client to construct or reconstruct her or his reality in regard to a challenging life situation. Inspired by its founders, Steve de Shazer, Insoo Berg and colleagues, solution-focused brief therapy is based on several assumptions—people are the experts about their lives; they are competent and have goals and solutions, but the change agenda must be established by the client (not the social worker) (DeJong, 2009). Aligned with a strengths-based perspective, interventions are directed toward identifying client system strengths and using those strengths to encourage the client's self-perception in a more functional light. Together, the client system and social worker then create an intervention plan that encompasses specific behavioral tasks aimed at the goal. The social worker's role is to help clients modify the ways they perceive the situation and interact with others. Typically, the client system has a previously successful experience on which to build for this situation.

In her work with Charlie, Emily employed a solution-focused approach. She first listened to him talk about an earlier goal that has been important to him. She then helped him reconnect with his earlier aspirations and recognize strengths he was not even aware he possessed. She and Charlie then collaborated to create behavioral strategies to accomplish his goals.

Solution-Focused Model in Generalist Practice   Solution-focused practice has been used primarily as a tool for working with individuals and families in clinical settings because of its emphasis on establishing individual goals and behavior change. Nevertheless, it can be used at all levels of generalist practice. At the group, organization, and community levels, the solution-focused social worker can help the group recognize its collective strengths and assets. In fact, the members can discover group strengths that do not exist on an individual level. The social worker can then help the group to agree on specific goals and mobilize to achieve those goals.

As an example, consider the case of a student who presents because of failing grades in academic work. The social worker asks if this is a recent situation, and the student responds that it is. The social worker uses a strengths-based, solution-focused brief therapeutic approach and asks the student to describe a time when he was making better grades. Notice that instead of focusing on things that are not going well, the social worker builds on the student's strengths. The social worker continues by asking the student to speculate as to why he was previously getting better grades. Upon hearing the student respond that his grades were better when he did his homework, asked for help from the teacher, and played fewer video games, the social worker may say, "So, you made better grades when you completed your homework, asked for help, and played fewer video games." Therein lies the solution. Box 7.2 lists some possible types of questions that can be used in a solution-focused approach.

Integration of Social Work Theory

In this chapter we have discussed each theory separately, but keep in mind that these theoretical perspectives are not mutually exclusive. Just the opposite, they can frequently complement one another. For example, the person-in-environment perspective provides the foundation for identifying strengths and seeing the client system as part of a larger environment, while the ecological and systems frameworks influence each other and enable the social worker to compartmentalize the distinctive environmental influences that impact the client's life experiences. Similarly, thinking systemically helps the social worker to focus on the client's relationships with other elements within the system.

The strengths-based and empowerment perspectives emanate from the ecological and systems models, while solution-focused practice is one application of these influences. These frameworks can also be integrated with other theoretical approaches to develop interventions for specific situations. Exhibit 7.3 depicts the way in which the theories and frameworks discussed in this chapter interrelate and guide one another.

Information integrated from other disciplines has also been instrumental in the development of social workers' knowledge and skills. **Eclecticism** is the process of using knowledge and skills derived from multiple theoretical concepts that are most appropriate to the client system, population, or situation at hand. The following

BOX 7.2

Questions for a Solution-Focused Approach

GOAL-FORMULATION QUESTIONS
- What will your days be like when you are no longer feeling depressed?
- What would have to be different in your relationship for you to feel satisfied?

MIRACLE QUESTIONS
- What would your life be like if you were able to reach your goal of graduating from college?
- What do you need in order to accomplish the goal of graduating from college, and how can I help you?

EXCEPTION FINDING QUESTIONS (WHAT WAS IT LIKE WHEN PROBLEMS DID NOT OCCUR)
- What was your family life like when your parents were not fighting?
- What is it like for the rest of you in the group when Joe is not angry and hostile?

SCALING QUESTIONS (USING A NUMERIC SCALE TO RATE PAST, PRESENT, AND FUTURE STATUS)
- On a scale of 1 to 10, how motivated are you to quit smoking? Where do you need to be to actually quit smoking? What do you need to do to get from 5 to 8?

COPING QUESTIONS
- When you feel like drinking again, what do you do to stop yourself?
- You and your children were homeless last year. What did you do to change that?
- How will you know when things are going well in your life? What will you be doing, who will you be with, and how will you be feeling, thinking, and acting?

WHAT'S BETTER QUESTIONS
- What is better in your life since we last met?
- How is your life better since you started taking your medication?

Source: Dejong, 2009

is a sampling of the theoretical influences that social work has gained from other professional disciplines:

- Theory from the field of sociology has aided the social work profession in understanding relationships between people and their environments, particularly with regard to class, culture, and inequality issues.

- Anthropological theory has helped social workers understand the origins and relationships of the wide diversity of groups served by social workers.

- Psychological theories have been invaluable for enhancing social workers' insights into human behavior and for developing therapeutic treatment approaches.

- Political science theories have been helpful in understanding issues related to government, the political process and environment, and power and control.

- Economic theory has helped the profession understand the ways in which the economy impacts the economic conditions in which client systems live and in the development of strategies for effecting change in the economic lives of persons living in poverty.

- Biological theory has been influential in several areas of social work, including human biological functioning and health and disease issues.

Theories from other disciplines and schools of thought have enhanced the development of effective intervention strategies for working with client and system issues that span the spectrum of our society. As social workers serve such a diverse and wide-ranging spectrum of society, multiple approaches are needed for use across populations, situations, and levels of practice. To adopt an eclectic approach, the social worker clearly must be well versed in a number of theoretical perspectives and processes.

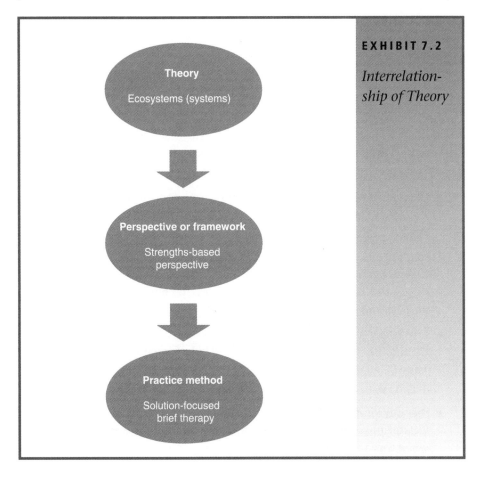

EXHIBIT 7.2

Interrelation-ship of Theory

Theory
Ecosystems (systems)

Perspective or framework
Strengths-based perspective

Practice method
Solution-focused brief therapy

CONCLUSION

This chapter has explored the role of the generalist social worker and the theoretical frameworks that guide and inform generalist social work practice. Applying these theoretical concepts to your practice can feel like an overwhelming challenge, particularly because there are so many theories from which to choose. Nevertheless, these constructs provide a basis on which to build your knowledge of effective and ethical social work practice.

Only a small number of the many available theoretical approaches are included in this chapter. As you continue the lifelong process of social work education, you will add other theoretical constructs to your repertoire of conceptual frameworks. For additional information on the social work profession and generalist practice, resources that may be helpful include the Council on Social Work Education's *Educational Policy and Accreditation Standards* (2009) and the National Association of Social Workers' *Code of Ethics* (2008).

MAIN POINTS

- Generalist social work practice provides for assessment and intervention at three levels: individuals and families, groups, and organizations and communities. The generalist social worker employs a variety of skills and plays many roles, including educator, advocate, and mediator.

- The person-in-environment perspective views the individual within the context of the environment in which she or he lives. This perspective is the foundation of social work theoretical approaches.

- The ecological perspective is used to understand the meaning of the interactions between client systems and the environment in which they exist.

- Building on the ecological model, systems and ecosystems theories are frameworks that help social workers understand and facilitate the change process that occurs for client systems within the context of the larger physical and social environment.

- Strengths-based and empowerment perspectives help the social worker identify the client system's strengths and use those strengths to frame goals that will build on their strengths and empower the client system to make changes.

- The solution-focused perspective has implications for practice at all levels because it enables the social worker to help clients reconstruct the ways in which they view their situation.

- At all three levels of generalist practice, these theoretical approaches can be combined to develop an intervention strategy that includes engagement and assessment of the client system, planning and implementation of the social work intervention, and evaluation of the social work intervention.

EXERCISES

We have explored theoretical frameworks to provide you with a basis for beginning your social work practice. Now it is your turn to apply your new knowledge in two exercises with the Sanchez Family interactive case (go to www.routledgesw.com/cases).

1. Read the following case scenario and identify the strengths that you perceive exist within the client situation. Link each of those strengths to one or more of the Principles of Strength perspectives described below. Lastly, review the scenario to describe the client situation from a deficits perspective.
   Principles of Strength:

   - *Every individual, group, family, and community has strengths.*

   - *Trauma and abuse, illness, and struggle may be injurious but they may also be sources of challenge and opportunity.*

   - *Assume that you do not know the upper limits of the capacity to grow and change and take individual, group, and community aspirations seriously.*

   - *We best serve clients by collaborating with them.*

   - *Every environment is full of resources.*

   You are the social worker at Our Lady of Guadalupe Church, which the Sanchez family has attended for years. During a recent church event, you noticed Gloria Sanchez wearing a long-sleeved turtleneck sweater on a particularly warm day. You speculate the reason for her attire is that she is covering up bruises. On numerous occasions, you have observed her husband, Leo, speaking to her in an extremely disrespectful manner and being demanding of her. The next time you see her you ask how things are going and she bursts into tears. She discloses to you that Leo has abused her throughout much of their marriage; she wants to leave him, but knows the teachings of the church oppose divorce. She shares that her sister, Carmen, is aware of the abuse but, for the present, has agreed not to tell the rest of the family. Carmen is very supportive, but is pushing her to "get help or get out." Gloria is terrified that her parents will learn about the abuse and blame her as they love Leo "like one of their own." Gloria has always felt close to her family and is saddened that she does not see them as often as she would like to. She visits less often out of fear that the family will suspect something is wrong.

CLIENT CHALLENGES	CLIENT STRENGTHS	PRINCIPLE(S) OF STRENGTHS PERSPECTIVE

2. In the previous exercise, you identified the strengths in Gloria's situation. Now, you will have the opportunity to consider Gloria's situation using a solution-focused approach. With your help, Gloria has identified the following areas of concern: being battered by her husband; thoughts of divorce; ensuring that the rest of her family does not learn about the violence; and concern that her relationship with her family is becoming distant. From a solution-focused perspective, consider each of these areas in terms of the strengths and resources possessed by Gloria or could be attained for or by her, her goals and a behavioral strategy to help her achieve the goal.

CHALLENGE	STRENGTH/RESOURCE POSSESSED	GLORIA'S GOAL	RESOURCES NEEDED	GOAL OR OBJECTIVE
Violent spouse				
Desire for divorce				
Family learning about the violence				
Losing her relationship with her family				

3. Review the case file for Junior Sanchez. Then select Celia Sanchez and answer Celia's Critical Thinking Questions.
4. Review the case file for Junior Sanchez. Then select Alejandro Sanchez and answer Alejandro's Critical Thinking Questions.

5. Locate the Case Study Tools and click on the Ecomap icon. Review the ecomap for the Sanchez family. Using the tool, create an ecomap for yourself. Provide a narrative analysis of your own ecomap, focusing on the strengths, areas for growth and change, and a future perspective on your life.

6. Go to the Riverton case at www.routledgesw.com/cases and review the case information. Begin your development of an intervention by: describing the system as you perceive it from a strengths-based perspective; identifying the barriers and challenges to change; and your thoughts on ways in which the Alvadora residents may be empowered to address their concerns about the state of their neighborhood.

CHAPTER 8

Fields of Social Work Practice

Like many students considering a career in social work, Emily was captivated with the range and diversity of employment possibilities. Through her social work classes, Emily learned that a BSW prepares her for generalist social work practice with a variety of persons and settings. The challenge for Emily then became narrowing her practice focus. Emily decided she needed to explore in depth the many and varied opportunities available to her as a BSW generalist social worker. In her investigation of the fields of social work practice, Emily used a number of strategies. She began by reading about fields of practice, using the Internet to learn about social work organizations and opportunities, talking to fellow students and faculty at her program, interviewing practicing social workers, and volunteering in a social service setting that provided her with a range of different experiences. Even as she progressed through this exploration, Emily could still see herself working in a number of different areas, but she felt confident that she was more aware of the breadth of opportunities that lie ahead for her.

Can you relate to Emily's dilemma? Social work is a profession that offers the potential to work in an array of fields. Many social workers are drawn to a particular field of practice as a result of life experiences or a strong interest in a particular setting or population. Have you considered the field or fields of practice that interest you? To get started in your investigation, Table 8.1 provides a sampling of the many fields of practice from which to choose.

For further insights into the realities of working in the field, in this chapter, eight social workers share their perspectives on the area of social work in which they practice. These "voices from the field" provide a window into the field of practice, the training and education required to work in that area, the rewards gained, challenges faced, and a perspective on the future of that field of social work practice. Written by the social workers themselves, these narratives are their views based on their own experiences. Each practitioner has a social work degree and is working with a different population and in a different setting, thus highlighting the

FIELD OF PRACTICE	SETTINGS
Mental health services	Community-based mental health centers
	In-patient-based psychiatric facilities
	Disaster relief programs
	Employee assistance programs
	Private practice
	Hospitals and rehabilitation programs
	Residential facilities
Medical social work	Hospitals and rehabilitation programs
	Community-based health care programs
	Community-based health education programs
Gerontological social work	Community-based service programs
	Hospitals and rehabilitation programs
	Residential facilities
	Adult day care programs
Chemical dependency and	Community-based treatment programs
addiction treatment	Hospital-based treatment programs
	Prevention and education programs
Child welfare services	Family service agencies
	Adoption programs
	Elementary and secondary schools
	Public child welfare agencies
School social work	Elementary and secondary schools
	Alternative school programs
International social work	U.S.-based immigrant and refugee programs
	Non-U.S.-based programs
	Disaster relief programs
	U.S.-based international programs
	Advocacy organizations
Domestic and family violence	Shelter-based programs
	Hospitals
	Legal system programs
	Community-based mental health programs
Criminal justice	Corrections settings
	Legal system programs
Crisis intervention	Disaster relief programs
	Victim assistance programs
Rural social work	Community service programs
	Hospitals and rehabilitation programs
Military social work	Military mental health and family service programs
	Deployment support programs
Community development	Non-profit and public sector
Community organizing	Community-based programs
Advocacy	Community-based programs
Policy Development and analysis	Non-profit and public sector programs

TABLE 8.1

Fields of Practice and Practice Settings

flexibility that social work degrees offer for working in a variety of settings with different populations throughout your career.

As you will learn in the three chapters that follow this chapter, social work interventions are built on the concept of planned change—a model that encompasses the stages of engagement of the client system, assessment of the situation to determine the strengths and barriers related to change, the planning and implementation of an intervention strategy, and the termination and evaluation of the helping relationship. As you follow the narratives contributed by the eight social workers in this chapter, you will gain an understanding of the planned change process that each embraces as they practice in their areas of social work practice.

GERONTOLOGICAL SOCIAL WORK PRACTICE

Practice with older adults, or **gerontological social work**, is a field of practice that is currently undergoing dramatic changes. With the anticipated increases in the older-adult population as the baby boomers reach their senior years and people live longer, the need for more health and social services is increasing. Currently, 13 percent of the U.S. population is age 65 or older (U.S. Census Bureau News, 2009). By 2030, all baby boomers will have reached age 65, making up nearly one-quarter of the U.S. population, and resulting in this population becoming larger than younger cohorts (He et al., 2005). More social workers will be needed to provide services to this population and their family members and caregivers, particularly in the areas of care coordination, case management, mental health services and supports, government program eligibility determination, care giving support and counseling (U.S. Department of Health and Human Services, 2006, p. 1).

Currently, less than 10 percent of social workers identify practice with older adults as their primary field of practice (Whitaker & Arrington, 2008). However, 78 percent of social workers report having contact with older clients (55+ years), while one-quarter have caseloads that are largely comprised of older adults (CHWS/CWS, 2006). Despite these statistics, only 7 percent of MSW students concentrate their education on gerontological social work practice, but over one-quarter of students in one survey reported taking an aging-related course as a undergraduate student and approximately 20% completed a graduate-level aging course (CSWE, 2006; Cummings et al., 2005). As the over-65 population reaches nearly one-quarter of the U.S. population, between 60,000 and 70,000 social workers will be needed in a wide range of fields, which is approximately double the number of social workers currently working in gerontological practice (CSWE, 2001). Moreover, exposure to gerontological issues during their education, attitudes toward older adults, and gaining gerontological social work skills predict the likelihood of a social worker pursuing employment with older adults (Cummings & Adler, 2007). Therefore, all social workers need increased awareness and skills for working with issues related to aging.

Practice Considerations with Older Adults

Through recent initiatives, social work educators have become aware of the need for increased emphasis on preparing students to work competently with older adults regardless of the setting in which they work. One such initiative, "Strengthening Aging and Gerontology Education for Social Work" (CSWE/SAGE-SW), has developed the following 10 competencies as being crucial for all social workers:

- Assess one's own values and biases regarding aging, death, and dying.

- Educate self to dispel the major myths about aging.

- Accept, respect, and recognize the right and need of older adults to make their own choices and decisions about their lives within the context of the law and safety concerns.

- Understand normal physical, psychological, and social changes in later life.

- Respect and address cultural, spiritual, and ethnic needs and beliefs of older adults and family members.

- Examine the diversity of attitudes toward aging, mental illness, and family roles.

- Understand the influence of aging on family dynamics.

- Use social work case management skills (such as brokering, advocacy, monitoring, and discharge planning) to link elders and their families to resources and services.

- Gather information regarding social history such as: social functioning, primary and secondary social supports, social activity level, social skills, financial status, cultural background, and social involvement.

- Identify ethical and professional boundary issues that commonly arise in work with older adults and their caregivers, such as client self-determination, end-of-life decisions, family conflicts, and guardianship.

Gerontological social workers practice with older adults in a variety of settings. Because much of the aging-related service delivery is provided by multiple disciplines, social workers often work directly with older adults and their families in host settings. A host setting is an organization whose primary mission is the provision of services other than social services (for example, health care or education). Such settings include hospitals; rehabilitation programs; residential care facilities (for example, skilled care and assisted living facilities, and senior independent living communities); adult day service programs; senior centers with congregate meal programs; home health agencies; and hospice programs. Gerontological social workers may work in agencies that provide case management services for older adults; they may investigate elder abuse, neglect, and exploitation; or provide supportive services for family members and caregivers.

Another important area of practice for gerontological social workers is policy practice. Influencing the development of legislation, policy, and programming for older adults is critical to the enhanced longevity and quality of life for the burgeoning older-adult population.

Carroll Rodriguez, BSW, Alzheimer's Association Chapter

I am the public policy director for a state coalition of Alzheimer's Association chapters (see Exhibit 8.1). I am charged with mobilizing others in an effort to bring about governmental and legislative changes that will benefit persons with Alzheimer's disease, their families, and their care partners. I work with the four state chapters, coordinating the state and national public policy activities for my state.

The route to becoming a state public policy director was not a straight one for me. Upon graduating with my BSW, I worked as a social worker in a skilled care nursing home and an adult day program. In these positions, I was responsible for facilitating support groups, working with older adults and their families, and coordinating admissions and care planning. Following a relocation with my family, I continued my gerontological social work career in community based services, working as a program supervisor with an area agency on aging.

In this position, I supervised senior center programs in rural communities and had the opportunity to open up several new senior centers in small communities that had not previously had services. From there, it was a natural progression for me to work for the Alzheimer's Association, where I started out working in the respite program in which I coordinated access to these much-needed services that provided a break for caregivers. These varied experiences gave me both valuable skills in working with families and insight into many different facets of care needed to maintain a quality of life for our older-adult population.

In my current position, I work to improve the laws and policies that govern the services provided to persons with Alzheimer's disease. Alzheimer's disease is one form of dementia (the terms are often used interchangeably), a progressive, degenerative disease of the brain for which there is no cure. As the most common form of dementia, it affects a person's memory, judgment, and ability to reason. More than 5.2 million Americans are living with Alzheimer's disease and millions more are impacted—the families and friends that serve as their care partners. A person with dementia will live an average of 8 years and as many as 20 years after the symptoms appear. As they advance through the disease process, long-term care and support are critical.

My experience as a social worker working with older adults prepared me well for working at the policy level. Having direct practice experience with this population in a variety of settings enables me to understand the needs of older adults and their

EXHIBIT 8.1

Alzheimer's Association

Alzheimer's Association St. Louis Chapter
9374 Olive Boulevard
St. Louis, Missouri 63132
www.alzstl.org
The mission of the Alzheimer's Association is to eliminate Alzheimer's disease
through the advancement of research and to enhance care and support for
individuals, their families, and caregivers. The association provides the following
services: Family Assistance Programs—Helpline, Care Consultation, Programs for
Individuals with Early Memory Loss, Support Groups, Respite Care Assistance, Family
& Community Education, and Professional Training.

care partners the gaps in the service delivery system, and the importance of ensuring
that policy-decision makers are well informed as they enact legislation and make
policy.

The Alzheimer's Association chapters are part of the nation's largest voluntary
health organization devoted to conquering Alzheimer's disease. Through a network
of more than seventy chapters across the country, individuals with the disease and
their care partners have access to a broad range of programs and services, and can
participate in support for research and advocacy. Because the association is such a
large organization that speaks on behalf of persons with Alzheimer's disease, we
have the opportunity to influence state and federal policies for this population.

State public policy activities and platform development begin with issue
identification. As I determine the areas for advocacy, I routinely ask the following

questions: What are the greatest unmet needs? Where are the gaps in services? How can we build an enhanced long-term care delivery system to meet the growing demands of an aging population? Answers to these questions can be found by listening to the voices of persons with the disease and their care partners.

Through focus groups, surveys, support group visits, and other means of communication, the coalition that I direct has identified three current areas of greatest need: (1) enhanced access to a continuum of long-term care services; (2) improved quality of care throughout the long-term care continuum; and (3) a cure for Alzheimer's disease. Identifying the conditions and needs is an essential first step in establishing the framework for development of a public policy platform.

Once a policy agenda is established, the next critical task is to develop potential solutions. This process involves coalition building and networking both internally, within the chapter network, and externally, with partners that have an interest in the issue. Health care providers, leadership within state agencies, researchers in the field of aging, and families with a vested interest in the issue are examples of partners that can aid in developing viable solutions and achievable goals.

Building on this process, I work with the coalition to outline a public policy platform that includes goals and objectives addressing the areas of focus. Some of the components that are necessary to advance a public policy initiative include drafting the language for proposed legislative bills; gaining sponsorship from legislators that are sensitive to and supportive of the issue; testifying at public hearings in front of legislators and voters; and building a broad base of supporters among voters, professionals, and legislators. Grassroots advocacy is at the core of this process. By mobilizing people that are passionate about an issue, a great deal can be accomplished, as shown by the following examples.

Every year, I travel with other advocates to my state capital and Washington, D.C., to talk with Congress about appropriations for funding research to find a cure for Alzheimer's disease, study the effects of this disease on individuals and their families, and to develop interventions to enhance their lives. Along with thousands of supporters, I write letters and e-mail and meet with legislators in the capitols and their home districts. As a result of these ongoing grassroots advocacy efforts, Congress has increased Alzheimer's research funding by more than $500 million over the last 13 years.

A current challenge for the families that I represent in my advocacy efforts is that both Medicare and private health insurance fail to address the chronic health care needs of persons with Alzheimer's disease. Medicaid serves as the safety net for long-term care services. The program supports community-based programs as well as nursing home care. Access to Medicaid services has become a primary area of focus for Alzheimer's advocates. Through grassroots efforts, we have worked to expand options, support, and access to home and community services.

A second area of challenge in my current advocacy work is promoting the quality of the care that is provided within those long-term care settings. More than half of all nursing home residents have some form of dementia, and the same holds true for assisted living facilities. My fellow advocates and I drafted and passed legislation in my state that requires all employees caring for persons with dementia to be trained in dementia care.

Working with a coalition of chapters to shape a public policy platform and mobilizing advocates to move that platform forward has required me to call upon a skill set acquired from both experience and education. With a BSW and 20 years of professional experience in the field of aging, I have learned the value of listening to others, the importance of negotiation and compromise, and the merits of networking and coalition building. However, of most importance is the realization that many voices can make change happen.

In terms of the future of my area of practice, it is projected that 14 million of today's baby boomers will develop Alzheimer's disease by midcentury. Costs for persons with Alzheimer's Disease will continue to increase as well. Annual public spending is projected by 2015 to be an estimated $189 billion (Medicare) and $30 billion (Medicaid); costs that will overwhelm our health care system and bankrupt both Medicare and Medicaid. Succinctly stated by the Alzheimer's Association, "We are facing a race against time." Now more than ever, there is a need for social workers to engage in public policy advocacy in support of persons with Alzheimer's disease and their care partners.

SOCIAL WORK PRACTICE WITH CHILDREN AND FAMILIES

Working with children and families is the second largest area of practice for social workers and is particularly popular with those with BSWs. Eleven percent of social workers report that they work in the area of child welfare and with families, but an additional 5 percent work with adolescents and 6 percent work in schools (Whitaker & Arrington, 2008).

Social work practice with children and families takes place in a wide variety of settings, including public child welfare agencies, residential care facilities, family service agencies, schools, mental health centers, chemical dependency and addiction treatment programs, agencies that serve persons with disabilities and health care settings. Services to children and families can be provided in settings that are publicly funded, nonprofit, and in the emerging for-profit area. Nearly half of social workers who work with children and families are employed in a private nonprofit setting with another 41 percent working in the public sector and the remaining 11 percent being in private for profit organizations (Whitaker & Arrington, 2008).

Practice Considerations with Children and Families

Social workers' responsibilities are equally as broad as the settings. They work in residential group homes as case managers, child care workers, and therapists. In public child welfare agencies, social workers investigate referrals about child abuse and neglect; and they work with children and families in the areas of alternative out-of-home care, prevention and adoption services, and family preservation and reunification programs. In private family service agencies, social workers also work with children and families in the areas of adoption, family preservation and reunification, alternative care, and in-home therapy programs. In agencies that provide services to persons with physical or mental illness, addictions, or disabilities, social workers complete intake assessments, develop and implement treatment plans and follow-up, provide individual and group therapy, and work with the children and/or their parents.

Greater emphasis has been given in recent years to the prevention of out-of-home placement for children and to strengthening the family's ability to function. As a result of this effort, specialized programs have been developed that focus on family preservation. The goal of family preservation programs is to enhance the family's ability to cope and manage. As social work education emphasizes a strengths-based, systems approach, social workers are well trained to serve as family preservation professionals. Social workers provide therapeutic case management, parenting education, and life skills services to families in both the family's home and agency settings.

School social work is another area of growth and opportunity for social workers. In schools, social workers conduct assessments, serve as liaisons between the school and the family, facilitate groups, and participate in multidisciplinary teams to develop individual educational plans for students. Through the provision of one-on-one and family services as well as educational and prevention programs, school social workers also provide support for those students at risk for poor academic and social outcomes.

One of the most serious issues confronting social workers who intervene with children and families is child abuse and neglect. **Child abuse** occurs when a child is subjected to physical and/or emotional injury and includes sexual abuse. **Child neglect** is considered to exist when the child's caregiver does not ensure that the child's emotional, physical, nutritional, educational, or shelter needs are being met. Public education and media attention has increased awareness of child abuse and neglect and the reporting process. Reports are made most frequently by school personnel. Other primary reporters include professionals from social service agencies, law enforcement, and health care organizations. Many professionals that work in these settings are legally mandated to report suspected cases of child abuse, neglect, or exploitation. Non-mandated reporters (for example, family, friends, neighbors, or observers) can make anonymous reports and are protected from prosecution as long as the report is not made with malicious intent. As a result of mandated reporting and increasing rates of reporting, the number of children entering the foster care system is increasing, with the number of children entering out-of-home placements each year exceeding the number that are returned to their homes. Working with a vulnerable population such as children who have been abused or neglected is not only consistent with the profession's mission, but children and families outcomes are improved by working with degreed social workers (NASW, 2005c). For these reasons, NASW's *Standards for social work practice in child welfare* (2005c) and 2009–2012 policy statement provide guidelines for competent practice with children and also call for better support for the social workers who work in this area.

Angela (Chierek) Bratcher, BSW, MSW, LCSW

Former social work position: Department of Social Services, Children's Division

Current social work position: Boys and Girls Town of Missouri

I received my bachelor's and master's degrees in social work. I have also completed the requirements to be a licensed clinical social worker. I was employed by the state Children's Division as a Social Service Worker II in a Child Abuse and Neglect unit for five years. I am currently employed at Boys and Girls Town of Missouri as a behavior specialist in the Fostering Futures program.

My position as a Social Service Worker II was the foundation of my experience in the social work field. My primary responsibility consisted of responding to mandated reports of suspected child abuse and neglect and preventive reports made through the agency's hotline. Mandated reports are made by professionals who work with children such as social workers, physicians, and day care workers, and are mandated by law to report suspected child abuse and neglect. A preventive report may be made by any concerned person and often relates to a family's need for services such as counseling or utility assistance referrals. Preventive reports do not usually contain any concerns of abuse or neglect by the child's parent or caretaker.

In general, child welfare workers are very focused on their role in the child protection system. It is essential to have professionals working for and with the children, since children cannot protect themselves. Using a strength-based approach, social workers working in child welfare agencies emphasize the strengths of the families with whom they are working, as this is important in achieving positive outcomes for families. An emphasis on teamwork is also a strength within the Child Abuse and Neglect unit and the community as a whole. Social workers support each other with resources to assist families and in the process of placing children in foster care. An increased emphasis is also being placed on implementing community support for children and families. By connecting children and families to their communities, a safety net is created for them in the event of another crisis.

My work was challenging and demanding as family situations vary—from substance abuse to the need for parenting, conflict management, or help with appropriate discipline. One of the first challenges for any worker is to engage families in their involvement with Children's Division. A family may be angry about the report, which can be an obstacle to their active involvement in the case.

Some issues cannot be addressed by providing services to families in their home. Severe physical and sexual abuse place the child's safety at immediate risk of suffering more abuse or neglect. In these cases, the child or children must either be temporarily placed with a relative with a safety plan to protect them, or the child must be taken into protective custody by the court and placed in foster care. If a child is temporarily placed with a relative, the allegations are investigated and a decision is made based on evidence compiled during the investigation. If the child is placed into protective custody, there will be an initial protective custody hearing to determine whether the child will remain in foster care. The foster care worker and the parents will develop a service plan to work toward reunification of the parents and child.

Properly supporting and providing services to families is challenging enough without the ongoing challenge of handling typically large caseloads. This requires concentrated focus on prioritizing the needs of some families over the needs of other families whose children are considered safe. Attracting and retaining workers with social work education who want to work in the field of child welfare is challenging as well. Not all child welfare agencies require service workers to have a social work degree, but our social work training makes us well suited for the field of child welfare because we are trained to fully focus on the needs of the family. I would like to see more degreed social workers working in these positions.

My experience in child welfare has taught me that the children who are placed in foster care often come from environments that lack structure and nurturance. These factors often result in behavior problems when a child is placed in a foster home. After five years working in public child welfare, I used my experience to gain employment as a behavior specialist in the Fostering Futures program. In my current position, my goal is to stabilize a child's placement using behavior management. Children in foster care can have a minimum number of placements in different homes or residential settings, or they can have many placements. Recurring placements is often another setback that children in foster care experience that this program seeks to prevent.

Each child referred to Fostering Futures has different behaviors that may result in disrupting their foster home placement. These behaviors may include temper tantrums, lying, stealing, talking back, difficulty following rules of the household, and substance use. Each child's behaviors are assessed through information gathered from the foster parent, case manager, the child and by direct observation by the specialist. I develop an individualized behavior plan to address the unique needs of each child. This plan serves as the guideline for implementing activities that address the child's behaviors through weekly home visits. The activities utilize therapeutic techniques including play therapy and art therapy which provide non-verbal outlets for feelings.

Through my work with children in foster care, I have discovered that children do want to improve their behavior. Acting-out behaviors are often just an outlet for the children's feelings of anger, loss and trauma associated with being in foster care. By teaching the children alternative strategies for dealing with their feelings, the children's behavior will eventually improve.

Another factor essential to stabilizing a child's foster care placement is the cooperation of foster parents. Although the training foster parents receive does inform them about the situations that children in foster care experience, they are often unprepared to handle the child's behaviors. I educate foster parents to understand the reasons behind the behaviors so they are more willing to work with the children instead of asking for the child to be removed from their home. By working with the foster parents on these issues and through consistency with implementation, the placement often becomes more stable. Foster parents have to be flexible and open to trying different techniques in handling a child's behavior instead of believing that one approach will work with every child.

The future of services for children in foster care is focusing on stabilization to reduce multiple placements. Improved education for foster parents is also needed so they understand the issues that children in foster care face and develop strategies for handling the issues. Nationally, greater emphasis needs to be put on permanency for children in foster care as stipulated by the 1997 Adoption and Safe Families Act. Many children are still lingering in foster care for several years without a permanent living arrangement, which does not allow children to obtain the security of a family.

Being a social worker who provides services to children in the child welfare system can be challenging and demanding, but also rewarding. As a beginning social worker working in children's services, I had a great opportunity to hone my organizational skills and learn a variety of different intervention strategies. This knowledge provided the framework for me to continue my work with children in foster care, by providing interventions that bring more stability to their lives.

SOCIAL WORK PRACTICE WITH IMMIGRANTS AND REFUGEES

The number of current U.S. residents born in other countries exceeded 38 million in 2007 (U.S. Census Bureau, 2009b). Persons born outside the United States who are living here may be in the country as a refugee or asylum seeker or here on an immigrant, student, business, or extended visa, or without documentation. In recent years, the largest numbers of immigrants were born in Mexico, China, the Philippines, El Salvador, Vietnam, and Korea with over one-quarter having entered the country since 2000 (U.S. Census Bureau, 2009).

Practice Considerations with Immigrants and Refugees

Social workers in the United States have always worked with an array of international issues, including providing services to people who immigrate to this country from their homelands. In the area of international adoptions, social workers assist families in applying, conduct home studies, act as liaison to the international adoption organization, and provide post adoption support services. Social workers also provide services in international emergency and disaster situations and in administering U.S.-based programs that provide services in the international community.

In addition to working with international issues, social workers play a prominent role in working with immigrants and refugees living in the United States. The settlement house movement focused originally on the provision of services to recent immigrants to the United States. Training social workers who are culturally competent and sensitive to the needs of the many and varied populations of persons that are new to this country is a priority for the profession.

Working with persons born in other countries will span the spectrum of the social work population, thus requiring U.S.-based social workers in virtually every field of practice to have the knowledge and skills for practicing with diverse populations. Social workers may work in direct practice with individuals and families that have immigrated to this country, or they may work in the policy and advocacy arena on behalf of entire communities of persons who have relocated to the United States. Policies toward newer residents are often conflicted, thus creating a need for social workers to become the voice for this population. Therefore NASW has called for the federal government to support immigrants and refugees through enactment of legislation and programming that ensures fair and equitable actions (NASW, 2009–2012d).

Suzanne LeLaurin, MSW, LCSW, International Institute

I am a social worker who works with persons who have emigrated from other countries to the United States. I am the senior vice president for individuals and families at a refugee resettlement agency. I oversee several departments that provide a variety of services to immigrants and their families. In the client services department, we provide case management, employment, social work and counseling services for newly arrived refugees. The education department is responsible for teaching English to speakers of other languages. The program development / quality assurance department is responsible for continuous quality improvement and staff training on grant requirements.

Social work is a second career for me. After spending over 20 years in the for-profit sector working for a large insurance company, I decided I wanted to work in the nonprofit sector, and chose to get my MSW because I want to help others gain access to needed services and enhance their quality of life. Since completing my MSW, I have obtained my license to practice clinical social work in my state.

In reflecting on my social work practice working with persons born in another country, I must include an emphasis on politics and advocacy. The United States is a country of immigrants, but as a society, we have conflicting views about the importance of immigrants to our country. In the mid-1990s, Congress passed legislation that restricted access by noncitizens who entered the United States legally to benefits available to U.S. citizens. There have been initiatives to ease those restrictions, especially since they were harming some of the most vulnerable persons in our society—seniors who had been unable to learn English sufficiently to obtain citizenship and were increasingly at risk of homelessness as well as despair (which pushed some of them to suicide).

With the horrifying terrorist attacks on the United States on 9/11/2001, many of the moves to welcome the immigrant to our shores shifted once again. Security tightened for all immigrants attempting to enter the United States. The effects were most pronounced with refugee migration—the largest population with which I work—as the number of refugees admitted dropped from almost 70,000 in fiscal year 2001 to fewer than 30,000 in 2002.

Advocacy became paramount in social work with immigrants, as the rise in anti-immigrant fever increased. My own agency worked with an advocacy group to accompany our clients to their preferred farmer's market and doctor's appointments, just to protect them from shouts of "go home, terrorist" and worse. One of my own staff, a former refugee herself, slept with her clothes on and a stick and her cell phone with her, for fear of intruders. Thankfully, the panic from 9/11 has died down, but the events of that horrible day gave new impetus to the strong anti-immigration sentiment of those fighting political gains for immigrants.

Counterbalancing the political forces to keep immigrants out of our country are the needs of employers. With the baby boom generation aging and birth rates decreasing in the United States, employers and policy experts are beginning to recognize that future growth in employment forces will depend on migration into our country. But during the recession of 2008–09, job opportunities were drying up for both American-born and foreign-born.

For the near future, it is likely that we will continue to see fewer refugees and other immigrants enter the United States. In spite of the lower numbers, however, we will still see those born in other countries in our midst, both to fuel our economy through a skilled workforce and because, unfortunately, we still experience war and civil unrest around the world, leading to refugees needing safe haven.

For those social workers interested in working with persons with diverse national origins, there will be many opportunities to provide a variety of social work services for refugees, those who are forced to flee their homelands due to civil unrest, persecution, and violence. These persons are considered "reluctant immigrants," as they did not choose to leave their homelands, but were forced to do so by circumstances beyond their control. Typically, they arrive here with little more than the clothes on their backs. This population needs and will continue to need our support in basic necessities (food, clothing, and shelter), learning the English language, employment, adapting to U.S. culture (while hopefully holding on to the richness of their own culture), and mental health services for coming to terms with the horrors of trauma and torture. These needs will also exist for migrant workers that come into the United States intent on making enough money to support their families, with a risk of exploitation by unscrupulous employers taking advantage of their undocumented status.

There is a growing need for cultural diversity training for those born in the United States that expands the definition of diversity beyond the traditional black-white-indigenous population categories into cultural diversity based on ethnicity. Our religious communities, while already pluralistic, will also shift beyond the dominant Judeo-Christian faiths, which will lead us to a need for diversity training for a variety of groups—other social service providers, employers, educators, medical professionals, and many more.

We also need to adapt our social work services to accommodate the needs of those whose cultural norms are different from those of the United States. Social workers must ask themselves questions like the ones I've asked myself. How do I, as a feminist, react to and serve a conservative Muslim woman who considers it immodest to show any parts of her body other than her hands and face; yet her clothing limits her ability to work in the only job I can find for her, such as a manufacturing job that requires clothing not get in the way of machines? How do I work with teenagers and parents experiencing family conflicts in which the teens are "Americanized" into thinking that adolescence is a time to "move away" from parents and become independent, while the parents come from a culture in which youth independence brings great shame on the family in their cultural community? How do I counsel an adult woman with an aging mother in need of long-term care, but who considers the idea of putting her mother in a skilled nursing facility a shameful rejection of her responsibilities as a dutiful and respectful daughter? Is self-esteem just a western construct, or does it have application in a culture that is more collectivist than individualistic? As social workers, we will all be challenged to serve those with different values and beliefs from our own, and these differences will be much more pronounced with those who were born in other cultures.

The great joy—and challenge—of working with persons from diverse national origins is that they help me see the world through a different cultural and political lens, influenced by their own life experiences, cultural norms, and beliefs that are so different from my own. I am in awe of the resilience and spirit of the refugees that come to this country, prepared to start building a whole new life after the one they knew was shattered and stolen from them. I am challenged to see my world through another person's eyes, and find myself questioning some of my own deeply held assumptions about my country and culture. The world has gotten so much smaller—and more exciting—for me after working with an international population for so many years.

SOCIAL WORK PRACTICE WITH CHEMICAL DEPENDENCY AND ADDICTION

An area of practice in which social workers have long been involved, chemical dependency and addiction treatment has undergone dramatic changes in recent years. Early substance abuse treatment efforts focused primarily on the rehabilitation of the persons addicted to alcohol, and the treatment was in the form of Alcoholics Anonymous, a model focused on mutual peer support. Inpatient treatment programs emerged during the 1970s for the treatment of alcoholism and other drug addictions. Restrictions imposed on treatment programs by the health insurance industry regarding the amount of reimbursement for treatment resulted in the elimination of many in-patient programs because clients were no longer able to afford the cost. In fact, nearly one-third of those seeking addictions treatment do not have insurance that will cover treatment (CHWS/CWS, 2006). As a result, chemical dependency and addiction treatment is now typically provided through a combination of short-term in-patient treatment followed by a period of out-patient treatment known as aftercare.

Practice Considerations in Chemical Dependency and Addiction

Despite the changes in the societal response to chemical dependency and addiction, the prevalence of chemical dependency and other addictions has not dissipated. As a result of the shift away from large in-patient programs, a relatively small number of social workers identify substance abuse (also referred to as alcohol, tobacco, and other drugs (ATOD) as their primary area of practice. Fewer than five percent of NASW members surveyed indicated addictions as their primary practice area (Whitaker & Arrington, 2008). Social workers who work in chemical dependency and addiction treatment programs are typically employed by private for-profit and private nonprofit organizations. Despite the relatively small number of social workers currently working in this field of practice, employment for social workers in this area is expected to increase by approximately 30 percent in the coming years (U.S. Department of Labor Bureau of Labor Statistics, 2009a).

Although a small percentage of social workers practice exclusively in the field of chemical dependency and addiction treatment, knowledge of addiction prevention and intervention is critical for social workers in virtually every field of practice. Substance use and abuse and addiction issues frequently overlap in such areas as mental illness, domestic violence, and corrections; therefore, social workers in these areas must be able to identify signs of chemical dependency and addiction. Because knowledge of substance abuse and addictions is essential for all social work practitioners, NASW has developed *Standards for Social Work Practice with Clients with Substance Use Disorders* (2005). This set of standards provides guidelines to all social workers regarding the need to understand addictions, appropriate and ethical interventions, and the role social workers can have in advocating and educating for client systems.

As you will read in the following narrative, the issue of dual diagnosis is prevalent in this area of the social worker's practice. **Dual diagnosis** occurs when the person is thought to be experiencing two diseases or conditions simultaneously, and the interaction of the two diseases can impede diagnosis and treatment.

Within chemical dependency and addiction treatment, dual diagnosis is typically the presence of mental illness and chemical dependence.

Jon Hudson, BSW, Chestnut Health Systems, Inc.

I am a BSW student completing my practicum at a large agency that provides treatment for adolescents with chemical dependency. I want to practice clinical social work, and because clinical work often involves chemical dependency issues, I need to have experience in this area. I find it an honor to work with these young people as they struggle with issues of chemical dependence. Although this is my first formal social work practice experience, I gained experience through volunteering and working part-time in several social service settings before beginning my practicum. My volunteer and employment experiences helped me to determine the areas of social work in which I would like to practice and the populations on which I want to focus my practice.

The residential program at my practicum site is separated by gender. I work in the capacity of a chemical dependence counselor on the male unit. In this setting, a substance abuse counselor provides treatment to individual clients and their families, facilitates group therapy, and works in teams with other counselors to maintain the daily routine of the treatment unit. The unit where I work houses 20 boys ranging in age from 13 to 17 years. Nearly all of the residents are court mandated to chemical dependency treatment, but the reasons for their sentences are not always related directly to use or abuse of substances.

More often, they are arrested for other crimes and discovered to be under the influence of substances during the arrest process. Most of the boys are from modest socioeconomic backgrounds, and their formal education has been interrupted as a result of their criminal activities and lack of family support. Some of the boys are dually diagnosed with a mental illness and chemical dependence. Working with persons who are dually diagnosed presents a special challenge in treatment, as both conditions must be addressed simultaneously.

Treatment of a person with a dual diagnosis usually results in a boy working with his counselor and a staff psychiatrist who provides medication and treatment for the mental illness. The counselor must be knowledgeable about the diagnosis and treatment of both conditions and balance the mental illness, chemical dependence, and, oftentimes, legal issues all at the same time.

Persons who are dually diagnosed may not be aware of the existence of a mental illness and be shocked to learn of it. The client may have been abusing drugs as a way to deal with the symptoms of mental illness and have difficulty accepting that he now has to grapple with two crises. Typically, the boy unwillingly enters the treatment program without knowing what to expect. As a result, he has no idea how to cope, and the news of a dual diagnosis puts extra stress on him. As a result, he may appear to be getting worse after the first few weeks in residence. I think the thing that touched me most was that learning that he has a dual diagnosis often makes the young man or boy feel more broken than he already feels.

A program such as the one in which I am completing my practicum provides judges with the option of sentencing alternatives that are more appropriate for developing young men and women. The fact that the boy or girl may have committed a crime, possibly several crimes, is secondary to the consideration that jail is not appropriate for everyone who commits a crime, especially children and adolescents. The program introduces the young people to treatment and healthy recovery before they have become entrenched in a maladaptive pattern of misuse of chemical substances. The longer a person is chemically dependent and actively using substances, the more difficult it is for her or him to break the cycle of dependence.

In my practicum, I am learning that there are special considerations when a client and a clinician are dealing with issues of chemical dependence. Many substances require a long time to clear the body. This can result in the person being in the treatment and recovery process longer, which increases the chances for long-term abstinence and recovery. In many parts of the world, the length of time a person is in treatment has become the leading issue in the search for new models of addiction treatment.

Traditional models of substance abuse treatment are based on the 12 steps of Alcoholics Anonymous and have complete abstinence as the primary goal. Since its beginnings in the 1930s, this model has been effective for millions of men and women suffering from chemical dependence. The model dictates that sufferers must first stop using chemicals and then admit they are chemically dependent and powerless over their substance of choice. One of the challenges that I have identified in this field of practice is that, although the 12-step model has a long-standing history, the addict must cease all drug use before she or he can move through recovery. I have observed that this approach works well for some in a self-help environment. In the framework of a treatment model, however, if the goal is to stop using and remain abstinent, cessation should not be a requirement to begin treatment.

In my practicum, I have been exposed to a new model of substance abuse treatment. The Harm Reduction model is finding success in many parts of the world, but is still controversial in the United States. Harm Reduction is based on the idea that the longer a person is engaged in the treatment and recovery process, the better her or his chances are for long-term recovery. Harm Reduction encourages the client to prioritize goals and does not require her or him to become and remain abstinent at any point. The user may see her or his problem as cocaine and not alcohol, for example, even though both are being used in a maladaptive pattern. The social worker using a Harm Reduction framework recognizes value in the client's theory and builds on that strength. Why does the social worker, who can clearly see that the person has a problem with cocaine and alcohol, concur with the client's theory of the problem? The social worker knows she or he can keep the client engaged in the recovery process longer by working on what the person sees as the problem, and the longer the person is engaged, the more likelihood of long-term change.

An example of a Harm Reduction program may be a needle exchange program in a city where the incidence of intravenous drug use is high. Opponents of the Harm Reduction approach claim that needle exchange does not work because it does not reduce the number of intravenous (IV) drug users. However, the incidence of new HIV infection is reduced, and this creates a safer, less harmful environment for everyone by reducing or eliminating the incidence of needle sharing. Needle exchange ensures that IV drug users are introduced to the treatment and recovery process; thus the seed is planted and the process begins.

I decided on social work as a profession because I believe in values of social justice, the dignity and worth of the person, a person's right to self-determination, and the importance of human relationships as outlined in the National Association of Social Workers *Code of Ethics* (2008). Through my coursework and practicum, I have learned to engage, assess, and intervene with client systems. Also of importance are the skills of critical thinking and evaluation.

Because I have learned the value of thinking critically about my practice, I have come to understand that treatment models for chemical dependence work can vary and are more effective with multidisciplinary professional teams that include social workers as integral, working parts of the models.

As a social worker I have been educated and trained in an approach that involves not only the person and her or his disorder. The social work perspective takes into consideration the person in her or his environment over time. This multidisciplinary approach transcends and includes approaches from the fields of psychology, sociology, anthropology, biology, and history. Social work theory helps me to understand that I need to integrate the biological, psychological, and social aspects of a person to understand her or his disease. In order to help a person in a competent and respectful manner, I need to know where the person lives, the education, family history, ethnic and cultural background, spiritual beliefs, and most importantly, the way in which the person perceives the condition or situation that prompted her or him to ask for help and the path to change.

SOCIAL WORK PRACTICE IN CRIMINAL JUSTICE

One area of **forensic social work**, social work practice in criminal justice, is a growing area for social work employment. Forensic social work is the practice of social work in areas relating to the law and legal systems, including the criminal and civil legal systems. Examples include child, older adult, and spouse/partner abuse; child custody; juvenile and adult criminal issues; and corrections.

Prompted by media and political attention, society has experienced an increased focus on crime and criminals. An increasing number of persons are being jailed, most in state and county facilities. Half of the residents of correctional facilities are awaiting trial, and many are persons of color and of low socioeconomic status. More than half of persons who encounter the criminal justice system are under the influence of alcohol or other substances during the time in which the crime for which they are accused was committed. For these reasons, NASW calls for social workers to be trained as culturally competent, forensic professionals who can develop intervention plans to address the client within the criminal justice system (NASW, 2009–2012d).

Practice Considerations in Criminal Justice

Social work practice in criminal justice encompasses a wide range of settings and issues. Social workers in this field of practice may work in adult or juvenile correctional facilities, community-based probation and parole agencies, mental health facilities, public defenders' offices, law firms, legal services organizations that represent the accused and the victims, juvenile or family court agencies, law enforcement agencies, or programs that respond to issues of domestic and family violence (Rome, 2008). Despite the fact that social workers have been involved in social work practice in criminal justice since the 1800s, the number of social workers that identify criminal justice as a primary area of practice is small (Rome, 2008; Whitaker & Arrington, 2008). However, because of the array of settings, some social workers may identify their primary practice of focus in a related area (for example, mental health or chemical dependency and addiction treatment). Practice in criminal justice is an employment option for BSW social workers. A relatively new area of focus for social workers interested in the legal system is to complete both a graduate social work and law degree.

Herbert Bernsen, MSW, County Department of Justice Services

I am the assistant director for a county Department of Justice Services (see Exhibit 8.2). I have a master's degree in social work. Through my involvement in the field of corrections, I have been designated a Certified Jail Manager by the American Jail Association. Because I have learned the importance of collaborating with others in the community whose services overlap with the criminal justice system, I am actively involved with several community organizations. I serve on the board of an Adult Basic Education program that provides GED teachers for inmates and am a board member for an organization that provides services to persons with developmental disabilities who encounter the criminal justice system.

I began my career in criminal justice social work while I was a student in the MSW program. I worked as a probation and parole officer and have continued in this field for the past 37 years. I have also served as a superintendent of the maximum and medium security correctional institutions.

My department is responsible for the operation of the county jail and the Community Corrections Division. The populations that we encounter are adult men and women, 17 years of age and older, charged with crimes ranging from felonies and misdemeanors to county ordinance violations. The capacity of the jail at which I work is 1,232 inmates. In 2008, 30,474 persons were booked at the jail, and the average daily population was 1186 inmates. The population consists primarily of those inmates awaiting trial, but inmates are sentenced to the jail for periods up to one year. For sentences exceeding one year, inmates are normally sent to the state prison system operated by the Department of Corrections.

The management philosophy used in our general population housing area is considered direct supervision. Correctional officers are stationed inside the housing area pods enabling officers to take a proactive role in controlling inmate behavior and minimizing tension. We find that assaults against staff and other inmates are significantly reduced in our current direct supervision facility compared to our previous linear design facility. In the more traditional linear facility, officers only intermittently observe inmates when they conduct patrols in front of their cells. In direct supervision facilities, the officer is inside the living area and she or he can often stop problems early before they escalate.

EXHIBIT 8.2

St. Louis County Department of Justice Services

St. Louis County Department of Justice Services
100 South Central Avenue
St. Louis, Missouri 63105
The St. Louis County Department of Justice Services is responsible for the operation of the St. Louis county jail and the Division of Community Corrections. The county jail provides 1,232 beds for the county's minimum, medium, and maximum security inmates. The Division of Community Corrections is located in a nearby building and is responsible for the operation of the Alternative Community Services Program, Mental Health Court and Probation Supervision Unit.

Photographs provided by Hellmuth, Obata, and Kassabaum, Inc.

Communication is the key skill for officers in dealing with inmates. Most inmates follow the rules because they want to live in a safe and secure environment. We set high expectations for inmate behavior, and this becomes a self-fulfilling prophecy. Inmates prefer to live in an environment in which the officer is the leader, not the toughest inmate. If an inmate consistently violates the rules, she or he is moved to an indirect housing unit with reduced privileges and restricted movement.

The most important part of the corrections department mission is to ensure inmate safety and security. As an administrator, I read daily reports and review incident reports. If there are numerous inmate assaults against other inmates or staff, we are not doing our job. Supervisors must make frequent inspections. Cells and inmate living areas must be routinely searched. If homemade weapons are being made, inmates cannot feel safe. Inmates are taught the rules and the possible sanctions for violating the rules. They also know that their right to a due process hearing to determine their guilt or innocence is affirmed.

The social worker in the corrections area works as a member of a multidisciplinary team. The social worker/case worker is responsible for conducting the initial assessment when the inmate is booked and processed into the jail setting. Often, this assessment involves crisis intervention, as the social worker must evaluate the inmate's current emotional state to identify issues such as suicidal ideation and mental illness. This assessment provides the basis for determining the part of the jail system in which the inmate will be housed. Second, social workers are responsible for coordinating and participating in the educational and treatment programs provided for the inmates. Casework also involves prioritizing the needs of the inmates through regular contact during their incarceration to assess how the inmate is functioning within the jail population and any issues that she or he is faced with from external sources (for example, family or financial). The social worker serves as a liaison with the legal system to monitor the inmate's case progress and with employers when inmates are participating in the work release program. Lastly, the social worker is often responsible for working with those inmates that need assistance upon release from jail to ensure that they are integrated effectively back into their communities.

One of the challenges of working in criminal justice is the high incidence of mental illness and drug abuse. In the early 1960s, there was an effort to deinstitutionalize vast numbers of persons with mental illness and provide the consequent community support and housing that would be needed. The community support for this effort fell woefully short. As a result, jails often became the place of last resort for those persons suffering from mental illness, not all of who had committed crimes. We have certainly needed to hire psychiatrists, psychologists, and social workers to work with persons diagnosed with mental illness inside our jails. Many of those experiencing mental illness do not, however, belong in jail in the first place.

Because I was aware of the inappropriate placement of many persons that suffered from mental illness, I was instrumental in forming a mental health court task force consisting of community mental health providers and criminal justice agencies. The goal of this task force was to establish a mental health court to divert persons with serious mental health disorders from the criminal justice system to appropriate mental health treatment and services in order to improve their mental health functioning and deter future criminal behavior. To ensure the provision of comprehensive services, we worked closely with the police department to implement their Crisis Intervention Team (CIT) program. In this program, police officers are trained to intervene in situations involving persons with mental illness. Our other partners included an advocacy group, the state mental health agency, a nonprofit mental health agency, and a university social work program along with judges, prosecutors, public defenders, probation officers, and our corrections department at the county jail.

Another challenge faced by social workers in criminal justice is the issue of substance abuse. Along with mental illness, the inmate population contains many persons that use and abuse alcohol and other drugs. My department has made a significant commitment to the treatment of substance abuse within the jail through the Choices Substance Abuse Recovery Program. Using a 12-step model, the program provides 90 days of treatment for male and female inmates with the goal of empowering participants to choose a lifestyle free of alcohol and other drug addictions and criminal behavior. During the past ten years, the Choices program served 2,120 inmates. Judges have embraced the program, and there has been a waiting list since the program's inception.

Each year, faculty and students at a local university evaluate the program, and each year the program consistently shows positive results. For example, during Years 2–9, seventy-two percent of those inmates who completed the program resided in the community without being arrested for a new crime or having their probation revoked or suspended. By the ninth year of the program, 91 percent of the participants successfully completed the program.

I have learned that providing educational opportunities is also important for helping inmates to initiate changes in their life. Local school districts provide instructors to prepare inmates to take the high school equivalency exam. Inmates have the opportunity to be tested. In 2008, 133 inmates took the GED test, and 90 received their diploma.

The successful operation of our jail and the programs that I have described here also depends on volunteers. There are currently over 300 active volunteers at the jail. Programs conducted by volunteers include creative writing, individual counseling, religious services, literacy assistance, leadership classes, substance abuse education, and support groups for substance abusers. The volunteers have a positive influence on the well-being of the inmates both inside and outside of confinement.

The field of social work in criminal justice has many challenges. Jails and prisons are being inundated with inmates with mental health and substance abuse problems. Jails and prisons have the highest rates of suicide in our society. In these times of scarce resources and reduced budgets, it is important to form partnerships with community leaders and organizations to provide services for inmate populations.

The future for social workers working in criminal justice is promising. There are a myriad of opportunities for correctional officers, social service staff, medical and mental health staff, and administrators in this field of practice. Innovations in inmate supervision and treatment, public health, technology, and community aftercare are examples of areas for growth and development. The vast majority of jail and prison inmates will be returning to their communities. The resources directed toward inmate populations during and after incarceration will pay significant dividends to the individuals, their families, and the community.

SOCIAL WORK PRACTICE IN HEALTH SETTINGS

The National Association of Social Workers reports that approximately 14 percent of social workers practice in health-related settings and this number is expected to increase by 24 percent in the coming years (Whitaker & Arrington, 2008; U.S. Department of Labor Bureau of Labor Statistics, 2009a). All areas of health care practice will grow faster than the average job growth. The growing older adult population and baby boomer generation account for a significant portion of these expected growth rates. With the shortened length of stay in hospitals and the increase of the older adult population, social workers are employed in more outpatient health care settings than inpatient (U. S. Department of Labor Bureau of Labor Statistics, 2009a).

Practice Considerations in Health Settings

Social workers who practice in any of the areas of health care social work, medical, mental health, substance abuse, or public health have the opportunity to work in a variety of organizations with a wide array of client systems and with a range of other professions. While health care social workers provide services across the lifespan from neo-natal intensive care to skilled nursing facilities, they share a common purpose: assist individuals and families function in response to health issues; prevent social and emotional issues from impacting health; and address service inadequacies (NASW, 2006–2009b). Social workers work in interprofessional teams in inpatient hospitals, out-patient medical clinics, health-specific educational and advocacy organizations, residential care facilities, skilled nursing facilities, rehabilitation settings, public health agencies, hospice, home health care, and mental health and substance abuse settings. Some of these organizations work with individuals across the lifespan, others are specific to adults, adolescents, or children. In other organizational settings, many are focused on a particular disease management such as HIV/AIDS, multiple sclerosis, Alzheimer's Disease, or diabetes. A shift toward providing services in the primary care setting is providing new opportunities for social workers who can engage in screening, assessments, and treatment protocols in the out-patient setting (Rock, 2009). With $155 million allocated by President Obama in 2009 to fund 126 new community health centers, social workers will have increased opportunities to serve the uninsured and underinsured in community settings.

Social work in the health field requires the social worker to have knowledge of the biological, psychological, spiritual and social aspects of human functioning along with the skills to work with other professionals that provide health care services. Understanding the distinct and overlapping roles of all the professions that work with the health care consumer population is key to being an effective health care social worker. Health care social work involves an integration of direct practice with individuals and families as well as an awareness of the impact of policies and the willingness to serve as an advocate for patients' needs. In an effort to ensure quality practice, NASW established *Standards for social work practice in health care settings* (2005d), which provide guidelines in the areas of ethics, social justice, cultural competence, privacy and confidentiality, theory, interprofessional practice, and documentation. These standards apply to health social workers in all settings.

Jane Sprankel, MSW, LCSW, Neighborhood Health Center

I have a master's degree in social work and am a social worker in the health field. In college, my first undergraduate major was education. I thought teaching would fill my desire to help people. I met some college students at a summer job and they were talking about their social work major. After I listened to what they were studying and their practicum experiences, a light bulb went on for me! I wanted to be a social worker. I changed my major and never looked back. My first practicum experience was in a community mental health center working with mental health consumers who had just been released from the state in-patient facility. While I have enjoyed all of the social work jobs I have had, it is health care where I have found my specialty.

As I pursued my MSW, I studied both macro and micro practice in health care. Upon completion of my MSW as I was considering the best place for me to begin my MSW career, a friend encouraged me to consider social work in a hospital. She said she found it interesting, fast paced, challenging, and it required the use of all social work skills, from policy to therapy. I took my friend's suggestion and entered the world of hospital social work. I discovered that her assessment of the work has been true throughout my career.

As an MSW social worker in the health field, I felt it was important to obtain the credentials that certify my competence as a social work professional. Therefore, I obtained my ACSW, a national credential that certifies me as a member of the NASW Academy of Certified Social Workers (ACSW), and a license to practice clinical social work in my state.

As a new hospital social worker, I began my work at a community-based hospital assigned to the rehabilitation/skilled nursing unit. The population I served was primarily older adults that experienced a health event and were in need of physical rehabilitation or skilled nursing care because they are no longer able to care for their own basic, daily needs. I was a member of an interprofessional team comprised of professionals in nursing; physical, occupational, and speech therapy; dietetics; and nurse case managers. My responsibilities were to assist with discharge planning, coping with illness and injury, patient and family education, and community resource referrals. During my time in this position, I developed a patient education program and support group for caregivers, became a part of an interprofessional team that provided diabetic education for patients and families, and facilitated a support group for patients with chronic pulmonary disease.

Along with the direct practice opportunities, I saw the impact of state and federal policy on our patients' ability to access services. Through professional organizations, I participated in working on changing Medicare and Medicaid policies. Through these experiences, the issues affecting older adults and their families became an area of increased interest for me. When I first began to work with older adults, I realized I saw them through my eyes and my age; but with more experience, I now see them through their eyes and their years of wisdom and living.

After four years in my first MSW social work position, I found myself wanting to specialize in the area of rehabilitation and obtained a position as rehabilitation social worker at an in-patient rehabilitation hospital. My work focused on young adults with spinal cord and brain injuries. Not unlike my previous responsibilities at the community hospital, I worked with patients and families in the areas of discharge planning, coping, patient/family education, and community resource referrals. As a member of the rehabilitation team, I participated in developing and maintaining program evaluation goals, team building, and staff education. I became active with the disability community, working on issues of access and services at the state and federal level.

In the nine years I worked as a rehabilitation social worker, I saw a trend in the aging of the population we were serving. People were living longer and were more susceptible to acquiring a spinal cord or brain injury. Because I had previously worked with older adults, I understood the dynamics of the developmental issues of this population and their families. These older adults and their families often faced different types of caregiving situations, discharge planning, and coping issues than the younger adults on the unit.

In 1999, I had the opportunity to be involved in a new project that was being developed to provide primary care and social services to new refugees and immigrants. I was intrigued with the idea of applying my health care social work skills in another area of the health care delivery system, the physician's office. I was also intrigued with working with non-English-speaking, new refugees and immigrants. My clients were primarily new refugees to the United States who may have arrived a few days or weeks prior to their visit to the community health care center. In most cases, the patients were coming from resettlement camps in their own or other countries willing to house them until they received approval to come to the United States. The health care they had received prior to coming here was often intermittent or minimal. These men, women, and children were entering a country they may have only known through the movies, a complex health care delivery system, and a culture different from their own.

My world as a social worker shifted dramatically with this new experience. I learned new skills, not the least of which was how to interview and provide counseling services through an interpreter. Because I was dealing with individuals and families from multiple countries, cultural competence took on a whole new meaning for me. I became acutely aware that, although I was a good health care social worker, I was going to have to reframe my practice to better meet the needs of this new clientele.

As I had the opportunity to get to know our clients and their health and social service needs, the nurse practitioner, physician, and I began to realize that many of our clients were suffering from post-traumatic stress disorder (PTSD). Hearing the stories of the war, their transitions during and after it, led us to understand that many of these people had suffered great physical harm, torture, and abuse at the hands of their captors. As the social worker on our team, I assisted these persons and their families in locating mental health professionals specially trained in war trauma and torture. Issues of access of care, policy implementation, and policy formulation became central to my practice with this population. Working as a part of a coalition of agencies serving refugees and immigrants, I was able to advocate for interpreter services provided by Medicaid that increased access to quality medical care.

In my current social work position at a university, I have the opportunity to work with BSW and MSW students as a mentor in health care social work. I assist as a field instructor for students in health care settings. I have taught courses in health policy and international social work in Mexico. I often serve as a guest lecturer on topics ranging from immigrant and refugee health to working with the elderly. I volunteer to be part of a team that provides training to medical interpreters to better serve the refugee and immigrant populations in my community. I currently serve on a community based committee that is working toward policy change for our elder refugees and immigrants so that they have better access to language skills, citizenship preparation and social and health services. I recently completed two terms on a board of directors that created an agency from the ground up to serve the mental health needs of refugees who experienced war torture and trauma. In addition, I recently completed three terms on a grants committee for a religious foundation that supported health and human service organizations. My practice as a health care social worker is a source of personal and professional satisfaction and has provided me with the expertise to serve as a mentor and teacher.

The future of social work in the health field is intimately tied to the aging population. The traditional settings of hospitals and clinics remain an arena in which social workers can work, but nontraditional settings, such as physicians' offices and ambulatory care centers, are increasingly becoming options for employment. Health care providers that work with diseases such as Alzheimer's, HIV/AIDS, multiple sclerosis, brain and spinal cord injury, stroke, cancer care have recognized the contributions of social workers and seek them to serve on their interprofessional teams. Rural health is another arena of practice for social workers. Local community hospitals and outpatient settings are in need of general practitioners to serve as part of the health care delivery team in the smaller communities. Social work students wishing to practice medical social work will likely find themselves practicing generalist social work and then specializing in one of many areas.

SOCIAL WORK PRACTICE IN MENTAL HEALTH SETTINGS

The social work profession is the largest provider of mental health services in the United States today, accounting for almost two-thirds of services. The remaining one-third are provided by psychiatrists, psychologists, and psychiatric nurses, as shown in Exhibit 8.3. Social work is recognized by the federal government as one of the four core mental health professions (Gibelman, 2004). As you might expect, mental health practice is also the largest area of practice for social workers, with over one-third of social workers reporting this category as their primary field of practice and 13 percent reporting they work in an out-patient mental health setting (Whitaker & Arrington, 2008). Moreover, social work practice in the area of mental health services is expected to grow by 30 percent in upcoming years (U.S. Department of Labor Bureau of Labor Statistics, 2009a).

After five years of practice as a social worker, the number of social workers that identify mental health as the setting in which they work begins to increase, supporting the idea that immediately following graduation, social workers gravitate to employment in the areas of aging, family and children services, and health settings and then shift their focus to the provision of more traditional clinical services after gaining experience. Mental health services are most often provided by social workers with an MSW or PhD. These social workers tend to be older, more experienced practitioners. Fewer social workers who are persons of color and of diverse ethnic groups identify themselves as mental health practitioners, creating a need for greater diversity among mental health providers (CHWS/CWS, 2006).

Practice Considerations in Mental Health Settings

Mental health services are provided in a variety of settings with diverse client populations. Social workers provide mental health services to children, adolescents, adults of all ages, families, groups, persons with physical and/or developmental disabilities; in correctional facilities, family service or mental health organizations, military and veterans programs, private practice, employee assistance programs, disaster relief programs, crisis intervention programs, victim assistance programs; and to persons from all races, ethnicities, and cultures. In sum, we are all potential consumers of mental health services provided by social workers.

Mental health services can be provided in the form of clinical therapy with individuals, families, and groups. Social workers facilitate support groups related to mental health issues, provide mental health education, and serve as advocates for those persons suffering from mental illness. More social workers providing mental health services are employed in out-patient mental health settings than in in-patient (hospital) settings (Whitaker & Arrington, 2008). Out-patient settings include public and nonprofit mental health centers and group and solo private practices.

A growing area of mental health practice for social workers is private practice. Seventeen percent of licensed social workers surveyed in 2004 reported they were engaged in private or group clinical practice, making this the third ranked setting in which social workers practice (CHWS/CWS, 2006). Nearly every major health insurance provider recognizes the graduate social work degree as a provider of mental health services, thus making clinical practice (private or agency based) a

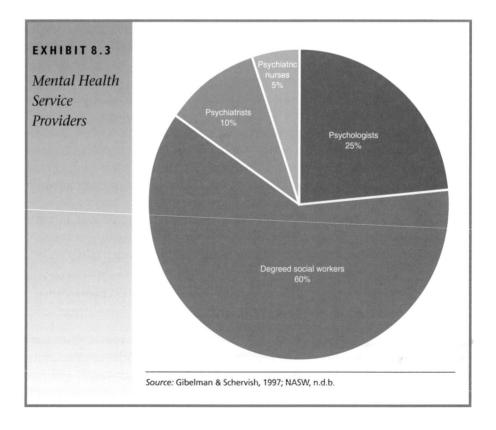

EXHIBIT 8.3

Mental Health Service Providers

Source: Gibelman & Schervish, 1997; NASW, n.d.b.

viable employment option for social workers with MSWs. Social workers in private clinical practice tend to garner the highest salaries within the social work practice community (CHWS/CWS, 2006).

Barbara Flory, MSW, LCSW

As a licensed clinical social worker, I was employed in a program for families that have experienced domestic violence. My education includes an undergraduate degree in human services and a graduate degree in social work from a private university. My postgraduate training includes a certificate in family conflict management from a state university, and family therapy training from a program accredited by the American Association of Marriage and Family Therapy. My combined experience of family therapy and mediation has prepared me for the unusual position that I held in today's social services environment.

For more than ten years, I was employed in a nonprofit mental health agency in a large metropolitan area. In my capacity as a program manager, I was responsible for all phases of program development, implementation, supervision of staff, and evaluation of program outcomes. Implemented in 1997, the program is a supervised visitation and custody exchange center implemented to meet the needs of family court and a special needs population of separated, divorced, and never-married families. The families are court mandated to participate in the programming out of three family court divisions: domestic relations (divorce and post-divorce child custody modifications), civil adult and child protection (time-limited protection orders sought by an adult), and juvenile dependency (child abuse and neglect cases resulting from a hotline call to child protection services). In rare cases, families were referred from the criminal child abuse and/or domestic violence dockets (e.g., domestic violence and/or child physical and/or sexual abuse cases that rose to a level that criminal prosecution was warranted).

As a public-private partnership between the local family court and the agency in which I worked, this formal collaboration required me to work at the interface between social services and the law, a unique position that requires knowledge beyond that which is traditionally a part of social work education.

Historically, supervised visitation between noncustodial parent and child is judicially ordered when the court determines that a child's safety is threatened by parental behavior. *Supervised visitation* is third-party guided contact between noncustodial parent and child for the purpose of maintaining or forming a relationship. Service delivery occurs on three levels to (1) ensure the safety of children when abuse is alleged, (2) reintroduce parent and child after a prolonged separation, and (3) introduce parent and child when no prior relationship exists. *Custody exchange transfer* is defined as the transfer of children from custodial to noncustodial parent for the purpose of temporary custody. In the context of child abuse and neglect, supervised visitation services have a well established history as a means to facilitate family reunification. Supervised visitation is a relatively new service within the domestic relations arena that is gaining credibility as an effective intervention when domestic violence is an issue. Over time, the judiciary has slowly embraced the practice of ordering supervised visitation on domestic violence cases to help ensure the protection of mothers and the children for whom they are responsible.

The population served was largely a violent group that engaged in psychological and/or physical aggression as a way to resolve interpersonal conflict. Approximately 70 percent of the client population had a history of abusive behavior, most often male-on-female intimate partner abuse (generally referred to as battering). In some instances, parental behavior excludes physical or sexual child abuse, and in other instances the children are abuse victims as well. Whichever the case, a violent home environment almost ensures diminished overall child well-being. Therefore, the program is structured to meet the unique physical and emotional safety needs of this abusive population.

In order to meet the needs of families, the program operated during non-traditional business hours, meaning evenings, weekends, and holidays, including Christmas day. Weekday and Sunday work hours started at 4:00 p.m. when parents began arriving to visit with their children under the supervision of a social worker. The social worker's responsibilities included ensuring children's safety during noncustodial parent/child visitation, teaching parenting skills and age appropriate communication skills, and facilitating attachment and bonding as needed. Modeling and coaching are two important skills that the social workers must possess to be successful in this practice area. Other noncustodial parents arrived at the center to pick up their children to spend time with them in an unprotected setting (for example, at home). The center was open on Saturday from 10:00 a.m. to 4:00 p.m., thus enabling parents to have flexible hours in which to spend time with their children.

Many parents who used the center had untreated, often undiagnosed, mental health disorders that contributed to their violent tendencies. Consequently, safety was paramount, and off-duty police officers had oversight responsibilities. A no-contact policy was necessary; that is, participating parents did not come face-to-face with each other while at the center, or communicate with each other outside the center.

It was encouraging to see that most parents could be good parents when offered the right circumstance. Unfortunately, sometimes circumstances dictated third-party intervention and court-restricted parental contact to mediate their violent behavior. The level of anger and distress exhibited by parents using the centers was often disproportionate to the event, resulting in violent outbursts with little provocation. I often found myself called upon to negotiate situations that were a crisis for overly stressed parents, whereas the situations were of little consequence for most parents. Consequently, staff members were hyper vigilant about safety and took all necessary precautions to ensure their personal safety as well as client system safety.

The program that I managed is only one small piece on a continuum of care needed to sustain families in the modern-day world. The agency in which I worked offered a broad scope of intervention services to include individual and family counseling, addictions treatment, workforce development, employee assistance services, suicide prevention, youth mentoring services, teen pregnancy prevention, and in-home geriatrics support services. I am fortunate that my employer valued and supported innovative programming.

Supervised visitation is an emerging field of practice in social services that enjoys both praise and criticism from mental health and legal professionals. There is limited research about the effectiveness of services, with my team and myself being among a handful of social workers that have conducted research in this field. As practitioners, in conjunction with a local graduate social work school, we conducted an exploratory study that showed that the service can be very efficacious in promoting noncustodial parent/child safe contact, reducing interparental violence and promoting child well-being (Dunn et al., 2004; Flory & Berg-Weger, 2003; Flory et al., 2001).

Since few social workers conduct research in their settings, my research experience and professional publications have resulted in private consulting roles, such as judicial training for a national organization and participation in a federal task force charged with developing standards and guidelines for the profession. The national task force of which I was a member demonstrated a commitment to shape an emerging field to meet public policy expectations, thus legitimizing services and helping to ensure the future evolution of the field.

Supervised visitation and safe custody exchange services emerged out of grassroots organizing that will support future programming, albeit at a limited level. Future expansion of services is largely in the hands of family courts faced with budgetary cuts due to shrinking state and federal budgets. There are, however, promising legislative efforts at the federal level to support noncustodial parental access to children. One effort has resulted in the development of some statewide networks of programs focused on keeping non-custodial fathers and their children connected. This effort is attuned to the fact that too many father's withdraw from their children's lives post-divorce, both emotionally and financially. Another federal effort is focused on developing centers designed to serve domestic violence victims and their children. This effort is attuned to the fact that battering does not stop after separation and/or divorce and the victims, ergo the children, remain vulnerable to abuse in the unprotected presence of the batterer. Both efforts recognize the benefits of keeping two parents safely involved in children's lives.

Like me, many social workers are employed in intense, highly conflictual, often violent, settings. Nothing in our training prepares us for the assaultive nature of the work, which often leads to vicarious traumatization of the professional. It was not until I left this area of practice that I realized just how stressful and debilitating the daily exposure to the stories of violence and the aggressive behaviors of the individuals were on my own psyche. Therefore, I learned that education in self-care is essential to support professionals who have chosen to work in this field. Developing awareness of the need to care for oneself is one of the real issues facing the profession that require attention by social workers of tomorrow.

After leaving this position, I became involved in the emerging field of collaborative family law. I chose this area of work—often referred to as a "peaceful" divorce process—because it is a stark contrast to the highly conflictual arena in which I worked, yet it allows me to continue to work with families in transition. The collaborative divorce process is a family law procedure in which the two divorcing parties agree that they will not go to court. The parties engage in a series of meetings with a team of divorce attorneys, mental health professionals, and accountants who work collaboratively to help the parties make fully-informed, carefully considered, settlement decisions that are consistent with the parties' priorities, goals, needs and interests. My former position in supervised visitation prepared me to train and work as a divorce coach and/or child specialist. My specialized knowledge about divorce as an emotional process, post-divorce communication issues, child custody parenting plans/schedules, and the effects of divorce on children helped me become an integral part of the team process. This remaking of a career as a solo clinical practitioner is an example of how specialized knowledge and skills developed in one social work domain can be transferred into another more personally desired area of practice.

My expertise in family and organizational systems and collaborative processes has opened doors to yet another area of social work practice. Currently, I am engaged as a consultant on a statewide strategic planning effort to reexamine and make alterations to improve the state's network of supervised visitation centers. I am also tasked with writing a policy and procedure manual that completes the state's standards for programming. The goal is to make service delivery more uniform, and thereby improve the quality of programming. I am also engaged in writing training curricula for this client; a documentation manual based on a hybrid model of case recording/note taking that I developed during my career that is specifically tailored to the supervised visitation profession.

As described herein, my career includes clinical therapy, parent and divorce coaching, mediation and conflict management, program development and implementation, program administration, staff supervision, research and teaching, system reform and consulting. The variety of work in which I am engaged is a good example of the depth and breadth of the social work education and the many opportunities an advanced degree in social work affords the social worker. My story demonstrates that the skills and knowledge that social workers possess are important tools that can be used in various ways to benefit the diverse client populations that we serve.

SOCIAL WORK PRACTICE IN RURAL SETTINGS

Rural communities are defined by the U.S. Census Bureau in the last official census in 2000 as those areas that lie outside of more densely populated areas known as urbanized areas or urban clusters. Social work practice in rural communities is an important area of practice, but one that can go unnoticed. Oftentimes, social workers may, in fact, be the only providers of mental health services in rural, non-metropolitan areas (Clark, 2003). The ratio of social workers varies across the U.S., but is particularly notable in states with more non-urban areas. For example, the number of licensed social workers per 100,000 persons ranges from a high of 408 (Maryland) to 23.7 (New Hampshire) (CHWS/CWS, 2006).

Chronic needs exist for social workers with expertise in mental health treatment (Gibelman, 2004). Social workers with BSW degrees tend to be more commonplace in rural communities than MSWs and doctoral-level social workers. They are thus required to function at multiple levels, for which they are prepared as generalists, and to be knowledgeable about a wider array of issues and resources than may be needed in an urban area.

Early pioneers in rural social work focused on political and policy changes that were needed to increase the availability of social work services in rural communities (Brown, 1933; Ginsberg, 1998; Martinez-Brawley, 1983). However, despite the small numbers of citizens and lack of services, rural communities are diverse populations. The Rural Social Work Caucus notes that social work employment opportunities in rural communities are on the rise.

Practice Considerations in Rural Settings

As generalist social work practice is the method best suited to practice in rural areas, social work educators are being called upon to include rural social work practice within social work curricula to enable students to understand the sophisticated level of skill and knowledge that are required for competent rural practice (NASW, 2009–2012k). Such a focus can help rural social workers to conceptualize the possible differences between urban and rural practice and incorporate these differences into the training of other social workers. A set of 19 assumptions has been developed by the Southern Regional Education Board Manpower Education and Training Project's Rural Task Force that includes guidelines for social workers in rural settings (Southern Regional Education Board, 1998). For example, rural communities may be diverse, but the people who live in them, as well as their needs, are more similar to people who live in urban areas than they are different. Although rural communities may lack basic services, greater priority is placed on services to sustain life than on those to enhance the quality of life. Rural communities have unique characteristics that can include geographically scattered poverty; existence of generational poverty; resistance to formal services and professionals, particularly those who are not members of the community; and more informal service networks.

Practice in small communities can provide social workers with a uniquely rewarding and challenging opportunity. In addition to being trained in generalist practice, social workers who practice in rural communities are required to develop knowledge, skills, and values appropriate for that community. These may include an understanding of the unique aspects of that community and the ability to use the community's customs and traditions as a basis for interventions; the willingness to respect the culture and values of the community; the ability to work within the informal network of services and resources; and the skills to develop new resources as needed (Southern Regional Education Board, 1998).

The social worker often plays overlapping roles in a small community. Whereas an urban setting typically offers a social worker anonymity, in smaller communities, social workers often have not only a history with, but also multiple ties to, persons to whom they will provide services. Such complex roles are not impossible in a larger community, but the potential is greater in a rural area due to the smaller population. Multiple roles can serve as both a strength and a liability in the social work relationship. Knowing a person's background, support system, and resources can be an asset in engaging her or him, assessing the situation, and developing and implementing an intervention. On the other hand, having extensive prior knowledge can compromise the social worker's professional objectivity.

Ellen Burkemper, PhD, MSW, LCSW, LMFT, RN, School of Social Work

For the last 25 years, I have provided a number of social work professional services in my small, rural community. I have found that social work practice in the small community is varied and requires that I be flexible and able to engage in services at the individual, family, group, and community levels. Through funding from the Department of Health, I participated in a program in which social workers obtain MSWs to provide mental health services through and in rural physicians' offices. Already a registered nurse, I was particularly well suited to this program, as I was familiar with the medical setting and terminology and lived in a rural community.

Upon completing my MSW, I had the opportunity to work in my community's mental health center as the center's coordinator and social work clinician. This practice opportunity brought forth all of my MSW generalist and clinical education and training. I was already knowledgeable about the services in my community and knew the local physicians and clergy that serve as the primary gatekeepers for referrals for mental health services. I felt this was a proactive way to bring the practice of social work to my community.

My responsibilities in the rural community mental health center included working with individuals, families, groups, organizations, and the community. Some of my practice activities included:

- Providing clinical services (therapy) for individuals and families.

- Working with other agencies to identify and develop community services.

- Representing the center at community meetings and events.

- Organizing fund-raising events.

- Collaborating with other programs involved in the provision of services to persons living with chronic and persistent mental illness.

- Making presentations to community groups on the services provided by the center.

- Serving as a member of the agency's advisory board.

- Writing newspaper articles regarding mental health concerns.

Due to a lack of funding and a need to consolidate services, the center closed after I had worked there for 10 years. Having the center close might have been a crisis, but I realized that I had gained considerable expertise in clinical and administrative practice. Because of the confidence that I had gained as a social worker, I decided to establish a private clinical practice as a solo practitioner. Concurrent with the opening of my private practice, I continued my education, ending with a doctoral degree in marriage and family therapy. I also began to work as a trainer and consultant for therapeutic foster parents for child protective services in my county.

The opportunities I have had to provide services in my small community have been rewarding. In small communities, there is a need for mental health services, and social workers are ideally suited to provide these services. As generalists, social workers are trained to engage in all levels of practice, and that versatility enables us to exercise our talents and education.

Working in a small community can present challenges. I had to be familiar with the NASW *Code of Ethics* (2008). In particular, rural social workers are knowledgeable about the special implications of the possible dual relationships that can occur in a small community. My family and I are active in my community, and living and working in a small community means that I am likely to run into clients while grocery shopping, attending weddings, church, professional gatherings, or school events. I learned to be careful to keep office work at the office. Of considerable importance is ensuring that client systems have knowingly provided informed consent for the social worker to discuss their cases with other professionals and that the social worker will not discuss them with friends, family members, or acquaintances. Clients must fully understand the social worker's role and functions, and the special implications of confidentiality in a small community. I talk with the client about the likelihood that we will encounter one another outside the professional social work setting. I inform clients that should that occur, I will not acknowledge them until they acknowledge me. By placing the decision to communicate in a public setting with clients, I am providing them with the right to self-determination.

Social workers are needed in small communities. Social workers that live and work in the small community have a view that is fuller than those who drive to the job and return home to other communities. Having been a member of a family in this farming community, my knowledge of the community helps me understand the culture in which the client system lives. This insight has provided me with a more efficient understanding of my clients' backgrounds, social environments, and rural ethic.

I see small-community social work as a viable field of practice. It offers the opportunity to engage in all levels of practice. In some cases, a benefit of rural practice is the ease of getting tasks accomplished due to the fewer numbers of individuals who need to be consulted. Social workers living and working in small communities are a minority, but rural areas can be an opportunity for employment, and for the expression of professional talents and education.

CONCLUSION

Although vastly different in terms of the settings in which they practice, populations with whom they work, and challenges they face, these "voices from the field" share a number of similarities and themes. Each social worker possesses a social work degree, not a degree in gerontology, substance abuse treatment, or counseling. Upon completion of the requirements for the social work degree, the social worker is, thus, equipped with a set of knowledge, skills, and values that enable her or him to practice at multiple levels with diverse populations in different settings. Specific knowledge of a population and setting is required, but the engagement, assessment, intervention, and evaluation process is common regardless of the targeted client system or setting.

Other similarities can be identified across the fields of practice. Having knowledge of aging issues is obviously important for working with older adults, but can be critical for working in every other field of practice described in this chapter. Because a significant amount of health care resources are devoted to older adults, knowledge of aging is essential for social workers in the health care setting (Clark, 2003). With increasing frequency, grandparents are rearing grandchildren or are living in three-generational households, thus requiring the social worker to have knowledge of those issues faced by the older adults in their clients' lives. Older adults can develop addictions or mental illness or become part of the criminal justice system as a perpetrator or victim. Older immigrants and refugees can present unique challenges as they strive to create a life in a new culture.

Advocacy and policy practice are two additional areas about which the social workers are united in their perceptions. In each of the narratives, the social worker states implicitly or explicitly that working on behalf of the client population is part of being an effective social worker. Advocacy is a vital skill, especially when resources are a critical factor and policies are limiting. The social workers who shared their stories highlight the need to advocate for improved services, more liberal policies, increased funding, and more effective treatment modalities. To achieve better access to services, social workers must be on the forefront of the legislative advocacy efforts for such issues as universal health insurance coverage, equity in mental health benefits, economic reform, and better access to services for those groups whose voices are not being heard by policy makers (for example, older adults, children, persons with disabilities, refugees and immigrants, battered women, and persons in the criminal justice system) (Clark, 2003). To be effective advocates, social workers must be knowledgeable about the functioning of organizations and communities, the workings of the political system, and the role of social and economic development (Mizrahi & Baskind, 2003).

Several of the narratives provide insights into the opportunities to build on the practice skills used with individuals and families in order to move into administrative and management roles. Herb, Suzanne, and Barbara all write of their administrative functions, but each is grounded in her or his knowledge of the issues that social workers that work with individuals, families, and groups face in working in their respective fields of practice.

Each of the social workers emphasizes a strengths-based perspective in terms of their fields of practice. Being able to identify the assets and resources that a client system or population possesses contributes to being an effective advocate, an ethical practitioner, and a partner with the client system in the change process. The narratives provide evidence of the importance of critical thinking as a valuable social work skill. In Jon's narrative on working in chemical dependency and addiction treatment, he describes a traditional treatment modality for substance abuse. Moreover, he voices skepticism regarding the effectiveness of that particular approach for all substance abusers and offers his insights into an alternative framework. Jon's social work training instilled in him the value of questioning and examining his social work practice so that all possibilities can be explored.

I want to point out that shortages do exist in several of the fields of practice described here. More social workers are needed to work with older adults, in chemical dependency and addiction treatment, and in the child welfare arena (Gibelman, 2004). Specifically, employment opportunities in the area of mental health, substance abuse treatment, and marriage and family therapy are expected to grow 30–34 percent from 2006–2016 (Dohm & Shniper, 2007). Although a variety of initiatives have been launched to increase the number of degreed social workers in aging and child welfare, for instance, still more initiatives are necessary to meet the needs of these and other areas. To gain the experience to respond to these emerging needs, social work students can seek out elective courses in working with specific populations and settings, gain field experiences in the areas in which a need exists, and participate in research to develop enhanced treatment approaches and policy recommendations (Mizrahi & Baskind, 2003).

You may not know the area of social work practice that is right for you. I encourage you to work in a variety of areas so that you can find the area or areas that are the best professional fit for you. You can begin by working with a population or in a setting that is familiar to you, but I also encourage you to explore an area or setting with which you are completely unfamiliar. Using a strengths-based approach, you can assess your strengths and explore areas in which those strengths can be assets. Check out the information provided in Box 8.1 to help you in your exploration.

BOX 8.1

Activities for Learning About Fields of Practice

Check out social work organizations:

- The website for NASW, located at http://www.naswdc.org, contains information about the organization and its activities as well as Issue Fact Sheets on specific fields of practice.
- Latino Social Workers Organization, a group for social workers to share experiences regarding education, employment, and the Latino community, located at: http://www.lswo.org.
- National Association of Black Social Workers, an organization committed to enhancing the quality of life and empowering people of African ancestry through advocacy, human service delivery, and research, is located at: http://www.nabsw.org.
- North American Puerto Rican and Hispanic Social Workers, a group for social workers and other human service professionals to strengthen, develop, and improve the resources and services that meet the needs of the Puerto Rican and Hispanic communities, located at: http://www.naprhsw.org.
- Rural Social Work Caucus, located at http://www.marson-and-associates.com, is an organization focused on issues related to rural social work practice.
- School Social Work Association of America, an organization of social workers working in public and private schools, located at: http://www.sswaa.org.
- International Federation of Social Workers, a global organization striving for social justice, human rights, and social development, located at: http://www.ifsw.org.

Read! There is a wealth of social work literature out there. Some possibilities of books for general reference and informational reading includes:

- Barker, R.L. (2003). *The social work dictionary*. Washington, DC: NASW Press.
- Doelling, C.N. (2004). *Social work career development (2nd edition)*. Washington, DC: NASW Press.
- Gibelman, M. (2004). *What social workers do (2nd edition)*. Washington, DC: NASW Press.
- Grobman, L.M. (2005). *Days in the lives of social workers (3rd edition)*. Harrisburg, PA: White Hat Communications.
- Grobman, L.M. (2007). *Days in the lives of gerontological social workers*. Harrisburg, PA: White Hat Communications.
- Grobman, L.M. (2005). *More days in the lives of social workers*. Harrisburg, PA: White Hat Communications.

BOX 8.1

continued

- LeCroy, C.W. (2002). *The call to social work—life stories*. Thousand Oaks, CA: Sage Publications. You can read a summary of this book along with excerpts from three social workers' life stories by visiting Dr. LeCroy's website at: http://www.public/ asu.edu/~lecroy/
- Mizrahi, T. & Davis, L.E. (2008). *Encyclopedia of social work (20th edition)*. Washington, DC & New York, NY: NASW Press and Oxford Press.
- National Association of Social Workers. (2009–2012). *Social work speaks. NASW policy statements 2009–2012 (8th edition)*. Washington, DC: NASW Press.
- Roberts, A.R. (2009). *Social workers' desk reference (2nd edition)*. Washington, DC: NASW Press.

While the list of social work-related journals is far too extensive to list here, you can check your school's library for a listing or review:

- Beebe, L. (1999). *Professional writing for the human services*. Washington, DC: NASW Press.
- National Association of Social Workers. (1997). *Author's guide to social work journals (5th edition)*. Washington, DC: NASW Press.

Several easily accessible and informative journals include:

- *BPD Update Online*. This online journal is published by the Baccalaureate Program Directors Association and is available at http://bpdupdateonline.bizland.com.
- *Journal of Social Work Values and Ethics*. Available at http://www.socialworker.com/ jswve, this online journal is dedicated to examining ethical and values issues that impact social work practice, research, and theory development.
- *The New Social Worker*. Published by White Hat Publications, this journal is targeted for social work students and new professionals and is available at: http:// www.socialworker.com.
- *Social Work*. The official publication of the National Association of Social Workers.
- *Social Work Today*. A biweekly magazine for social workers. For free subscription information, go to: http://www.socialworktoday.com.

For all your social work projects, check into these social work-related databases:

- http://www.findarticles.com A constantly updated, free search engine, articles can be printed in their entirety at no cost.
- http://blogs.nyu.edu/socialwork/ip This website provides news and new scholarship from around the world that is relevant for social work practice.
- http://cosw.sc.edu/swan/ Search engine for social resources for social work faculty, students, and professionals.

Government documents—http://www.pueblo.gsa.gov and http:// www.access.gpo.gov.

MAIN POINTS

- Social workers' range of knowledge and skills should include knowledge of human behavior and biology; the philosophy of other disciplines; awareness of cultures, faith traditions, laws, policies, and social systems; and the ability to work with a diverse population of clients and other professionals.

- With a social work degree, you can practice in a variety of different fields within the same career, including mental health, chemical dependency, and criminal justice. Within the field, you work with a variety of client systems at various levels.

- Eight social workers present their experiences in eight different fields, from working with older adults to working in a rural community, with the goal of sharing the diversity, challenges, and rewards of the social work profession.

- The diverse fields are held together by the commonality of social work practice. For example, working with older adults requires knowledge of medical and health issues. Working in mental health involves interactions with the legal and health systems.

- Although opportunities in the fields of practice presented here are increasing, other growth areas for employment exist in employee assistance programs, forensic social work, and school social work.

EXERCISES

1. Using the Sanchez Family interactive case (go to www.routledgesw.com/cases), review the case file for Junior Sanchez. Then select Roberto Salazar and answer Roberto's Critical Thinking Questions.
2. Review the case file for Junior Sanchez. Then select Emilia Sanchez and answer Emilia's Critical Thinking Questions.
3. Review the case file for Junior Sanchez. Then select Gloria Sanchez Quintanilla and answer Gloria's Critical Thinking Questions.
4. Go to the Carla Washburn interactive case at www.routledgesw.com/cases. In working with Mrs. Washburn, develop a list of questions you have about working with older adults. Utilizing the section in this chapter and other sources you can locate, identify the specific gerontological knowledge and skills needed for providing social work services to an older adult.
5. Go to the National Association of Social Workers Web site at www.naswdc.org. Click on Issue Fact Sheets and read about the various fields of practice that are included in this chapter. From the Issue Fact Sheets, develop a list of areas about which you would like to have more information.

6. With assistance from your instructor, identify a social work student with whom you can conduct an interview regarding her/his primary field of practice interests. Your assignment is to dialogue with your fellow student to gain insight into the reasons she/he has chosen social work for a career, the pros and cons of majoring in social work, and the life and academic experiences that she/he perceives to be helpful in pursuing a social work career.

7. You may also want to consider interviewing a social work practitioner. Your instructor may again be of assistance in identifying a social worker with whom you can conduct an interview regarding her/his primary field of practice interests. Your assignment is to develop a set of questions to pose to the social work professional and conduct an interview regarding her or his training, experiences, philosophy, and practice wisdom.

8. You have been given the opportunity to read about various fields of action in social work practice. Imagine that you are working in one of these fields of practice. Given your previous experience, respond to the following questions:

    a. How might you see political, economic, and social issues impact your work?

    b. What are the potential "isms" that you might encounter in this field of practice?

    c. How might you adjust to the issues that you identified in the previous two questions?

CHAPTER 9

Social Work Practice with Individuals and Families

Emily's career has taken her down many paths, but the knowledge and skills she developed for working with individuals and families have proved invaluable in all her practice experiences. She has learned to develop rapport, establish trust, build relationships, conduct interviews, and employ skills of engagement, assessment, intervention, and evaluation, and these skills have formed the foundation of Emily's social work career. Emily has applied these skills when working with children, families, young adults, and older adult client systems.

In this chapter, we explore the area of **individual and family social work practice**. Providing services to individuals, couples, and families is the cornerstone of social work practice. Also known as **micro practice**, working one-on-one with individuals and families is the primary focus of most practicing social workers.

In fact, almost all (96 per cent) of social work practitioners spend a portion of their time providing direct services to clients with over two-thirds reporting direct services with individuals and families as their primary practice area where they spend more than half of their overall work time (CHWS/CWS, 2006; Whitaker & Arrington, 2008). Social work practice with individuals, couples, and families is an area that continues to have increasing opportunities. Not surprisingly, a larger proportion of younger and more recently graduated social workers are employed in direct practice areas, while many older, more experienced social workers often move into supervisory, administrative, management, teaching, and research positions.

Practitioners who work with individuals and families continue to work primarily in traditional settings such as health and mental health and family service settings, but they are also found in educational, religious, and correctional settings. This chapter focuses on the history and meaning of this level of practice. It also identifies practice skills that are essential for direct practice with individuals and families.

HISTORICAL PERSPECTIVE ON SOCIAL WORK PRACTICE WITH INDIVIDUALS AND FAMILIES

As you learned in Chapter 2, the history of social work is, in many ways, the history of social work practice with individuals and families. The friendly visitors, outdoor relief, and eventually, the Charity Organization Society movement of the 19th century all served as the forerunners of modern-day social work practice with individuals and families. Focused on providing aid to the individual or family unit, the work of these early practitioners evolved into a methodology referred to as **social casework**. Recall from Chapter 1 that this is a method of social work practice in which social workers, through direct contact with the client system, help individuals and families to resolve personal challenges. Using the medical profession as a model, Mary Richmond, in her 1917 book, *Social Diagnosis*, introduced the concept of social diagnosis as a method for the friendly visitors to objectively gather information and make assessments.

This concept became the model for the social casework that social workers practice today. Moving beyond the concept of social diagnosis, Richmond's 1922 book, *What Is Social Case Work?* provided the basis for the teaching and practice of social casework for many decades to come. Richmond proposed social casework as a method for helping individuals adjust to their situations by identifying needs, goals, and resources (McNutt & Floersch, 2008). Early caseworkers were trained in the idea that one approach—social casework—could be used to help individuals and families resolve problems caused by "deviations from accepted standards of normal social life" (Brieland, 1995, p. 2251). For example, social workers who engaged in casework during this period may have worked with an immigrant family to obtain housing and jobs, helped a widow to obtain financial assistance, or facilitated the adoption of an orphaned child.

Introduced later, the concepts of person-in-environment, ecological, and systems constructs were embraced by the social work profession. However, social casework continued to be the prevailing model for social work practice well into the 20th century. This exclusive focus on the individual changed when the social upheaval of the 1960s brought the issues of race, ethnicity, poverty, and human rights to the forefront of societal attention (McNutt & Floersch, 2008). This attention prompted social workers to incorporate a broader, more holistic perspective when intervening with client systems.

Contemporary concepts for practice with individuals and families emerged as a result of the changes of the 1960s and 1970s. Practice with individuals and families then shifted to include the emergence of the ecological model that encompassed the environmental perspective, the need for research to support and guide practice, and the birth of the generalist model. The generalist model emphasized an ecological, systemic, and strengths-based approach to working with individuals, groups, and communities. From that basis, social workers can develop a broad-based set of skills for working with any population.

THE CHANGE PROCESS IN SOCIAL WORK PRACTICE WITH INDIVIDUALS AND FAMILIES

Change is the goal of the social worker's involvement with client systems at all levels of practice. Change for the client system involves embracing new attitudes or behaviors. Within the context of the social work relationship, establishing goals for change is a key component of the plan developed to achieve the goals set by the client system. Change is a part of the intervention and is agreed upon by the social worker and the client system.

Social workers become involved in a wide variety of change efforts in working with individuals and families. For example, social workers help client systems in such situations as:

- Beginning or ending a phase of life, for example, marriage, divorce, parenting, career change, caring for a family member, retirement, or grief.

- Relationship difficulties, for example, friendship, family, marital, parent/child, or employment.

- Life crises, for example, physical or mental health problems, violence, natural or economic disasters, or legal problems.

- Chemical dependency and addictions, for example, alcohol, drugs, food, gambling, sexual, or spending.

All interventions revolve around **planned change**, a process in which the social worker and client collaborate to plan and then execute a series of actions designed to enhance the client's functioning and well-being. Planned change for interventions with individuals, families, groups, organizations, and communities consists of four phases: engagement, assessment, intervention, and evaluation. See Exhibit 9.1 for a depiction of the planned change model.

Change is a fluid process that involves unexpected starts and stops. The client system may be able to establish goals for change, but the process may be interrupted when real-life factors intervene; for example, the client may be seeking employment, but her or his car breaks down or child care arrangements fall through. The social worker's responsibility is to monitor and support the change process by helping the individual anticipate and respond to challenges and crises that affect the change process.

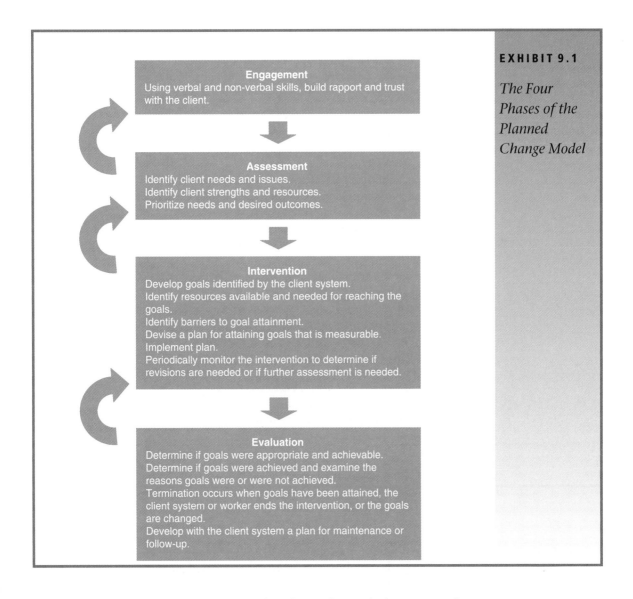

EXHIBIT 9.1

The Four Phases of the Planned Change Model

Engagement
Using verbal and non-verbal skills, build rapport and trust with the client.

Assessment
Identify client needs and issues.
Identify client strengths and resources.
Prioritize needs and desired outcomes.

Intervention
Develop goals identified by the client system.
Identify resources available and needed for reaching the goals.
Identify barriers to goal attainment.
Devise a plan for attaining goals that is measurable.
Implement plan.
Periodically monitor the intervention to determine if revisions are needed or if further assessment is needed.

Evaluation
Determine if goals were appropriate and achievable.
Determine if goals were achieved and examine the reasons goals were or were not achieved.
Termination occurs when goals have been attained, the client system or worker ends the intervention, or the goals are changed.
Develop with the client system a plan for maintenance or follow-up.

To facilitate planned change, the social worker understands the situation from the perspective of the client system. Some clients want to change something in their lives and feel capable of doing so, whereas others who desire change feel incapable of doing so. Still other clients perceive no need for change. The saying *"starting where the client is"* guides social workers in gaining insight into the client's perception of the problem and the desired goal. This approach helps the social worker understand the client system's motivation and capacity for change and will prevent the social worker from making assumptions regarding the client's thoughts, feelings, and values. Understanding the client's stance on change can serve to deter the social worker from imposing her or his desired goals on the client.

BOX 9.1

Checklist of Personal Communication Styles

You may use the following checklist of personal communication styles to assess your own communication style. After answering the questions, identify those areas that may warrant attention in order to enhance your communication as a social worker.

- Are you more comfortable listening or talking?
- Do you view your role being to give advice or explore options?
- When listening to someone describe a difficulty or challenge, do you feel compelled to immediately offer solutions?
- Do you find it difficult to pay attention when others are talking?
- Do you find that while others are talking, you are thinking of what you are going to say next?
- Do you find that you notice non-verbal communication as well as the verbal message?
- Do you become so consumed with the details of a "story" that you miss the essence of the story?
- Do you have a difficult time listening to a "story" without interjecting your own personal experiences or biases?
- How do you determine if you got the essence of the story?
- Do you find that you are easily distracted when conversing with another person (i.e., watching other activities, thinking of things you have to do later, etc.)?
- How do you react to people who have difficulty communicating in a straightforward manner (i.e., non-focused, tangential, etc.), are uncommunicative, or hostile?
- Does your speech include "ums," "ers," "you knows?"
- Do you feel that you communicate in a straightforward manner?
- What is your non-verbal communication style—use of hands and gestures, volume and tempo of your voice, posture, etc.?

Source: Adapted from Corey & Corey, 1998, p. 69.

The social worker is a collaborator in the planned change process. Recall from Chapter 7 that the strengths-based perspective is based on the belief that the client is the expert on her or his life, and the social worker's role is to support and empower the client to enhance her or his function and well-being. Staying true to this social work approach often requires social workers to take stock of their thoughts and feelings about the client's situation, choices, and goals. As one example of this process, Box 9.1 provides a checklist of questions that you can use to inventory your personal communication style.

To use the strengths-based perspective properly, social workers must consistently compare the client's goals with their own to ensure that the goals being worked toward are the client's and not the social worker's. As we all know from our personal experiences, our motivation is likely to be much higher when the goal we are working toward is one in which we are invested and one that we think has the most possibility for success. Because social workers sometimes work with clients who did not voluntarily seek assistance, goals can be quite different.

The goals of the client who is not voluntarily seeking services may be to end the professional relationship as soon as possible. Even with that apparent disparity of goals, the social worker's responsibility is to "start where the client is" and identify the common ground on which to build a working relationship. In this case, the common ground may be the mutual desire to terminate the relationship.

SKILLS FOR SOCIAL WORK PRACTICE WITH INDIVIDUALS AND FAMILIES

To practice social work with empathy and efficacy, the social worker must possess a repertoire of specialized skills. In this section, we explore beginning social work skills for each of the four phases of the planned change intervention—engagement, assessment, intervention, and evaluation. These basic skills are essential for practice at all levels, and they serve as the foundation for the more advanced skills that social workers develop to address specific situations.

While working at the sexual assault response program, Emily responded to a call from a convenience store manager late one night. A woman had come to the store and asked to use the telephone. Her swollen face and bleeding lip suggested that she had been physically assaulted. Recognizing the customer from previous visits to the store, the manager asked if she could help. The woman, Victoria, burst into tears and told the manager she had been attacked by a man she did not know as she was entering her apartment. He dragged her into some bushes, beat and sexually assaulted her, and then left her in the bushes as he fled on foot. Victoria agreed to allow the manager to call Emily's agency, but not the police.

Emily first met Victoria in the manager's office. As Emily entered the room, she observed Victoria lying on a couch in a fetal position and crying. When Emily moved toward her and said her name, Victoria visibly flinched. Emily recognized that as a result of the trauma that Victoria had experienced, building trust with Victoria was critical to being able to help her.

Emily's first step was to sit down near Victoria, but not too close to threaten her. She told Victoria who she was and that she was there to help in any way that she could. She asked Victoria if she could get her a tissue. As she spoke to Victoria, Emily spoke slowly in a warm and soft tone. She leaned forward toward Victoria but made no attempt to touch her. She told Victoria that the manager had informed her that Victoria had been attacked. Emily then suggested that if Victoria was willing and when she was ready, they go to the hospital so that Victoria could be examined and could call the police to report the assault. Emily was careful not to use graphic, medical, or legal jargon at this point, focusing instead on helping Victoria to feel safe.

Emily sat with Victoria for an hour before Victoria said she was ready to go to the hospital. Emily assured Victoria that she would stay with her through the examination and the police interview. As Victoria rose from the couch, Emily asked for Victoria's permission to physically assist her in getting up and walking to the car. During the trip to the hospital, Emily explained to Victoria what she could expect when they reached the hospital. She continued to speak softly, calmly, and with empathy, assuring Victoria that she was now safe and in control of the procedure.

Engagement of Individuals and Families

In order to conduct a complete and accurate assessment of the client system, the social worker's first task is to establish a working relationship that encompasses rapport, trust, and respect—three distinct phenomena. Rapport is the client's perception that she or he and the social worker have established a congenial relationship that promotes a sense of trust in which the client can share personal information (Shulman, 2009). When the social worker respects the client, she or he will treat the client with esteem and dignity. Engaging the client is the first step in building a successful relationship.

Engagement is the process of eliciting information in an open and trusting manner using both verbal and nonverbal communication. To engage the client system and build rapport, the social worker should attend to the following aspects of verbal communication:

- Speak at a pace that the client can easily follow, particularly with clients whose first language is different from yours or clients that have a hearing impairment.

- Speak at a level that the client can easily hear, but not too loud.

- Speak with warmth and empathy.

- Use language appropriate to the client's culture, ethnicity, and social group, but do not attempt to use language that is unfamiliar to you.

- Use language appropriate to the client's educational level.

- Avoid professional jargon that may be unfamiliar to the client.

- Use respectful language to refer to individuals and groups, paying particular attention to avoiding language that promotes the isms.

- Patiently listen while the client tells her or his story without interrupting, prompting, or interjecting words.

- Avoid "ums," "you knows," and other unnecessary language.

Attention to nonverbal communication is as important as verbal communication characteristics. Important nonverbal issues to consider include:

- Ensure that you and the client are both physically on the same level (for example, both sitting).

- Maintain direct eye contact, when culturally appropriate. When working with a family or small group, maintain equal eye contact with all members of the group. To look at one or more persons more than others can imply a preference or bias and can hamper your ability to establish trust with all members.

- Look at the client while speaking instead of looking out the window, at forms, or the client's chart, for example.

- Maintain physical and emotional focus on the client when the client speaks, as opposed to thinking ahead to the next question or comment.

- Avoid distractive behaviors (for example, playing with pencil/hair, swinging leg, tapping on the desk, checking your phone/computer).

- Directly face the client.

- Lean slightly forward to indicate attentiveness.

- Use nonverbal gestures that are typical and comfortable, but ensure that they are not excessive to the point of distraction.

- Demonstrate appropriate facial expressions such as interest, warmth, and varied responses that are appropriate to the client's remarks. Facial expressions should be consistent with the words.

Assessment of Individuals and Families

Emily stayed with Victoria through the physical examination, the collection of evidence for the rape kit, and the police interview. Because these events took several hours, Emily had an opportunity to become more familiar with Victoria's situation. She learned that Victoria had moved to the city to attend college. She was now a management trainee at a department store in the mall and lived alone in a ground-floor apartment. She was engaged, but her fiancé lived in another state and visited only once a month. Her family was in her hometown several hours away. By asking questions in a gentle, unobtrusive manner, Emily was able to begin the assessment process. Emily was careful not to ask questions that were not relevant to gathering information for responding to Victoria's immediate need of safety. Emily learned that Victoria's attacker likely knew where she lived and possibly that she lived alone. She learned that Victoria had friends from school and work, but did not know anyone at her apartment complex, as she had just recently moved there. Victoria admitted that she was terrified to return to her apartment, but she did not want to leave town because she had work and school commitments.

Assessment is the professional activity conducted with the client that provides the basis for understanding the client system's situation and planning the intervention. In conducting an assessment at the individual, family, group, or community level, the social worker uses theoretical frameworks to guide the gathering of relevant information and the evaluation of the information to determine its meaning for the client system. At the same time, the worker must evaluate the level of functioning for the system—with a focus on strengths—as well as the resources available to the system. When the social worker has completed this process, she or he works with the client to define and prioritize the issues to be addressed within the intervention. They then begin to develop the intervention, paying specific attention to the time frame, the necessary resources, appropriate strategies and activities, and desired outcomes (Meyer, 1995).

In order to develop an accurate assessment and intervention plan, the assessment process, when possible, should be multi-faceted so that it may capture the complexity of the client's life. Information should be gathered from multiple sources, including the client and collaterals (e.g., family members, friends, health and social service providers, and other professionals); archives (e.g., medical, legal, or educational records); direct observation of activities; and standardized measures (O'Hare, 2009).

While an array of diverse methods and sources of information are needed to fully understand the client system, much of the information is gathered through an interview with the client; therefore, the next step in the assessment process is for the social worker to consider the types and quality of questions to ask the client. Questions should be focused on gathering only that information relevant to the situation at hand (and not just interesting). They should be grounded in the strengths-based perspective, and they should convey a sense of genuine support and empathy to the client. To elicit as much relevant information as possible and to optimize client comfort, assessments should also emphasize the following (Collins & Coleman, 2000):

- *A balance of open-ended questions and responses and closed-ended questions and responses:* **Open-ended questions** and responses (questions that ask what, how, and feelings questions) are helpful for gathering information and affirming the client's control of the situation. **Closed-ended questions** and responses (questions that can be answered by yes, no, or short answers) are more directive and allow the social worker to control the interview.

- *Avoidance of excessive questioning:* A good rule to follow is to ask no more than two questions in succession without pausing for reflection.

- *Periodic reflection:* Recapping or paraphrasing the client's response, known as **reflection**, enables the social worker to clarify her or his understanding of the client's words. Recapping not only makes the client feel validated and understood, but also enables her or him to clarify any misunderstandings by the social worker. At the same time, it enables the social worker to consider the information that has been shared and to plan for future comments and directions for the interview.

- *Silence:* Not speaking is an important social work skill. Pausing after asking a question enables the client to consider her or his response in a thoughtful manner.

In addition to these guidelines, there are numerous behaviors that social workers should either embrace or avoid in developing an assessment. Table 9.1 gives additional examples of assessment that are effective and those that should be avoided.

When conducting an assessment with a family, the social worker employs the same skill set that is appropriate for use with individuals, but with several additional considerations for the challenges inherent in assessing family issues. The family is a system, and working with a family essentially means working with a group and can be overwhelming at first. The family assessment provides the social worker and the family with insights regarding patterns of individual behaviors, family functioning, relationships, communication patterns, and dynamics among family members.

The first step in conducting a family assessment is to determine the composition of the family. This process requires the social worker to have a broad concept of family, given that the definition of family has changed considerably in recent years. The accepted social work definition of **family** is a group of persons, usually residing together, who acknowledge a sense of responsibility for one another and function as a unit. As defined by the U.S. Census Bureau (2009), the number of households increased 11 percent between 2000 and 2007 and "family" households (co-residents related by birth, marriage, or adoption) rose 9 percent. During the same period, however, nonfamily households grew by 15 percent and one-person households grew by 17 percent, suggesting that social workers need to rethink traditional definitions of family.

Adopting a broad definition of family helps the social worker to conduct a thorough family assessment. Social workers routinely intervene with family units that do not conform to the traditional definition of family. Examples are gay, lesbian, bisexual, and transgendered couples; people who share a residence but are not biologically or legally related; blended families that include the children of multiple marriages or relationships; single parents; grandparents serving as parents; multi-generational family units; and foster and other kinship relationships.

TABLE 9.1	ASSESSMENT "DON'T'S"	EXAMPLE	ASSESSMENT "DO'S"
Assessment "Don'ts" and "Do's"	Excessive utterances, excessive head nodding	Frequent use of "That's good." "Really?"	Occasional use of these comments can serve as prompters or encouragers.
	"Why" questions	"Why did you hit your son?"	"What were you feeling when you struck your son?"
	Use of poor grammar (e.g., "that," "it," etc.)	"What did it feel like when it happened?"	"How did you feel when your daughter told you about the abuse?"
	Closed questions	"Do you want to tell me what brought you here today?"	"What brought you here today?"
	Talking more than clients talk	Social worker does the majority of the talking.	Client does the majority of the talking.
	Machine gun questioning— series of "grilling" questions	"Where were you when that happened? How did it feel? What did she say?"	The client's response should guide the next question.
	Leading questions	"I'm sure you told him that you would leave him if he didn't stop drinking, didn't you?"	"What did you say to your husband about his drinking?"
	Placating	"Now, Mrs. Smith, there is nothing to worry about."	"Mrs. Smith, I will be here to support you through this experience."
	Minimizing	"I'm sure you're keeping so busy that you don't really miss him that much."	"Missing a loved one who dies is a normal reaction."
	Rescuing	"I'll make sure that you don't get evicted."	"How can I help you with your housing situation?"
	Fidgeting	Twirling hair, playing with a pen/pencil, or moving about in the chair.	Movement is a normal action, just not to the point of distraction.
	Poor attending skills	Looking out the window, through papers, or responding to a beeper.	Focusing on the client during the encounter is essential to the social work relationship.
	Giggling at inappropriate times or during silences	Giggling, in general, conveys an unprofessional air and is offensive.	Laughing with the client at appropriate times is supportive.

ASSESSMENT "DON'T'S"	EXAMPLE	ASSESSMENT "DO'S"	**TABLE 9.1** *continued*
Use of repetitive words (e.g., "you know," "like," "okay," "uh huh")	"I'm like, you know, happy to set another appointment with you, okay?"	"I will be happy to schedule another appointment with you."	
Advice giving	"I definitely think you should have the procedure."	"Let's explore the pro's and con's of having the procedure."	
Multiple, double-barreled questions	"When did you separate?" "Have you filed for divorce?" (Client may not know which to answer or answer one and leave worker with the wrong impression.)	Ask a question, wait for a response, and continue.	
Slouching	Slouching implies a posture that suggests this is a casual relationship and the worker may not be taking the situation seriously.	Sitting upright and leaning slightly forward suggests a professional, interested posture.	
Letting the client ramble	Allowing the client to wander off the topic to the point that assessment cannot be completed.	Clients can often provide useful information while talking, but the social worker should monitor.	
Mimicking cultural traits or language or client's behaviors	Using language or gestures that are not typical, but done only for the benefit of the client.	Use appropriate language, but do not "experiment" on the client.	
Taking sides with the clients	"I know you meant well."	"My role is to be objective and neutral."	
Giving false reassurances or agreeing when that is inappropriate or unknown	"I'm sure the doctor will be able to give you good news on your tests."	"If you would like, I can be with you when you get your test results."	
Ignoring cues about the client's subjective experiences and only focusing on the objective issues (i.e., getting the form completed)	"Now, what was your annual income last year?" (asked while client is sobbing)	"You seem very upset. Would you like to talk about it?"	

TABLE 9.1 *continued*	ASSESSMENT "DON'T'S"	EXAMPLE	ASSESSMENT "DO'S"
	Judgmental responses	"I am sure you want to take care of your mother at home instead of putting her in a nursing home."	"Have you thought about your mother's care? Let's discuss the options."
	Inappropriate use of humor	"You know how they (fill in the group) can be."	If initiated by the client, the social worker should confront the inappropriate humor.
	Premature problem-solving	"I've heard enough. Let me tell you what I think."	"I need more information before we can discuss options."
	Criticizing or belittling clients or condescending behaviors	"You're not being fair." "You shouldn't worry about that."	"You seemed concerned about that."
	Over-reliance on "chit-chat"	Anything beyond the usual greeting and pleasantries is too much casual conversation.	Greeting the client, asking about her/his well-being and responding briefly to her/his inquiries is appropriate.
	Overprotecting clients by avoiding clear cues to implicit information	"I think there may be some concern about your son's academic performance." (when, in fact, the son is failing)	"I am concerned that your son's grades are below the level needed for him to pass."
	Inappropriate response to information shared by client	With wide eyes, "Wow, you have got to be kidding!"	Empathetically stated, "You must have been surprised."
	Communicating displeasure when a client does not appear grateful	"I hope you know how difficult it was to get you an appointment today."	Commenting on a client's lack of gratitude is not appropriate.

Source: Adapted from Collins & Coleman, 2000.

When conducting a family assessment, the social worker must determine which family members are to be included in the change effort. Several factors may contribute to the composition, including the goal(s) of the persons seeking services, the willingness and availability of family members to participate, and the relationships of the family members with one another. For example, in an adoption process, all members of the family should be involved, as the addition of a new member will affect everyone. Engaging with each family member can be particularly difficult if one or more members has not voluntarily sought the services of a social worker or has different needs and agendas for the intervention. Involuntary participants may feel anger, resentment, or hostility.

The skills of engagement described in this section become critical as the social worker strives to establish rapport with each family member and the family unit as a whole, while observing the interactions among family members and between the family and their external environment.

Intervention with Individuals and Families

Using the information that she had gathered from Victoria during the assessment process, Emily developed an immediate and short-term plan for intervention with the agreement that Victoria would allow Emily to follow up the next day. With Emily's help, Victoria was able to state that her immediate need was a safe place to stay. In response, Emily arranged with one of Victoria's friends from work for Victoria to stay with her. Being sensitive to the trauma that Victoria had experienced, Emily did not want to overwhelm her with a request to establish long-range goals.

Over the next several weeks, Emily had regular contact with Victoria. Emily told Victoria that she was there to support her through this period, but their goal will include phasing Emily out of Victoria's life as Victoria recovers and regains emotional strength. Together, they established a list of objectives as prioritized by Victoria. Victoria wanted to return to living independently, feel safe, and be able to talk with her family and fiancé about her experience. Emily identified several types of services that would be most helpful to Victoria. Working together toward the goals identified by Victoria, Emily helped Victoria to relocate to a new third floor apartment. Emily referred Victoria to several services that helped her to meet her goals: the community police program for an in-home safety assessment, a support group for survivors of sexual assault, and a clinical social worker to help her address her feelings of guilt and violation and to work with Victoria's family and fiancé.

Once the social worker has engaged with the client and gathered relevant information to assess the client's situation, the worker and the client can jointly begin the process of planning and carrying out the intervention. **Intervention** is the phase of the social work relationship in which the actual work is completed. During the assessment phase, the social worker and the client system engage in the process of identifying needs, issues, strengths, and resources. Using that information, they next focus on prioritizing the client's needs and mobilizing the client's strengths and resources to facilitate the desired change.

The social work intervention involves two steps: planning and implementation. In planning an intervention, the social worker and the client identify the areas of change on which the client system wants to focus the intervention. Initially, the goals may be broad or overwhelming. Through discussion, the social worker and the client system will prioritize the goals and define each goal in specific behavioral and achievable terms. This is the point in the intervention in which the social worker and the client negotiate and document a contract that is mutually agreed upon, clear, measurable, and specific.

Once the intervention is planned, the next step is implementation. Reviewing the contract on a regular basis enables the client and the social worker to monitor progress and determine whether the goals and strategies are realistic or if they should be changed or eliminated. Applying the concepts of the strengths-based approach to planning and implementation, the social worker recognizes the client as the expert on her or his life and respects the client's right to self-determination in facilitating the change process. Exhibit 9.2 provides additional information on the planning and implementation phase.

Developing social work interventions with families brings the focus on the family as the client system. Building on the skills used with individuals, family interventions may be more complex as the focus may encompass the immediate and/or extended family along with formal and informal support networks. *Family Group Conference (FGC)* is a relatively new approach that can be used in situations involving children, adults, or intergenerational families. FGC brings together professionals, client systems, extended family, and others in the support networks to discuss and collaborate together to determine the optimal way to serve the client system (Brodie & Gadling-Cole, 2008).

The intervention phase can be a time of gratification and fulfillment, but it can also be a time of challenges. Changing lifelong behaviors and patterns of interaction is sometimes difficult and even painful for clients. Social workers, too, can be challenged when clients are unable or unready to change their lifestyles. Nevertheless, when social workers and clients commit to mutually agreed-upon goals and agree to make adjustments as needed, the intervention can produce a positive outcome. A written contract, mutually agreed upon by both the social worker and the client, is a valuable tool in the development and implementation of an intervention. Contracting with a client system can help the social worker and client to clarify their purpose, respective roles and expectations (Shulman, 2009). Box 9.2 provides an example of a contract format that can be used to develop goals and strategies for the planned change effort. Although the intervention phase may seem to be the culmination of the client–social worker relationship, evaluation and termination of the intervention are equally important.

EXHIBIT 9.2

*Steps in Social
Work
Intervention*

Planning Phase

- Involve the client in the implementation planning process. Ask the client to identify areas of concern or desired change.
- Prioritize the client's concerns based on the client's desired goals for change. You may suggest options, while recognizing the client's right to self-determination.
- Using behavioral terms, reflect the client's priorities back to the client so they may be translated into specific needs, tasks or behaviors for change. This process might require you to move the client from generally conceptualized priorities to specific ones that can be translated into operatonalized goals and activities.
- Determine the level(s) of intervention or strategy—individual, couple, family, group, and/or organizational—that is most appropriate for each need, recognizing that any change has the potential to impact others.
- Establish measurable and achievable goals. These goals should be clear, specific, and attainable given the client's strengths and resources.
- Articulate objectives (the strategies for attaining the desired goals) and action steps to be taken by client system and the social worker.
- Formalize a contract specifying the steps to be taken by the client and the social worker and the time frame. Contracts can be framed in implicit, oral, or written terms. Written contracts are the most specific form and are helpful strategies for monitoring the progress of the change effort toward attaining the client's goals. Regardless of the form, the contents of the contract should be clear, specific, measurable, include a timeframe, and within the reach of the client and social worker. See Box 9.2 for an example of a written contract.

Implementation Phase

- Complete the tasks contracted for during the planning phase.
- Monitor the contract at regular intervals to determine if the goals are still viable or if they need to be adjusted, terminated, or deleted from the contract.

Source: Adapted from Kirst-Ashman & Hull, 2006; Sheafor & Horejsi, 2008; and Shulman, 2009.

Evaluation and Termination of Individuals and Families

After Emily worked with Victoria for three months, she reminded Victoria that their goal was to terminate the relationship when Victoria felt she no longer needed Emily's support. The two of them took this opportunity to evaluate their work together. Using the contract they had negotiated as a basis for their evaluation, they reviewed each of the objectives. By that time, Victoria had settled into her new apartment. With the community police officer's help, she had taken a number of personal and environmental safety measures. She was regularly attending the sexual assault survivor support group and had seen the clinical social worker three times. She wanted to continue with the support group because she felt they understood her fears, setbacks, and uneasiness in talking about the event with others. Because the goals that they established were specific and measurable, Emily and Victoria were able to determine that their work together was a success and Victoria was ready to terminate her relationship with Emily.

Evaluation is the process by which the social worker and client system assess the progress and success of the planned change effort and determine whether it is time to terminate the relationship. In order for the social worker and the client to conduct a meaningful evaluation, the assessment and intervention phases must have been conducted in a comprehensive, well-conceived, and collaborative manner. In turn, these phases can be completed successfully only if the goals and objectives were developed with specificity and clear-cut strategies for measurement.

Evaluations can occur in two forms. Process evaluations focus on assessing the social work intervention itself (for example, the dynamics of the social worker–client system relationship), while outcome evaluations are targeted at determining the success of the intervention in attaining the defined goals (Shulman, 2009). The social worker may want to conduct periodic evaluations throughout the course of the intervention to monitor its progress. If progress is not being made, the social worker and client can refocus the intervention strategy in a direction that is more likely to promote a successful outcome.

Although periodic evaluations are helpful, evaluating the intervention at the time agreed upon in the contract is critical. This allows the social worker and client to address some fundamental questions: Can the relationship be terminated because the goals have been successfully achieved? Were the goals not achieved and should they be renegotiated? Should the relationship be terminated because there is no longer a need? Determining whether the intervention facilitated the change that the client desired also serves as a way of evaluating the social worker's practice (for example, is the social worker offering appropriate and helpful input?). Using the contract as a basis for evaluation, the social worker and client can scrutinize each aspect of the intervention to determine whether the social worker upheld her or his commitment to the client and the change effort, adhered to professional ethical standards, and met the obligations to which she or he contracted.

As in so many areas of social work practice, a variety and combination of methods and skills are available for conducting evaluations. Some specific strategies for measuring the success of practice approaches include evaluating programs and change. Measuring clients' attitudes and behaviors before, during, and following an intervention provides evidence of change. Obtaining the client's feedback regarding services and benefits is a common strategy for evaluation. Client satisfaction measures should be interpreted with caution, however, as satisfaction, or lack thereof, does not necessarily determine success or effectiveness.

Client Names(s):

Victoria H.

Client System's Description of Issues to be Addressed:

Feel safe

Remain independent

Goals and Tasks:

Goal	Client Tasks/Date	Social Worker Tasks/Date
1. Arrange for safe alternative housing.	Inquire about apartment above ground floor.	Provide referral to community police program.
2. Talk with my family and fiancé about the rape.	Attend survivor support group and meet with therapist.	Provide referral to survivor support group and therapist specializing in rape trauma.
3. Assume control of my life.	Journal daily and share journal with social worker.	Provide support as needed.

Date Contract will be reviewed

3 months from date of contract

I agree with the above stated goals, to complete the contracted tasks, and participate in a review and evaluation of the contract on the specified date.

Victoria	Emily
Client	Social Worker

Date	Date

BOX 9.2

Sample Contract for Client System and Social Worker Intervention Planning

Another effective strategy is to monitor change through the life of a contract. Developing the contract to identify mutual goals, strengths, and resources; strategies for achieving the goals; and barriers to goal achievement will give the social worker and client a working document for evaluating change throughout the intervention.

In addition to the contract, social workers typically document each encounter that occurs with and about the client system. Such documentation may be recorded in writing or electronic form and cannot, under most circumstances, be shared or released without the consent of the client or the client's legal representative (e.g., parent or guardian). Documentation can be utilized for a variety of purposes, including: accountability (to supervisors, funders, or legal system); monitoring client progress; and improving the social worker's practice skills (Kagle, 2009). Therefore, documenting such information as facts related to the situation, your observations, and client activities can become key to the evaluation process.

Agencies that fund social work programs and services have placed increasing importance on evaluating social workers' services as a way to determine funding levels. In other words, social workers can no longer just try to "help people." Rather, they now must verify that people were helped, and they must identify change that occurred as a result of the intervention. Within the profession itself, evaluating social work methods and practices enables social work educators to develop curricula that will train new social workers to be effective and efficient.

After completing their evaluation of their work together, Emily and Victoria planned for termination. They agreed they would meet one more time. At that meeting, they again reviewed the goals they had established and the progress that Victoria had made in meeting her goals. They discussed plans for handling situations in which Victoria felt her safety was being threatened, and they anticipated such events as the anniversary of the rape and her upcoming marriage. Emily offered Victoria the option to contact her in the future if she felt a need to talk or just to let Emily know how she was doing. Emily commended Victoria on her strength in handling this situation, and she told Victoria she appreciated Victoria's willingness to work with her. Victoria told Emily that she had been a "lifesaver" and she would forever be grateful to her. She admitted that she would miss Emily, and she was grateful to know that she could call Emily if she felt a need to talk with her.

Termination, defined as the official breaking off of the social worker–client relationship, is the goal from the first encounter. Failure to establish termination as the ultimate objective can lead to situations in which the client becomes dependent on the social worker. Individuals and families can come to feel comfortable in their relationships with the social worker and be reluctant to lose the support and caring that the worker provides. Because the mission of social work is to empower clients to enhance their functioning and well-being, social workers are obligated to engage the client, assess the situation, plan and carry out an intervention, evaluate the intervention, and then terminate the planned change relationship. The social worker who empowers the client to make changes in her or his life and devises a plan for maintaining that change provides a greater service than a worker who creates a relationship in which the client continues to look to the worker for help with each life crisis. Of course, if future events create a real need for assistance, services can be resumed.

Terminations occur for a variety of reasons and in a variety of ways. The social work relationship can be terminated in the following situations:

- The goals have successfully been achieved.

- The client withdraws from the relationship because she or he no longer agrees with the plan established within the contract.

- The client is no longer eligible to receive services.

- The social worker feels that the goals cannot be achieved or the client is unwilling to comply with the contract.

- The social worker or agency is no longer the most appropriate service provider for the client.

- The social worker leaves the agency.

Ideally, the concept of termination is introduced at the first social worker–client encounter. It is then built into the intervention, routinely discussed, and carried out in a planned manner. Planned terminations enable the client to enter into the contract and work through the intervention with a clear focus on the desired outcome, knowing that when the specified goals are reached, the planned change relationship will be terminated. Determining the point at which termination can occur often influences the planning and implementation of the intervention. For example, when working with a person who identifies self-sufficiency as a priority, the social worker can design an intervention aimed toward independent living and economic stability. When the person has secured housing and a regular income, the planned change relationship can then be successfully terminated.

Successful termination of the social work relationship includes the following processes:

- Reviewing the goals and objectives included in the contract to determine whether these goals have been met, to identify barriers to meeting the goals, and consider future goals.

- Developing a plan for maintaining change after the relationship has been terminated. This plan must anticipate issues such as the client's response should the crisis occur again, as well as the skills, resources, and strengths developed and needed for the client's response.

- Discussing continued professional contact between the social worker and the client, anticipating such questions as when and under what conditions future contact would be acceptable and the appropriate parameters for that contact.

- Expressing feelings about ending the relationship. The nature of the social work relationship can be intense and personal, and both the client and social worker can feel anxious or sad about ending that part of their lives. Therefore, discussing feelings is an important ingredient in a successful termination.

A skillfully facilitated termination can be gratifying for both the client system and the social worker. Client systems can achieve a sense of closure and, if permitted by agency policy, can be reassured that they can contact the social worker in the future if the need arises. Also feeling a sense of closure, the social worker can end the planned change relationship with the client, having addressed the progress, developed a maintenance plan, and discussed their feelings about the work they have completed together.

CONCLUSION

Social work practice with individuals and families can be approached systematically using the steps of engagement, assessment, intervention, and evaluation. Although such an approach provides a structure for working with individuals and families, facilitating a planned change is not always straightforward, simple, or without complications. During the intervention phase, the social worker should routinely revisit the original assessment to determine whether it is accurate.

Working with client systems whose lives can be steeped in crises, unexpected twists and turns, and external pressures requires social workers to be flexible and patient. Social workers must be willing to renegotiate or delay plans for interventions in order to respond to unplanned changes in the planned change effort. The change process is not typically a linear process, but a fluid one that requires returning to steps that may previously have been addressed or completed.

In the next two chapters, we explore the process of engagement, assessment, intervention, and evaluation in the context of social work practice with groups, organizations, and communities. Although the client systems at the group and community levels are larger, the same basic premise provides the foundation for the social work intervention. Having the knowledge and skills to build rapport and trust, gather information, develop a planned change effort, and evaluate and terminate the intervention is the same regardless of the size or makeup of the client system.

This chapter has provided you with the framework from which you can expand your social work knowledge and skills. The agency in which you work will determine the specific assessment tools, intervention protocols, and evaluation methods that you will use, but having a well-grounded knowledge of the change process will enable you to transfer the knowledge and skills to the setting.

MAIN POINTS

- Direct social work practice with individuals and families is the process of working one-on-one with the client system to identify and assess a need and develop a plan for facilitating a change.

- The client system's investment in the change process is key to the success of the social work intervention. The social worker is a collaborator in the planned change process.

- Developing a social work intervention using the strengths perspective is essential for identifying the assets and resources possessed by the client system and for planning a successful intervention.

- Social workers practicing with individuals and families use a variety of skills within the context of engagement, assessment, intervention, and evaluation.

- Engagement is the building of rapport and trust with the client system.

- Assessment includes gathering information about the client system and the client's perception of her or his strengths, resources, and needs.

- With the client, the social worker plans an intervention that includes determining desired goals, priorities, barriers to change, and strategies for making change.

- Evaluation consists of assessing the progress and/or success of change and the change process, the effectiveness of the social work intervention, and readiness to terminate the client–worker relationship.

EXERCISES

1. It is now your turn to apply the knowledge of individual and family social work practices that you have acquired by reading this chapter. Using either the Sanchez Family interactive case or the Carla Washburn case (go to www.routledgesw.com/cases), you will have the opportunity to experience a social work relationship from engagement through evaluation.
   a. Locate the Case Study Tools and select Biopsychosocial. Review each of the four perspectives. Open the panel for the Sanchez family and review each of the four biopsychosocial perspectives. Select one of the biopsychosocial perspectives, click on a topic in the center circle to select it, and answer each of

the questions that appear. After you have completed these questions, complete Tasks 1–3 for this section.

b. Go to the Intervene tab. Continuing with the client that you selected in the assessment phase, develop an intervention plan. Following the prompts, define goals and needs, identify Tasks for the client and social worker, and complete the timeline. Complete Tasks 1–3 for this section.

Next, go to the Case Study Tools and select the Interaction Matrix. Match the client with whom you were working previously with the members of her/his family by clicking on Plot the Interaction. Identify the issues or barriers that exist between your client and her/his family members.

c. Go to the Evaluate tab. Continuing with your selected client, complete Tasks 1–3 for that specific client.

2. This chapter highlighted the importance of "starting where the client is." Review the following scenario and prepare a response to the questions that follow:

Mr. J. is a 61-year-old male. He was diagnosed with probable dementia of the Alzheimer's type. Mr. J. is experiencing increasing memory problems; he has been unable to find his car in the mall parking lot on three occasions, and has begun to lose his possessions (e.g., glasses, keys, etc.) on a regular basis. He works as a shipping and receiving foreman for a discount chain store. Given that the typical course of Alzheimer's disease is eight to ten years from time of diagnosis to death, the physician has recommended that Mr. J. consider early retirement within the next year and that he be evaluated by the Department of Motor Vehicles to determine if he is safe to drive. The physician has asked you to follow up with Mr. J. and his family to implement these recommendations. Mr. J. and his family—which includes his wife and adult son—are adamantly opposed to both recommendations, stating that his forgetfulness is just normal aging and that everyone misplaces small items and gets lost in large parking lots. Where do you begin?

a. Describe the way in which you would start where the client is.

b. Reflect on the possible strengths and challenges related to starting where the client is in the scenario you have just read.

3. Write a script as though it were a play. The script will focus on a social worker interviewing an individual or family client system. Include in the script the questions that the social worker would ask in her/his assessment of the individual or family. Also include the facial and body language of the social worker and the client system. Include the client system's responses to the social worker. At the close of the script, draw an ecomap of the individual or family system and identify the individual and family strengths and areas for growth and change.

4. Describe a change you have made in your life, how you were able to do so, why you made the change, and the long term effects of the change on you and those in your environment. Discuss how this experience might impact your work and professional development.

CHAPTER 10

Social Work Practice with Groups

Over a period of time, Emily began to notice that the clients staying at the shelter for women who had experienced partner abuse and their children shared a common concern regarding parenting. In working with the women with children, Emily heard many women voice apprehension about the effects of domestic violence on their children. Emily was uncertain as to the most effective method for addressing this issue. After talking to co-workers and conducting research regarding options, Emily determined three possible strategies for responding to the need for parenting information:

1. *the Community-wide Domestic Violence Coalition could develop a program;*

2. *Emily could approach a local clinical social worker about forming a therapy group for women who had been victims of domestic violence, and parenting could be incorporated as a therapeutic goal; or*

3. *Emily's agency could form a support group for current and former residents of the shelter.*

In this chapter, we will learn more about each of the options Emily proposed and the one that best met the needs of Emily's clients.

Working with groups has long been a part of social work practice. Also referred to as **mezzo (meso)** practice, **group work** is a practice method in which the social worker works with a multiperson client system to develop a planned change effort that meets the needs of the group. The goals of group work focus on addressing individual issues, a need for information and education, support, or social problems. The social worker's role in a group can be as a initiator, facilitator, therapist, resource person, consultant, or evaluator.

Social work practice with groups emphasizes group interdependence, interaction, and support as the vehicle for change. Group practice is built on the concept that change occurs as a result of the ongoing and changing group dynamics and group members' interactions with one another. Thus, group social work practice has a dual role—the group and the individual change as a result of the group intervention (Schopler & Galinsky, 1995). Essentially, the strength of group work is that a group can accomplish more as a group than a person can alone, whether the desired change is on the individual or community level. Moreover, the concept of "people helping people" can be empowering, depathologize problems and stigmas, and reduce social and emotional isolation (Gitterman & Knight, 2000, p. 15). As Kurland (2007) offers:

> the very act of forming a group is a statement of our belief that every member of the group has something to offer the others, something to give to others, not just to get from them. (p. 12)

Group work is increasingly a part of most social workers' career experiences. While only eighteen percent of social workers identify group work as their primary area of practice (Whitaker & Arrington, 2008), most social workers engage in some form of group social work practice as a part of their social work positions and view group work as just one of many activities in which they engage. The NASW *Code of Ethics* (2008) includes working with groups as one of the ethical principles for social work practice. The *Code* charges social workers to strengthen relationships and the well-being of people at all levels of social work practice, including social groups. The *Code* also mandates that social workers practice with competence, thus providing the basis for all social workers to have knowledge and skills for working with groups.

This chapter highlights the historical development of group work as a method of social work intervention and the role of group work within generalist social work practice. We will explore the types of group work methods along with an introduction to skills needed to effectively deliver group services.

HISTORICAL PERSPECTIVE ON SOCIAL WORK PRACTICE WITH GROUPS

First used in the settlement house movement of the late 1890s, a group approach was most effective for the reform of such social problems as inadequate housing and working conditions, a concept still present in contemporary community-based organizations (Schopler & Galinsky, 1995). Group work for the promotion of recreational and educational activities then emerged after World War I. Mary Richmond, known primarily for her contributions to the development of practice with individuals and families, began to draw attention to the practice of group work during the 1920s, but it was not until the 1930s that group work was recognized within the profession as a method for intervention (Brieland, 1995). Before the introduction of training specific to group social work practice, group work was considered primarily a recreational or nonprofessional activity.

The term group work was first used in 1927 and provided the basis for introducing curricula to train social workers in professional group facilitation (Brieland, 1995). By the 1930s and 1940s, group work had become an intervention method for professional social workers working with hospitalized patients, persons with developmental disabilities and mental illness, and returning World War II veterans. The Great Depression of the 1930s contributed to the growth of social work practice with groups as social workers mobilized groups for the purpose of social change and coping with the devastation of the depression (Garvin, 1997). However, controversy regarding group work's place within social work practice continued as professionals debated whether group work was a recreational activity, a social work method, or a separate profession.

Interest in incorporating group methods into social work practice continued to grow and expand into more settings over the next several decades. During the 1960s, the profession began to view group work as a part of social work practice and began to promote a similar skill set for casework and group work (Garvin, 1997). By the 1970s, social workers were participating in a variety of experimental groups focused on self-improvement. Over the next 20 years, group work became an integrated part of social work practice for social workers addressing clients' challenges and issues at the individual and family, organizational, and community levels.

Group social work practice is now recognized as part of the profession's mission to empower and promote well-being through the social worker's serving in the roles of broker, teacher/educator, enabler, advocate, mobilizer, mediator, and case manager. Group work has evolved into an area of social work practice that can meet the multiple demands of the profession because it can be applied in a range of settings, with diverse populations, uses a variety of practice approaches, and is applicable for intervention at the individual, group, and community levels (Garvin & Galinsky, 2008). The profession recognizes the value of educating all social workers in group knowledge and skills. As a result, all social work students are exposed to group work theory and practice through coursework and field experiences. In recognition of the importance of social workers having competence in the areas of group work, the Association for the Advancement of Social Work with Groups (AASWG) has developed standards for social work practice with groups (2005). Listed in Box 10.1, the standards specify the core knowledge and values needed for social work practice with groups.

MODELS OF CHANGE IN SOCIAL WORK PRACTICE WITH GROUPS

Building on the knowledge and skill base established for working with individuals and families, group work practice has evolved into distinct change approaches with

BOX 10.1

*Standards for
Social Work
Practice with
Groups*

Core Values and Knowledge
- Core values emphasize respect for the persons and their autonomy and creation of a socially just society.
- Core knowledge includes knowledge of: individuals; groups and small group behavior; function of the group worker.

Pre Group Phase: Planning, Recruitment, and New Group Formation
- Work in this phase includes: identifying aspirations, needs, and goals; determining group structure and process; recruiting and orienting members; and developing group purpose and methods.

Group Work in the Beginning Phase
- Work in this phase includes establishing a beginning contract, cultivating group cohesion, and shaping norms of participation.

Group work in the Middle Phase
- Work in this phase includes assisting progress on individual and group goals; attending to group dynamics/processes; and assisting members to identify and access resources from inside and outside the group.

Group Work in the Ending Phase
- Work in this phase includes preparing members for group ending; identifying gains and changes; discussing impact of the group on systems outside the group and the movement the group has made over time; and identifying direct and indirect signs of members' and worker's reactions to ending; evaluating achievement; and helping members make connections and apply new knowledge and skills.

Source: Excerpted from AASWG, 2006.

similar theoretical underpinnings. Three models for group work were introduced at a 1966 meeting of the Council on Social Work Education that continue to influence contemporary social work practice with groups (Garvin, 1997). The three models include goals related to social issues, remediation, and reciprocity. Influenced by the collective works of a variety of scholars, all three models are grounded in systems theory and emphasize a goal oriented outcome. More recently, a fourth model has been added. The task group model also emphasizes a goal-oriented focus (Toseland & Horton, 2008). As this century unfolds, group social work practice has become integrated into social work practice that draws on an eclectic variety of theoretical frameworks.

Each of the models described in this section has multiple uses and similarities. As you will learn from Emily's situation, one issue can be addressed by more than one intervention. While distinct in nature, each group shares the similarity that change can occur as a result of the group effort and could not be reached as effectively with only individual efforts.

Social Goals Groups

Aimed at facilitating social change on the organizational or community level, social goals groups, or social action groups, originated from the early work of reformers, but continue to be a primary approach used by social workers striving to achieve social change today. Rooted in the concepts of social responsibility, social action, democracy, and social justice, a social goals group strives to change society by changing social structures (Toseland & Horton, 2008). A key component of social work practice with organizations and communities, social goals groups may be established for the purposes of accomplishing specific tasks, carrying out the goals of an organization, changing a law or policy, or developing a new program. The social worker may serve as initiator, participant, or consultant of a social change group. Professionals or nonprofessional persons may lead social action groups. Typically, the group's goals determine the leadership.

Groups whose aim is goal specific can be short term if there is no need for the group to continue once the goal is achieved or the time limit has expired for the goal to be achieved. For goal-specific groups that have an ongoing mission, longevity may be indefinite.

The following are examples of task-oriented social action groups.

- *Neighborhood groups that promote a safe environment:* Such a group may hold regular meetings to strategize ways to improve and monitor neighborhood safety. The group may be composed of neighborhood residents, social service professionals who work in the neighborhood, and law enforcement personnel. Such a group is likely to be long term, but the focus may shift from establishing a plan for safety to one of maintaining the plan. Due to their involvement in the community, social workers are often in a position to identify the need for a neighborhood group; so they may serve to mobilize the group, but not to lead the group. Neighborhood residents with an investment in their community are usually most effective as group leaders.

- *Members of the Alzheimer's Association:* Such a group may be formed to lobby legislators to introduce and pass legislation requiring mandatory dementia education for long-term residential care workers caring for patients with Alzheimer's disease. This group may be composed of family members of persons suffering from dementia, representatives from the residential long-term care industry, and health and social service professionals. This group may exist over multiple legislative sessions, but the lifetime of the group will be determined by the success or failure of proposed legislation. Should the legislation be enacted, the group may refocus its efforts on implementing and monitoring the mandatory educational requirements, or they may redirect their efforts to other legislation to protect persons living with dementia. The social worker's employment position or personal interest in the issue will determine her or his role.

- *Child welfare workers from various public and private agencies that monitor the foster care system:* To ensure that children in the foster care system have timely and permanent plans developed, such a group might meet regularly to provide oversight of all foster care cases in a city, county, or region. Group members can include professionals from multiple professions, such as social work, education, health, and law. This group essentially provides a quality assurance function and could exist indefinitely. The social worker's role may be as a leader, facilitator, chair, participant, or a combination of these roles.

Faced with the dilemma regarding the best approach for strengthening the parenting needs of women receiving services from the domestic violence program, Emily asked to have the issue placed on the agenda for the monthly meeting of the Community-wide Domestic Violence Coalition. This group of social, medical, and legal service professionals had organized for the purpose of enhancing communication among the community's domestic violence services, influencing legislation, and training members of the community to respond effectively to victims of domestic violence. Because they developed programs to address specific domestic violence–related needs, Emily thought the group might be appropriate for creating a program for parenting. After hearing Emily's proposal that such a program be developed, Coalition members determined that the provision of direct client services was outside the purview of their mission. Coalition members felt that such a service should be provided by individual agencies to simplify such issues as leadership, funding, and comfort level of potential participants.

Remedial Groups

With an exclusive emphasis on problem-focused individual growth and change, remedial, or therapeutic, goals groups are professionally facilitated groups aimed at helping group members enhance their social functioning. Also known as treatment groups, group therapy, group psychotherapy, and clinical group work, the goal for the person in a remedial goals group is to eliminate or cope with a specific social, emotional, or behavioral issue (Barker, 2003). Clinically oriented group work was first incorporated into social work practice in rehabilitation settings (Garvin, 1997). As discussed in the next section on reciprocal groups, not all group work focused on individual growth and change is in therapeutic or treatment groups. The distinguishing factor for therapeutic groups is the presence of a professional group leader and the development of treatment goals specific to individual change.

Group dynamics—interacting with other group members, hearing their experiences, and strategizing personal attitudinal and behavioral change—is influential in promoting change within the group members, but group goals are secondary to the goals of each group member. Problem-solving, behavior change, restored functioning, and development of coping skills are typically the focus of a remedial group (Toseland & Horton, 2008).The role for the social worker is typically as a leader or facilitator. Social workers may also serve as co-leaders of certain types of therapy groups, particularly in cases of single gendered groups, groups that are conflictual in nature, or groups that encompass emotionally sensitive issues.

Therapeutic groups often arise when a professional identifies several individuals within the agency's client population that share a common presenting issue. In the case of the mothers at Emily's shelter, Emily determined that the agency was serving a number of clients who shared a common concern. Therapeutic groups may meet for a specified number of sessions or weeks or have an open-ended time limit or number of sessions. They may also be closed or open: Closed groups have a designated group membership that does not change during the lifetime of the group, whereas group members can move in and out of open groups as needs arise.

The following are examples of groups that might be formed for the purpose of therapeutically focused group work.

- *Persons hospitalized for mental illness:* Social workers working in psychiatric facilities often conduct group therapy on a daily or weekly basis with patients hospitalized for newly diagnosed or chronic or persistent mental illness. These social worker–led groups usually supplement individual therapy, but the interactions among group members serve to support and enhance individual treatment. The group itself is typically open and ongoing, the membership changing with admissions to and discharges from the facility. Group membership may be determined by diagnosis, time and duration of admission, or gender.

- *Survivors of childhood incest:* A group composed of persons who are survivors of incest is likely to be single gendered due to the emotional intensity of the issue and the fact that incest raises considerable trust problems for the survivors. A survivor group may be formed within an agency by the administrative or clinical staff and can either be time limited or ongoing and open or closed. In determining the type and timing of a survivor group, the social worker is sensitive to the nature of the trauma and the situations of the individual members of the group.

- *Male batterers:* A group of men identified by the social service or legal system as batterers can be composed of involuntary or voluntary members. Involuntary groups, particularly ones with members that have a history of violence, can be challenging groups to facilitate due to members' hostility and resentment regarding their participation in the group. A group for batterers is typically a highly structured group with a focus on behavioral change. Such groups are often led by co-facilitators to enable a balanced response to disputes and angry outbursts. Behaviorally focused groups are typically time limited and closed in order to enhance the therapist's ability to provide information and promote individual change and group cohesion.

Emily considered forming a therapy group to respond to the need for parenting information for the shelter's residents. With a BSW, Emily was not trained to conduct a therapy group, so she explored the possibility of co-leading a treatment group with a local clinical social worker in private practice. Emily developed a concept that the therapist would offer a weekly therapy group for women who had been battered by their partners. The voluntary, open-ended group would be accessible to women in the community, and the therapist could incorporate parenting issues for children who have also been victimized by domestic violence. After discussing her proposal with the clinical social worker, Emily and the clinical social worker jointly agreed that a therapy group was one effective approach for addressing the women's feelings regarding their life experience, and parenting issues would naturally become a part of the discussion. The two social workers agreed that they would not include a formal parenting education curriculum in this group.

Reciprocal Groups

Also referred to as the mutual aid, self-help, and support group model, reciprocal groups emphasize the concept of common goals, interests and exchange as the basis for change. Group members come together out of a shared interest or experience. Personal growth and change occur as a result of group members sharing those commonalities, exchanging support with one another, and receiving information about their shared issue. Receiving support from others who have similar experiences can be validating and empowering for the membership. Based on a member's needs and personality, support groups can be used to augment individual treatment or can be beneficial as a stand-alone resource. Reciprocal aid groups differ from therapy groups in several areas: (1) leaders can be professional or nonprofessional, (2) individual members do not typically have specified treatment goals, and (3) the intervention occurs as a result of the members' interpersonal relationships.

The group and the reasons for its origins often determine the social worker's role. Being on the forefront of service delivery, the social worker may identify a common need among her or his clients and be instrumental in creating the opportunity for a support group to meet at the agency. The social worker may serve initially as the group's facilitator and turn that role over to the group itself. The leader's role can be multi-faceted. She or he can serve as a mediator between group members, encourage an environment to enable members to work as a group, and facilitate interactions between members to support individuals in meeting their goals (Toseland & Horton, 2008). Support groups are typically less formal than therapy groups and are open so that members can move in and out of the group as they feel a need.

The following are examples of self-help, support-focused groups.

- *Addictions groups:* The 12-step model that originated with Alcoholics Anonymous is an example of a self-help group with members providing the leadership. Addictions self-help groups have expanded beyond alcohol to include other drugs, food, gambling, and sexual behavior. Social workers can play a leadership role in addictions groups, but in a traditional 12-step model, there is no formal or professional leadership. Most addictions-focused groups are open ended, with members using the group to sustain their recovery process. Members may stop participating as they feel confident in their behavioral change.

- *Adoption or sibling groups:* Groups for families that are acquiring new members through adoption, remarriage, or birth may focus on providing education about such issues as the adoption or birth, but they also provide an opportunity for the members to identify and share their feelings about the change.

- *Disease/health condition groups:* Groups for persons suffering from a particular health condition are often facilitated by hospital social workers or social workers in organizations that advocate for and educate the public on specific health concerns. Groups are formed for persons with a variety of conditions, such as cancer, multiple sclerosis, strokes, and pregnancy.

- *Significant-other groups:* Support groups for the families and friends of persons experiencing a particular life event or health condition have increased in recent years. For example, such groups provide considerable support for the family and friends of persons newly diagnosed with an illness or injury; gays, lesbians, bisexuals, and transgendered persons; persons that have been victimized by an assault or disaster; and persons experiencing an addiction.

Investigating the third option in her pursuit of a parenting program, Emily approached the administration of her own agency. Emily described the need that she and other workers had identified among the mothers being served by the agency and the results of her research and consultation. She proposed that the agency offer a psychoeducational group (one that includes both education and emotional support) so that the clients could be exposed to parenting education, share their concerns, and strategize about ways to respond to their children's experience with domestic violence. Emily felt she could make a greater impact on this issue through a group, as she could provide information on parenting, a group experience could complement the individual work she and her co-workers were engaging in with each woman, and the women could support one another. The agency director agreed with Emily's assessment and gave approval for Emily to develop the group and advertise it to her co-workers and former and current residents. Although several potentially viable options for responding to a client need emerged from Emily's ideas and research, she was confident that the support group approach could provide the parenting support and information needed by the mothers.

Task Groups

A fourth model of group practice, the task group model, brings together features of the three previously described models. The focus of a task group is to work toward completing a task, action, or goal that has been previously agreed on by the group members (Furman et al., 2009). The task group is a collaboration aimed at creating solutions to specific problems or issues that exist for a group larger than the task group itself (Toseland & Horton, 2008). The group utilizes reciprocal respect, information sharing, and decision-making process to achieve the mutually-agreed upon goals. Like the other models described, a task group can encompass a focused goal (social goals model), returning stability or function (remediation model), or mutual support (reciprocal model).

Building on a strengths-based foundation, the social worker strives to help group members identify their strengths and potential contributions. The social worker's roles also include facilitating group communication, consensus, and progress toward the agreed-upon goals. While typically structured with a designated leader, agenda, and work plan, task groups can also be meetings that involve brainstorming, planning, and conflict resolution (Furman et al., 2009).

Examples of task groups include:

- *Individual Education Plan (IEP):* School and community staff along with parents or guardians meet regularly to discuss the educational and social progress of students who have special needs. The social worker brings a systemic and strengths-based perspective to this interprofessional team.

- *Senior Immigrant Project:* A group of co-workers at a community-based agency serving older adults wants to provide culturally appropriate services to the growing population of older immigrants that live in the area. The social work convenes a group to collaborate on a grant proposal to submit to a private foundation to develop a program for the older adults and their families.

- *Volunteer Appreciation Task Force:* The volunteer coordinator at the food pantry calls a meeting of the staff to develop plans to show appreciation to the agency's volunteers for the countless hours spent helping the organization collect, sort, and distribute food donations. By consensus, the group developed a plan to host a dinner where they would prepare the food and serve the volunteers.

SKILLS FOR SOCIAL WORK PRACTICE WITH GROUPS

Social work practice with groups builds on many of the skills that are used in working with individuals and families. In fact, regardless of the social work group model being delivered, they all share five commonalities: (1) systems approach; (2) understanding of group dynamics; (3) intervention approach; (4) intervention processes; and (5) commitment to evidence of effectiveness (Garvin & Galinsky, 2008). Establishing a group for persons with a common cause, need, or agenda does not ensure that the group process will be mutually beneficial for all members (Shulman, 2009).

Without understanding the concepts and power of group practice, the social worker may attempt to be the sole "helper" in the group; whereas using group practice skills, the social worker understands the entire group serves as helpers (Gitterman & Knight, 2000). Group work also uses the skills of engagement, assessment, intervention, and evaluation that were introduced in Chapter 9. We will focus on these skills as they apply to the phases of group work. Despite the type, makeup, purpose, or structure of a group, all group experiences have three phases—beginning, middle, and end. The beginning phase encompasses engagement and assessment activities, the middle phase includes the intervention, and the ending phase involves evaluation and termination. As the group intervention moves through the planned change effort, social workers often notice that conflict becomes a normal part of the group process and can be a part of the intervention itself.

First, the group must be formed and membership determined. When social workers have the opportunity to determine group membership, they may be able to ease the process of engaging group members by attending to the factors that influence group dynamics. Forming a group that is optimally configured in terms of goals, member characteristics, and logistical issues contributes to group and worker cohesion, enabling the group to progress more quickly to the tasks at hand. However, social workers may not always have free rein in determining group members. The following factors that affect group membership may or may not be influenced by the social worker:

- Individual and group eligibility criteria and goals determine who may be eligible or interested in joining the group.

- The pool of group members from which the social worker can draw will vary.

- Logistical issues such as time, location, cost, duration, and accessibility (for example, open versus closed) should accommodate group members' needs.

- Optimal size, for example, is 6 to 8 members for a therapy group, while 15 to 20 is acceptable for support and educational groups. Task groups range from small to very large.

- Some groups thrive on a mixture of personality types, ages, and gender, while other groups need homogeneity of personality types for a successful experience. For example, young children can be in mixed gender groups, but adolescents may find mixed gender groups uncomfortable, particularly if issues of sexuality are to be discussed.

Once Emily had permission to form a parenting support group for current and former shelter clients, she began by gathering information from her co-workers regarding their perceptions of client needs in the area of parenting. She also obtained input from clients at one of the weekly house meetings in which staff and current clients discuss house issues. Her idea was favorably received, and she went ahead with the planning. The group was scheduled for a time and location that Emily felt best served the clients. She arranged for the group members' children to be supervised by a volunteer. Emily created flyers to post around the house and to mail to those former clients that she knew it was safe to contact. For their safety, women who return to live with batterers cannot always be contacted by the social worker. Because this group has a psychoeducational focus, Emily felt that diversity in age, race, and ethnicity would be an asset.

During the first session, Emily began by explaining the origins and purpose of the group. She asked each member to introduce herself and say as much or as little about herself as she wished and to state one goal she had for herself in joining this group. Next, Emily and the group developed some general rules related to frequency of sessions, attendance, speaking out of turn, handling conflicts, and sharing information about group members outside the group meeting. Because Emily knew each of the group members from her stay at the shelter, the first session was comfortable, and the members began to bond with one another.

Engagement of Groups

The first step in engaging the group is to perceive the group as the client system. Although groups are made up of individual members and the social worker engages each of those individual members, she or he engages the entire group as well. Regardless of the type of group work being practiced, the beginning stage includes group formation and first meeting activities:

- *Introductions:* Group members have the opportunity to introduce themselves by the name they wish to be called during group meetings and to share with the group any information they feel is relevant for the group experience. Social goals and task group members may share their particular knowledge or expertise that brought them to the group.

- *Explaining the purpose of the group:* The person who convened the group (this may be the group leader) is responsible for explaining the reason the group has been formed and to share her or his role and expectations for participating in the group.

- *Establishing group rules, norms, and boundaries:* An important step in engaging group members is to provide the opportunity for each person to voice her or his feelings about individual and group goals and expectations for the group experience. Enabling all the members of a group to contribute to a set of group rules, norms, and boundaries enhances their connection to the leader and to one another, thus motivating them to continue with the group's work. For example, group members may choose to establish rules regarding attendance, timeliness, conflict management, sharing information outside the group, and even responsibility for refreshments.

- *Attending to group members:* Just as attending skills are important for engaging individuals, a similar skill set is required for developing effective group work skills. Focusing on verbal and nonverbal engaging skills to enhance communication, clarify exchanges, and create an environment in which the person feels safe is somewhat more complex at the group level, as the social worker attends to all members of the group at the same time. Keeping the perspective that group work involves facilitating relationships with individual group members and the group itself helps to distinguish the group practitioner in a group setting from a worker who works with individuals (Shulman, 2009). During this early phase of group development, social workers also want to be aware of and sensitive to members' feelings about participating in a group (AASWG, 2006).

    The engagement, or beginning, phase in group practice is essential for the process of building group cohesion and trust. Being part of a group process requires the individual to take risks in sharing thoughts, feelings, and ideas. Members of groups that are effectively engaged by the group leader are likely to feel a higher level of connection to each other and the leader and trust the safety of the group process.

Assessment of Groups

Despite the fact that Emily knew all of the group members before they joined the group, she needed to assess their current situations and, specifically, their concerns and strengths in the area of parenting children exposed to domestic violence. Emily began her assessment of the group members as they introduced themselves, shared their stories, and stated their expectations for the group. This process enabled Emily to learn about the level of violence to which the children had been exposed, the way in which the mothers had handled that exposure, whether the children had been physically abused as well, and behaviors exhibited by the children that concerned the mother.

In addition to assessing each individual, Emily was able to assess the group members in terms of their strengths as parents and the areas in which they could build on those strengths to enhance their parenting skills. Other factors she thought about were the members' investment in the group process, their ability to bond with and support one another, and how they might handle emotional and conflictual situations that could occur within the group.

Following engagement, the next phase of the group process is the assessment of individuals within the group as well as the group as a whole. In addition to identifying individual members' goals, the social worker's role is to help members determine a set of goals for the group. Focusing on the following issues will help to achieve this:

- *Group development:* The social worker's role is to determine whether the group's level of cohesion can support mutual goal setting and sharing that will result in a positive impact on group members (Schopler & Galinsky, 1995). Therefore, assessment of group bonding is critical. The social worker can help group members become aware of their commonalities and their ability to support the goals of the individual members as well as the group. Even the process of establishing group norms, rules, and goals can provide the social worker with information for assessing individual members' communication and interpersonal styles as well as the group's ability to function collectively.

- *Group diversity:* As part of the assessment of group development, the social worker is aware of the influence of member diversity on the group building and work processes (AASWG, 2006). Group member characteristics that can impact group dynamics include race, ethnicity, gender, cultural background, age, values, and professional affiliation. The group process can be a useful strategy for increasing awareness of and educating individuals on stereotypes and diversity issues.

- *Group members' strengths and resources:* In conducting initial and ongoing group assessment, the social worker helps both individuals and the group as a whole to identify strengths, resources, and areas for growth and change. Different from individual assessment, group assessment shifts the emphasis to members of the group, who ask questions, share experiences and insights, and identify resources previously unknown to other members or the social worker.

- *Balance of personal and group goals:* Each group member shares her or his motivation for participating in the group experience and identifies her or his expectations for that participation. The social worker is aware that the change process is a *group* process and balances attention appropriately with each group member. The social worker helps link personal needs to group needs and goals (AASWG, 2006). Group members can be a resource for identifying the concerns and priorities of other members, thus involving all members of the group in the personal change process. Such a strategy fosters development of individual assessment as well as group cohesion. To achieve balance and involvement of all members, the worker uses a combination of open- and closed-ended questions and encourages other members to engage in questioning one another as well.

Ongoing assessment is particularly important in group practice. Because the group experience involves a variety of individual personalities and life experiences, the goals, concerns, and dynamics change constantly. The social worker's role in practice with groups is to be aware of the interactions among group members and to monitor individual and group process and progress. Individual and group goals and group structure (for example, rules, norms, or membership) may change as a result of ongoing assessment. Vigilance and flexibility regarding changing group dynamics allow group members and the social worker to develop plans and interventions to fit the changing needs of the group members as well as the group itself. Ongoing assessment is also a facet of the evaluation process that enables the client and social worker to monitor individual and group progress toward goals.

Intervention with Groups

Using the individual and group goals identified by the group members, Emily proposed that each session have two components: education and support. Each meeting would begin with a "checking in" period in which the members could share successes or ask for help with their parenting. The second half of the session would include a presentation by Emily or another professional on a topic specific to parenting children that have experienced trauma. Together, Emily and the group developed a list of possible topics to cover, being flexible in case additional topics arose. Throughout each session, Emily monitored the interactions of the group members with her and one another and noted individual growth and change. Emily routinely provided feedback to the group on her observations and asked the members to do the same with her and one another.

As with social work interventions at the individual and family practice level, group interventions occur in two phases: planning and implementation. Working with a group in the middle phases of its life, the social worker continues to help establish individual and group goals and begins to develop a plan for achieving those goals.

Keeping in mind the dual emphasis of individual and group goals is necessary for both planning and implementing. Even if the group is able to develop a mutually agreed-upon set of group goals, individual perceptions of the tasks and activities needed to achieve those goals may vary considerably. In addition, the group may reach consensus on group goals, but individual goals are bound to be distinct and unique, just as the group members are distinct and unique persons. Moreover, both individual and group goals may change over the lifetime of the group, requiring the group leader to be aware of and responsive to the need for periodical review of goals. The social worker is responsible for monitoring and overseeing the changing balance of issues.

Planning activities at the group level include establishing goals and documenting the agenda for the group experience.

- *Establishing goals:* The social worker helps the group create goals for the individual within the group and the group itself, using specific and measurable tasks and outcomes. Working with all group members, the social worker provides input into the development of the goals, weighs the advantages and disadvantages of proposed goals, identifies barriers and available and needed resources, and provides links between the individual and group proposals (AASWG, 2006).

- *Documenting the agenda for the group experience:* For remedial and reciprocal goals groups, developing individual and group working agreements helps the participant focus on her or his personal commitment as well as the commitment to the larger group. For social action and task groups, the agreement can be in the form of a working statement of the purpose, goals, and activities of the group while delineating the roles of the individual members. Box 10.2 shows an example of a working agreement, similar to the individual contract in Chapter 9, that can be used in remedial, reciprocal, and social action goals groups.

Implementation of individual and group goals begins by taking action. The social worker and group members put into action the individual and group goals that have been established. As they proceed, the social worker and the group engage in ongoing assessment of their individual and collective work toward individual and group goals to determine whether goals need to be revised.

The implementation stage of group practice may provide the greatest challenges for the social worker and group members, as this stage involves the actual changing

Group Members:

Olivia M.   Tammy R.

Shirley B.   Megan S.

Cynthia W.   Angela G.

Group Goals as Agreed on by All Group Members:

Identify our strengths as mothers

Improve parenting skills

Have a safe place to talk about our experiences

Group Rules and Expectations:

Group will meet weekly; members attend as needed

Members will respect one another's right to speak

All information shared will be confidential

Individual Group Member Goals and Tasks:

Group Member	Goal	Client Tasks/Date	Social Worker Tasks/Date
Olivia	1. Be able to share my situation with others	I will share at least one personal item each meeting	Each meeting, I will support Olivia by asking if she would like to share
	2. Identify my strengths as a parent	I will report at least one positive thing I did during the week as a mother	I will provide information on "parenting without spanking"
	3.		

Date Contract Will Be Reviewed:

8 weeks from today

I agree with the above stated goals, to complete the contracted tasks, and participate in a review and evaluation of the contract on the specified date.

Olivia M.   Emily
Client   Social Worker

Date   Date

of attitudes, behaviors, and completion of tasks. The social worker watches for and addresses individual and group issues that can impede the work of the group. Let us look at some aspects of group dynamics and suggestions for addressing them:

- *Conflict:* Differences may arise as members work toward the contracted goals at varying paces, and conflict can occur concerning individual and group values or when needs change. The social worker may often be confronted with member-to-member conflict as well as member-to-social worker conflict. The social worker can model conflict resolution by responding directly to the conflict and involving group members in facilitating a positive outcome.

- *Violation of group rules and norms:* Even if rules are clearly outlined during the group's early development, members may find themselves unable to comply or to fulfill expectations. Responsibility for confronting violations falls to the group leader. Asking the group to review the previously established rules and to address the infraction empowers the group to act as a unit in determining an appropriate response.

- *Disruptive members:* Group process can suffer from having members that create obstacles to achieving the desired goals. Behaviors that impede the group's progress include talking too much or too little, not fulfilling obligations (for example, attendance or tasks), and being overly critical. A group leader minimizes the disruption by monitoring for such behaviors and addressing the disruptive behaviors either within the group session itself or outside the group meeting. Offering alternative strategies for interacting with the group and modeling appropriate behaviors while in the group provide members with options for appropriate interaction.

The purpose and goals of the group influence the development and implementation of the intervention. For example, an intervention for an anger management group focused on teaching the members appropriate skills for handling their anger may be highly structured and formalized, whereas a group for persons recently widowed may be less structured to foster the sharing of feelings and supporting one another. Despite the type of intervention, relevant strategies are needed that build on individual and group strengths, meet individual and group needs, and focus on specific and measurable outcomes.

Evaluation and Termination of Groups

During the beginning phase of the group's work, Emily and the members agreed the group would meet weekly for eight weeks, and at that point they would evaluate the future of the group. The members also completed a standardized parenting questionnaire at the first and eighth sessions to determine a baseline and changes in parenting style and knowledge. At the eighth session, the group asked that Emily continue the group, but open it to other current and former shelter residents to join. Through these two evaluation strategies, Emily and the group members were able to assess both individual and group goals and make decisions for the future.

The final phase of group work includes evaluation and possible group termination. This segment of group work provides the opportunity to integrate the process of the group experience with the content addressed during the group interactions, thus enabling the social worker and the group members to review learning and changes that occurred (Shulman, 1999). Evaluation at the group level can be more complicated than when working with individuals. Individual and group goals are evaluated along with the group process. In general, strategies for evaluating a group experience evolve from the structure of the group, goals, and intervention tasks and activities. For example, structured groups benefit from more formalized evaluations, while less structured groups (for example, ongoing support groups) may be able to informally evaluate process and progress on a regular basis.

Evaluation is part of the group process from the time the group is formed, but building evaluation into the ending phase serves a variety of functions. Evaluating progress toward individual and group goals can be empowering. The social worker and group members identify personal and group changes that have occurred, assess the impact of the group experience on the members' lives, and determine whether future intervention is needed (AASWG, 2006). On the other hand, individual or group goals may not have been achieved, and an evaluation provides an examination of that outcome as well, to determine whether the goals or the intervention were not appropriate or resources were not available (Schopler & Galinsky, 1995).

To capture the complexities of the group experience, a multifaceted plan for conducting a group evaluation might include the following:

- Audio- or videotaping, with group members' informed consent, to enable the social worker to observe group dynamics and her or his skills.

- Obtaining information from group members in such areas as needs assessments, measures of attitudes or behaviors, or physical measures before and after the group experience.

- Obtaining group member feedback regarding satisfaction with the group experience and the leadership.

- Reviewing individual and group goals.

- Reviewing processes used to accomplish goals.

Groups that are time limited or based on a specific goal or activity may terminate as a group at this stage. In these situations, the termination process encompasses the entire group. On the other hand, open-ended groups may not terminate as a group, but individuals terminate as they leave the group. Therefore, evaluation may occur for the individual at the time of her or his departure from the group, but this can still involve those members that are not leaving the group.

In addition to assessing change in any type of group, the social worker facilitates group termination and follow-up using a common set of skills:

- The social worker and group members share feelings about ending the group experience and leaving the group.

- Plans for maintaining change are developed.

- Group members discuss their feelings about having contact after termination from the group (for example, returning to the group, having contact outside the group, or having group reunions).

Although social work practice with groups requires specialized skills for engagement, assessment, intervention, and evaluation, each phase uses those skills developed for working with individuals and families. At the group level, the processes of engagement, assessment, intervention, and evaluation can be fluid and dynamic, particularly in groups that are open ended or in groups in which the goal or purpose may change after the group is formed. Monitoring individual and group progress toward goal achievement requires the social worker to move back and forth comfortably between phases of work.

CONCLUSION

Groups can be a powerful experience for both the social worker and the members of the group. Groups often achieve far greater accomplishments than a person could alone, but a group intervention is not for every person or every issue. The effective social worker uses her or his engagement and assessment skills to determine whether a group intervention is the optimal approach to use in a given situation.

While emphasizing the group, the social worker uses the skills of engagement, assessment, intervention, and evaluation that were introduced in Chapter 9 for work with individuals. In group practice, the social worker must simultaneously build rapport with the individual group members and facilitate group cohesiveness, being careful not to focus too much attention on one group member or issue. While balancing individual and group needs, the skill set required for group practice is not unique to group work; it is the purpose of those skills that are unique to group work (Ephross & Greif, 2009). With leadership from a social worker, group members can come together to provide input into the development of the individual and group intervention plan and participate in a groupwide evaluation of the experience. Working with a group of people at one time may seem like a daunting task, but the social worker's skill in viewing strengths from a systemic perspective can be an asset.

MAIN POINTS

- Group work is a method of practice in which the social worker works with a group of persons to address individual issues; a need for information and education; support; or social conditions. Introduced in 1927, group work soon became an established part of the social work educational curriculum.

- The main group work models are in the areas of social action, individual growth (or remediation), self-help and support (or reciprocity), and tasks. The goal of a social action group is to initiate or change a policy, law, or program; individual growth groups emphasize clinically oriented treatment for a personal issue or concern; support groups are mutual aid groups based on a common life experience; and task groups complete a pre-determined goal that is typically focused outside the group members themselves.

- In the practice of social work with groups, the social worker forms the group, facilitates a group meeting or session, provides resources for the group, or works with the group to develop strategies to meet the desired goals.

- The outcomes for the group are based on the individual members' ability and willingness to be interdependent and interact with one another for the purpose of achieving the goals. Although change occurs for the individual members of the group, the focus of the intervention is on the group as a whole.

- As with social work practice with individuals and families, skills for group work focus on the areas of engagement, assessment, intervention, and evaluation.

EXERCISES

1. Below are descriptions of three groups in which the Sanchez family (interactive case at www.routledgesw.com/cases) may be participants. Read the descriptions and, utilizing the group practice models highlighted in this chapter, complete the items that follow the descriptions.

Group 1—Grandparents Raising Grandchildren
Hector and Celia are members of a group for grandparents rearing grandchildren. The group, which meets for a monthly potluck meal, shares strategies and resources related to rearing grandchildren. The group was organized by a social worker who

has custody of her granddaughter. Occasionally, the group meeting includes a presentation by a professional on a topic of interest to the group (e.g., legal and financial issues and childrearing strategies).

Group 2—Women's Group

Celia Sanchez is a member of a group for persons experiencing depression. The group meets weekly for 90 minutes at the mental health center. Facilitated by two clinical social workers, the group is comprised of eight women who were referred by other mental health professionals. Celia was referred by the social worker working with Hector and her to facilitate Joey's adoption. The adoption social worker noted that Celia had experienced episodic depression throughout her life and was currently reporting depressive symptoms. Each group member was interviewed by the group leaders to determine her appropriateness for the group. The group addresses such issues as identifying causes and symptoms of depression, treatment strategies, and strategies for coping with depression.

Group 3—Grandparents for Justice

Through their involvement with the grandparents group, Celia and Hector became members of a group in their state that is working for improving the state laws that determine the rights of grandparents. The group was formed by several grandparents who struggled with the state's child welfare system to gain custody of their grandchildren. The group's goal is to see legislation passed that will protect the rights of grandparents.

Part I: Identify the Model:

Group 1—Grandparents Raising Grandchildren

Type of Group ———————————————————————

Indicators that identify the type of group

   1)

   2)

   3)

Group 2—Women's Group

Type of Group ———————————————————————

Indicators that identify the type of group

   1)

   2)

   3)

Group 3—Grandparents for Justice

Type of Group ———————————————————————

Indicators that identify the type of group

   1)

   2)

   3)

2. After completing the previous exercise, select one of the group scenarios. Using that scenario, identify skills appropriate for each phase of the group process.

Engagement
   1)
   2)
   3)

Assessment Skills
   1)
   2)
   3)

Intervention Skills
   1)
   2)
   3)

Evaluation and Termination Skills
   1)
   2)
   3)

3. As you read in the first exercise, Hector and Celia have become involved in a group working for improving the state laws that dictate the rights of grandparents. Using the knowledge that you have gained regarding the types of group process and the phases of the group process, develop a list of strategies that the group might use to develop a plan and focus local and state attention on their issue.

4. Go to the Riverton interactive case at www.routledgesw.com/cases. As a new resident and social worker in the Alvadora neighborhood of Riverton, you have become aware of the neighbors' concerns. While there is concern for the issues of public drinking and its accompanying problems, there have been no attempts to organize the residents for action. Using a social goals approach, your task is to convene a group of neighborhood residents who will develop a plan to advocate with City officials to address the problems. After familiarizing yourself with the residents, determine the potential strengths and contributions of each of the residents. From a social goals perspective, develop a plan for organizing a group and provide strategies for recruiting members and creating a goal.

5. Go to the Carla Washburn interactive case at www.routledgesw.com/cases. Following the death of her husband, Carla Washburn joined a widows' group at her church. Not only was she able to benefit from participation in this group, she was able to help other widows with their adjustments as well. With the loss of her grandson, Mrs. Washburn has once again found herself grieving the loss of a loved one. Respond to the following:

a. How could a group experience benefit the client system in her current grief?
b. Describe the group model that you would recommend for Mrs. Washburn.
c. Develop a draft of a contract that you would negotiate with Mrs. Washburn if she were to join a group.

Social Work Practice with Organizations and Communities and Policy Practice

In Chapter 7, Emily worked with Marietta to arrange home-based services so that she could continue independent living. Home health care is one of the services that Emily arranged for Marietta to receive. As a result of policy changes in the reimbursement of home health agencies for services provided to recipients, a number of the older adults with whom Emily worked, including Marietta, had their home health services decreased or terminated altogether. Emily began to see negative consequences occurring for these older adults. Some of the older adults were no longer able to live independently and had to move in with family members or into a residential care facility, thus losing their independence.

Viewing her role as an advocate as well as a case manager, Emily compiled case examples detailing the negative effects of the policy changes. With her agency's support, Emily shared her data with a community coalition of agencies and organizations that engage in legislative advocacy on issues related to older adults. The advocacy group used Emily's data in their campaign to introduce legislation that would increase the reimbursement rates for service providers for older adults receiving home health services. Emily worked with the advocacy group to prepare testimony for a legislative committee. She arranged for family members of the home health care recipients to travel to the state capitol and testify before the committee on the negative impact of the cutbacks. As a result of this collaborative effort, legislation was passed to increase reimbursement for home health services for older adults.

In the previous chapters, we examined social work practice on the individual, family, and group levels. In this chapter, we explore social work practice that targets change efforts at the organizational, community, and societal levels. Also referred to as **macro practice, community-level social work practice** is a method of social work practice that promotes changes in practices, policies, and legislation that impact groups of people in an organization, community, state, country, or even the world. Macro-level interventions are often initiated in response to government incentives (e.g., economic stimulus of 2009); significant funding decreases (e.g., Medicaid cuts); or a large-scale social movement to address oppression (e.g., the Apartheid in South Africa) (Gibelman, 2004). When policies are punitive or bureaucracies are large and impersonal, the social worker can serve as an advocate for the client system in facilitating change in the system that is intended to serve the client system. Community-level practice serves a range of purposes, including: improving the quality of life; advocacy; human social and economic development; service and program planning; service integration; political and social action; and social justice (Weil & Gamble, 2009, p. 883).

Influencing social change encompasses a range of different practice approaches and interventions. Although many of the terms and concepts that describe social work practice with organizations and communities are used interchangeably, they are, in fact, distinct practice approaches and are not synonymous. The advocacy effort made by Emily on behalf of her client, Marietta, which brought about the policy change, is an example of one of the many roles that a social worker can play while practicing at the organizational and community level. Table 11.1 (see pp. 270–271) provides descriptions of various activities performed by social workers practicing with organizations and communities.

Social workers have worked for change at the organizational, community, and societal levels throughout the history of the profession. While 14 percent of practicing social workers describe their primary practice focus is macro practice, organizational and community practice is also often combined with direct practice. In fact, over half (51 per cent) of social workers surveyed report spending their time in direct services to clients, but the remaining time spent is such activities as administration, management, supervision, consultation, training, planning, teaching, research, project management, policy/legislative development, fundraising/grantwriting and community organizing (Whitaker & Arrington, 2008, p.8). Exhibit 11.1 provides descriptions of macro practice activities. As you know, social workers commonly begin their careers by working with individuals and families and then move into areas that include administration, management, teaching, or research. This career path means that administrators, supervisors, and teachers have insight into the issues and challenges of social work practice with individuals and families.

Although organizational and community-level practice may not be their primary focus, all social workers are ethically and professionally obligated to advocate for social justice. The NASW *Code of Ethics* (2008) prominently addresses ethical obligations to practice at the organizational and community level. Four of the six ethical principles emphasize this responsibility. For social work practice at the community level, the *Code* charges social workers with the responsibility to (1)

Administration and management	18.0%	**EXHIBIT 11.1**
Supervision	5.0%	*Social Workers'*
Consultation	5.0%	*Primary*
Planning	4.0%	*Activities with*
Training	4.0%	*Organizations*
Teaching	3.0%	*and*
Research	2.0%	*Communities*
Fundraising and grantwriting	1.0%	
Community organizing and advocacy	1.0%	
Policy/legislative development	1.0%	

Source: Whitaker & Arrington, 2008.

promote social change "with and on behalf of vulnerable and oppressed individuals and groups" in the areas of poverty, unemployment, discrimination, and other areas of social injustice; (2) serve both client systems and the larger society and address the needs of organizations and communities as well as individuals, families, and groups; and (3) practice with integrity within organizations (NASW, 2008).

Addressing social injustice is considered to be a social work responsibility because social injustice "harms people and limits their opportunities to live as fully human persons with inherent worth and dignity" (Horejsi, 2002, p. 12). Moreover, Standard 6 of the *Code of Ethics* focuses on social work practice within the broader society in the areas of

- social welfare;

- public participation through influencing policies and institutions;

- public emergencies; and

- social and political action through working toward equity in access to resources, opportunities, and policies.

In this chapter, we explore the third level of generalist practice, beginning with a review of the historical development of social work practice with organizations and communities. To understand the underpinnings of the many and varied facets of working with organizations and communities, we will examine the models of change used in this level of practice and the skills that are essential for being an effective practitioner.

TABLE 11.1	SOCIAL WORK APPROACH/INTERVENTION	DEFINITION
Types of Social Work Practice with Organizations and Communities: Focus on Neighborhood and Community Safety	Neighborhood and community organizing. *Example:* Activities aimed at improving the safety for residents of a neighborhood or community.	Facilitating the creation or maintenance of a "collective body" within a specified geographic area that shares a common concern related to a social problem to work toward resolution of the shared concern.
	Organizing functional communities. *Example:* Activities aimed at providing public information and education on personal and a community-wide basis.	Facilitating change within a community of shared interests, a functional organizer helps to raise awareness aimed at changing attitudes or behaviors.
	Community, social, economic, and sustainable development. *Example:* Activities focused on increasing revenue in a community through development of neighborhood watch programs to enhance customer safety.	Planned, systemic process for developing or improving standard of living or infrastructures (e.g., economic, physical, or social) within a geographic or interest-based community.
	Program development and community liaison. *Example:* Creation of a relationship with a group of neighborhood residents to develop a program to address personal, home, and business safety.	Providing leadership at the agency level to identify, develop and attain goals, seek and allocate resources, supervise personnel, and oversee service delivery.
	Social planning. *Example:* Prompted by community complaints, city administrators study the crime statistics and patterns of the area to determine the trends in and types of crime and conduct a community needs assessment.	Systematic, data-driven, and evidence-based process for achieving social change uses experts or professionals who identify a need and conduct an assessment, develop a plan for service delivery, and implement an evaluation.

HISTORICAL PERSPECTIVE ON SOCIAL WORK PRACTICE WITH ORGANIZATIONS AND COMMUNITIES

The origins of social work practice with organizations and communities can be found in the early efforts of the Charity Organization Society and settlement house movements. Charity Organization Society workers advocated for change with organizations regarding the sharing of client information, while early settlement

SOCIAL WORK APPROACH/INTERVENTION	DEFINITION	TABLE 11.1
		continued
Coalitions. *Example:* Organizations that serve older adult populations collaborate on a program to educate older adults on safety issues and provide safe escort and transportation services to older adults.	Coalitions bring together groups and organizations that are committed to a common cause or concern. Alliances are often able to have a greater impact on decision-makers.	
Political and social action. *Example:* Supporting candidates who are committed to increasing community policing and safety.	Activities that build political pressure to resolve a social problem or address a social need at the institutional or policy level. Electoral activities involve working to elect candidates who support issues important to a group, organization, or community or working to pass legislation important to a group, organization, or community.	
Movements for progressive change. *Example:* Advocacy groups across the country unite to address the issue of hate crimes being perpetrated on the gay, lesbian, bisexual, and transgendered community.	Large-scale community, national, and international efforts focused on addressing social injustices targeting specific populations.	

Sources: Barker, 2003; Butterfield & Chisanga, 2008; Sager, 2008; Streeter et al., 2008; Weil & Gamble, 2009.

house activists fought for improved living conditions for the poor through legislative advocacy (Brieland, 1995). In fact, Jane Addams and her colleagues at Hull House were the first to engage in large-scale advocacy efforts to address sanitation problems in Chicago, resulting in Addams's appointment as sanitation inspector (Quam, 2008). The first settlement house workers also worked to improve the living conditions of surrounding neighborhoods.

The role of community practice continued to grow throughout the first half of the 20th century. The Great Depression of the 1930s, in particular, focused the country on the need for community-level interventions to address the issues of widespread poverty, unemployment, and hunger. Through the New Deal programs, the federal government assumed responsibility for the development and implementation of community-level interventions for the first time in U.S. history. The social upheaval of the 1960s galvanized the role of community organization and advocacy for the social work profession. Social workers were involved in advocacy efforts in the areas of civil rights, employment, the Vietnam War, and welfare rights.

With an emphasis on social work practice with individuals and families, interest in organizational and community change waxed and waned through the 1970s and 1980s. By the 1990s, the efforts of several social work organizations had created a resurgence of interest in such arenas as political campaigns and advocacy. Acknowledging the need for social workers to have competence at multiple levels of intervention contributed to the development of the generalist social work practice model in which social workers strive to address social problems with individuals, families, groups, *and* communities. Such recognition has enabled the social work profession to reach a point in the 21st century in which practice at the organizational and community level is an integral part of the profession.

Social workers practicing at the organizational and community level often face funding challenges; however, the profession's commitment to community organization, advocacy, and other organizational and community-level service activities remains strong. The Council on Social Work Education has shown its commitment to ensuring that all social workers have knowledge and skills for organizational and community practice in the current curriculum guidelines, which state that social workers should be prepared to work with organizations and communities as well as individuals and families and to be competent in policy practice to promote effective service delivery (2008).

MODELS OF CHANGE IN SOCIAL WORK PRACTICE WITH ORGANIZATIONS AND COMMUNITIES

Aimed at facilitating change within systems of all types and sizes, social work practice with organizations and communities can be achieved using a variety of approaches. Achieving change within a system is a challenging endeavor due to the many and varied persons, policies, and needs involved. In order to facilitate systemwide change, social workers need to determine whether the system is ready for a change or alternatives can be explored. If a change is viable, the social worker's role may focus on identifying the key persons and resources that are needed to facilitate the change process.

In an effort to address social injustices at the organizational or community level, social workers are instrumental in working toward change within political, social, and economic systems. The concept of community is thus defined to include the physical or geographic environment or a social group or organization. Upon defining the community to be targeted and the goal of the change effort, the social worker selects the most appropriate approach to achieve the desired outcome. Models of community organization have been developed that enable social workers to match the community, the goals, and the strategies for intervention. Described in the following pages, these models include: (1) neighborhood and community organizing; (2) organizing functional communities; (3) community, social, economic, and sustainable development; (4) program development and community liaison; (5) social planning; (6) coalitions; (7) political and social action; and (8) movements for progressive change (Streeter et al., 2008).

Neighborhood and Community Organizing

Aimed at improving the quality of life in a specific geographic locale, the concept of community organizing can have multiple meanings depending on the issues and goals of a particular group or need. Building a sense of community connections among residents to achieve a desired change is a primary focus of this model of practice. Common to most efforts to build community is the concept that a community is complex and dynamic and growth begins with recognizing the community's existing infrastructure, the potential collaborations, and capacity for change (Milligan, 2008). Blending community development, social planning, and social action, residents join together with one another and with professionals to mobilize and build community resources to enhance the economic and social functioning of an area.

Examples of community organizing initiatives include:

- *Organizing for better housing:* Residents of an apartment complex request help from a community-based social services agency in getting needed repairs made to their apartment buildings. The landlord has refused to replace inefficient, potentially dangerous heating and cooling equipment, maintain the exterior of the buildings, and replace hallway and outdoor lighting. With the assistance of the residents, the agency's social worker conducts an on-site assessment of their concerns and contacts a local attorney in the housing division of a legal services agency. Together, the legal services attorney and the social worker compile a report and form a team made up of the attorney, the social worker, and representatives from the residents' group. The team present the report to the landlord, and the landlord promises to make repairs. Repairs are not made within the six month period promised. With the social worker's help, the residents organize a picket outside the landlord's office. The changes are then made promptly.

- *Organizing for better transportation:* A neighborhood group unites around the issue of having the public transportation system extend to their neighborhood so that access to and from the neighborhood is enhanced.

Functional Community Organizing

In addition to being a geographic area, communities can also be interest-based communities. These functional communities are groups that share commonalities such as ethnicity, values, faith traditions, or socioeconomic levels (Butterfield &

Chisanga, 2008). Similar to organizing a neighborhood, the focus of the change effort in functional community organizing is to identify and raise awareness regarding the need for an action, provide education, change attitudes or behaviors, and organizing and leading an advocacy effort for change (Weil & Gamble, 2009).

Examples of functional community organizing include:

- *Students Organizing for Students:* A group of social work students who have been completing a service learning project in a faith-based after school program discover that the children are having difficulty getting to the program from their elementary schools. The social work students organize a campaign to help the children's parents advocate for the school district to include the program on its route.

- *Faith Community Organizing for Immigrants and Refugees:* The ministerial alliance in a community becomes aware that a group of immigrants and refugees are struggling to find a building in which to hold their religious services. The alliance comes together to offer their individual facilities to be used on a rotating basis until such time the community of immigrants and refugees are able to raise funds to obtain a permanent home for their services.

Community, Social, Economic, and Sustainable Development

Change efforts in the community development approach can be focused on spatial-based or interest-based communities (Butterfield & Chisanga, 2008). This approach assumes that members of the community are invested in enhancing the environment in which they live, and efforts are typically aimed at a specific problem or need that exists. By developing goals related to community cohesion, capability, and competence, building a sense of community, also known as capacity development, is the desired outcome of this approach (Rothman, 2008).

Effectiveness of a development change intervention is increased as member participation increases. Change is based on the assumption that community members can engage in a cooperative, self-help process with one another and with outside individuals and groups because they desire change and can change. In essence, the client system and the change agent system are the same population. The change effort can be directed toward such areas as economic development or community empowerment (Butterfield & Chisanga, 2008).

The social worker's role in community development varies from initiator to participant. As a professional working in the community and interacting with a range of people and groups, the social worker may be in a unique position to identify a community need that residents or members of the community do not view as a community-wide problem. Therefore, the social worker may initiate a social change effort by mobilizing key persons within the community, following the social goals model of group practice described in Chapter 10. The social worker may train a community member to assume leadership and then relinquish the leadership role to the community. In situations in which community members identify the condition needing change, the social worker helps to facilitate the change. The social worker may also be a participant in the change effort based on her or his residence in the community, position within an organization, or as an outside consultant to the change effort due to a particular expertise or by virtue of membership in the community.

Let us look at some examples of community development change efforts.

- *Neighborhood residents concerned about health care access:* The decreasing accessibility to health care of residents in a neighborhood largely composed of older adults living on limited incomes comes to the attention of a social worker in a community center. With the help of the agency's neighborhood advisory committee, the social worker conducts a needs assessment to determine the extent of access problems and learns that many older adults have not seen a physician regularly since the nearby clinic closed several years earlier. The advisory committee approaches the local medical school to propose opening a small free clinic in the agency to serve outpatient needs. The medical school faculty seizes the opportunity to provide a training site for medical students, and a partnership is born.

- *Refugee-owned businesses:* Clients and former clients of a refugee resettlement agency approach social work staff about refugee-owned business owners being harassed. In recent months, a number of the refugee-owned businesses have been vandalized. With the support of the local business owners, the social worker convenes a task force comprising representatives from the refugee-owned businesses, Chamber of Commerce members, law enforcement personnel, and the community development agency. The task force conducts an assessment of the neighborhood and finds the problem to be widespread. They agree to address the issues of vandalism, increased security, and community relations. The social worker assists initially by chairing the task force, but later works to identify a leader from the refugee business community to assume that role.

In community development activities, the experts are the members of the community. The social worker's role is to support and assist the community in developing and implementing a change to enhance the lives of those in the community.

Program Development and Community Liaison

Development at the program level can originate in several areas. Social workers working in direct services may identify a need that is not being filled by their or another organization. Current or former recipients of services may bring attention to the need for a new or expanded service.

The role for the social worker can be multi-faceted. The social worker may be the person who draws attention to the need for a service to be implemented. She or he may then be the one who develops and implements the service. Conversely, the social worker may be approached to aid in the development of a service, thus serving as a liaison for her or his organization. Social workers can engage in program or funding proposal development, advocacy, and facilitator roles (Streeter et al., 2008).

Examples in which social workers may engage in program development and serving as a liaison to the community include:

- *Service Expansion:* Former recipients of services provided by an urban domestic violence program initiate an expansion into their rural community by contacting the agency and requesting that a satellite office be opened in their area. The domestic violence program conducts its own needs assessment to determine that the rural community lacks services for women who are victims of abuse, approaches key persons in the community for support, and establishes the program. A social worker working for the shelter may be called on to conduct the needs assessment, develop the program, or to manage the satellite program. A social worker may also be a key person in the rural community, whose support and involvement can help the program to gain acceptance.

- *Programming for Pre-schoolers:* A BSW practicum student works as part of an inter-agency team to develop educational and social programs for children who are 3 to 5 years old. The agency provides childcare and programming for children up to age 3 and for children 5 and older, but parents of children age 3 to 5 must find other child care and programs within the community. The BSW student worked with a group to develop a needs assessment and a program proposal that included a proposal for funding (Bollig, 2009).

Social Planning

Within a **planning** approach, change efforts are aimed at policy-level or community-wide change that may be orchestrated by professionals, outside consultants, and influential decision makers and may not involve members of the community themselves as the initiators of the change effort. Those who are impacted by the planning effort should, however, be involved in the planning itself (Rothman, 2008). Social planning is implemented to address a special need within the community. Based on the belief that experts, who have access to empirical data and technical expertise, best orchestrate change, social planning involves social change at the institutional and bureaucratic levels (versus at the community level).

The social worker's role may be as a member of a professional team involved in identifying issues, collecting data, analyzing policy, and planning a program to address needs. With the profession's values and knowledge of planned change efforts and training in identification, assessment, resource development and management, and human needs, social workers' participation in social planning is an asset (Sager, 2008).

The following are examples of social planning change efforts:

- *Neighborhood redevelopment:* Municipal officials, concerned about the deterioration of one of the city's historic neighborhoods, conducts a community assessment to determine the extent of decline. Upon determining that the number of businesses, owner-occupied households, and the tax base have drastically decreased, the city's Office of Community and Economic Development applies for federal funding to restore the neighborhood. The funding enables the city to offer tax breaks for new homeowners, low-interest loans for new business owners, funds for rehabilitation and beautification of buildings, and grants for development of social service programs. The social worker may be in a position to gather and analyze data, facilitate the interactions of local officials, publicize the redevelopment effort, review applications, and oversee program development.

- *International social work education:* Dramatic social, political, and economic changes in former communist countries have created a need to restructure the social service delivery system within the countries. Recognizing that the expertise to build a social service system based on democratic ideology did not exist within the professional community of these countries, social workers from the United States are called in to assist in the rebuilding effort. The social worker's role in this change effort is to serve as a trainer, facilitator, educator, and consultant, working with professionals to develop organizational practices, fund-raising mechanisms, and evaluation processes that are consistent with the new social structure.

- *Rural domestic violence services:* Consider the earlier example of the domestic violence agency establishing a satellite program in a rural community from a different perspective: Instead of the idea originating with the former recipients of services, an example of a social planning effort may be the result of hospital staff identifying a need. Noticing an increase in the number of women presenting to the emergency room who report being abused by their partners, the hospital staff determine that local services are needed. The nearest domestic violence program is 30 miles away in the county seat. The hospital administrator contacts that program and asks for their help in establishing a satellite program at the hospital. The administrator and shelter director apply for a grant to provide start-up funding for a hospital-based social worker to provide services for women who are seen at the hospital for abuse-related injuries. Once that program is in place, an advisory group is formed and plans are made to seek long-term funding to keep the program running on a permanent basis.

Coalitions

The concept of "strength in numbers" is the basis for coalition development. Coalitions are collaborative initiatives that unite such groups as agency professionals, client systems, governmental organizations, educational institutions, and legislative groups around a common interest or goal. Building a coalition is typically aimed at impacting a large-scale change over a long period of time that involves influencing the decision-making process and focuses on accessing resources (Streeter et al., 2008).

The social worker may initiate the building of a coalition or participate as a member of a coalition. With skills in micro-, mezzo-, and macro-level practice, social workers are well positioned to serve in coalition leadership, mediation, and organizing roles (Streeter et al., 2008).

Coalition building examples may include:

- *Coalition for Community Development:* Building on the previous example of neighborhood redevelopment, a social worker working in an agency in that neighborhood may invite resident associations, social service organizations, and representatives from the faith community to come together as a coalition to advocate for the funding organization to approve the request for neighborhood redevelopment.

- *Coalition for Human Rights:* A social work student returned from completing a practicum experience in a country in which women's rights were being oppressed utilizes her network of students interested in social justice issues to build a coalition for increasing awareness of this issue. She invites student organizations from across her campus to co-sponsor an educational and awareness raising event outside the student center. The event included providing information on the oppression women were experiencing, signing petitions to be sent to legislators, and needs of the women in that region of the world.

Political and Social Action

Aimed at addressing a social injustice, **political and social action** change efforts increase political pressure on decision-making processes so that oppressed groups receive equitable services, resources, and power. Social action often involves advocating for rights on behalf of or with a group that does not have a strong voice within the decision-making process. Advocacy can occur at the organizational, community, governmental, and legislative levels and may involve a range of activities, from public education campaigns to confrontational meetings and public protests. Working from a systems framework enables the social worker to grasp the meaning and inadequacies of the client-system interaction and to facilitate change that will enhance the functioning of both parts of the system (Shulman, 2009). Social workers also help candidates to get elected to political office.

Social action is typically accomplished through lobbying or mobilizing (Mondros, 2009). When engaged in lobby activities, social activists may also choose to direct their resources toward the passage of legislation or election of political candidates who support political agendas favoring the agency or organizational mission. Mobilizers focus on long-term change efforts such as reducing the number of HIV/AIDS cases through the provision of education, public awareness, health care strategies, and improving access to health care.

The following are examples of political and social action change efforts.

- *Welfare reform:* In the wake of budget cuts that reduced the state's public cash assistance programs, the director of a statewide welfare rights organization puts together a coalition of welfare recipients, social service professionals, and the ministerial alliance to engage in a high-profile advocacy effort. Pooling their resources, the coalition mounts a campaign that includes letters, e-mail, local visits, and telephone calls to legislators; educational sessions to teach effective lobbying techniques to faith groups; trips to the state capital to lobby key legislators; and public service announcements to air on radio and television. The social worker may be involved in any of these activities directly or indirectly as a facilitator.

- *Political action:* The political action committee for NASW members (PACE—Political Action for Candidate Election) has chapters in every state. On behalf of NASW members, state chapter PACE committees endorse candidates at the local and state level, and the national PACE committee endorses candidates at the national level. Candidates are endorsed based on their platform on issues related to the social work profession. NASW members participate in campaigns, assist with voter registration, and contribute to campaigns.

Movements for Progressive Change

The social work profession has a long and rich history of participation in and support of social movements aimed at promoting social justice, creating program and policies that support elimination of oppression and discrimination, and fostering opportunities for groups and communities who have previously been unable to access services or rights. Such movements are large-scale and impact change on the national and international level. The movement to gain the vote for women and the civil rights movement are historical examples of major initiatives within our society that have addressed the need for progressive change.

The following are examples of current social movements:

- *Gay Rights Movements*: Beginning in the 1960s and 1970s, many in our society have been engaged in seeking rights for persons who are gay, lesbian, bisexual, and transgendered to be able to live without discrimination, adopt children, and marry.

- *Immigration Rights:* Many people across the U.S. have been advocating for the comprehensive reform of immigration laws and rights.

In terms of identifying and intervening with organizational and community issues, social workers have a unique vantage point because of the profession's commitment to social justice, enhancement of client and community well-being and functioning, and empowerment. Having a working knowledge of the models of change described here enables the generalist social worker to effect change at the organizational and societal level. Knowledge of multiple approaches further provides the social work practitioner with the ability to move back and forth among the models and use the aspects of each model that will best meet the need. Social workers can also be involved personally with social movements.

Focused on the issue of neighborhood and community safety, Box 11.1 provides descriptions and examples of community-level interventions that social work students, faculty, and professionals can be involved in to make a difference.

SKILLS FOR SOCIAL WORK PRACTICE WITH ORGANIZATIONS AND COMMUNITIES

Organizations and communities are made up of persons and groups; therefore, effective practice with organizations and communities is built on the skills learned in working with individuals, families, and groups. Similar to social work practice with groups, the client in organizational and community practice is a group of individuals. For example, the client system may be residents in a neighborhood or community; social service agencies seeking adequate funding; or persons that share a common diagnosis, life event or style, or need.

As in social work practice with individuals, families, and groups, practice with organizations and communities encompasses multifaceted and varied roles. The role of the social worker in an organizational or community intervention is the same as it is at other levels of practice, but focuses on a larger client system. For example, the social worker may function in one or more of the following ways:

- *Broker:* In a brokering capacity, the social worker working with organizations and communities forms connections through the building of collaborations, coalitions, networks, and partnerships.

- **Enabler:** Community-level practitioners empower clients and others to participate in change by organizing and coordinating the efforts of individuals and groups committed to a common issue or concern. As many of the tasks and activities of organizational and community practice involve group meetings, social workers require skills to facilitate meetings, including planning, agenda development, and leading. Also included in the enabler role is evaluation. As funding sources increasingly require verification that funding is supporting programs that are making a positive impact, social workers are required to develop and carry out evaluations, analyze findings, and compile evaluation reports to staff, boards of directors, and funders.

- *Advocate:* Advocacy involves articulating the needs of a group to those in decision-making positions in the form that is most effective with the targeted decision makers (for example, press releases, letters, lobbying, public education campaigns, demonstrations, political lobbying, and petitions). Advocates must be willing to take risks and have realistic expectations regarding success. Legislative advocacy requires an array of strategies: providing research and technical information, understanding legislators' biases, having insights into all perspectives on the issues, and presenting issues in ways that can be embraced by the legislators (Reisch, 2009).

- **Mobilizer:** Grant writing and organizing fund-raising campaigns (for example, events, mailings, and telethons) are examples of activities engaged in by social workers in the mobilizing role. This role also encompasses program development and planning. Organizational and community practice often involves establishing new or expanding programs, which means identifying the need for a program, conceptualizing and designing the program, securing funding or administrative support, overseeing program operations, and evaluating program outcomes.

- *Mediator or negotiator:* Through reflective listening, the social worker can aid opposing groups in establishing a common ground and a mutually agreed-upon resolution of the issues. In the role of mediator, the social worker serves as an unbiased party, while the role of negotiator typically involves the social worker having a preference for one side over the other.

- *Administrator:* Social work administration activities include overseeing program development and operations, budgets, fund-raising, and personnel.

BOX 11.1

Making a Difference: Influencing State Policy

WHAT STUDENTS AND FACULTY CAN DO!

- Get out of your comfort zone.
- Ask your professors for advocacy and policy assignments.
- Identify an issue or problem that you want to change.
- Form a group at work or school to help you advocate.
- Contact your legislators and ask them to help you introduce a bill.
- Develop fact sheets and policy briefs.
- Identify and track a bill in the state legislature that affects your field agency.
- Enter the national contest, "State Policy Plus," for cash and commitment.
- Plan a social work "rally day" at the state legislature annually.
- Serve as an intern in the office of a state legislator.
- Visit state senators and representatives personally or as a class and inform them of your concerns on a particular bill.
- Organize a group to prepare testimony at a public hearing or subcommittee.
- Write letters to your state legislators.
- Track state legislation using the Internet. Visit www.statepolicy.org.
- Work with your state chapter of NASW in lobbying for its legislative agenda.
- Design a research project analyzing the current impact of state welfare reform.
- Join a coalition or advocacy group and assist them in setting their agenda.
- Organize a forum or luncheon for state legislators, lobbyists, service providers, and clients on a proposed bill or policy.
- Prepare and deliver testimony before a legislative committee.
- Analyze and compare a particular policy or bill among all 50 states or internally.
- Write position papers for candidates who are campaigning for legislative office.
- Volunteer to work in a political campaign to support a candidate.
- Conduct a survey of candidates or legislators on their views about proposed bills or significant issues.
- Persevere and be very determined.

Source: Robert Schneider, Virginia Commonwealth University.

Just as with individual, family, and group work, social work at the organizational and community level can be practiced using the concepts of engagement, assessment, intervention, and evaluation as a method for structuring social work practice processes and activities. The roles just described can be used within each phase of the social work intervention at the organizational or community level.

As a BSW student, Emily completed a practicum at a multiservice community center that provides social services to the residents of an urban neighborhood. Emily had the opportunity to gain generalist social work experiences working with children in the after-school program, taking applications for the utility assistance program, and co-facilitating a job skills group with mothers in the welfare-to-work program. To provide Emily with organizational and community experiences, the field instructor invited her to participate in the Neighborhood Advisory Council. This group provided input to the staff on the needs of the community.

During Emily's first meeting with the Neighborhood Advisory Council, one of the neighborhood resident council members suggested that neighborhood children and youth needed access to an after-school tutoring program. The council voted to create an ad hoc committee to explore the development of a tutoring program. Together with her field instructor, Caroline, Emily served as co-chair of the ad hoc committee. The committee began to investigate the possibility of adding tutoring to the services provided by the center.

The ad hoc committee chair's first task was to identify persons that would have an interest in this issue of tutoring and could provide support for launching the program. The first meeting was scheduled at the center (in the room that could house the tutoring program) with representatives from the center's Children and Youth Department, the school district's Office of Administration, the council, and neighborhood parents. Participants introduced themselves and described their personal or professional role. Caroline explained the reason for forming the ad hoc committee, the purpose of the gathering, and asked each member to share her or his thoughts (or the feelings of the constituency being represented by the member) regarding the need for a tutoring program. Although the group was generally in agreement on the concept of a tutoring program, questions were raised regarding neighborhood residents' support for a tutoring program, resources needed to mount a program, and staff or volunteers to operate the program. Emily volunteered to conduct a needs assessment and research best practices in tutoring programs and report back to the committee at the next month's meeting.

Engagement of Organizations and Communities

Organizational and community-level concerns or needs are often addressed in a fragmented manner in which all relevant parties are not communicating with one another, and key participants may not be involved in the change process. In order to effectively work at this level, social workers use a systems approach and involve all those persons that can influence the change or can be affected by the change.

As with group work, the first step in engaging the client system is to identify the persons and groups that can contribute to the change effort. Several different groups may be involved, depending on the type and goal of the organizational or community change effort. For example, a welfare rights coalition (group one) may be representing welfare recipients (group two), and front-line workers in the welfare agency that have insight into the needs of the target group are in a third group. A group may come together naturally, as in the case of the earlier example of refugee business owners, or may have to be formed, as in the case of the neighborhood redevelopment example. Criteria for determining participants relate to those contributions that each person or group can make to the change effort. Contributions may come in the form of knowledge, resources, influence, funding, credibility, or access to other groups or resources.

During the engagement phase of an organizational and community change effort, all participants have the opportunity to articulate the needs, resources, contributions, and barriers to participation for themselves or the groups they represent. In addition, each participant contributes to the development of the purpose, goals, decision-making process, and allocation of resources and responsibilities. A key to sustaining participants' investment in the change process is to ensure that each participant has a clear understanding of the tasks and activities for which she or he is responsible and ensure that the individuals are invested in the goals of the group. Each participant's contribution is affirmed and valued in the process.

The social work skills of reflective listening, interpreting both verbal and non-verbal communications, and negotiation can contribute to the group's ability to bond around a common concern. As with social work practice at the individual, family, and group levels, the social worker practicing at the community and organizational level will use empathy and rapport-building skills to engage with individuals and groups.

Assessment of Organizations and Communities

In formulating a strengths-based assessment approach, Emily and her field instructor developed the following plan:

- Clarification of purpose: *The council wanted to know if there was an interest in and need for a tutoring program as well as the viability of launching and sustaining such a program.*

- Data collection strategy: *In an effort to determine neighborhood interest and need for a tutoring program, Emily and Caroline developed a multimodal approach to collecting data. To ascertain community attitudes regarding a tutoring program, Emily and a representative from the residents' committee conducted a door-to-door survey of 50 neighborhood households using a survey developed by Emily and approved by the committee. Next, Emily contacted the local Board of Education to gather information on existing tutoring resources in the area and the process for creating a tutoring program that would build on current resources. Emily then contacted other tutoring programs and gathered information regarding development, staffing, funding, and evaluation. Additionally, she consulted the scholarly literature on tutoring programs.*

- Compilation of data: *Emily compiled information from the various sources, contacted possible volunteer sources, and at the next committee meeting, presented a written and verbal report highlighting the interest, assets, and potential outcomes for a neighborhood-based tutoring program.*

An essential component of developing a plan of intervention for effecting change within an organization or community is the assessment process. The first assessment activity is to identify the organization or community targeted for change. Once identified, the organization is assessed to determine whether change is needed, desired, feasible, and sustainable. The assessment and goal setting phases of the community intervention may actually be an important aspect of the overall intervention, particularly when the members of the community are invited to contribute to identifying the issues and concerns and participating in the gathering of information (Tropman, 2008). Gaining familiarity with the target group and identifying and organizing a core group of supporters can, in fact, contribute to the change process. Assessment of organization and community needs encompasses an array of activities, including determination of goals in order to identify the information to be gathered and the way in which the information will be used. Macro practitioners should assume the possibility of resistance, passive as well as active, with any change effort and incorporate that into the assessment process (Mizrahi, 2009).

The next step is to develop and conduct an assessment. Mulroy (2008, pp. 385–386) provides five principles for assessment that can serve as guidelines for conducting a community-level assessment: (1) value participation from diverse constituencies; (2) use multiple methods (quantitative and qualitative data); (3) encourage civic participation and technical elements; (4) keep the assessment realistic; and (5) value asset-building. At the organizational and community level, having a plan for gathering information or data is critical for the future phase of organizing, analyzing, and interpreting the data. Data that is useful in the development of a plan includes in-person, telephone, or mail surveys; focus groups; official government data; agency records on services provided; and in-depth interviews with key stakeholders.

The assessment could then focus on the following:

- *Strengths and available resources:* Identify the availability of existing resources and assets possessed by the target group or community.

- *Organizational and community attitudes:* Having input from the key players and others involved in the change process contributes to the development of the plan and intervention and, ultimately, to the success or failure of a change effort.

- *Barriers to change:* An extension of identifying attitudes toward change, determining the existence of any obstacles to change is included as part of the planning process. Barriers may include such factors as attitudes, perceptions, funding, political support, space, and participation.

- *Viability of sustaining a change:* Determining the organization's or community's ability to maintain a change is critical information to have before implementing a change plan.

- *Assessment of similar change efforts:* Identifying organizations and communities that have developed similar programs, policies, or changes and evaluating the success or failure of those efforts and factors that led to their ending are included within a needs assessment.

Intervention with Organizations and Communities

Using the data from Emily's needs assessment, the ad hoc committee developed the following plan:

- *Goal: Develop a plan to establish a tutoring program building on the assets and capacities of the neighborhood residents, and implement it by the start of the next school year.*

- *Objectives: Using information gathered from the board of education and other tutoring programs, develop a schedule, curricular plan, budget, and staffing coverage.*

- *Present plan to the ad hoc committee and council for approval.*

- *Publicize the program to neighborhood parents and youth and school personnel.*

After receiving approval of the plan from both the ad hoc committee and the council, Emily and Caroline implemented the intervention by developing a curricular plan for tutoring and a training program for the tutors; obtained funding from the agency for supplies and refreshments; recruited volunteers to serve as tutors; advertised the program to parents, youth, and teachers; and prepared the room designated for the program. Once the program was under way, Emily served as on-site supervisor, and she and Caroline met weekly with the volunteer tutors. With permission from students' parents, Emily contacted teachers on a monthly basis to monitor student performance.

Organizational and community interventions comprise planning and implementing activities that involve balancing multiple sets of needs, agendas, and resources. The social worker's role may be to negotiate a plan and intervention between groups whose goals and perceived obligations conflict. Having a realistic understanding of the organizations, policies, and limitations involved in accomplishing the goals can help the social worker create viable alternatives for addressing the need(s) identified during the needs assessment. With the skills that a generalist social worker possesses, helping the opposing parties to establish a common goal and to compromise regarding the intervention plan may fall within the purview of the social worker's responsibilities to the group.

Goal development means prioritizing the needs identified during the needs assessment process and articulating overall goals while attending to the individual needs of constituent groups. In organizational and community interventions, practitioners ensure that the goals address the needs of all involved participants and that responsibility for meeting the objectives is equitably shared by all groups. Although participants may contribute different skills, resources, or influence, all participants have a clear role that contributes to the achievement of the established goal. Moreover, each objective that relates to the overall goal should be specific and measurable so that the change effort can be evaluated.

Just as with micro- and mezzo-level interventions, a priority in establishing goals is achievability. The strategies for action contain specific objectives toward achieving the desired change. The goals, action strategies, and evaluation methods are mutually agreed upon, documented, and shared with all relevant constituencies. As members of the change effort carry out the tasks and activities designed to meet the goals, regular communication and ongoing evaluation are used to monitor progress.

Evaluation and Termination of Organizations and Communities

Evaluation of the tutoring program began with the development of the program plans. The needs assessment yielded information to suggest that a program was needed; therefore, creating the program fulfilled that need. However, simply creating a service to meet a need does not equate to success. Maintaining regular contact with the volunteers, students' parents, and teachers provided ongoing input into such issues as student participation, parent and student satisfaction with the program, and student performance at school. Documenting the input from the involved groups enabled Emily and Caroline to report to the council that the tutoring program was meeting a neighborhood need and to recommend continuation.

Evaluation of organizational and community interventions is an ongoing and complex process. Because many interventions are long-term change efforts that are implemented over months or years with a large and varied number of persons and groups involved, evaluation may be compartmentalized and conducted on an ongoing basis. Evaluation strategies that are applicable for organizational and community interventions include:

- Review of the needs assessment and goals to determine whether identified needs and goals have been met.

- Pre- and post-intervention measures to determine whether change occurred and the extent of change.

Program outcomes and continuous quality assurance can be evaluated by assessing such change-related efforts as quantity and quality of services provided, revenue generated, decreased spending, or behavior change.

Termination of organizational and community-level change may indicate success or failure of the change effort. As in the case of program development, the intervention can be terminated when the program is operational, but with a stabilization effort incorporated to enable the program to be sustained. In an advocacy effort, termination may occur when a policy is or is not changed or law is or is not enacted. In these situations, the change effort may shift to focus on the implementation of the change. In other situations, termination is moot because the purpose of the intervention is to facilitate an ongoing change.

CONCLUSION

Social workers have skills that can influence large-scale changes in organizations, communities, and the society as a whole. To facilitate change at these levels, social workers use the knowledge and skills learned for working with individuals, families, and groups but apply them on a larger scale. Working at the organizational and community level, social workers have to advocate on behalf of a client, develop a new program, obtain funding, interpret data for program evaluation, or analyze the impact of a new policy on their clients. Therefore, social workers must keep abreast of the policy issues that are being proposed that could affect the lives of the persons they serve. Working at the organizational and community level often requires the social worker to have vision and patience—vision to see the possibility of large-scale change and patience to traverse the multiple and complex steps to achieve the change.

For additional information on social work practice with organizations and communities, check out the following groups and websites:

- Influencing State Policy (www.statepolicy.org) is an organization for social work students, faculty, and professionals that provides information on advocacy and current legislation.

- NASW (www.naswdc.org) provides the latest information on the association's advocacy efforts, issues, updates, and political action. See information on the NASW publication *Social Work Speaks: NASW Policy Statements, 2009–2012*, a comprehensive guide to social and political issues that affect the social work profession.

- Association for Community Organization and Social Administration (http://acosa.org) is an organization for community organizers, planning activists, administrators, policy practice specialists, students, and faculty.

- International Federation of Social Workers (http://www.ifsw.org) is a global organization striving for social justice, human rights, and social development.

- Alliance for Justice (http://www.afj.org) is an association of organizations focused on civil rights in the areas of mental health, women, children, consumers, and the environment. This group sponsors the First Monday Campaign, an effort to raise awareness about public policy and advocacy.

- National Budget Simulation is a website that will allow you to see the impact of budget decision-making on the federal budget. To learn more about the budget simulation, go to: http://www.nathannewman.org/nbs/.

MAIN POINTS

- Social work practice with organizations and communities is defined as working toward large-scale change in a practice, policy, program, or law that affects people's lives.

- The roots of the social work profession are well grounded in practice at the organizational and community level as evidenced by the work of the settlement house workers whose goal it was to improve the living conditions for persons in the neighborhoods in which they worked.

- Models for facilitating change within organizations and communities include: neighborhood and community organizing; organizing functional communities; community, social, economic, and sustainable development, program development and community liaison; social planning; coalitions; political and social action; and movements for progressive change. Development activities bring about change in a specific geographic or functional area; planning focuses on organizing a group of people to facilitate change that may span different groups, but affect people experiencing similar life situations; the goal of a social action intervention is to organize people around a particular issue in a effort to influence decision making related to that issue.

- As at the other two levels of social work practice, skills for working with organizations and communities use the approaches of engagement, assessment, intervention, and evaluation.

- Specific social work skills needed for organizational and community practice include negotiation, fund-raising, collaboration, organization, advocacy, analysis, administration, program planning, evaluation, and supervision.

EXERCISES

1. In the Sanchez Family interactive case (go to www.routledgesw.com), go to the Engage tab and locate the Case Study Tools. Select the Town Map. After familiarizing yourself with the community in which the Sanchez family lives, select one of the family members and identify those community resources that could be accessed by her/him to address the need(s) that you have identified for that individual. What are the assets of the community for meeting the needs that you have identified for the family?

2. Complete Task 3 in the Engage tab.

3. You have learned from the Sanchez Family case that Hector and Celia have two children with disabilities. As you know from Chapter 10, they have become involved in a community group that advocates for additional funding for children with disabilities. Based on the knowledge you have gained from the current chapter, strategize about ways in which this group can be successful in launching a fundraising campaign.

4. In the Riverton interactive case (go to www.routledgesw.com), go to the Engage tab and locate the Case Study Tools. Select the Riverton Town Map. Using the Town Map, complete the Critical Thinking Questions for each of the four areas: Engage, Assess, Intervention, and Evaluation.

5. If you have worked through the Riverton case, you will now be familiar with the many aspects of the community system, including potential partners for developing an intervention to address the issue of the Alvadora neighborhood being used for drinking and disposing of refuse. Because of your professional knowledge and your personal investment, you have been asked by your agency to establish a taskforce to "clean up Alvadora."

   a. Identify key stakeholders to invite to join the taskforce who will be effective in establishing common goals for the area.

   b. Develop a preliminary and prioritized strategy for the group.

6. Because laws impact the lives of everyone in our society, but particularly those persons served by social workers, having an awareness of legislative activity in your state is essential for effective social work practice. Go to the Internet site for Influencing State Policy at www.statepolicy.org and click on the resources button. Click on All State-Local Government Servers. Select a state and explore the current legislative activities for that state. You might want to investigate current and pending legislation that can impact the client systems with whom social workers work. Select one legislative issue and prepare a two-minute presentation on an example of that state's policy and deliver it orally in class. Bring a one-page written version of the two-minute presentation to class with enough copies for your fellow students and the instructor.

   (*Source:* R. Schneider, Virginia Commonwealth University, 2002)

7. Advocacy is an important social work skill and one that requires the social worker to be able to articulate her/his points on behalf of the client or issue being advocated. In this exercise, you will have the opportunity to advocate for an issue that has been written about in a newspaper or other publication. Using the Internet or a hard copy of a newspaper or publication, identify an article that describes an issue, event, or pending legislation about which you have an opposing view. Write a letter to the editor of that publication articulating your point of view. The following guidelines may help you in making your points and being published.

WRITING STRONG COMMENTARIES: Share your opinion, make a point, keep it clear

Commentaries, or "op-eds," are important ways to build the reputation of the school or college the writer represents. The opinion page is one of the most popular sections of a newspaper. Commentaries also offer excellent ways to highlight opinions. But opinion page editors tell us the **first** reason they reject commentaries or "op-eds" is because they are too balanced or only offer facts and figures. A good opinion piece isn't a survey of both sides of an issue, but a strong, concise argument. The **second** reason op-eds often are turned down is that writers have failed to grab the reader's attention in the first sentence. Instead they alienate the reader by delaying the point of the piece until the end.

   Below are some tips that will help you the next time you write an op-ed.

Timeliness is key. An opinion piece is usually only as hot as the news of the day.
Take a position. Facts and figures are OK to back your case, but don't rely on them. Don't be afraid to offer your opinion.
Clarity is crucial. Keep your sentences short, simple and to the point. Use language the average person can understand. Avoid jargon suited only to your expertise.
The first sentence is the most important. Summarize your thesis and tell the readers why they should care.

Do not forget the last sentence. Give your ending as much thought as your start. A concise summary is vital.

Offer solutions. Don't just address the problem, but discuss ways it can be fixed.

Keep it short. Most pieces should not be more than 500–600 words.

(*Sources:* Saint Louis University Marketing and Communications)

CHAPTER 12

The Social Work Profession

Emily has been fortunate to provide a range of services to a diverse group of people in a variety of agency settings. Her social work degrees have enabled her to easily secure employment with each of her transitions. She values being part of a profession that not only embraces people with empathy and compassion but also provides her with the knowledge, skills, and values to empower others to enhance their lives. As Emily's story ends, yours begins.

As you have learned in this introductory course, social work as a profession has a long and rich history. But you might also want to know where the profession of social work is going in the future. Where will the jobs be? What will these jobs pay? What type of preparation will social workers need to be effective in the coming decades? In this final chapter, we will complete our exploration of the social work profession by considering the future trends and opportunities for the social work profession, examining the route to becoming a social worker, and, most importantly, moving toward answering the question: Is social work a career for you?

PROFESSIONAL OUTLOOK FOR SOCIAL WORKERS

> *Social work does not exist in a vacuum. As much as any profession, social work activity is woven into the very fabric of society. Social work acts and reacts to that which transpires in society.*
> —ALLEN-MEARES & DEROOS (1997, p. 384)

As we consider social work practice in the 21st century, the future looks bright for the profession. Employment opportunities continue to expand, compensation for social workers is increasing, and society recognizes the valuable contributions that social workers can and do make to the well-being of people they serve. As the social work profession enters its second century, the profession will continue to be viewed as a major service profession and, as noted in the opening quotation, remain an integral part of society. In fact, employment opportunities for social workers are expected to increase at a rate twice that of any other career area with growth particularly targeted in the areas of aging, home healthcare, substance abuse treatment, school social work, and private social services organizations (U.S. Department of Labor Bureau of Labor Statistics (BLS), 2008–2009). Projections suggest that the future of social work will have a distinctive focus on the concerns of women, children, older adults, and immigrant populations as these continue to be the persons in our society that are most vulnerable and at risk of negative outcomes. Social work will continue to be somewhat unique among major professions, as its members are predominantly women, and women increasingly hold many of the leadership positions.

There continues to be substantial participation by men. Social work will continue to be a profession that emphasizes diversity and will be involved in public controversy, because social workers are often involved in sensitive and highly publicized social issues.

Employment Trends and Opportunities

The future appears extremely promising in terms of increasing employment opportunities for social workers. Increases in diversity of all kinds—ethnic, cultural, age, and family structure—will continue to provide expanded opportunities for social workers. The U.S. Bureau of Labor Statistics projects a 59 percent increase in the category of social assistance employment which includes social workers, counselors, health educators, adult literacy and remedial education teachers, and social and human service assistants (US Department of Labor, 2007). For social workers interested in working in the area of advocacy and grantmaking, and civic organizations, a 14 percent increase in employment is expected between 2006 and 2016 (BLS, 2008).

Social workers in the United States already number approximately 600,000. This number is expected to reach 727,000 by 2016, an overall growth of approximately 18 to 30 percent depending on area of practice (BLS, 2008–2009). The Bureau of Labor Statistics projections of the fastest growing occupations for 2006–2016 suggest a 34 percent increase in employment for baccalaureate substance abuse and behavioral disorder counselors (2007). At the master's level, mental health and substance abuse treatment opportunities for social workers are anticipated to increase by 30 percent. Additionally, increases are expected for social workers in child, family, and school areas (19 percent) and medical and public health (24 percent) (Dohm & Shniper, 2007). Employment prospects are expected to be most competitive in urban areas, but social work positions in rural communities will continue to provide significant opportunities for social workers, in general, and BSWs, in particular.

Projections for growth have been consistently positive in recent years. The popular press has proclaimed social work along with other social and public service-related opportunities to be one of the hot careers on the rise. Here is a sampling of these reports:

- In response to the economic recession, the *Wall Street Journal* (April 12, 2009) projects increases in such social work-related areas as public service and government. *The Journal*'s on-line Career Journal also lists social work as one of the "Best Careers" (Wall Street Journal, 2006).

- One of four hottest fields created by the aging of the baby boomers, with opportunities in patient advocacy and gerontological social work (McCleary, 2002). Social workers will be needed as members of teams to serve the Baby Boomer generation as they age (Worldwidelearn.com).

- One of "seven hot sectors in these hard times" by *Rolling Stone* (Mulrine, 2002).

- One of the careers with the largest expected growth between 2000 and 2010 (Eisenberg, 2002).

- Mental health and substance abuse social workers are included on the list of Hottest Careers for College Graduates through 2016 with 62,000 jobs expected to be available (Collegeboard.com, 2009).

In addition to increasing opportunities to work with older adults and their families, other settings expected to experience growth and employ larger numbers of social workers at all levels in the early part of the 21st century include agencies that provide services in child protection, disabilities, HIV/AIDS, and chemical dependency and addictions. Social work employment opportunities in the criminal justice system, particularly with adolescents, will continue to grow, as will social work positions within elementary and secondary school systems. Private practice (in which self-employed clinical social workers provide individual, family, and group treatment) will be another growth area for social workers with MSWs. The focus will be on the provision of intensive, short-term interventions, increased group interventions, and advocacy, particularly at the policy level (Austin, 1997).

The funding crises that have plagued the social work profession for much of its history will continue to dictate the growth that is realized in these settings. The need for social workers will remain constant, however. Our legislators and funding sources will determine whether the resources required to meet the need will be present as well, making advocacy efforts critical as an area of social work focus.

Areas of Practice   The provision of mental health services is expected to remain the primary area of practice for social workers, as evidenced by the fact that students enrolled in social work programs identify mental health as the largest area of concentration (18.6 percent in 2006 (CSWE)) and over one-third of social work practitioners report their primary area of practice as mental health (Whitaker & Arrington, 2008).

As noted, a significant area of growth for social workers is in the area of gerontological social work, especially in community-based and hospital-based medical and residential services (Rosen & Zlotnik, 2001). As a result of increasing pressure on physicians to maintain shorter hospitalizations, patients are being returned to their homes with greater needs for in-home health services. Social workers serve as key members of the multidisciplinary team of health professionals that work with older adults and their families to provide adequate home- and community-based care. Funding has been made available to social work educators in recent years to provide students with knowledge, skills, and values so they may work effectively with older adults and their families regardless of the area in which they specialize.

With the privatization of many social service systems, a number of social workers are expected to leave the public and nonprofit sectors to work in forprofit and nonprofit organizations. Privatizing social services shifts administrative responsibility for delivery to a privately owned company that contracts with governmental agencies and private insurance companies. These contract agencies then provide the services at a lower cost, as there are typically fewer bureaucratic requirements. In particular, employment opportunities have been expanding in the for-profit sector of mental health, medical facilities, and home-based care for persons with disabilities and older adults (Gibelman & Schervish, 1997).

Salaries   Almost all students want to know the salaries they can expect when they choose social work as a career. Although it is common knowledge that social work salaries, like many other human service-related careers, have historically lagged behind other professions, the salaries for social workers are improving. In recent years, the profession as a whole has united to campaign for higher salaries and compensations and has realized some success in this area. The statistics presented here are broad-based, nationwide salary ranges that differ considerably by region, field of service, educational level, and experience; but they serve as a useful reference point.

The U.S. Department of Labor reports that median annual salaries for all social workers in 2006 ranged from the low $30,000s to upper-$40,000s. Specifically, the median annual salary for social workers employed in child, family, and school settings was $37,480; in medical and public health settings it was $43,040; and in mental health and chemical dependency services, $35,410 (2008–2009). To give you an idea of the range of salaries for particular fields, Box 12.1 lists salaries for several categories within the main divisions of child, family, and school services; health care services; and mental health and chemical dependency services.

A 2006 survey reported the median annual salary for the profession to be $33,540 (BSWs), $49,570 (MSWs), and $65,700 (doctoral level) (CHWS/CWS, 2006). Exhibit 12.1 provides a breakdown of projected social work salaries. In examining the differences between the salaries of social workers with BSWs and MSWs, geographic locale and type of setting influence salaries. For the 310,000 licensed social workers in the U.S., the annual incomes are typically higher than those social workers who do not obtain licensure. BSWs typically earn over 30 percent less than those social workers with a graduate degree and social workers in rural areas earn more than 20 percent less than those working in metropolitan areas (CHWS/CWS, 2006).

Overall, a survey of licensed social work salaries are comparable to professions that are considered comparable (e.g., elementary and secondary teachers, school counselors, clergy, counselors, and nurses). BSW salaries are on par with non-social work counselors in substance abuse and mental health, while MSWs earn salaries comparable to teachers, librarians, nurses, and school counselors (CHWS/CWS, 2006). A variety of explanations have been offered for these lower salaries. Professions that are made up largely of women (for example, nursing and education) routinely receive lower levels of compensation. The social work profession is approximately 85 percent female. Second, social workers are typically employed in organizations that may struggle for financial stability, thus paying lower salaries. As many social workers feel drawn to the profession out of a commitment to working in services for and with the disenfranchised, social workers are undervalued by dominant society in the area of compensation. Despite these challenges, 90 percent of social workers surveyed report feeling they are helping their clients to improve their quality of life; more than two-thirds view their salaries as "adequate" to "very adequate;" and the same number perceive they are respected and supported in their work setting (CHWS/CWS, 2006).

Although these explanations may be, to varying degrees, a valid commentary on the state of the social work profession's salary status, they can also serve as a call to social workers to engage in more aggressive advocacy for the profession.

Social workers provide valuable, much-needed services to a large segment of our population and therefore deserve recognition and compensation for the work they do. Social workers routinely focus professional advocacy efforts on behalf of client systems, but to maintain high-quality education and training opportunities social workers also need to advocate for salaries that recognize the valuable services provided.

Societal Perceptions of the Social Work Profession

Social work is a profession that is visible and valued within our society. Validation of that statement comes from the fact that social workers are employed in an increasingly wide-ranging number and type of settings and are being sought to fill needs in the social service delivery system.

In addition to the traditional settings that have been described throughout this book, social workers are entering the political arena. Over 170 social workers have been elected in recent years to political office at the local, state, and national levels. For a listing of social workers in elected office and information on getting involved,

BOX 12.1

*Social Work
Salaries in
2006*

Child, Family, and School Services
    $32,590/year (residential care facilities)
    $43,500/year (individual and family services)
    $39,000/year (state government)
    $43,500/year (local government)
    $48,360/year (elementary and secondary schools)

Medical and Public Health Care Services
    $35,510/year (individual and family services)
    $38,550/year (nursing and personal care facilities)
    $41,590/year (local government)
    $44,470/year (home health care services)
    $48,420/year (hospitals)

Mental Health and Substance Abuse Treatment Services
    $30,590/year (residential programs)
    $34,920/year (individual and family services)
    $34,290/year (outpatient mental health and substance abuse centers)
    $39,240/year (psychiatric and substance abuse hospitals)
    $39,550/year (local government)

Source: U.S. Department of Labor Bureau of Labor Statistics, 2008–2009.

visit the NASW-PACE website at http://socialworkers.org/ pace. Social workers are also being called on to use their knowledge and skills to develop national policy. As an example, a social worker was added to the staff of Senator Hillary Clinton to design policy on older adult issues. State government officials also recognize the need to increase the number of social workers.

Additional support for the positive perception of the social work profession comes from a recent study conducted by a group of MSW students in a research class at Arizona State University. Using randomly selected telephone numbers, students conducted 386 telephone interviews with local residents in their community and asked questions about the respondents' knowledge and perceptions of the social work profession (LeCroy & Stinson, 2003; O'Neill, 2003). Viewed as a boon to the profession, here are some of the respondents' perceptions:

- 97 percent perceive that social workers are valuable to the community.
- 96 percent see social workers as a source of comfort in times of need.
- 92 percent believe that social workers work with all socioeconomic groups.
- 91 percent perceive social workers as protectors of children.
- 82 percent report they would be generally happy if their children became social workers.

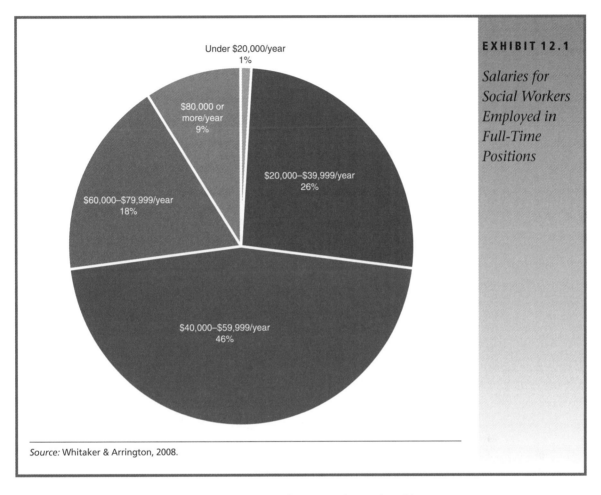

Source: Whitaker & Arrington, 2008.

- 80 percent feel social workers are important for society's social problems.

- 79 percent responded that social workers engage in family therapy.

- 67 percent personally know a social worker.

- 59 percent view social workers as agents of social change (for example, have the ability to influence policy).

- 59 percent report that the information they have received about social workers is positive.

- 56 percent have had personal experience with a social worker.

- 53 percent believe that a bachelor's degree is appropriate for the practice of social work.

- 8 percent view the role of social workers being to disburse "welfare payment."

Although this profile of public perceptions of social workers is encouraging, social workers will continue to advocate for the profession by educating the public regarding the role that they play in society. They do this by taking every opportunity to represent the profession favorably in the public eye. For instance, they write letters, make telephone calls, send e-mail messages, blog, and twitter when social workers are negatively portrayed in the news, on television, and in the movies. They can ensure that when the media highlight social workers, they are identified as degreed social workers. Conversely, when a person who does not possess a social work degree is identified in the media as a social worker, professional social workers challenge that label and provide clarification that only those persons who have been awarded social work degrees from CSWE-accredited programs are social workers.

PROFESSIONAL SOCIALIZATION

Developing the knowledge, skills, and values needed for social work practice is only one aspect of becoming a social work professional. Along with learning the theories and methods of practice, becoming a social work professional involves being socialized into the profession. Professional socialization involves becoming acquainted with the values, norms, and culture of the profession, establishing a professional identity, identifying with the social work profession, feeling comfortable with that self-identity, and understanding the role of social work within the community and society. Being a social worker becomes part of who you are.

You have begun your socialization process by gaining an overview of the profession; experiencing social work through class discussions and exercises; possibly volunteering or working in a social service agency; and hopefully, interacting with other social work students and social work practitioners. In the following sections, we explore the next steps in the professional socialization process.

Social Work Education: Pursuing a Degree

Do you see yourself as a social worker? Some students know before they begin their first social work course that they want to be a social worker. For others, the feeling of connection comes later in other courses or their field experience. Professional identification begins with introspection and soul searching. Essentially, you are asking yourself, "Is social work the right career for me?" "Do I see myself working in those settings that I have been learning about and doing the work I have been reading about and seeing?" The decision to become a social worker lies solely in your hands, but if you are unsure, a number of activities may help you determine whether you identify with the social work profession.

As you learned in the discussion on the social work degree in the first chapter of this book, to become a social worker requires a bachelor's or master's degree in social work awarded by a college or university accredited by the CSWE. In 2009, there were 698 social work programs accredited by the CSWE—195 MSW and 470 BSW programs, with 21 and 12 programs, respectively, in candidacy (an application for accreditation is in process) (CSWE, 2009). Approximately 30,000 BSW and MSW degrees are awarded each year in the U.S. (CHWS/CWS, 2006). Due to anticipated retirements and the growing need for services for older adults and children, this number is not expected to meet the needs of our society. While the majority (70 per cent) of social workers expect to remain in their positions, 13 percent are planning to retire within the next two years, leaving over 50,000 vacancies and making social work one of the professions most impacted by upcoming retirements (CHWS/CWS, 2006; Dohm, 2000).

Bachelor of Social Work   Social work courses at the BSW level focus on preparing generalist social work practitioners. A brief description of the social work curriculum follows. As was briefly noted in Chapter 1, the Council on Social Work Education *Educational policy and accreditation standards* (2008) provides competency-based guidelines for BSW and MSW social work curricula that are summarized below, but individual social work progams determine the best model for delivering coursework in that social work program.

- *The Social Work Curriculum and Professional Practice:* Grounded in a liberal arts foundation, a competency-based social work education at the baccalaureate level prepares graduates for generalist practice, while at the master's level, practitioners are trained for advanced practice in a specific area of concentration.

- *Core Competencies:* Competency-based education is focused on student learning outcomes that are measurable and relevant to the social work foundations of knowledge, values, and skills in the practice areas of individuals, families, groups, organizations, and communities. The ten competencies that have been determined as important for social work practitioners include:

  - *Identify as a professional social worker and conduct oneself accordingly*—social workers are committed to: (1) advocating for client access to the services of social work; (2) practicing personal reflection and self-correction to assure continual professional development; (3) attending to professional roles and boundaries; (4) demonstrating professional demeanor in behavior, appearance, and communication; (5) engaging in career-long learning; and (6) using supervision and consultation.

  - *Apply social work ethical principles to guide professional practice*—social workers have knowledge about the profession's value base, ethical standards, and relevant laws.

o *Apply critical thinking to informal and communicate professional judgments*—social workers have knowledge of principles of logic, scientific inquiry, and reasoned discernment and use critical thinking along with creativity and curiosity.

o *Engage diversity and difference in practice*—social workers understand diversity, its impact on the human experience and that diversity encompasses age, class, color, culture, disability, ethnicity, gender, gender identity and expression, immigration status, political ideology, race, religion, sex, and sexual orientation.

o *Advance human rights and social and economic justice*—social workers are committed to the belief that all persons have basic human rights including freedom, safety, privacy, adequate standard of living, health care, and education.

o *Engage in research-informed practice and practice-informed research*—social workers use practice experiences to inform research and research to inform practice, policy, and delivery of services.

o *Apply knowledge of human behavior and the social environment*—understanding human behavior across the lifespan and systems in which people live are essential for social work practice.

o *Engage in policy practice to advance social and economic well-being and to deliver effective social work services*—social workers are prepared to understand the history and structure of policies that impact client system and engage in **policy practice**.

o *Respond to contexts that shape practice*—in order to respond to the evolving and dynamic nature of society and social work practice, social workers must be informed about current issues, events and service delivery methods.

o *Engage, assess, intervene, and evaluate with individuals, families, groups, organizations, and communities*—social workers have the knowledge and skills to practice at multiple levels and with a range of populations, but practice in any context includes engagement, assessment, intervention, and evaluation.

o *Field education:* Known as the signature pedagogy, field education is the integration of theory and practice that occurs when the student is able to apply the knowledge and skills learned in the classroom in an agency-based social service setting. Under the supervision of social work practitioners, students gain experience in engaging, assessing, intervening in, and evaluating client systems that include individuals, families, groups, organizations, and communities.

Content for BSW courses builds on the content of the other courses required in a liberal arts curriculum. Although programs vary considerably, courses typically taken by social work majors at the bachelor's level include English, communications, human biology, history, mathematics and/or statistics, political science and/or economics, fine arts, sociology and/or anthropology, foreign language, psychology, and philosophy. Each of these areas of study is key to becoming an articulate, effective social worker who has a broad base of knowledge about people, culture, and society. The competent social worker understands the way in which the human body and mind function, the role of culture in our society, the impact of the economy and the political system on the lives of the people that social workers serve, and the use of statistical analysis for the purposes of funding and evaluation. The arts and humanities courses that social work students take provide an understanding of the motivations of human beings.

In addition to the general liberal arts courses and required social work courses, social work students complete elective coursework in individual areas of interest. Most BSW programs offer electives, but students can also choose to take their elective coursework in other departments to round out their knowledge base. Using our past to look into the future, you can seek out elective coursework, readings, projects, and experiences to enable you to approach your social work career armed with a broad-based repertoire of skills. There are a variety of areas you may want to cultivate during your social work training.

- Critical thinking skills, which are essential for effective social work practice, come from a broad understanding of the liberal arts. They empower the social worker to question, discuss, and test assumptions and knowledge in the quest for social work practice competence (Gambrill, 1997).

- Coursework in economics can strengthen your understanding of the impact of a shifting labor market on psychosocial issues (for example, chemical dependency and addiction, domestic violence, multiculturalism, and physical and mental health problems) (Reisch & Gorin, 2001).

- Having an understanding of the legal system can be invaluable to a practicing social worker. Most fields of social work practice intersect at some point with the legal system. Client systems may encounter the legal system as a victim of crime or the accused, when they need guardianship, have end-of-life decisions that require legal intervention, or need legal help with immigration concerns.

- The integration of policy knowledge and skills into social work practice places individual, family, and group concerns within a larger societal context (Jacobson, 2001).

- Knowledge of aging and effective practice methods for working with older adults and their families will be essential for social work practice in the coming decades as the baby boomers become older adults (CSWE/SAGE-SW, 2001).

- Knowledge of community practice education is needed, particularly in classrooms that promote multidisciplinary education and communication and in assessment and intervention at the community level.

- Social workers need leadership skills to be on the forefront of policy development instead of reacting to established policies.

- Communications skills, such as public speaking, working with the media, and providing testimony, are essential for being effective advocates for the social worker's constituencies.

- Applied research skills are important for conducting agency or community-based research, including the ability to conduct needs assessments and develop and evaluate programs with measurable outcomes.

- Knowledge of the global community is a critical area for the contemporary social work professional. Whether you gain proficiency in a second or third language, experience a study abroad semester or course, complete a practicum focused on an international population, or a combination of these options, becoming skilled in working with diverse populations and cultures is essential.

- The time has come for social workers to be particularly skilled in the areas of collaboration, coalition building, and service coordination skills to strengthen the voice of those client systems often unheard by policy makers and to serve as a bridge between those in power and those not in power (Reisch, 1997).

In order for social workers to maintain knowledge and skills that are relevant for societal needs of the time, they require regular, ongoing education. Completing a BSW degree involves a comprehensive education based on the foundations of generalist social work knowledge, skills, and values. Areas for intervention and employment opportunities are extremely varied and constantly in a state of change. Social workers require education and training to enable them to be responsive to the changing society.

Master of Social Work   At the graduate level, coursework is delineated into two levels: foundation and concentration. The foundation coursework, comparable to the generalist courses completed as part of the BSW, consists of social work practice with individuals, families, groups, organizations, and communities; human behavior and the social environment; social policy; research methods; and the field experience. Also typically infused and integrated throughout the foundation coursework are the areas of social work values and ethics, understanding and respect for diversity, populations at risk, and social and economic justice.

At the master's level, following the successful completion of the foundation coursework, students select an area of concentration in which to focus their course of study. Each social work program establishes these areas of specialized study, but the curriculum typically includes advanced coursework in the areas introduced at the foundation level: practice, human behavior, policy, research, and field experiences. Although the diversity of concentration areas is wide ranging throughout MSW programs, areas of specialization you are likely to find include children, youth, and family practice; mental and physical health practice; gerontology; administration; community and policy practice; and social and economic development. Many schools offer **advanced standing** into MSW programs to students who have graduated from a CSWE-accredited BSW program. Their coursework may be applied to part or all of the foundation coursework, thus decreasing the total number of credits required to complete the MSW degree. With advanced standing, students may complete their master's degree in a shorter period of time or take more elective coursework in areas of interest.

Additional options for completing both the BSW and MSW degrees are the five-year and Bridge programs offered at some institutions. The five-year program typically involves the student's completing a joint BSW and MSW degree within a structured five-year plan. The Bridge program typically enables the student to complete three years in another major or institution and begin MSW coursework during the senior year of the undergraduate experience.

Current Issues Influencing Social Work Training for the Future

Because social work is a profession that responds to the personal and societal needs and concerns of the times, social work knowledge and education must also reflect current societal changes and needs. As you have learned, economic downturns present an array of challenges for social workers and the client systems being served, but as one social worker notes: "Times like this push people to re-examine their core values, those core values of caring for each other. Those values fit very well with the core values of social work" (Smith, 2009). As we progress through the 21st century, some new opportunities are emerging for social workers.

Over 400 social workers gathered for the historic 2005 Social Work Congress with the goal of developing a "common agenda for the social work profession for the next decade." From that gathering, twelve imperatives for the next decade were established (Clark et al., 2006):

- Assure excellence in aging knowledge, skills, and competencies at all levels of social work education, practice, and research.

- Participate in politics and policy where major decisions are being made about behavioral health.

- Assure a qualified social work labor force to serve children.

- Take the lead in advocating for quality universal health care.

- Elevate the public's awareness of the efficacy and cost-effectiveness of social work practice in healthcare.

- Address the impact of racism, other forms of oppression, social injustice, and other human rights violations through social work education and practice.

- Increase the value proposition of social work by raising standards and increasing academic rigor of social work education programs.

- Moblize the social work profession to actively engage in politics, policy, and social action, emphasizing the strategic use of power.

- Strengthen social work's ability to influence the corporate and political landscape at the federal, state, and local levels.

- Continuously acknowledge, recognize, confront, and address pervasive racism within social work practice at the individual, agency, and institutional levels.

- Promote culturally competent social work interventions and research methodologies in the areas of social justice, well-being, and cost-benefit outcomes.

- Connect research and practice through partnerships among researchers, the field, and communities.

Throughout this book, a number of the issues addressed in the imperatives have been highlighted. Following is a discussion of the issues and opportunities related to a selected sample of the imperatives that will impact the social work profession and career opportunities.

Health Care Social Work Practice   Social work is becoming more integrated within the health care delivery system; therefore, social workers need knowledge, skills, and values to understand the biopsychosocial and spiritual dynamics that impact people's lives. For example:

- As social workers become more involved in older adult and end-of-life issues, in prolonging life, in psychopharmacology, and genetic counseling, knowledge of biochemistry, neuroscience, and genetics will be a marketable asset.

- As researchers investigate the biological causes of some mental illnesses, social workers, as primary providers of mental health treatment, need an understanding of the interrelatedness of the biological and psychological aspects of mental illness (Austin, 1997).

- Social workers already play a significant role in the provision of interprofessional physical and mental health and social services to persons across the spectrum of the service delivery system. To prepare for practice in an interprofessional setting, social workers need skills in teamwork, contracting, group process, leadership, and conflict resolution (Abramson, 2009).

Gerontological Social Work Practice As you have read throughout this book, the Baby Boomer generation (those persons born between 1946 and 1964) have already changed our society in significant ways, but their entrance into older adulthood will impact the face of aging more than we have previously known. This group is the largest generational cohort in our history and, as older adults, they will be healthier, more technologically sophisticated, and informed consumers; will work longer; and require more focused, specialized services and care. Social workers will be needed as part of interprofessional teams to meet the needs of this population in a variety of settings. Opportunities have begun to emerge and will continue to increase in a variety of practice areas:

- For the fast-growing older adult population, social workers will be needed particularly in the areas of mental and physical health services.

- To serve the older adults who live in alternative living arrangements in retirement, social workers will be needed in residential care facilities, to include assisted living, skilled care and hospice.

- With improvements in medical care and access, older adults of racial, ethnic, and cultural groups are living longer, social work opportunities exist for working with healthy, productive older adults in direct practice, administrative, and policy areas.

- Baccalaureate social workers will be in high demand for their skills to work effectively in direct practice and advocacy roles with older adults and caregivers, both caregivers of children and older adults (Williams & Joyner, 2008).

Technology and Social Work No longer a novelty but a part of our daily lives, technology is a necessary skill area for social workers. Social workers must have increasing levels of technological sophistication for providing services, record keeping, data analysis for funding and program evaluation, communication, and distance education. Computer technology has enabled social workers to conduct online therapy and support groups, facilitate discussion/chat rooms for clients interested in similar issues, provide long-distance social work education and training, maintain up-to-date knowledge of legislation and policies, and reach numerous policy makers in a matter of seconds around the world. In short, technology has enhanced social workers' abilities to reach more people more often in less time. However, we must use technology in an ethical and responsible manner. Social workers are ethically obligated to ensure integrity at all times when using technology. For example, confidentiality is essential when communicating with or about client systems via a cell phone, e-mail, and text messaging. Websites should be checked to ensure they are credible and secure sources of information. Social networking sites (Facebook, MySpace, LinkedIn, and micro-blogging) present the profession with both opportunity and risk. While these forms of communication and potential intervention enable increased access for both clients and providers, the ethical obligation for privacy may be virtually impossible to maintain, making informed consent critical (Sfiligoj, 2009).

In an effort to ensure that social workers and client systems have access to and appropriately and ethically use technology, the National Association of Social Workers and the Association of Social Work Boards developed Standards for Technology and Social Work Practice (2005). The standards encompass such technology-related issues as competent, appropriate, legal, and ethical use of technology; accurate representation of self when using electronic communications; strict adherence to privacy of communication; advocacy for community access to helpful technology; and understanding of the dynamics of electronic communications.

Examples of knowledge, skills, and opportunities related to technology include:

- Technological enhancements enable social workers to conduct groups and meetings in a virtual environment through telephone/video/web conferencing and Internet groups (e.g., chat rooms, bulletin boards, email, and list-serves). Social workers must be aware of group dynamics in the absence, in some cases of verbal and non-verbal communications (Toseland & Horton, 2008).

- Just as traditional records are subject to scrutiny, electronic records (e.g., notes, emails, and postings) may be utilized in legal proceedings and insurance determinations; therefore, social workers must be sensitive to the information included in these forms.

- Opportunities for social work interventions exist in the areas of online support, advocacy, fundraising, education, policy development, innovative services, and one-on-one support available for crises (Smith, 2009).

Disaster Response and Crisis Intervention   Disaster is defined as an extraordinary natural or human-made event that can bring harm to property and human life, while disaster syndrome is considered to be the phases experienced by a disaster or crisis survivor (i.e., preimpact, impact, postimpact and disillusionment or long-term impact) (Barker, 2003). Social workers are increasingly on the scene in times of disaster and crisis to provide support and mental health services. For example, over 40 percent of the volunteers trained by the American Red Cross to provide mental health services in emergency and disaster situations are professional social workers (NASW, 2005a).

Social workers' knowledge and skills in crisis intervention make them valuable assets for working with persons traumatized by a disaster or crisis. Disaster response can be framed within the planned change process of engagement, assessment, intervention, and termination (resolution) (Bliss & Meehan, 2008). However, a specialized skill set is needed as well that includes: knowledge of stress and coping responses; ability to individualize an intervention to the situation and the phase of recovery with sensitivity and context of the circumstances; and ability to support other disaster responders (NASW, 2009–2012c).

Practice issues relevant for disaster and crisis preparedness and response include:

- Social workers are prominently represented in the aftermath of such natural disasters as Hurricane Katrina and have contributed to the profession's knowledge and skill base regarding disaster and crisis response. Critical skills needed in working with survivors include listening, anticipating and normalizing reactions and recovery, recognizing resilience; and building on strengths (McPartlin, 2006).

- Social workers are needed to work with those members of the military involved in deployments and combat, and their families. Social workers have accompanied troops in virtually every deployment in recent times and are working with the families on the home front before, during, and after the deployment.

- Social workers working in crisis and disaster response must be vigilant about attending to their own self-care. Crisis/disaster work can be intense and emotionally challenging for the responders. As helping professionals, social workers recognize the obligation to care for self to avoid burnout, also known as compassion fatigue. Strategies can include: healthy lifestyle habits (e.g., exercise, nutrition, and sleep), relaxation, supervision, continuing education and spiritual or meditation practices (Arrington, 2008; Wharton, 2008).

International Social Work and Multilingualism   With increased focus on international and global issues both within the U.S. and around the world, social workers will continue to play a larger role both domestically and internationally. Social work employment opportunities will continue to grow within the U.S. in virtually every area of the social service delivery system, particularly in community-based social service agencies that serve immigrant and refugee populations, health care facilities, schools. Internationally, social workers have established a presence within the nongovernmental organizational (NGO) community with 95 percent of program director and coordinator positions in twenty NGOs held by degreed social workers (Clairborne, 2004).

As the U.S. population continues to become increasingly diverse, having written and verbal proficiency in multiple languages enables a social worker to communicate more effectively with client systems. When we think about being bilingual in the United States today, Spanish is typically the first language that comes to mind. Although Spanish follows English as the second most common language spoken, there is a need for social workers who are fluent in other languages as well, including Russian, Bosnian, and American Sign Language.

- If you are considering a career working in the international arena, having certain experiences are key; therefore internationally-focused knowledge and skills from such areas listed here are helpful: coursework; volunteer/service or paid internships; personal cultural experiences; multilanguage fluency; and community organization, fundraising, and clinical skills (McLaughlin, 2007).

- Opportunities continue to grow for social workers to assume leadership and administrative roles in international organizations located both in the U.S. and abroad.

- Maintaining awareness of global issues is critical regardless of the setting in which you practice social work. You are obligated to be aware of international and global issues as they impact every facet of our society and our practice.

Child Welfare Services The professionalization of child welfare services is at a critical point in the United States. Historically, due to large caseloads and inadequate salaries, child welfare agencies in nearly every state are challenged to have competent and appropriately trained professionals to work in the area of child welfare. Although turnover rates are considerably less for degreed social workers that work in child welfare, many states do not require a social work degree for these positions; thus, the national turnover rate is 30–40 percent annually (U.S. General Accounting Office, 2003). High turnover results in less effective and inconsistent services for children and families.

More social workers, at both the BSW and MSW level, are needed to develop knowledge and skills to work in child welfare services. Employment opportunities for social workers who want to work with children are expected to grow faster than the average for all professions (14–20 per cent) (BLS, 2008–2009).

Practice issues that are relevant for this field of practice include:

- Qualified and competent social workers are needed to respond to the needs of children who are born into poverty (one every 33 seconds or one in every six), are abused or neglected (nearly one million a year), or are being reared by grandparents (2.5 million) (Children's Defense Fund, 2008).

- Career possibilities for generalist, baccalaureate social workers in the area of child welfare include micro, mezzo, and macro opportunities. For instance, social workers skills at all levels can be utilized in public or private agencies in child protective services, family preservation, and foster care.

- To increase and strengthen the workforce, in general, and in certain areas such as child welfare services, student loan forgiveness programs have been offered. Information on loan forgiveness programs may be available at the federal and state levels, NASW (http://www.socialworkers.org/loanforgiveness/) and your college or university's student financial services office. The following resources are a sample of such resources:

  - National Health Service Corp—http://nhsc.bhpr.hrsa.gov/join_us/lrp.cfm.

  - U.S. Department of Education's Income Contingent Repayment (ICR) Program—www.ed.gov.

  - U.S. Department of Education—http://www.ed.gov; http://www.gov/finaid/info/find/edpicks.jhtml?src=ov.

  - Smart Student Guide to Financial Aid—http://www.finaid.org/.

  - Income Contingent Repayment—http://www.finaid.org/loans/icr.phtml.

  - Volunteer organizations—http://www.finaid.org/loans/forgiveness.phtml.

  - Military—http://www.finaid.org/loans/forgiveness.phtml.

  - Income Based Repayment and Public Service Loan Forgiveness—http://www.ibrinfo.org.

Your state may have loan forgiveness for certain areas of social work practice such as children and family, health care or **school social work**. To inquire about these opportunities, check with your NASW state chapter or your state's department of professional licensing. Advocacy is not just for the clients and the communities we serve but also for our professional concerns. Loan forgiveness is one of those professional concerns. Social workers can become advocates for the profession by writing to legislators to advocate for legislation that supports loan forgiveness for social workers.

Making Social Work Your Career

Having gained insight into some of the societal and social work practice challenges and opportunities that are on the horizon for social workers in the future, let us end the journey by turning our attention to your socialization as a social work professional within this context of future needs and issues. Box 12.2 provides an

BOX 12.2

*Activities to
Promote
Professional
Identification*

- *Network:* Through social work organizations, get acquainted with other social workers who have interests similar to your own. Join a social work listserv or chat room for the opportunity to converse with other social work students and faculty. See if your school has a student social work association or student/faculty special interest groups (for example, social workers interested in working with older adults or a group for students that are gay, lesbian, bisexual, or transgendered). If you join a group, get involved! There is no better way to get connected than to serve in a leadership position.

- *Join NASW:* You can get a discounted student membership rate as well as a transitional rate following graduation. As a member, you receive a monthly newspaper, *NASW News,* the journal, *Social Work,* your local chapter newsletter, and the opportunity to join one of the Specialty Practice Sections, including aging; alcohol, tobacco, and other drugs; child welfare; health; mental health; poverty and social justice; private practice; and school social work. Membership in one of the Specialty Practice Sections provides several benefits: two newsletters per year that include sections on the trends, specific activities, and practice updates of interest to members of that section and online forums for section members to network with one another. In addition, each NASW chapter and the national chapter have student representation—think about running for one of those positions. The NASW website (naswdc.org) has a wealth of information on the profession. For example, check out 50 Ways to Use your Social Work Degree at http://50ways.socialworkblog.org/ to read the stories of 50 practitioners, view a video on the profession, learn surprising facts about social work, and even calculate your future salary.

- *Get more experience:* You may have been required to complete a community service experience for this introductory course, but consider the value of gaining even more experience in the social service field. You can continue volunteering at the site where you completed your community service, gain a different experience by volunteering at another organization, or even seek paid employment at an agency. Many social service organizations have part- or full-time positions for students seeking to gain social service experience.

array of possibilities for you to gain more information and experience with the social work profession. Key to your success in determining whether the social work profession is for you is gaining experience. Volunteer and service-related activities are valuable opportunities for developing insights into the world of social work. Working as a volunteer in a social service setting can provide you with access to social workers who can share with you the rewards and realities of being a social worker.

Although formalized education is an essential part of your professional socialization as a social worker, many informal aspects of your educational experience are equally important for your professional development. One group of graduating BSW students share their wisdom for optimizing your social work professionalization experience during your time as a social work student (Clewes, 2001):

- Be prepared to grow and change by being open minded and having your values and beliefs challenged, but do not plan to change anyone but yourself.

- Maximize your learning opportunities by challenging yourself and recognizing that every person that comes into your life can teach you something. Venture into areas of learning that are new for you.

- Ask for help when you need it, and see mistakes as opportunities for learning.

- Be prepared for your social work program to change you and provide you with the tools to go out and continue this change.

Your social work training will be a lifelong process; therefore, the list of educational and professional socialization opportunities provided here is just the beginning. Our society is in a constant state of flux, and the knowledge and skills needed by social workers must be regularly updated and refined over the course of their career. Stated before the dawn of the 21st century, Reeser's (1996) charge that the social worker of the 21st century would need a broad array of knowledge and skills to enable her or him to work with equal effectiveness on private issues (individual, family, and group work) and public issues (organizational and community practice) continues to be true today.

CONCLUSION

Is a career in social work for you? Social work is a unique helping profession that is dually committed to providing social services, such as emergency shelter, while advocating for change to alleviate social problems, such as lobbying for affordable housing policies. Social work is a profession striving to make a difference as its members work for positive social change and serve vulnerable groups within our society. It is a fulfilling profession shaped by the totality of the social worker's life experiences and professional knowledge, skills, and values. You can begin the process of identifying with the social work profession as early as this first social work course and revisit that process many times throughout your career.

You are almost at the end of your first social work course. You have been exposed to a wide range of information about the profession of social work and have, hopefully, gained a sense of what a career in social work would entail. Your task now is to determine how your journey will continue. I would like to end our time together by asking you to consider the inspirational theme for Social Work Month 2009 (NASW, 2009):

Social Work: Purpose and Possibility defines the social work profession. People who become social workers do so because they seek a purpose for their career, and recognize that there are many different paths where a social work degree might lead. Social workers are passionate, purpose-driven individuals who want to do an excellent service for individuals and communities.

MAIN POINTS

- The outlook for the social work profession is promising. Employment trends suggest that social work jobs will be expanding into new areas, particularly related to aging and racial and ethnic diversity, although provision of mental health services will continue to be the primary area of practice for social work professionals.

- The current median annual salary for social workers is in the mid-$30,000 to upper-$40,000 range.

- Societal perceptions of the social work profession are improving, but social workers must stay focused on self-advocacy efforts to ensure that such perceptions continue to improve.

- The BSW prepares social workers to function as generalist practitioners. Both the BSW and MSW foundation curricula encompass a broad spectrum of content that includes human behavior, social policy, research, and social work practice and is integrated through the field experience.

- Socialization as a social work professional encompasses the formal educational process along with the informal strategies for developing a professional identity. Be prepared for a lifelong process of growth and change if you decide to pursue a career in social work.

EXERCISES

1. Go to the Evaluate tab in the Sanchez Family interactive case (at www.routledgesw.com/cases). Review the Evaluation Introduction and complete Task 1 for the entire Sanchez Family case (notebook review).
2. To conduct an overall review of the Sanchez Family case, complete Task 2, which includes intervention evaluation, case closed, and final thoughts. In the final thoughts section, reflect on the work you have done with the Sanchez family throughout this class. How would you know that you were effective in your work? For example, would you ask the family to complete a satisfaction survey? Would you review the goals the family set for themselves and measure progress against those goals? If you failed to reach certain goals, how would you respond?

3. Complete Task 3. Bid farewell to the Sanchez family and consider all that you have learned from them.

4. You are now familiar with social work interventions at the micro, mezzo, and macro levels. Referring to the community's concerns in the Riverton neighborhood of Alvadora (interactive case at www.routledge.com/cases), identify an issue or challenge and develop an intervention that can be approached from all three levels of social work practice.

5. Along with completing an introductory social work course and learning about the social work profession, talking with practicing social workers is an excellent strategy for determining if social work is the right career for you. With the help of your instructor for this course or other faculty in the social work program, identify a social work practitioner that you can interview in person at her/his agency. Consider an area of social work that is of interest to you and select a practicing social worker that works in that area. Examples might include:

Health/medical	Child welfare	Gerontology
Policy	Community organizing	Administration
Advocacy	Mental health	School social work
Law/justice system	Children and families	Adoption
Substance abuse treatment	Domestic violence	Youth

After you have identified a social worker to interview, contact the person by telephone or e-mail to request the interview. Be certain to discuss a convenient time and duration for the interview. Confirm the interview time and location. You may want to e-mail or mail your questions to the interviewee before the interview. Don't forget to send a thank you note after the interview.

Upon completion of the interview, reflect on the information that you learned from the social worker and submit that to your instructor. Summarize the information you gained, but also reflect on your thoughts and reactions to what you learned. Note: You may want to consider audiotaping the interview to help with your reflection paper.

Here are some suggestions to get you started in your interview. Do not feel limited to these suggestions. Be creative and inquisitive!

- Tell me about your journey into social work. What about social work appealed to you? How did you decide to become a social worker?

- What is your educational background for being a social worker?

- What social work experiences have you had, including practical and paid employment?

- How did you determine the area(s) in which you wanted to work?

- Tell me about your current social work position. What are your responsibilities? How long have you been employed in this position?
- What do you like/dislike about your job?
- What are the positive aspects of being a social worker?
- What are the negative aspects of being a social worker?
- What suggestions would you offer to someone who is considering a social work career?
- Based on what you now know, what suggestions do you have for courses or field experiences that a social work student might seek out during training?

Here are some suggestions for you to consider as you reflect on this experience:

- Before the interview, how would you describe/define social work?
- Did the social worker you interviewed confirm or change your perception of the social work profession?
- What about the social worker's job appealed or did not appeal to you? Can you see yourself working in the area or job of the social worker you interviewed? Why or why not?
- What new information did you learn about social work that you did not previously know?
- Did the social worker discuss how she/he applies the values of the social work profession?
- Did the social worker discuss any ethical conflicts that she/he has encountered? How would you handle similar situations?

6. Discuss your current perception of social work. Issues to consider: has your attitude/perception changed since the beginning of the semester; if so, how; what is your perception of the future of social work.
7. The following may be completed as a group or in-class exercise.

Lydia Dennyson: A Social Work Planned Change Intervention

Focused around a case study of Lydia Dennyson, this exercise brings together the range of social work knowledge that you have gained through this course. In order to determine an appropriate intervention plan for the client system, you will first need to learn about the aging-related changes that occur in her life and the impact of those changes on her ability to maintain a functional quality of life. In order to develop a viable plan for intervention, you will need to learn about resources in your community at the individual and family, organizational and community level that can be developed or mobilized for the benefit of the client system and policies that impact older adults and their families.

Background Information

Mrs. Dennyson is an 82-year-old woman who lives alone in the home she shared for four decades with her husband, now deceased for the past eleven years. She has remained in the home since the death of her husband and has, until recently, been highly functional, active, and productive. She retired at age 66 from her career as a Human Resources specialist for a large corporation. With the retirement income from both her husband and herself, she has been financially comfortable—able to travel to visit family, update her home and car, and pursue her cultural and social interests. She has three children, all of whom live several hundred miles away. She sees them several times a year, but typically only around holidays and on periodic visits to their homes.

Over the past several years, Mrs. Dennyson has begun to experience increased difficulty with her vision. Attributing this to "normal" aging, she did not seek specialized medical care. She has been compensating for her visual impairment in many areas of her life. She developed a strict routine from which she seldom strayed, and generally hid from family, friends, and her physician that she was becoming less functional. In the area of driving, she limited her driving to daylight, non-peak hours, stayed close to her home, and used only those routes familiar to her. It was not until she was involved in a motor vehicle incident that she was responsible for that the severity of her impairment was discovered.

During a follow-up with her physician, she was informed by the physician that she was no longer safe to drive because she had a degenerating visual condition. While she possessed limited understanding of this diagnosis and its future implications, she informed the physician that she had no one who could help her and she had no choice but to continue driving. The physician cautioned her against driving in the future.

Over the ensuing months, Mrs. Dennyson discontinued virtually all of her social, volunteer, and religious activities, travel, and health-related appointments. When her daughter, Janice, came to visit, she was appalled to see the condition of her mother, the house, and the car. Her usually well-kept mother was disheveled, somewhat confused, and significantly thinner. The previously immaculate house was in disarray and the car was covered with scratches, dents, and evidence of multiple fender-benders. Upon further inspection, Janice found multiple unpaid bills, late payment notices, and large sums of cash hidden throughout the house.

Despite the fact that her mother denies any problems and insists that she will continue living in the home alone, Janice is obviously distraught and has no idea what to do. She contacts the Senior Services Center and asks for an immediate appointment for her mother to be seen. You are the case manager assigned to see Mrs. Dennyson.

The Intervention

Utilizing a strengths-based intervention plan that encompasses the steps of engagement, assessment, intervention and termination/evaluation, your task is to develop an intervention plan for Mrs. Dennyson, identify the practice implications for each phase, and consider the lessons learned from this experience.

Phase I—Engagement of the client system

- Who is your client?
- How do you engage the client system?
- How do you interact with the non-client "actors" in this system?

Practice implications for the Engagement phase

- ✓ What additional information is needed?
- ✓ What are the sources of the information?
- ✓ What are your initial impressions?
- ✓ What knowledge is needed?
- ✓ What skills are needed?

Phase II—Assessment

- What are the strengths of the client system?
- What are the goals and needs of the client system?
- What community and family resources are available to meet those goals and needs?
- What are the barriers to reaching those goals and needs?
- What is your assessment of the client system's goals and needs?

Practice implications for the Assessment phase

- ✓ What knowledge is needed?
- ✓ What skills are needed?
- ✓ Are you aware of the client system's values?
- ✓ What is your ethical obligation in this situation?
- ✓ What is your legal obligation in this situation?
- ✓ Who are potential partners in gathering information?
- ✓ How might you manage conflicting goals within the client system?
- ✓ What policies might impact the case?

Phase III—Intervention

- What is an intervention plan that is realistic and potentially helpful to this situation—for the client, the daughter, and the service delivery system?
- How does the intervention plan build on the strengths of the client system?
- Are there adequate and viable resources available to fulfill the plan—at the individual, family, organizational, or community levels?
- What new or different resources are needed to implement the intervention plan?
- What are the barriers to obtaining those resources?

- What is an appropriate timeframe for the implementation of this intervention plan?
- Are the barriers at the individual, family, or community level?
- What policies impact the situation?

Practice implications for the Intervention phase
- ✓ What knowledge is needed?
- ✓ What skills are needed?
- ✓ Who are potential partners in developing and implementing an appropriate intervention plan?
- ✓ Is the intervention plan achievable? Measurable? Ethical?
- ✓ How might you manage conflicting views of the intervention plan?

Phase IV—Termination and Evaluation
- What constitutes a successful intervention (i.e., how will you know when you have completed the intervention)?
- What evaluation process would help you to gauge the success of the intervention?

Practice implications for the Termination and Evaluation phase
- ✓ What knowledge is needed?
- ✓ What skills are needed?
- ✓ How will the intervention be evaluated?

Lessons Learned—Upon completing the planned change process, consider the following:

- What information did you realize that you possessed?
- What information did you realized you needed?
- What knowledge did you realize you possessed?
- What knowledge did you realize you needed?
- What skills did you realize you possessed?
- What skills did you realize you needed?
- What are the value and ethical issues related to this scenario?
- What are the legal implications of this scenario?
- What is your knowledge of community resources?
- What is your awareness of strategies to develop or mobilize needed community resources?
- What policy information about older adults did you realize that you possess?
- What policy information about older adults did you realize that you need?

REFERENCES

Abramson, J. (2009). Interdisciplinary team practice. In Roberts, A.R. *Social workers' desk reference* (2nd ed.) (pp. 44–50). New York: Oxford Press.

Akin, J. (1998). *100 skills of the professional social worker.* Tallahassee, FL: NASW Florida chapter.

Albelda, R., Folbre, N., & the Center for Popular Economics. (1996). *The war on the poor: A defense manual.* New York: The New Press.

Allen-Meares, P. (2000). Our professional values and the changing environment. *Journal of Social Work Education, 36*(2), 179–182.

Allen-Meares, P., & DeRoos, Y. (1997). The future of the social work profession. In M. Reisch & E. Gambrill (eds.), *Social work in the 21st century* (pp. 376–386). Thousand Oaks, CA: Pine Forge Press.

Arrington, P. (2008). *Stress at work: How do social workers cope? NASW Membership Workforce Study.* Washington, DC: NASW.

Association for the Advancement of Social Work with Groups, Inc. (2006). *Standards for social work practice with groups* (2nd edition) [Online]. Available: http://www.aaswg.org.

Association of Baccalaureate Social Work Program Directors. (n.d.). Generalist practice [Online]. Available: http://www.bpdonline.org.

Austin, D.M. (1997). The profession of social work in the second century. In M. Reisch & E. Gambrill (eds.), *Social work in the 21st century* (pp. 396–407). Thousand Oaks, CA: Pine Forge Press.

Bakely, DC (1976). *If . . . a big word with the poor.* Newton, KS: Faith and Life Press.

Baldino, R.G. (2000). Wearing multiple hats as a social worker. *The New Social Worker, 7*(2), 25.

Barker, R.L. (1999). *The social work dictionary* (4th ed.). Washington, DC: NASW Press.

Barker, R.L. (2003). *The social work dictionary* (5th ed.). Washington, DC: NASW Press.

Barth, M.C. (2001). *The labor market for social workers: A first look.* Prepared for the John A. Hartford Foundation, Inc.

Begun, B. (2000, January 1). USA: The way we'll live then. *Newsweek,* 34–35.

Blank, B.T. (1998). Settlement houses: Old idea in new form builds communities. *The New Social Worker, 5*(3), 4–7.

Blank, B.T. (2006). Racism—the challenge for social workers. *The New Social Worker, 13*(4), 10–13.

Bliss, D.L. & Meehan, J. (2008). Blueprint for creating a social work-centered disaster relief initiative. *Journal of Social Service Research, 34*(3), 73–85.

Blundo, R. (2008). Strengths-based framework. In Mizrahi, T. & Davis, L.E., *Encyclopedia of social work* (20th ed.) (pp. 4:173–177). Washington, DC and New York: NASW Press and Oxford University Press.

Boes, M. & van Wormer, K. (2009). Social work with lesbian, gay, bisexual, and transgendered clients. In Roberts, A.R. *Social workers' desk reference* (2nd ed.) (pp. 934–938). New York: Oxford Press.

Bollig, K. (2009). Personal communication. April 2, 2009.

Boyd, K. (1996). There IS a job market for BSW graduates. *The New Social Worker, 3*(2), 18–19.

Braddock, D. (1999). Occupational employment projections to 2008. *Monthly Labor Review, 122,* 51–77.

Brieland, D. (1995). Social work practice: History and evolution. In R.L. Edwards, *Encyclopedia of social work* (19th ed.) (pp. 2247–2257). Washington, DC: NASW Press.

Brodie, K. & Gadling-Cole, C. (2008). Family group conferencing with African-American families. In C. Waites, *Social work practice with African American families: An intergenerational perspective* (pp. 123–143). New York: Routledge.

Brown, J. (1933). *The rural community and social casework*. New York: Family Welfare Association of America.

Burkemper, E. (2004). Informed consent in social work ethics education: Guiding student education with an informed consent template. *Journal of Teaching in Social Work, 24*(1/2), 141–160.

Butterfield, A.K.J. & Chisanga, B. (2008). Community development. In Mizrahi, T. & Davis, L.E., *Encyclopedia of social work* (20th ed.) (pp. 1:375–381). Washington, DC and New York: NASW Press and Oxford University Press.

Center for Health Workforce Studies & Center for Workforce Studies. (2006). *Licensed social workers in the US, 2004*. Rensselaer, NY and Washington, DC: University of Albany School of Public Health Center for Health Workforce Studies and NASW Center for Workforce Studies.

Center on Budget and Policy Priorities. (2003). Poverty increases and median income declines for second consecutive year [Online]. Available: http://www.cbpp.org/9-26-03pov.htm.

Center on Budget and Policy Priorities. (2009). *American Recovery and Reinvestment Act of 2009: State-by-state estimates of key provisions affecting low- and moderate-income individuals*. Washington, DC: Center on Budget and Policy Priorities.

Chace, W.M. (1989). The language of action. *Wesleyan LXII*(2), 36.

Children's Defense Fund. (2008). *State of America's Children 2008—Highlights*. Washington, DC: Children's Defense Fund.

Claiborne, N. (2004). Presence of social workers in nongovernment organizations. *Social Work, 49*(2), 207–218.

Clark, E.J. (2003). The future of social work. In R.A. English, *Encyclopedia of social work* (19th ed., 2003 supplement) (pp. 61–70). Washington, DC: NASW Press.

Clark, E.J., Weismiller, T., Whitaker, T., Waller, G.W., Zlotnik, J.L., & Corbett, B. (2006). *2005 social work congress—final report*. Washington, DC: NASW.

Clark, S. (2007). Social work students' perceptions of poverty. *Journal of Human Behavior in the Social Environment, 16*(1/2), 149–166.

Clewes, R. (2001). Experto credite: New social work graduates share their wisdom. *The New Social Worker, 8*(4), 14–16.

Collegeboard.com. (2009). Hottest careers for college graduates: Experts predict where the jobs will be in 2016 [Online]. Available: http://www.collegeboard.com/student/csearch/majors_careers/236.html.

Collins, D., & Coleman, H. (2000). Eliminating bad habits in the social work interview. *The New Social Worker, 7*(4), 12–15.

Colon, E., Appleby, G.A., & Hamilton, J. (2007). Affirmative practice with people who are culturally diverse and oppressed. In G.A. Appleby, E. Colon, & J. Hamilton (eds.), *Diversity, oppression, and social functioning: Person-in-environment assessment and intervention* (2nd ed.) (pp. 294–311). Boston: Allyn & Bacon.

Congress, E.P. (2009). The culturagram. In A.R. Roberts & J. Watkins (ed.), *Social workers' desk reference* (2nd ed.) (pp. 969–975). New York: Oxford University Press.

Corbett, B.S. (2008). Distinctive dates in social welfare history. In Mizrahi, T. & Davis, L.E., *Encyclopedia of social work* (20th ed.) (pp. 4:403–424). Washington, DC and New York: NASW Press and Oxford University Press.

Corcoran, J. (2008). Direct practice. In Mizrahi, T. & Davis, L.E., *Encyclopedia of social work* (20th ed.) (pp. 2:31–36). Washington, DC and NY: NASW Press and Oxford University Press.

Corey, M.S., & Corey, G. (1998). *Becoming a helper* (3rd ed.). Pacific Grove, CA: Brooks/Cole Thomson Learning.

Council on Social Work Education/SAGE-SW. (2001). *Strengthening the impact of social work to improve the quality of life for older adults and their families: Blueprint for the new millennium*. Washington, DC: Author.

Council on Social Work Education. (2004) [Online]. Available: http://www.cswe.org.

Council on Social Work Education. (2006). *Statistics on social work education in the United States: A summary*. Alexandria, VA: CSWE.

Council on Social Work Education. (2008). *Educational policy and accreditation standards*. Washington, DC: Author.

Council on Social Work Education. (2009). Guide to the economic stimulus bill. Available at: http://www.cswe.org/NR

Coven, M. (2005). An introduction to TANF [Online]. Washington, DC: Center on Budget and Policy Priorities. Available: http://www.cbpp.org.

Cummings, S.M. & Adler, G. (2007). Predictors of social workers employment in gerontological work. *Educational Gerontology*, *33*, 925–938.

Cummings, S.M., Adler, G., & DeCoster, V.A. (2005). Factors influencing graduate-social-work students' interests in working with elders. *Educational Gerontology*, *31*, 643–544.

Dale, M.L. (2001). Your summer vacation—or is it? The value of experiential learning as part of the new social worker's career campaign. *The New Social Worker*, *8*(1), 4–6.

Daniel, C.L. (2008). From liberal pluralism to critical multiculturalism: The need for a paradigm shift in multicultural education for social work practice in the United States. *Journal of Progressive Human Services*, *19*(1), 19–38.

Danziger, S. (2002). Approaching the limit: Early national lessons from welfare reform. In B.A. Weber, G.J. Duncan, & L.A. Whitener (eds.), *Rural dimensions of welfare reform* (pp. 25–49). Kalamazoo, MI: W.E. Upjohn Institute for Employment Research.

D'Aprix, A.S., Boynton, L.A., Carver, B., & Urso, C. (2001). When the ideal meets the real: Resolving ethical dilemmas in the real world. *The New Social Worker*, *8*(2), 20–23.

Day, J.C. (1996). *Population projections of the United States by age, sex, race, and Hispanic origin: 1995 to 2050*. U.S. Bureau of the Census, Current Population Reports, P25–1130. Washington, DC: U.S. Government Printing Office.

DeJong. P. (2009). Solution-focused therapy. In A.R. Roberts & J. Watkins (ed.), *Social workers' desk reference* (2nd ed.) (pp. 253–258). New York: Oxford University Press.

DeNavas-Wait, C., Proctor, B.D., & Smith, J.C. (2008). Income, poverty, and health insurance coverage in the United States: 2007. U.S. Census Bureau, Current Population Reports, P60–235. Washington, DC: U.S. Government Printing Office.

Dickinson, N.S. (1997). Federal social legislation from 1994 to 1997. In R.L. Edwards, *Encyclopedia of social work* (19th ed., 1997 supplement) (pp. 125–131). Washington, DC: NASW Press.

Doelling, C., Matz, B., & Kuehne, J. (1999). *Job market of 1998 MSW graduates*. Prepared by the Social Work Career Development Group.

Dohm, A. (2000). Gauging the labor force effects of retiring baby-boomers. *Monthly Labor Review*, pp. 17–25.

Dohm, A. & Shniper, L. (2007). Occupational employment projections to 2016. *Monthly Labor Review*, 86–125.

Dolgoff, R., Loewenberg, F.M., & Harrington, D. (2009). *Ethical decisions for social work practice* (8th edition). Belmont, CA: Thomson Brooks/Cole.

Dunlap, K.M., & Strom-Gottfried, K. (1998a). Everyday ethics and values for social workers (Part 1 in a series on ethics). *The New Social Worker*, *5*(1), pp. 16–18.

Dunlap, K.M., & Strom-Gottfried, K. (1998b). Maintaining confidence in confidentiality (Part 3 in a series on ethics). *The New Social Worker*, *5*(3), pp. 10–12, 19.

Dunn, C. (2002). The importance of cultural competence for social workers. *The New Social Worker*, *9*(2), 4–5.

Dunn, J.H., Flory, B.E., Berg-Weger, M., & Milstead, M. (2004). An exploratory study of supervised access and custody exchange services: The children's experience. *Family Court Review. An Interdisciplinary Journal*, *42*(1), pp. 60–73.

Economic Policy Institute. (2009). Basic family budget calculator [Online]. Available: http://www.epi.org/content/budget_calculator.

Eisenberg, D. (2002, May 6). The coming job boom. *Time*, 40–44.

Ephross, P.H. & Greif, G.L. (2009). Group process and group work techniques. In A.R. Roberts & J. Watkins (ed.), *Social workers' desk reference* (2nd ed.) (pp. 679–685). New York: Oxford University Press.

Flexner, A. (1915). *Is social work a profession? Proceedings of the National Conference of Charities and Correction* (pp. 576–590). Chicago: Hildmann Printing.

Flory, B.E., & Berg-Weger, M. (2003). Children of high conflict custody disputes: Striving for social justice in adult focused litigation. *Social Thought*, *22*(2/3). (Also published in Stretch, J.J., Burkemper, E.M., Hutchison, W.J., & Wilson, J. (2003). *Practicing justice* (pp. 205–219). New York: Haworth Press.)

Flory, B.E., Dunn, J., Berg-Weger, M., & Milstead, M. (2001). An exploratory study of supervised access and custody exchange services: The parental experience. *Family and Conciliation Court Review: An Interdisciplinary Journal*, *39*(4), 469–482.

Frumkin, M., & Lloyd, G.A. (1995). Social work education. In R.L. Edwards, *Encyclopedia of social work* (19th ed.) (pp. 2238–2246). Washington, DC: NASW Press.

Furman, J. & Parrott, S. (2007). *A $7.25 minimum wage would be a useful step in helping working families escape poverty*. Washington, D.C: Center on Budget and Policy Priorities.

Furman, R., Rowan, D., & Bender, K. (2009). *An experiential approach to group work*. Chicago, IL: Lyceum Books, Inc.

Gambrill, E. (1997). Social work education: Current concerns and possible future. In M. Reisch & E. Gambrill (eds.), *Social work in the 21st century* (pp. 317–327). Thousand Oaks, CA: Pine Forge Press.

Garvin, C.D. (1997). *Contemporary group work*. Boston: Allyn & Bacon.

Garvin, C.D. & Galinsky, M.J. (2008). Groups. In Mizrahi, T. & Davis, L.E., *Encyclopedia of Social Work* (20th ed.) (pp. 2:287–298). Washington, DC and New York: NASW Press and Oxford University Press.

Gates, T. (2006). Challenging heterosexism: Six suggestions for social work practice. *The New Social Worker*, *13*(3), 4–5.

Germain, C.B., & Gitterman, A. (1980). *The life model of social work practice*. New York: Columbia University Press.

Germain, C.B., & Gitterman, A. (1995). Ecological perspective. In R.L. Edwards, *Encyclopedia of social work* (19th ed.) (pp. 816–824). Washington, DC: NASW Press.

Gibelman, M. (2004). *What social workers do* (2nd ed.). Washington, DC: NASW Press.

Gibelman, M., & Schervish, P.H. (1997). *Who we are: A second look*. Washington, DC: NASW Press.

Ginsberg, L. (1998). Introduction: An overview of rural social work. In L. Ginsberg (ed.), *Social work in rural communities* (3rd ed.) (pp. 3–22). Alexandria, VA: Council on Social Work Education.

Ginsberg, L.H. (2001). *Careers in social work* (2nd ed.). Boston: Allyn & Bacon.

Gitterman, A. & Germain, A. (2008). Ecological framework. In Mizrahi, T. & Davis, L.E., *Encyclopedia of social work* (20th ed.) (pp. 2:97–102). Washington, DC and New York: NASW Press and Oxford University Press.

Gitterman, A., & Knight, C. (2000). The power of group work. *The New Social Worker*, (2), 15–18.

Golden, G.K. (2008). White privilege and the mental health profession. *The New Social Worker*, *15*(2), 4–5.

Goode, T.D. & Jones, W. (2006). *A definition of linguistic competence*. Washington, DC: Georgetown University National Center for Cultural Competence.

Green, G.P., & Haines, A. (2002). *Asset building in community development*. Thousand Oaks, CA: Sage Publications.

Gummer, B. (1995). Social planning. In R.L. Edwards, *Encyclopedia of social work* (19th ed.) (pp. 2180–2186). Washington, DC: NASW Press.

Gutiérrez, L., & Nagda, B.A. (1996). The multicultural imperative in human services organizations: Issues for the twenty-first century. In P.R. Raffoul & C.A. McNeece (eds.), *Future issues for social work practice* (pp. 203–213). Boston: Allyn & Bacon.

Hagen, J.L. & Lawrence, C.K. (2008). Temporary assistance to needy families. In Mizrahi, T. & Davis, L.E., *Encyclopedia of social work* (20th ed.) (pp. 4:225–229). Washington, DC and New York: NASW Press and Oxford University Press.

Hartman, A. (1978). Diagrammatic assessment of family relationships. *Social Casework*, *59*, 465–476.

Haynes, K.S. (1996). The future of political social work. In P.R. Raffoul & C.A. McNeece (eds.), *Future issues for social work practice* (pp. 266–276). Boston: Allyn & Bacon.

He, W., Sengupta, M., Velkoff, V.A. & DeBarros, K.A. (2005). *Current Population Reports, P23–209, 65+ in the United States: 2005*. Washington, DC:

U.S. Census Bureau, U.S. Government Printing Office.

Hepworth, D.H., Rooney, R.H., Rooney, G.D., Strom-Gottfried, K., & Larsen, J. (2010). *Direct social work practice: Theory and skills* (8th ed.). Belmont, CA: Brooks/Cole.

Hernandez, V.R. (2008). Generalist and advanced generalist practice. In Mizrahi, T. & Davis, L.E., *Encyclopedia of social work* (20th ed.) (pp. 2:260–268). Washington, DC and New York: NASW Press and Oxford University Press.

Hoefer, R. (2008). Social welfare expenditures. In Mizrahi, T. & Davis, L.E., *Encyclopedia of social work* (20th ed.) (pp. 4:101–107). Washington, DC and New York: NASW Press and Oxford University Press.

Hoffman, K.S., Lubben, J.E., Ouellette, P.M., Westhuis, D., Shaffer, G.L., Hutchison, E.D., Alvarez, A.R., Biegel, D.E., & Colby, I.C. (2008). Social work education: Overview. In Mizrahi, T. & Davis, L.E., *Encyclopedia of Social Work* (20th ed.) (pp. 4:107–137). Washington, DC and New York: NASW Press and Oxford University Press.

Hopps, J.G., & Collins, P.M. (1995). Social work profession overview. In R.L. Edwards, *Encyclopedia of social work* (19th ed.) (pp. 2266–2282). Washington, DC: NASW Press.

Hopps, J.G., Lowe, T.B., Stuart, P.H., Weismiller, T., & Whitaker, T. (2008). Social work profession. In Mizrahi, T. & Davis, L.E., *Encyclopedia of social work* (20th ed.) (pp. 4:138–168). Washington, DC and New York: NASW Press and Oxford University Press.

Horejsi, C.R. (2002). Social and economic justice: The basics. *The New Social Worker*, 9(4), 10–12.

Jacobson, W. (2001). Beyond therapy: Bringing social work back to human services reform. *Social Work*, 46(1), 51–61.

Johnson, N. (2001). A hand up. How state earned income tax credits help working families escape poverty in 2001: Summary [Online]. Center on Budget and Policy Priorities. Available: http://www.cbpp.org/10-18-01sfp.htm.

Kagle, J.D. (2009). Record-keeping. In A.R. Roberts & J. Watkins (ed.), *Social workers' desk reference* (2nd ed.) (pp. 28–32). New York: Oxford University Press.

Kane, M.N. (2008). When I'm 75 years old: Perceptions of social work students. *Social Work in Health Care*, 47(2), 185–213.

Kendall, K.A. (2000). *Social work education: Its origins in Europe*. Alexandria, VA: Council on Social Work Education.

Kindle, P.A. (2006). The inherent value of social work. *The New Social Worker*, 13(4), 17.

King, M.L. Jr. (1963, June 23). Speech at the Great March on Detroit.

Kirst-Ashman, K.K. & Hull, G.H. (2006). *Understanding generalist practice* (4th ed.). Belmon, CA: Thomson Brooks/Cole.

Kondrat, M.E. (2008). Person-in-environment. In Mizrahi, T. & Davis, L.E., *Encyclopedia of social work* (20th ed.) (pp. 3:348–354). Washington, DC and New York: NASW Press and Oxford University Press.

Kosberg, J.I., & Kaufman, A.V. (2002). Gerontological social work: Issues and imperatives for education and practice. *Electronic Journal of Social Work*, 1(1), February 15.

Kosmin, B.A., & Mayer, E. (2001). *American religious identification survey, 2001*. New York: The Graduate Center of the City University of New York.

Kurland, R. (2007). Debunking the "blood theory" of social work with groups: Group workers *are* made and not born. *Social Work with Groups*, 30(1), 11–24.

Landon, P.S. (1995). Generalist and advanced generalist practice. In R.L. Edwards, *Encyclopedia of social work* (19th ed.) (pp. 1101–1107). Washington, DC: NASW Press.

Lazere, E., Frernstad, S., & Goldberg, H. (2002). States and counties are taking steps to help low-income working families make ends meet and move up the economic ladder [Online]. Center for Budget and Policy Priorities. Available: http://www.cbpp.org/5–18–01wel.htm.

LeCroy, C.W., & Stinson, E.L. (2003). Public's perception of social workers. Paper presented at 2003 Society for Social Work and Research, Washington, DC.

Leighninger, L. (2000). *Creating a new profession: The beginnings of social work education in the United States*. Alexandria, VA: Council on Social Work Education.

Levitis, J. & Koulish, J. (2008). *State earned income tax credits: 2008 legislative update*. Washington, DC: Center on Budget and Policy Priorities.

Logan, S.M.L. (2003). Issues of multiculturalism: Multicultural practice, cultural diversity, and competency. In R.A. English, *Encyclopedia of social work* (19th ed., 2003 supplement) (pp. 95–105). Washington, DC: NASW Press.

Lohr, S. (2009, April 11). With finance disgraced, which career will be king? NYtimes.com/business [Online]. Available: NYtimes.com/business: http://www.nytimes.com/2009/04/12/weekinreview/12lohr.html?_r=1&ref=weekinreview.

Longres, J.F. (2008). Richmond, Mary Ellen (1861–1928). In Mizrahi, T. & Davis, L.E., *Encyclopedia of social work* (20th ed.) (p. 4:368). Washington, DC and New York: NASW Press and Oxford University Press.

Mackelprang, R.W., & Salsgiver, R.O. (1999). *Disability: A diversity model approach in human service practice*. Pacific Grove, CA: Brooks/Cole.

Mackelprang, R.W., Patchner, L.S., DeWeaver, K.L., Clute, M.A., & Sullivan, W.P. (2008). Disability. In Mizrahi, T. & Davis, L.E., *Encyclopedia of social work* (20th ed.) (pp. 2:36–43). Washington, DC and New York: NASW Press and Oxford University Press.

Marson, S.M., & MacLeod, E.H. (1996). The first social worker. *The New Social Worker, 3*(2), 11.

Martinez-Brawley, E. (1983). *Seven decades of rural social work*. New York: Praeger.

McCleary, K. (2002, October). Help wanted. *Good Housekeeping, 235*(4), 77–78, 80.

McLaughlin, A. (2007). How to snag a job in international social work. *The New Social Worker, 14*(2), 26–27.

McNutt, J. & Floersch, J. (2008). Social work practice. In Mizrahi, T. & Davis, L.E., *Encyclopedia of Social Work* (20th ed.) (pp. 4:138–144). Washington, DC and New York: NASW Press and Oxford University Press.

McPartlin, T.K. (2006). Notes from the Gulf: A social worker reflects on hurricane relief. *The New Social Worker, 13*(1), 18, 23.

Meyer, C.H. (1995). Assessment. In R.L. Edwards, *Encyclopedia of social work* (19th ed.) (pp. 260–270). Washington, DC: NASW Press.

Miller, W.R. & Rollnick, S. (2002). *Motivational interviewing: Preparing people for change* (2nd ed.). NY: The Guilford Press.

Milligan, S.E. (2008). Community building. In Mizrahi, T. & Davis, L.E., *Encyclopedia of social work* (20th ed.) (pp. 1:371–375). Washington, DC and New York: NASW Press and Oxford University Press.

Minahan, A. (1981). Purpose and objectives of social work revisited. *Social Work, 26*(1), 5–6.

Mindell, C.L. (2007). Religious bigotry and religious minorities. In G.A. Appleby, E. Colon, & J. Hamilton (eds.), *Diversity, oppression, and social functioning: Person-in-environment assessment and intervention* (2nd ed.) (pp. 226–246). Boston: Allyn & Bacon.

Mizrahi, T. (2009). Community organizing principles and practice guidelines. In A.R. Roberts & J. Watkins (ed.), *Social workers' desk reference* (2nd ed.) (pp. 872–881). New York: Oxford University Press.

Mizrahi, T. & Baskind, F. (2003). Social work education and the future. In R.A. English, *Encyclopedia of social work* (19th ed., 2003 supplement) (pp. 137–149). Washington, DC: NASW Press.

Mizrahi, T. & Davis, L.E. (2008). *Encyclopedia of Social Work* (20th ed.). Washington, DC and New York: NASW Press and Oxford University Press.

Mondros, J.B. (2009). Principles and practice guidelines for social action. In A.R. Roberts & J. Watkins (ed.), *Social workers' desk reference* (2nd ed.) (pp. 901–906). New York: Oxford University Press.

Mulrine, A. (2002, March 14). Where the jobs are. *Rolling Stone, 891*, 62.

Mulroy, E.A. (2008). Community needs assessment. In Mizrahi, T. & Davis, L.E., *Encyclopedia of social work* (20th ed.) (pp. 1:385–387). Washington, DC and New York: NASW Press and Oxford University Press.

Murdock, S.H., & Michael, M. (1996). Future demographic change: The demand for social welfare services in the twenty-first century. In P.R. Raffoul & C.A. McNeece (eds.), *Future issues for social work practice* (pp. 3–18). Boston: Allyn & Bacon.

Nagle, A. & Johnson, N. (2006). *A hand up: How state earned income tax credits help working families escape poverty in 2006*. Washington, DC: Center on Budget and Policy Priorities.

NASW News. (2003, February). Practitioners surveyed; incomes increased. *NASW News, 48*(2), 1, 8.

National Association of Social Workers. (n.d.a). *Issue fact sheets. Diversity & cultural competence* [Online]. Available: http://www.naswdc.org.

National Association of Social Workers. (n.d.b). *Issues fact sheets. Mental health* [Online]. Available: http://www.naswdc.org.

National Association of Social Workers. (1973). *Standards for social service manpower*. Washington, DC: NASW.

National Association of Social Workers. (1998). *Milestones in the development of social work and social welfare*. Washington, DC: Author.

National Association of Social Workers. (2004a). [Online]. Available: http://www.naswdc.org.

National Association of Social Workers. (2004b). *Social work profession and issue fact sheets* [Online]. Available: http://www.naswdc.org.

National Association of Social Workers. (2005a). *Facts about social work*. Available at: http//www.socialworkers.org/pressroom/swm2005/facts.asp.

National Association of Social Workers. (2005b). Government relations update [Online]. Available: http://www.naswdc.org/advocacy/updates/default.asp.

National Association of Social Workers. (2005c). *NASW standards for social work practice in child welfare*. Washington, DC: NASW Press.

National Association of Social Workers. (2005d). *NASW standards for social work practice in health care settings*. Washington, DC: NASW Press.

National Association of Social Workers. (2005e). *NASW standards for social work practice with clients with substance use disorders*. Washington, DC: NASW Press.

National Association of Social Workers. (2006–2009a). Economic Policy. *Social work speaks: National Association of Social Workers policy statements 2006–2009*. Washington, DC: NASW Press.

National Association of Social Workers. (2006–2009b). Health care. *Social work speaks: National Association of Social Workers policy statements 2006–2009*. Washington, DC: NASW Press.

National Association of Social Workers. (2006–2009c). Cultural and linguistic competences in the social work profession. *Social work speaks: National Association of Social Workers policy statements 2006–2009*. Washington, DC: NASW Press.

National Association of Social Workers. (2007). *Indicators for the achievement of the NASW Standards for Cultural Competence in Social Work Practice*. Washington, DC: NASW.

National Association of Social Workers. (2008). *Code of ethics*. Washington, DC: NASW. Available at: http://www.naswdc.org

National Association of Social Workers. (2009a). *General facts about social work*. Available at: http://www.socialworkers.org/pressroom/swMonth/2009/swfacts.asp.

National Association of Social Workers. (2009b). *Social work profession* [Online]. Available: http://www.socialworkers.org/profession/overview.asp.

National Association of Social Workers. (2009–2012a). Confidentiality and information utilization. *Social work speaks: National Association of Social Workers policy statements 2009–2012*. Washington, DC: NASW Press.

National Association of Social Workers. (2009–2012b). Deprofessionalization and reclassification. *Social work speaks: National Association of Social Workers policy statements 2009–2012*. Washington, DC: NASW Press.

National Association of Social Workers. (2009–2012c). Disasters. *Social work speaks: National Association of Social Workers policy statements 2009–2012*. Washington, DC: NASW Press.

National Association of Social Workers. (2009–2012d). Immigrants and refugees. *Social work speaks: National Association of Social Workers policy statements 2009–2012*. Washington, DC: NASW Press.

National Association of Social Workers. (2009–2012e). Language and cultural diversity in the United States. *Social work speaks: National Association of Social Workers policy statements 2009–2012*. Washington, DC: NASW Press.

National Association of Social Workers. (2009–2012f). Lesbian, gay, and bisexual issues. *Social work speaks: National Association of Social Workers policy statements 2009–2012.* Washington, DC: NASW Press.

National Association of Social Workers. (2009–2012g). People with disabilities. *Social work speaks: National Association of Social Workers policy statements 2009–2012.* Washington, DC: NASW Press.

National Association of Social Workers. (2009–2012h). Poverty and economic justice. *Social work speaks: National Association of Social Workers policy statements 2009–2012.* Washington, DC: NASW Press.

National Association of Social Workers. (2009–2012i). Public child welfare. *Social work speaks: National Association of Social Workers policy statements 2009–2012.* Washington, DC: NASW Press.

National Association of Social Workers. (2009–2012j). Racism. *Social work speaks: National Association of Social Workers policy statements 2009–2012.* Washington, DC: NASW Press.

National Association of Social Workers. (2009–2012k). Rural social work. *Social work speaks: National Association of Social Workers policy statements 2009–2012.* Washington, DC: NASW Press.

National Association of Social Workers. (2009–2012l). Social work in the criminal justice system. *Social work speaks: National Association of Social Workers policy statements 2009–2012.* Washington, DC: NASW Press.

National Association of Social Workers. (2009–2012m). Transgender and gender identity issues. *Social work speaks: National Association of Social Workers policy statements 2006–2009.* Washington, DC: NASW Press.

National Association of Social Workers. (2009–2012n). Welfare reform. *Social work speaks: National Association of Social Workers policy statements 2009–2012.* Washington, DC: NASW Press.

National Association of Social Workers. (2009–2012o). Women's issues. *Social work speaks: National Association of Social Workers policy statements 2009–2012.* Washington, DC: NASW Press.

National Association of Social Workers and Association of Social Work Boards. (2005). *NASW and ASWB standards for technology and social work practice* Washington, DC: NASW Press.

National Association of Social Workers Center for Workforce Studies. (2005). *Assuring the sufficiency of a frontline workforce: A national study of licensed social workers.* Washington, DC: NASW.

National Association of Social Workers National Committee on Racial and Ethnic Diversity. (2001). *NASW standards for cultural competence in social work practice* [Online]. Available: http://www.naswdc.org.

National Center for Health Statistics. (2003) [Online]. Available: http://www.cdc.gov/nchs.

National Public Radio/Henry J. Kaiser Family Foundation/Harvard University Kennedy School of Government. (2001). *Poverty in America* [Online]. Available: http://www.kff.org.

O'Hare, T. (2009). *Essential skills of social work practice: Assessment, intervention, and evaluation.* Chicago, IL: Lyceum Books.

Okun, B.F., Fried, J., & Okun, M.L. (1999). *Understanding diversity: A learning-as-practice primer.* Pacific Grove, CA: Brooks/Cole.

O'Neill, J.V. (2003). Profession perceived favorably by public. *NASW News, 48*(3).

Ozawa, M.N. (1997). Demographic changes and their implications. In M. Reisch & E. Gambrill (eds.), *Social work in the 21st century* (pp. 8–27). Thousand Oaks, CA: Pine Forge Press.

Pace, P.R. (2009). Recovery Act to impact social services. *NASW News, 54*(4), pp. 1,6.

Paraquad. (n.d.). *Words with dignity* [Online]. Available: http://www.paraquad.org.

Parrott, S. (2008). *Recession could cause large increases in poverty and push millions into deep poverty.* Washington, DC: Center on Budget and Policy Priorities.

Peck, S. (1999). Who are we? *The New Social Worker, 6*(1), 4–6.

Peterson, J. (2002). *Feminist perspectives on TANF reauthorization: An introduction to key issues for the future of welfare reform* [Online]. Institute for Women's Policy Research. Available: http://www.iwpr.org.

Pinderhughes, E. (1995). Direct practice overview. In R.L. Edwards, *Encyclopedia of social work* (19th ed.) (pp. 740–751). Washington, DC: NASW Press.

Quam, L. (2008). Addams, Jane (1860–1935). In Mizrahi, T. & Davis, L.E., *Encyclopedia of social work* (20th ed.) (pp. 4:318–319). Washington, DC and New York: NASW Press and Oxford University Press.

Raffoul, P.R. (1996). Social work and the future: Some final thoughts. In P.R. Raffoul & C.A. McNeece (eds.), *Future issues for social work practice* (pp. 293–300). Boston: Allyn & Bacon.

Ramanathan, C.S., & Link, R.J. (1999). Future visions for global studies in social work. In C.S. Ramanathan & R.J. Link, *All our futures: Principles and resources for social work practice in a global era* (pp. 219–237). Belmont, CA: Wadsworth.

Rank, M.R. (1994). *Living on the edge: The realities of welfare in America.* New York: Columbia University Press.

Rank, M.R. (2006). Toward a new understanding of American poverty. *Journal of Law and Policy, 20*(17), 17–51.

Rank, M.R. (2008). Poverty. In Mizrahi, T. & Davis, L.E., *Encyclopedia of social work* (20th ed.) (pp. 3:387–395). Washington, DC and New York: NASW Press and Oxford University Press.

Rank, M.R. & Hirschl, T.A. (2001a). The occurrence of poverty across the life cycle: Evidence from the PSID. *Journal of Policy Analysis and Management, 20*(4), 737–755.

Rank, M.R., & Hirschl, T.A. (2001b). Rags or riches? Estimating the probabilities of poverty and affluence across the adult American life span. *Social Science Quarterly, 82*(4), pp. 651–669.

Rank, M.R., & Hirschl, T.A. (2002). Welfare use as a life course event: Toward a new understanding of the U.S. safety net. *Social Work, 47*(3), 237–248.

Rauscher, L., & McClintock, M. (1997). Ableism curriculum design. In M. Adams, L.A. Bell, & P. Griffin (eds.), *Teaching for diversity and social justice* (pp. 198–229). New York: Routledge.

Reamer, F.G. (1995). Ethics and values. In R.L. Edwards, *Encyclopedia of social work* (19th ed.) (pp. 893–908). Washington, DC: NASW Press.

Reamer, F.G. (2001). *Ethics education in social work.* Alexandria, VA: Council on Social Work Education.

Reamer, F.G. (2006). *Ethical standards in social work.* Washington, DC: NASW Press.

Reamer. F.G. (2008a). Ethics and values. In Mizrahi, T. & Davis, L.E., *Encyclopedia of social work* (20th ed.) (pp. 2:143–151). Washington, DC and New York: NASW Press and Oxford University Press.

Reamer, F.G. (2008b) Ethical standards in social work: The NASW Code of Ethics. In Mizrahi, T. & Davis, L.E., *Encyclopedia of social work* (20th ed.) (pp. 4:391–397). Washington, DC and New York: NASW Press and Oxford University Press.

Reamer, F.G. (2009a). Ethical issues in social work. In A.R. Roberts (ed.), *Social workers' desk reference* (2nd ed.) (pp. 115–120). New York: Oxford University Press.

Reamer, F.G. (2009b). *The social work ethics casebook: Cases and commentary.* Washington, DC: NASW Press.

Recovery.gov. (2009). Your money at work. Available at: http://www.recovery.gov/

Reeser, L. (1996). The future of professionalism and activism in social work. In P.R. Raffoul & C.A. McNeece (eds.), *Future issues for social work practice* (pp. 240–253). Boston: Allyn & Bacon.

Reid, P.N. (1995). Social welfare history. In R.L. Edwards, *Encyclopedia of social work* (19th ed.) (pp. 2206–2225). Washington, DC: NASW Press.

Reisch, M. (1997). The political context of social work. In M. Reisch & E. Gambrill (eds.), *Social work in the 21st century* (pp. 80–92). Thousand Oaks, CA: Pine Forge Press.

Reisch, M. (2000). Social work and politics in the new century. *Social Work, 45*(4), 293–297.

Reisch, M. (2009). Legislative advocacy to empower oppressed and vulnerable groups. In A.R. Roberts & J. Watkins (ed.), *Social workers' desk reference* (2nd ed.) (pp. 893–900). New York: Oxford University Press.

Reisch, M., & Gorin, S.H. (2001). Nature of work and future of the social work profession. *Social Work, 46*(1), 9–19.

Reisch, M., & Jarman-Rohde, L. (2000). The future of social work in the United States: Implications for field education. *Journal of Social Work Education, 36*(2), 201–214.

Richmond, M. (1897). The need of a training school in applied philanthropy. In *Proceedings of the (1897) National Conference of Charities and Correction* (pp. 181–186). Boston: Geo. H. Ellis.

Richmond, M. (1917). *Social diagnosis.* New York: Russell Sage Foundation.

Richmond, M. (1922). *What is social casework?* New York: Russell Sage Foundation.

Rock, B.D. (2009). Social work in health care for the 21st century. In A.R. Roberts (ed.), *Social workers' desk reference* (2nd ed.) (pp. 10–15). New York: Oxford University Press.

Rome, S.H. (2008). Forensic social work. In Mizrahi, T. & Davis, L.E., *Encyclopedia of Social Work* (20th ed.) (pp. 2:221–223). Washington, DC and New York: NASW Press and Oxford University Press.

Rose, N. (1997). The future economic landscape: Implications for social work practice and education. In M. Reisch & E. Gambrill (eds.), *Social work in the 21st century* (pp. 28–38). Thousand Oaks, CA: Pine Forge Press.

Rosen, A.L., & Zlotnik, J.L. (2001). Demographics and reality: The "disconnect" in social work education. In E.O. Cox, E. Kelchner, & R. Chapin (eds.), *Gerontological social work practice: Issues, challenges, and potential* (pp. 81–97). New York: Haworth Press.

Rothman, J. (2008). Multi mode of community intervention. In J. Rothman, J. Erlich, & J. Tropman, *Strategies of community intervention* (7th ed.) (pp. 141–170). Peosta, IA: Eddie Bowers Publishing Co., Inc.

Sager, J.S. (2008). Social planning. In Mizrahi, T. & Davis, L.E., *Encyclopedia of social work* (20th ed.) (pp. 4:56–61). Washington, DC and New York: NASW Press and Oxford University Press.

Saint Louis University. (2009). *Writing strong commentaries*. Saint Louis, MO: Marketing and Communications.

Saleebey, D. (1996). The strengths perspective in social work practice: Extensions and cautions. *Social Work*, *41*(3), 296–305.

Saleebey, D. (2006). *The strengths perspective in social work practice* (4th edition). Boston: Allyn & Bacon.

Sanfort, J.R. (2000). Developing new skills for community practice in an era of policy devolution. *Journal of Social Work Education*, *36*(2), 183–185.

Scharlach, A., Damron-Rodriguez, J.A., Robinson, B., & Feldman, R. (2000). Educating social workers for an aging society: A vision for the 21st century. *Journal of Social Work Education*, *36*, 521–537.

Schlesinger, E.G., & Devore, W. (1995). Ethnic-sensitive practice. In R.L. Edwards, *Encyclopedia of social work* (19th ed.) (pp. 902–908). Washington, DC: NASW Press.

Schneider, R. (2002). Influencing "state" policy: Social work arena for the 21st century. *The Social Policy Journal*, *1*(1), 113–116.

Schopler, J.H., & Galinsky, M.J. (1995). Group practice overview. In R.L. Edwards, *Encyclopedia of social work* (19th ed.) (pp. 1129–1142). Washington, DC: NASW Press.

Schott, L. (2008). Summary of final TANF rules. Some improvement around the margins. Washington, DC: Center on Budget and Policy Priorities.

Schott, L. & Levinson, Z. (2008). *TANF benefits are low and have not kept pace with inflation*. Washington, DC: Center on Budget and Policy Priorities.

Seccombe, K. (1999). *"So you think I drive a Cadillac?" Welfare recipients' perspective on the system and its reform*. Boston: Allyn & Bacon.

Segal, E.A. (2007). *Social welfare policy and social programs: A values perspective*. Belmont, CA: Thomson Brooks/Cole.

Senkowsky, S. (1996a). Religion and social work. *The New Social Worker*, *5*(4), pp. 8–9.

Senkowsky, S. (1996b). Social work's religious roots. *The New Social Worker*, *3*(2), 10.

Sfiligoj, H. (2009). New technology transforming profession, *NASW News*, *54*(4), p. 4.

Sheafor, B.W. & Horejsi, C.R. (2008). *Techniques and guidelines for social work practice* (8th edition). Boston, MA: Allyn & Bacon.

Sheridan, M.J. (2002). Spiritual and religious issues in practice. In A.R. Roberts & J. Watkins (ed.), *Social workers' desk reference* (pp. 567–571). New York: Oxford University Press.

Sherman, A. (2009). *Tax credit provisions in house and senate recovery packages would lessen growth in poverty*. Washington, DC: Center on Budget and Policy Priorities.

Sherman, A., Greenstein, R., & Parrott, S. (2008). *Poverty and share of Americans without health insurance were higher in 2007—and median income for working-age households was lower-than at bottom of last recession*. Washington, DC: Center for Budget and Policy Priorities.

Sherraden, M. (1990). *Assets and the poor: A new American welfare policy*. Armonk, NY: M.E. Sharp, Inc.

Sherraden, M. (2008). *IDAs and asset-building policy: Lessons and directions.* St. Louis, MO: Washington University in St. Louis Center for Social Development.

Shulman, L. (1999). *The skills of helping individuals, families, groups, and communities* (4th ed.). Washington, DC: NASW Press.

Shulman, L. (2009). *The skills of helping individuals, families, groups, and communities* (6th ed.). Belmont, CA: Brooks/Cole, Cengage Learning.

Siegel, J. (1996). *Aging into the 21st century.* Washington, DC: Administration on Aging, Dept. of Health & Human Services.

Simmons, C.S., Diaz, L., Jackson, V. & Takahashi, R. (2008). NASW cultural competency indicators: A new tool for the social work profession. *Journal of Ethnic and Cultural Diversity in Social Work, 17*(1), 4–20.

Smith, C.J. (2009). Hard times steer some toward social work [Online]. Available; http://blog/syracus.com/progress_impact/2009/02.

Smith, M.L., (2009). What my "LED ball" reveals about the future of technology and social work: A farewell aloha. *The New Social Worker, 16*(1), 30–33.

Southern Regional Education Board Manpower Education and Training Project's Rural Task Force. (1998). Educational assumptions for rural social work. In L. Ginsberg (ed.), *Social work in rural communities* (3rd ed.) (pp. 23–26). Alexandria, VA: Council on Social Work Education.

Statistical Abstract of the United States. (2000). [Online]. Available: http://www.census.gov/statab/www.

Streeter, C.L., Gamble, D.N., & Weil, M. (2008). Community. In Mizrahi, T. & Davis, L.E., *Encyclopedia of Social Work* (20th ed.) (p. 1:355–368). Washington, DC and New York: NASW Press and Oxford University Press.

Strom-Gottfried, K., & Dunlap, K.M. (1998). How to keep boundary issues from compromising your practice (Part 2 in a series on ethics). *The New Social Worker, 5*(2), pp. 10–13.

Strom-Gottfried, K., & Dunlap, K.M. (1999). Unraveling ethical dilemmas. *The New Social Worker, 6*(2), pp. 8–12.

Syers, M. (2008). Flexner, Abraham (1866–1959). In Mizrahi, T. & Davis, L.E., *Encyclopedia of Social Work* (20th ed.) (p. 4:338). Washington, DC and New York: NASW Press and Oxford University Press.

Toseland, R.W. & Horton, H. (2008). Group work. In Mizrahi, T. & Davis, L.E., *Encyclopedia of Social Work* (20th ed.) (p. 2:298–308). Washington, DC and New York: NASW Press and Oxford University Press.

Tropman, J. (2008). Phases of helping. In J. Rothman, J. Erlich, & J. Tropman, *Strategies of community intervention* (7th ed.) (pp. 127–133). Peosta, IA: Eddie Bowers Publishing Co., Inc.

Urban Experience in Chicago: Hull House and its neighborhoods, 1889–1963 [Online]. Available: http://uic.edu/jaddams/hull/urbanexp/contents.htm.

U.S. Census Bureau. (2001). Households and families: 2000. Census 2000 Brief [Online]. Available: http://www.census.gov.

U.S. Census Bureau. (2003). *Poverty in the United States: 2002.* Current Population Reports, Series P60-222. Washington, DC: Government Printing Office.

U.S. Census Bureau. (2004). United States Census 2000 [Online]. Available: http://www.census.gov.

U.S. Census Bureau. (2008a). Families and living arrangements [Online]. Available: http://www.census.gov/population/wwwsocdemo/hhfam.html.

U.S. Census Bureau. (2008b). *Income, Poverty, and Health Insurance Coverage in the United States: 2007* [Online]. Available: http://www.census.gov/prod/2008pubs/.

U.S. Census Bureau. (2008c). Poverty: 2007 highlights [Online]. Available: http://www.census.gov/hhes.www/poverty/poverty07/pov07hi.html.

U.S. Census Bureau. (2008d). Income, earnings, and poverty data from the 2007 American Community Survey [Online]. Available: http://www.census.gov/prod/2008pubs/acs-09.pdf.

U.S. Census Bureau. (2009a). 2009 Statistical Abstract [Online]. Available: http://www.census.gov/compendia/statab.

U.S. Census Bureau. (2009b). Census Bureau data show characteristics of the US foreignborn population [Online]. Available: http://www.census.gov/Press-Release/www.realeases.

U.S. Census Bureau News. (2009c). Older Americans Month: May 2009 [Online]. Available: http://www.census.gov.

U.S. Census Bureau. (2009d). Population and household economic topics [Online]. Available: http://www.census/gov/population/www/index.html.

U.S. Committee for Refugees and Immigrants. (2008). World Refugee Survey [Online]. Available: http://www.refugees.org.

U.S. Department of Agriculture. (2009). Economic stimulus-adjustment to the maximum supplemental nutrition assistance program (SNAP) monthly allotments [Online]. Available: http://www.fns.usda.gov/fsp/rules/Memo/09/021809.pdf.

U.S. Department of Health and Human Services. (2004). Protecting the privacy of patients' health information [Online]. Available: http://www.hhs.gov/news/facts/privacy.html.

U.S. Department of Health and Human Services. (2006a). TANF 7th Annual Report to Congress [Online]. Available: http://www.hhhs.gov/programs/ofa/datareports/annualreport7/.

U.S. Department of Health and Human Services. (2006b). The supply and demand of professional social workers providing long-term care services: Report to Congress [Online]. Available: http://aspe.hhs.gov/daltcp/reports/2006/Swsupply.htm#ref7.

U.S. Department of Health and Human Services. (2009). The 2009 HHS poverty guidelines [Online]. Available: http://www.aspe.hhs.gov/poverty/09poverty.htm.

U.S. Department of Health and Human Services Health Resources and Services Administration, Maternal and Child Health Bureau. (2008). *Women's Health USA 2008*. Rockville, Maryland: U.S. Department of Health and Human Services.

U.S. Department of Labor. (2007). *Career guide to industries, 2008–2009 edition: Social assistance, except child day care* [Online]. Available: http://www.bls.gov/oco/cg/cgso40.htm.

U.S. Department of Labor. (2008). *Career guide to industries, 2008–2009 edition. Advocacy, grantmaking, and civic organizations* [Online]. Available: http://www.bls.gov/oco/cg/cgso54.htm.

U.S. Department of Labor. (2009a). Employment situation summary [Online]. Available: http://www.bls.gov/news.release/empsit.nr0.htm

U.S. Department of Labor. (2009b). Minimum wage laws in the states—January 1, 2009 [Online]. Employment Standards Administration Wage and Hour Division. Available: http://www.dol.gov.

U.S. Department of Labor Bureau of Labor Statistics. (2002a). *Occupational outlook handbook* [Online]. Available: http://stats.bls.gov/oco/ocos060.htm.

U.S. Department of Labor Bureau of Labor Statistics. (2002b). *Occupation report* [Online]. Available: http://stats.bls.gov.

U.S. Department of Labor Bureau of Labor Statistics. (2009). *Career guide to industries 2008–2009 edition* [Online]. Available: http://data.bls.gov/cgibin/print.pl/oco/cg/cgs040.h4m.

U.S. Department of Labor Bureau of Labor Statistics. (2008–2009). *Occupational outlook handbook, 2008–09 Edition*, Social Workers [Online]. Available: http://www.bls.gov/oco/ocos060.htm.

U.S. General Accounting Office. (2003). *HHS could play a greater role in helping child welfare agencies recruit and retain staff (GAO-03-357)* [Online]. Available: www.gao.gov.

Van Soest, D. (2008). Oppression. In Mizrahi, T. & Davis, L.E., *Encyclopedia of social work* (20th ed.) (pp. 3:322–324). Washington, DC and New York: NASW Press and Oxford University Press.

Vaughn, M., Fu, Q., DeLisi, M., Beaver, K., Perron, B. & Howard, M. (2009). Are personality disorders associated with social welfare burden in the United States? Results from the National Epidemiologic Survey on Alcohol and Related Conditions. *Journal of Personality Disorders*.

Wahab, S. (2005). Motivational interviewing and social work practice. *Journal of Social Work*, 5(1), 45–60.

Wall Street Journal. (2006). *2006 Best Careers* [Online]. Available: CareerJournal.com.

Walsh, J. (2010). *Theories for direct social work practice* (2nd ed). Belmont, CA: Wadsworth Cengage Learning.

Walton, S. (1996). Getting real: Mastering the art of helping others. In *America's best graduate schools* (p. 63). Washington, DC: *U.S. News and World Report*.

Wambach, K.G., & Van Soest, D. (1997). Oppression. In R.L. Edwards, *Encyclopedia of social work* (19th ed.,

1997 supplement) (pp. 243–252). Washington, DC: NASW Press.

Weil, M.O. & Gamble, D.N. (2009). Community practice model for the twenty-first century. In A.R. Roberts (ed.), *Social workers' desk reference* (2nd ed.) (pp. 882–892). New York: Oxford University Press.

Wharton, T.C. (2008). Compassion fatigue: Being an ethical social worker. *The New Social Worker, 15*(1), pp. 4–7.

Whitaker, T. (2008). *Who wants to be a social worker? Career influences and timing.* NASW Membership Workforce Study. Washington, DC: National Association of Social Workers.

Whitaker, T. & Arrington, P. (2008). *Social workers at work. NASW Membership Workforce Study.* Washington, DC: National Association of Social workers.

Williams, L.D. & Joyner, M. (2008). Baccalaureate social workers. In Mizrahi, T. & Davis, L.E., *Encyclopedia of social work* (20th ed.) (pp. 1:185–188). Washington, DC and New York: NASW Press and Oxford University Press.

Wilshere, P.J. (1997). Personal values: Professional questions. *The New Social Worker, 4*(1), p. 13.

Worden, B. (2007). Women and sexist oppression. In G.A. Appleby, E. Colon, & J. Hamilton (eds), *Diversity, oppression, and social functioning: Person-in-environment assessment and intervention* (2nd ed) (pp. 93–114). Boston: Allyn & Bacon.

Worldbank Group. (2003). Understanding poverty [Online]. Available: http://www.worldbank.org/poverty/mission/up1.htm.

Worldwidelearn.com. (2009). Five biggest trends impacting the job market [Online]. Available: http://www.worldwidelearn.com/online-education-guide.

Yeskel, F., & Leondar-Wright, B. (1997). Classism curriculum design. In M. Adams, L.A. Bell, & P. Griffin (eds.), *Teaching for diversity and social justice* (pp. 231–260). New York: Routledge.

CREDITS

Akin, Jim, "100 Skills for Social Workers." (1995) NASW-Florida Chapter. Reprinted with permission of the National Association of Social Workers, Inc.

Bakely, Donald C. (1976). "If . . . A Big Word with the Poor." Faith and Life Press. Reprinted with permission.

Branding, Ronice E. "Action Continuum." Adapted from the National Conference for Community and Justice—St. Louis Region. Reprinted with permission.

Collins, D. & H. Coleman. (2000). "Eliminating Bad Habits in the Social Work Interview," *The New Social Worker*, 7(4). 12–15. Reprinted with permission.

D'Aprix, A.S., L.A. Boynton, B. Carver & C. Urso. (2001). "When the Ideal Meets the Real: Resolving Ethical Dilemmas in the Real World," *The New Social Worker*, 8(2). 20–23.

Germain, C.B. & A. Gitterman. (1995). "Ecological perspective." In R.L. Edwards, *Encyclopedia of Social Work*, 19th Edition. Washington, DC: NASW Press. 816–824. Reprinted with permission of the National Association of Social Workers, Inc.

Gitterman, A. & Germain, A. (2008). Ecological framework. In Mizrahi, T. & Davis, L.E., *Encyclopedia of social work* (20th ed.) (pp. 2:97–102). Washington, DC and New York: NASW Press and Oxford University Press.

Hartman, A. (1978). "Diagrammatic Assessment of Family Relationships." *Social Casework*, 59(8). 470. Reprinted with permission from *Families in Society* (www.familiesinsociety.org), published by the Alliance for Children and Families.

Lynch, Darlene and Robert Vernon, "You'll Need a Social Worker." © 2001. Reprinted with permission. For free distribution information visit http://hsmedia.biz.

Saint Louis University, Department of Marketing and Communications.

Saleebey, Dennis. (1996). "The Strengths Perspective in Social Work Practice: Extensions and Cautions." *Social Work*, 41(3). 296–305.

Schneider, Robert, "Influencing State Policy." Reprinted with permission. For more information visit http://www.statepolicy.org.

Wesleyan University Library, Special Collections & Archives.

GLOSSARY/INDEX

Note: Page numbers ending in *e* refer to exhibits. Page numbers ending in *t* refer to tables.

group work, 248
for inmates, 199–200
practice considerations, 205–207
rural setting case study, 212–214
salaries, 298
service providers, 6, 206e
settings, 11e, 179t, 206
mezzo (meso) social work practice: Working with a group of individuals toward the goal of planned change, 243
see also **group work**
micro social work practice: Working with individuals, couples, and families in direct social work practice toward the goal of planned change, 220
see also **individual and family social work practice**
military social work, 179t, 271, 309
minimum wage, 54
mobilizer: A social work role in which the social work facilitates the organization of individuals or groups to gain access to needed resources or attain a goal, 281
Mothers' Pension program, 32
motivational interviewing, 169
movements for progressive change, 271t, 279–280
MSW
see **Master of Social Work (MSW)**
multiculturalism: The practice of embracing and honoring the values, beliefs, and culture of others, 106–107
multilingualism, 14, 309–310
Muslims, 79, 80e

(NASW)
see also *Code of Ethics* (NASW)
National Association of Social Workers (NASW): The professional organization for the social work profession that serves to provide information, education to the profession and advocate on behalf of its members, 1, 4, 289
education policy, 14
establishment of, 41
on forensic training, 197
on gender equity, 78
on immigrants and refugees, 190
joining, 312
language policy, 95
on LGBT discrimination, 113
on multiculturalism, 107
political agenda, 85, 297–298
on poverty, 65–66

Standards for Cultural Competence in Social Work Practice, 96, 97–98, 159
Standards for social work practice in child welfare, 187
Standards for social work practice in health care settings, 202
Standards for Social Work Practice with Clients with Substance Use Disorders, 193
Standards of Technology and Social Work Practice, 308
National Budget Simulation, 289
National Urban League, 32
National Youth Administration (NYA), 33
negotiator
see mediator
neighborhoods
coalitions for redevelopment, 278
and community organizing, 270t, 273, 282
group work, 247
social planning, 277
networking, 312
New Deal, 32–33, 60, 271
Nixon, Richard, 35, 61
nonprofit organizations
see private practice

Obama, Barak, 37, 64, 85, 86, 202
OBRA (Omnibus Budget Reconciliation Act 1981), 35–36, 62
Older Americans Act, 1965, 35, 61
Omnibus Budget Reconciliation Act (OBRA), 1981, 35–36, 62
open-ended questions: Eliciting information from a client system through asking questions that address feelings, 228
see also **closed-ended questions**
oppression: The restriction by one group over an individual or another group in the areas of activities, access to resources or ability to exercise their rights, 81–84, 83e, 102
organizing functional communities, 270t, 273–274
"outdoor relief", 25, 221

PACE (Political Action for Candidate Election), 85, 279
Patten, Simon, 38, 40e
People:Environment (P:E): Perspective that emphasizes the interrelationship between individuals and the environment in which they live, 159
person first language: Language in which the person is noted first followed by the situation or condition